FINAL RESTING PLACES

UnCivil Wars

FINAL RESTING PLACES

Reflections on the Meaning of Civil War Graves

Edited by Brian Matthew Jordan and Jonathan W. White

Foreword by David W. Blight

THE UNIVERSITY OF GEORGIA PRESS   ATHENS

Athens, Georgia 30602
www.ugapress.org

Designed by Erin Kirk
Set in Walbaum
Printed and bound by Friesens
The paper in this book meets the guidelines for permanence and durability of the Committee on Production Guidelines for Book Longevity of the Council on Library Resources.

Most University of Georgia Press titles are available from popular e-book vendors.

Printed in Canada
23 24 25 26 27 P 5 4 3 2 1

Library of Congress Cataloging-in-Publication Data

Names: Jordan, Brian Matthew, 1986– editor. | White, Jonathan W., 1979– editor. | Blight, David W., writer of foreword.
Title: Final resting places : reflections on the meaning of Civil War graves / edited by Brian Matthew Jordan and Jonathan W. White ; foreword by David W. Blight.
Description: Athens : The University of Georgia Press, [2023] | Series: UnCivil wars | Includes bibliographical references and index.
Identifiers: LCCN 2023019307 | ISBN 9780820364551 (hardback) | ISBN 9780820364568 (paperback) | ISBN 9780820364575 (epub) | ISBN 9780820364582 (adobe pdf)
Subjects: LCSH: United States—History—Civil War, 1861–1865—Monuments. | Soldiers' monuments—United States. | War cemeteries—United States. | Soldiers' bodies, Disposition of—United States—History—19th century. | United States—History—Civil War, 1861–1865—Casualties.
Classification: LLC E641 .F56 2023 | DDC 973.7/6—dc23/eng/20230512
LC record available at https://lccn.loc.gov/2023019307

Contents

Foreword

From Every Point of the Compass out of the Countless Graves

DAVID W. BLIGHT

In a 1961 interview, when asked yet again how the Civil War was remembered and discussed in his youth in and around Guthrie, Kentucky, hard on the Tennessee border, Robert Penn Warren remarked that it had been "part of the emotional furniture" of his life. Warren had grown up as a boy frequently visiting his Confederate veteran grandfather, Gabriel Penn, and listening intently to the old man's stories of his troops, his personal experiences as a cavalryman, and tales steeped in Lost Cause ideology.[1] As a writer and poet, Warren would grow to craft as penetrating and authentically tragic a story about the meaning of the Civil War as perhaps any American author. Warren hated sentimentality and melodrama; he much preferred probing the depths of the human condition, of the tragic, fated character of life and history, and indeed, the buried and living legacies of the Civil War that gave him his historical imagination.

Warren found in the Civil War and its afterlives a natural lode of limitless ore from which to fashion art in verse, fiction, and nonfiction prose. He wrote as if he took inspiration from the very ground, indeed the graves of the war dead strewn across the land, some in well-kept, adorned official cemeteries, and some simply part of the dust, the vegetation, the rocks that form the land of the border region in which he was born and raised.

In a reminiscence, Warren recalled roving around with a boyhood friend through the scraggy hillsides and woods around his grandfather's farm one summer. The youths believed they were traversing some of "the dark and bloody ground" on which the Civil War had been fought. They stumbled upon some "bones," and on another occasion a depression in the ground they imagined had been a soldier's grave. Later, in his series of "Kentucky Mountain Farm" poems, Warren saw history buried in, as well as emerging from, the "rocks" of those fields and hills.

In the cycles of geology, of stone breaking down and reforming, Warren saw a metaphor for history: "The hills are weary, the lean men have passed; / The rocks are stricken, and the frost has torn / Away their ridged fundaments at last, / So that the fractured atoms now are borne." Then in the poem "History among the Rocks," he imagined further long-ago scenes:

> Think how a body, naked and lean
> And white as the splintered sycamore, would go
> Tumbling and turning, hushed in the end,
> With hair afloat in waters that gently bend
> To ocean where the blind tides flow . . .
>
> In these autumn orchards once young men lay dead . . .
> Grey coats, blue coats. Young men on the mountainside
> Clambered, fought. Heels muddied the rocky spring.
> Their reason is hard to guess, remembering
> Blood on their black mustaches in moonlight.
> Their reason is hard to guess and a long time past:
> The apple falls, falling in the quiet night.[2]

How many Americans over more than half a century have wandered in battlefield parks, or in remote hills or landscapes of the border South, or even in formal cemeteries, and pondered the dead of 1861–65, as Warren does in this haunting poem? How have they been moved or puzzled by the scale of the dead in moonlight, or wondered about the "reason" they fought? How many times has the wanderer been deflected from a sense of meaning of the sacrifice, of any sort of cause and effect, by the character of memorials, by the beauty of landscapes that now perfectly hide the smell, the taste, the sound, and the hideous sights of the real war that happened there?

Humankind has left its dead, from war and every other cause, strewn through geological time and space. Graves, real and imagined, are everywhere in American soil from our Civil War. And Warren warned us in an essay, appropriately entitled "A Sense of the Past," that for present and future-minded Americans, never eager to look too deeply at their own savage past, they are walking, often unaware, on minefields. History is waiting for us even in the ground when we least may expect it. "Some explosively recalcitrant fact gets left out of the fine scheme," Warren wrote about Civil War memory, "and this fact, like an unexploded grenade in a rubbish heap, is likely to cause trouble."[3] In one recurring racial, political, or legal reckoning after another, we are reminded that those grenades will and do go off as we contend with the unfinished legacies of slavery, the war, and Reconstruction.

No one left a more powerful expression of the meaning of the Civil War dead than Walt Whitman, nurse and bard of the suffering and dying soldiers. The wounded and the dead never left his consciousness. In "Old War Dreams," Whitman combined a remembrance laced with elegiac tragedy and romance:

> In midnight sleep of many a face of anguish,
> Of the look at first of the mortally wounded, (of that indescribable
> Look,)
> Of the dead on their backs with arms extended wide,
> I dream, I dream, I dream.

Over and over, in many words, Whitman declared the dead in their graves his "companions." His art was intensely personal, rooted in experience; but he sang as though from a nation's heart as well as his own. In "Ashes of Soldiers," Whitman summoned the dead to a gathering of collective love and purpose that the nation no longer could achieve:

> Noiseless as mists and vapors,
> From their graves in the trenches ascending,
> From cemeteries all through Virginia and Tennessee,
> From every point of the compass out of the countless graves,
> In wafted clouds, in myriads large, or squads of twos or threes or
> Single ones they come,
> And silently gather around me.[4]

If only the Civil War graves could draw us to such gatherings today, to grand civic expressions of reinventing the America that all those dead died to reinvent in the 1860s, knowingly or not. Would that we could hear Whitman's summons, in our grand pluralistic cacophony of people, and find in all those honored dead yet another rebirth. This collection of marvelous essays about Civil War graves and cemeteries, written by some of the most distinguished and imaginative historians of our era, compiled and edited expertly by Brian Jordan and Jonathan White, takes a large step in suggesting the many places we might begin that rebirth. Perhaps we need to spend more time amidst the rocks, walking the hillsides, imagining the graves anew, and then face the reasons why they died.

FINAL RESTING PLACES

Introduction

BRIAN MATTHEW JORDAN AND
JONATHAN W. WHITE

On the afternoon of January 12, 1862, taking advantage of a respite from the biting temperatures of a gray Virginia winter, nineteen-year-old Lucy Buck—together with her father and sister—roved among the rows of freshly made soldiers' graves near her home in Front Royal. As she surveyed the "heaps of earth" marked with "rough head and foot boards," the vast scope and scale of the Civil War—then just nine months old—became agonizingly manifest. "There under my very feet they rested so still," she told her diary, "I could scarce realize that those whose arms had been strong in the conflict, whose feet had been so swift in the battle, were now lying all so powerless." In comparison to the dead, Buck mused that she "might boast of a giant's strength."[1]

The Civil War did few things better or more efficiently than make final resting places. Between 1861 and 1865, more than half a million soldiers succumbed to chronic diseases, enemy bullets, or the effects of captivity. The war planted bodies on battlefields and in boneyards; beneath obedient rows of military headstones; and amid the crowded, anonymizing disorder of mass graves. Some bodies were lost at sea, while time eroded the traces of men hastily deposited in makeshift graves. Remains were scattered across farms and behind earthen works, often planted where they fell. As the seat of the conflict's eastern theater, the Old Dominion became one vast cemetery. "Death is nothing here," the poet Walt Whitman marveled as he surveyed the field hospitals around Fredericksburg in December 1862. "As you step out in the morning from your tent to wash your face you see before you on a stretcher a shapeless extended object . . .

it is the corpse of some wounded or sick soldier," he wrote. "Perhaps there is a row of three or four of these corpses lying covered over. No one makes an ado. There is a detail of men made to bury them; all useless ceremony is omitted."[2]

In Whitman's reckoning, the "stern realities" of battle rendered "the old etiquets a cumber and a nuisance." And yet Civil War Americans were no strangers to death and dying. In the antebellum years, epidemics made regular, deadly romps through especially unhygienic cities; astoundingly high rates of infant mortality supplied still other unwelcome opportunities to contemplate life's ephemerality. Coroners and census takers made death more visible by massing mortality statistics. Meanwhile, sprawling rural cemeteries became the preferred pastoral escapes of both northerners and southerners; these cypress- and maple-shaded mazes of granite and bronze kept death close at hand. By the time the war began tallying casualties, Americans understood that graves were sacred spots that could afford the dead afterlives on earth. The soldiers that Lucy Buck paid tribute to in the Shenandoah Valley could no longer lend manpower to the war effort, but their rude graves resounded with meaning. Contrary to the young Virginian's conviction, the dead were anything but "powerless."[3]

Final Resting Places roves among Civil War graves to render legible their enduring power. Ranging from a small, family plot in rural North Carolina to the magnificent marble rotunda of Grant's Tomb—tiptoeing among tombstones from chilly New England to tropical Brazil—each chapter features a leading scholar meditating on the long shadows cast by the Civil War dead. We afforded wide latitude to our contributors, inviting them to tell compelling stories and take us to unexpected places. Acknowledging the evocative power of Civil War graves, we encouraged the authors to embrace the tool of autobiography if they felt it appropriate. As such, many of the essays reveal as much about the production of history as they do about the past.

Recent historians have turned renewed attention on death and dying in the Civil War era. Drew Gilpin Faust's *This Republic of Suffering* (2008) powerfully revealed all that death demanded of the living. Civil War Americans transmuted the gruesome ends many soldiers met on distant battlefields into culturally recognizable and ultimately reassuring "good deaths." Faust's book further demonstrated how the war's mass casualties augmented the size and scope of the federal government, brokering a new

The Civil War did few things better or more efficiently than create final resting places. Stretching as far as the eye can see, rows of freshly made soldiers' graves near the General Hospital at City Point, Virginia, await their headstones. Courtesy of the Library of Congress.

relationship between individuals and the state. "The meaning of the war," she wrote, "had come to inhere in its cost." That cost grew significantly higher at the dawn of the sesquicentennial. In 2011 a "census-based" count of the Civil War dead conducted by historical demographer J. David Hacker resulted in an upwardly revised tally of the conflict's human toll. Even noncombat deaths—long neglected—have now been cataloged in Brian Steel Wills's *Inglorious Passages* (2017). As still other scholars recover the nonlinear trajectories of battlefield injuries, the lingering effects of chronic diseases, and the unhygienic conditions faced by freedom-seeking enslaved refugees, it seems quite likely that a full accounting of the Civil War dead—a project first undertaken by Union veterans—is not yet finished.[4]

A related body of scholarship has considered how postwar Americans made sense of death on such a staggering scale. William Blair, John Neff, and Caroline Janney have identified cemeteries as key terrain in the protracted battles over the Civil War's meaning and legacy. Taken together, their books have demonstrated how "cities of the dead" posed obstacles to reconciliation,

Photographer Timothy H. O'Sullivan captured the "unfinished work" of the burial crews at Gettysburg, who piled dead Confederates into trenches where they fell. Courtesy of the Library of Congress.

promoted dueling visions of Civil War memory, and seeded the pernicious myths of the Lost Cause. By surveying the diversity of Civil War graves and bringing a select few into focus, *Final Resting Places* lends texture and depth to these findings.[5]

No less than battlefields, soldier monuments, popular prints, literary works, or filmic representations, graves were unique sites where narratives of the war were constantly made and remade. Thomas Nast famously exploited the emotive power of graves to critique both the wartime movement for "peace without victory" and the postwar drive for sectional reconciliation. In "Compromise with the South," a pungent *Harper's Weekly* illustration that the cartoonist "dedicated" to the 1864 Democratic National Convention, a one-legged Yankee veteran stands astride the grave of a dead comrade. Over the grave, marked by a crude headboard lettered with the words "In Memory of the Union Heroes in a Useless War," the amputee extends a conciliatory hand to an immodest Jefferson Davis. A small, rural churchyard in northeastern Pennsylvania offers another example. There lies buried Lt. James Stewart Robinson, who had been shot and killed by a draft dodger in nearby Benton Township.

The weather-beaten marker placed by the soldier's family reports matter-of-factly that Robinson "Was shot by a Rebel sympathizer in Benton Tp Columbia Co. Pa while assisting a U.S. officer in attempting to arrest deserters."[6]

African Americans keenly appreciated the capacity of graves to actuate memories and promote political action. As self-appointed custodians of the Union dead, Black Americans did their best to keep and preserve Union gravesites; they also laureled the final resting places of northern veterans with flowers and wreaths ("choice emblems alike of pure hearts and brave spirits," as Frederick Douglass put it) on Memorial Day. The significance of these acts of remembrance would in no way be lost on white southerners. A few years after the war, several white women in

Republicans charged Democrats with treason for calling the war a "failure" in their party platform at the Chicago Convention in 1864. In "Compromise with the South," Thomas Nast depicted Lady Liberty and a wounded Union veteran bowing in grief over a grave that had been erected "In Memory of Our Union-Heroes Who Fell in a Useless War." Confederate president Jefferson Davis stands triumphantly on the fresh grave as scenes of destruction, murder, and enslavement crowd the background. Courtesy of the Library of Congress.

During the presidential election of 1864, Democratic operatives from New York were arrested for casting fraudulent ballots in soldiers' names. In this cartoon, Thomas Nast captures how such election fraud desecrated the memories of Union soldiers who had died in the war. Collection of Jonathan W. White.

Marianna, Florida, stripped decorations from the grave of a Maine lieutenant killed during Brig. Gen. Alexander Asboth's late-war mounted raid on the city. According to several eyewitnesses, the women "tore them into tatters, threw them into the street and trampled on them, walking backwards and forwards."[7]

Elsewhere throughout the defeated South, recalcitrant rebels testified to the political afterlife of Civil War graves by defiling them. In December 1865 an army quartermaster noted the "constant depredation of headboards" marking Union soldiers' burial sites around Nashville. Months later, that same official attributed the deplorable condition of Yankee graves near Memphis to "the disloyal character" of the locals. At Camp Dick Robinson in Kentucky, the final resting places of federal soldiers were "nearly all in bad condition"—the headboards either "knocked down and destroyed" or choked with briars. Likewise, the skeletons of U.S. troops killed during the operations around Atlanta were routinely "ploughed up" by local farmers or "rooted out" by hogs; in one location, ex-rebels heaped the exposed remains of their former enemies in a "promiscuous pile." These not infrequent outrages figured significantly in the decision to

establish a network of federal burying grounds at or near sites of major battles. "The primary idea in the establishment of National Cemeteries," Brig. Gen. James Lowry Donaldson explained, "is to secure the remains [of Union soldiers] from desecration, when it cannot otherwise be done."[8]

The federal government's herculean effort to locate, collect, and consecrate Union graves after the Civil War bespoke the widely shared belief that gravesites could convey meaning to the living. Frederick Douglass acknowledged as much in an 1871 speech that he delivered in Arlington, Virginia, at the Tomb of the Civil War Unknowns—a granite vault holding the remains of more than two thousand unknown Union soldiers. "There is, in the very air of this resting-ground of the unknown dead," he began, "a silent, subtle and all-pervading eloquence, far more touching, impressive, and thrilling than living lips have ever uttered . . . it is now whispering lessons of all that is precious, priceless, holiest, and most enduring in human existence." Douglass trusted that the monument before him—and the rows of military headstones all around him—would serve as eternal reminders that "victory to the rebellion meant death to the republic."[9]

Ten months after Appomattox, the celebrated sketch artist Alfred R. Waud captured an all-too-familiar scene for the readers of *Harper's Weekly*: a war widow pausing at the grave of her soldier husband.

Monument to the Unknown Dead, Arlington National Cemetery, Arlington, Virginia, ca. 1900. Courtesy of the Library of Congress.

While Civil War graves were sites of civic memory for the nation at large, they were also places of personal mourning for grieving families. While troves of wartime letters, old photographs, and lovingly preserved personal effects could afford the dead afterlives on earth, their surviving kin yearned for the closure and dignity of a gravesite. Families lacking the means to convey the bodies of deceased loved ones back home often settled for the simple knowledge of the location where their soldiers were interred. Understanding the importance of this information, burial details did their best to supply it. A few days after the rebels ensnared his Bay State regiment in Antietam's West Woods, Pvt. Roland Bowen penned a devastating letter to the father of his dead comrade, Pvt. Henry Ainsworth. Bowen apologized that he was "too late" to place the dead soldier's body in an individual grave; however, he assured the bereft father that he would always remember the boy's final resting place. "The trench in which Henry is buried is situated near a log cabin just out side the garden fence," he wrote. "The trench was 25 feet long, 6 feet wide and about 3 feet deep. The corpses were buried by Co., that is the members of each Co. are put together. Co. H was buried first in the upper end of the trench next to the woods. They are laid in two tiers, one on top the other. . . . Henry is the third corpse from the upper end on the top tier next to the woods."[10]

Yet for far too many families, such knowledge was not immediately—or ever—forthcoming. More than two decades after the war, in an index of the anguish that such uncertainty could invite, the brother of a twenty-three-year-old New Yorker mortally wounded at Second Bull Run sent a despairing missive to the quartermaster general. "I wish you would give me information where he died, where he is Buried, the number of the Grave, &c," Michael Brandle wrote. The official reply arrived three weeks later. "By direction of the Quartermaster General, you are respectfully informed that a careful examination of the records in this Office, fails to show the interment of the soldier named in a National Cemetery." Very likely, the soldier's remains were "classed among those Unknown" and removed to Arlington; still, the search would endure.[11]

At least two major themes course through this book. First, the essayists point to the power of place. They muse over stark juxtapositions—as well as silence, absence, and erasure. Historically, these juxtapositions and erasures were quite deliberate. The Grand Army of the Republic, the largest fraternal organization for honorably discharged Union veterans, was the only nonsegregated social guild in the late nineteenth century. Its flag festooned burial plots were some of the only places where Americans could find Blacks and whites interred next to one another. At Camp Lawton, a rebel military prison in Georgia, Confederate captors denied Union soldiers branding irons—ensuring that the more than five hundred graves crowding the stockade would be marked with unadorned wooden stakes. Elsewhere, the graves of enslaved persons—no less than those occupied by victims of racist and guerrilla violence—were consigned to oblivion. In its own, perverse way, forgetting is a form of remembering.[12]

Second, the contributors to this collection remind us that Civil War graves have served as a prism through which successive generations have viewed and understood the conflict; their significance and potency as symbols have changed dramatically

Bust of Robert Smalls at the entrance of Tabernacle Baptist Church Cemetery, Beaufort, South Carolina. Photograph by Chloe Baker.

Stephen A. Douglas Tomb and Memorial, Chicago, Illinois. Douglas, an avowed white supremacist, died in 1861. His tomb was completed in 1881. It stands on land he once owned, which became Camp Douglas during the Civil War. The ninety-six-foot-tall memorial is now in a predominantly Black neighborhood, and some have called for its removal. Photograph by David Wiegers.

over time. Today, Arlington National Cemetery is one of the most revered locations in our civic landscape—a place that affirms heroism, valor, and a shared sense of national purpose. Yet the cemetery began as an attempt to humiliate Robert E. Lee: to deliver to his doorstep—quite literally—the human costs of his treasonous rebellion.[13] Within the last decade, Lee's own gravesite (on the campus of the university he led after the Civil War) has invited controversy. The remains of the infamous rebel cavalryman Nathan Bedford Forrest, after years of repose beneath an imposing equestrian statue in Memphis, were exhumed and moved across the state to a museum owned and operated by the Sons of Confederate Veterans.

Owing to the number and variety of the graves produced by the Civil War, this book cannot be comprehensive. While we solicited essays that would amplify the range and diversity of wartime experiences, loyalties, and identities—including pieces on soldiers and civilians, officers and enlisted men, guerrillas and regulars, the free and the enslaved—perceptive readers will doubtless note the absence of many iconic gravesites that, but for the constraints of space, might have been reasonably included. Essayists do not pause at Lincoln's Tomb, ponder the burial site of Stonewall Jackson's amputated arm, or salute Thaddeus Stevens, the Radical Republican congressman who, in selecting a nonsegregated cemetery in Lancaster, Pennsylvania, wished to "illustrate in my death the principles I advocated through a long life—equality of man before his Creator." Still, we hope that taken together, the pieces presented here invite further reflection on the personal and political consequences of our nation's defining conflict.

The Lincoln Tomb at Oak Ridge Cemetery in Springfield, Illinois, features bronze replicas of famous Lincoln statues that depict Lincoln at various points in his life. It was completed in 1874 and restored between 1899 and 1901, at which point Lincoln's remains were buried beneath ten feet of concrete in order to prevent attempts to steal Lincoln's body, which had been attempted in 1876. Photograph by David Wiegers.

"The Soldier's Memorial," produced by Currier & Ives, features a woman dressed in mourning garb pausing at the grave of a Union soldier. Grieving families could purchase one of these hand-colored lithographs and inscribe it with the name and regiment of their fallen soldier as well as the date and location of his death. Courtesy of the Library of Congress.

In 1867 the remains of Confederate general Ambrose Powell Hill were removed from his original battlefield burial site to Richmond's Hollywood Cemetery. In 1891 they were reinterred beneath this statue of the general on the streets of Richmond. The presence of the grave complicated the city government's effort to remove the statue in 2020. In October 2022 a state judge cleared the way for Hill's remains to be removed to Fairview Cemetery in Culpeper and for the monument to be donated to the Black History Museum and Cultural Center of Virginia. Courtesy of Frank Jastrzembski.

A friendly-fire incident at the battle of Chancellorsville resulted in the amputation of "Stonewall" Jackson's left arm, which was buried at Ellwood Manor. The site was marked with this granite slab in the early twentieth century. Photograph by Chris Mackowski.

1

Common Soldiers and Sailors

A Hollywood Grave

GLENN W. LAFANTASIE

There is a great void that comes to those who experience the death of a loved one. In death's aftermath, it is impossible to feel whole. It's as if a huge portion of one's self has been cleaved away. Eventually, those who survive the death of someone they've loved realize that their world will never be the same, that their loss is permanent, and sadness will come in waves, especially when one least expects it. There is no real end to grief. Thomas Mann, the German novelist, was correct when he wrote: "It is a fact that a man's dying is more the survivors' affair than his own."[1]

That proved to be the case for William C. Oates, the colonel of the 15th Alabama Infantry at Gettysburg. In the late afternoon of July 2, 1863, he and his men hastily withdrew from the slopes of Little Round Top, while the 20th Maine Regiment, led by Col. Joshua L. Chamberlain, came barreling down upon them with fixed bayonets, driving the Confederates into the nearby woods and up the steep hillsides of Big Round Top. Yet Oates knew that his regiment's retreat meant something more than simply a defeat in battle. As the Alabamians fell back, Oates was forced to leave behind his younger brother, John, who lay with mortal wounds between the craggy boulders that formed Little Round Top's southeastern face. Colonel Oates, thirty-one years old, wanted to rescue John, twenty-nine, but he collapsed from heat prostration halfway up Big Round Top and required help to get back on his feet and up to the safety of the hill's summit. That dark night, the eerie moans of the wounded filled the air with a relentless, discordant dirge of human suffering.[2] Much

Col. William C. Oates. From William C. Oates, *The War between the Union and the Confederacy* (New York: Neale, 1905).

later he learned that John had died in a Union field hospital, east of Little Round Top.

William and John grew up together in the 1830s on a hardscrabble farm in Pike County, Alabama, not far from the Chattahoochee River in the southeastern region of the state. According to William's unpublished autobiography, he and his brother were the closest in age among the Oates brood, and their bond tightened as childhood merged into adulthood. Like William, John became an attorney and joined his older brother in a fairly thriving practice in Abbeville, Henry County.[3] "No brothers loved each other better," wrote William long after the war.[4]

Before war's end, William Oates received a nearly fatal wound during the siege of Petersburg that cost him his right arm. It took time for him to recover, but when he did, he resumed his law practice in Abbeville. Later, when he was elected as a seven-term U.S. congressman and served as a one-term governor of the state, he got married, moved to Montgomery, and assembled a fortune based on his vast real estate holdings. Yet all of his success mattered little to him when he compared it to the personally devastating loss of his brother.[5]

Oates never forgave himself for having left his wounded brother behind on the Gettysburg battlefield. Every year, he dreaded the arrival of July 2, the anniversary of the day his brother was mortally wounded, and December 24, the anniversary of his brother's birth. One Christmas Eve, Oates wrote his son to tell him how the night brought forth a perennial ache in his heart. Downstairs, Oates's wife hosted a large, and sometimes boisterous, party of people imbued with Christmas spirit and spiritous liquors. Oates ignored the festivities and concentrated on writing John's story, which he had never previously revealed to his son. He could feel nothing but "sad over his fate." Entrapped in his wrenching memories of his lost brother, Oates concluded the letter by writing: "He was a noble young man and died for his country and in a just cause as he and I both saw it." The fact that he never knew where John had been buried bothered him more and more over the years, but he lacked any knowledge of how he might go about locating his brother's final resting place.[6]

Decades after Appomattox, the Civil War still gripped William C. Oates's thoughts, memories, and labors. For several years, from the end of the Spanish-American War, in which he had served as a brigadier general, to 1904, Oates unsuccessfully tried to erect a monument to his regiment, the 15th Alabama, on the slopes of Little Round Top. He intended it specifically as a memorial to his brother John and to the rest of the soldiers who had fought with the 15th Alabama on that once bloody hillside. But his attempt—which took place over frustrating years of red tape and bureaucratic obfuscations—failed when the Gettysburg National Military Park commissioners, who administered the park for the War Department, refused to approve his request. Oates finally gave up. Today there is still no monument to the 15th Alabama on Little Round Top.[7]

In the summer of 2004, while working on the last chapter of my Oates biography, I hit a wall. It wasn't really writer's block; it was an entirely different phenomenon—call it an instinct, a vague feeling, that I had missed something important about Oates's final years. I had no idea what it could be. I told my wife, Donna, about the impasse, and her advice was to stop anguishing over it and just let it be for a while. So, that's precisely what I did. Meanwhile, I asked an editor in New York—a friend of a friend—if she'd be willing to read what I'd written so far and critique it. She agreed and soon wrote back to me in a three-page, single-spaced letter that made my heart sink when I opened the envelope, but which turned out to be the best advice I've ever received as a writer. She let me know that I had written a good biography of William Oates, but, she said, I was telling the wrong story. The *real* story, she said, was about the two brothers, William and John, and how one survived the Civil War and the other didn't. I showed Donna the letter, and she enthusiastically agreed with the editor. As a result, I decided to revise the whole manuscript, pulling everything I knew about John to the forefront. The manuscript remained a biography of William Oates, but it now had a greater emphasis on his relationship with John.[8]

But I still confronted difficulties in drafting the final chapter. Maybe, like other biographers, I was reluctant to let my subject die. One day, though, when I was looking for something else in a 1910 issue of the *Southern Historical Society Papers* (a postwar magazine and propaganda machine devoted to the Lost Cause and all things Confederate), I spotted an article entitled "Monument to Confederates." The short piece announced that a marble stone would be erected at Point Lookout, Maryland, to memorialize the 3,384 dead Confederate soldiers and sailors who had died there in a prisoner-of-war camp. The article went on to say: "This work has been in progress during the past four years, under the direction, first, of Colonel William Elliott, of South Carolina, the [federal] Commissioner for that purpose, appointed in March, 1906, by President [Theodore] Roosevelt. Upon the death of Colonel Elliott, the President appointed as Commissioner in his stead, former Governor *William C. Oates*, of Alabama."[9] *What?!?* I exclaimed out loud. Until that moment, I had been working on the Oates biography for fifteen years, on and off. Never before had I encountered a reference to the Office of the Commissioner for Locating and Marking Confederate Graves and, to wit, that Oates had worked as its chair. Quite frankly, I was dumbfounded.

After Donna helped pick me up from the floor, she said: "You see? Your writer's block was meant to be. It gave you time to stumble upon something about Oates you never knew before." I would never have thought about it quite like that. Donna had a rare gift of making all life seem mystical and mysterious. She was right, of course, as subsequent events would show.

Living close to Washington, DC, at the time, I knew what I must do. I hightailed it to the National Archives, where one of its research consultants found the records of the federal commission.[10] There were about a dozen archival boxes in the collection, many of them containing William Oates's correspondence as commissioner. I couldn't believe my good fortune. The boxes before me contained not only records that I had never seen before, but those records told the full story of how Oates, the man who had lamented the loss of his brother for decade after decade, put the memory of his wrenching war behind him, finding, at last, the emotional closure and relief he had so desperately sought. For William Oates, the worst day of his life took place on July 2, 1863. But forty-seven years later, he discovered the means by which his soul—and his broken heart—could finally find peace.

During the first few years of the twentieth century, Confederate veteran organizations called for a uniform system of federal care for all Confederate graves in northern cemeteries, especially the graves in or near prisoner-of-war camps. The president's appointment of Oates to the commission must have come as a great surprise to the aging Alabamian, now in his seventies, for he had not asked for the position. What's more, the president was a Republican; Oates was a Bourbon Democrat.

Although he had been laid low in the winter of 1908 with a bout of pneumonia, Oates took over as commissioner the following spring. His capable assistant was L. Frank Nye, the local son of a hardware merchant and a graduate of Georgetown University. A dedicated worker without the fussiness of most bureaucrats, Nye did most of the research, kept all the files straight, and generally kept the commission moving forward and making progress. The two men worked well as a team.[11]

There was an advantage to his position that Oates never could have foreseen. Reading the commission's prodigious files, he discovered that his predecessor had visited Gettysburg and had learned that Confederate graves had been mapped and marked by Dr. John W. C. O'Neal of Gettysburg, and that two other men from the town, Samuel Weaver and his son Rufus B. Weaver, had worked with ladies' memorial associations to exhume the Confederate dead on the battlefield and reinter them in cemeteries in the South. In February 1909 Oates corresponded with O'Neal and Rufus Weaver and told them of his quest to find where his brother John was buried. He soon learned that John had died at the Union army's Fifth Corps hospital set up on Michael Fiscel's farm, which was located east of the Round Tops.[12] Then a letter from Dr. Weaver arrived. "It affords me great pleasure," wrote Weaver, "to reply that my records of the removal of the remains of the Confederate dead show that, on Sept. 10th, 1872, the remains of Lt. J. A. Oat[e]s, 15th Alabama Regt., were shipped to Richmond, Va., and there interred in Hollywood Cemetery." Weaver explained that John Oates's remains could not be distinguished from the remains of eleven other Confederates buried at the Fiscel farm, so all twelve bodily remains were shipped together to Richmond in a wooden box labeled with the letter A.[13]

Oates was elated. After all this time, after so many years of mourning for his brother, he was about to find him at last. Oates had Nye write in March to Bettie Ellyson, the recently installed president of the Ladies' Memorial Association, which was the organization responsible for removing the Confederate dead from Gettysburg and for maintaining the graves in Richmond's Hollywood Cemetery. In the letter, Nye—writing over Oates's signature—asked for the location in the cemetery where Box A had been placed.[14] Several weeks passed by, but neither Oates nor Nye received any answer from Richmond.

It was a difficult time for Oates. He complained about failing eyesight, and that summer, in a letter to his son Will, he claimed that he could scarcely see at all. The senior Oates turned all his case files over to Will and ceased practicing law.[15] At last, in the winter of 1910, Mrs. Ellyson's reply arrived at the commission's office in Washington. Although she claimed not to know much about the reinterment of the Gettysburg fallen, she did tell him this: "The box marked A is on Gettysburg Hill in Hollywood in [the] Soldiers' part, near the Monument the Ladies from Philadelphia erected in memory of our soldiers who were buried up there [i.e., in Gettysburg]." She said that if Oates wished to visit the cemetery, she would be glad to meet him "and show you about where your brother is buried."[16]

It is a mystery why Oates simply did not get on a train and go to Richmond to see for himself where John was buried. Despite his eye troubles, he could have managed the trip with little difficulty. Instead, he sent Nye to the Hollywood Cemetery. Interestingly enough, Nye—either knowingly or unwittingly—made his trip so

Monument to the Confederate Dead, ca. 1905, Hollywood Cemetery, Richmond, Virginia. Courtesy of the Library of Congress.

Monument to the Gettysburg Dead, Hollywood Cemetery, Richmond, Virginia. Photograph by Jonathan W. White

that he was in Richmond on July 2, 1910, the forty-seventh anniversary of the 15th Alabama's assault on Little Round Top. Nye found his own way around the burial grounds to the Gettysburg section where Mrs. Ellyson had said Box A had been buried. Nye later wrote to Ellyson: "While I was not able to report to General Oates the exact location of the grave of his brother, yet I could tell him of the excellent condition in which this section of the cemetery is maintained."[17] It didn't matter to Oates. It was enough for him to know, once and for all, where John was laid to rest.

Oates's long search for his brother was over. By mid-July, when he finally learned that there was no hope of ever finding his brother's individual gravesite, Oates became seriously ill and bedridden. His health began to decline rapidly. It was as if his mission in life had been accomplished, and now it was time for rest and peace. Then the end finally came. Half an hour past noon on September 9, 1910, he died quietly in his bed at his Montgomery home. He was buried, with military honors, in Oakwood Cemetery, on the outskirts of the city.[18] Eventually, a tall stone obelisk, with a larger-than-life bronze statue of him, was erected over his grave. It is an impressive memorial. There stands Oates as he had appeared in the postwar years, dressed in civilian attire, wearing a handsome three-piece suit, his right sleeve hanging limp by his side. But most people who visit the cemetery do so to see the grave of Hank Williams, the country music singer.

Richmond, like Rome, is built on seven hills. There are, of course, no ancient structures in the Virginia capital, unless one counts St. John's Episcopal Church, built in 1741, as ancient. It was a warm, sunny day in October 2008 when Donna and I—on our way to Tidewater for a few days—decided to take a detour to find Hollywood Cemetery and John Oates's burial site. The cemetery, established in 1847, sits on one of the seven hills and overlooks, from a high bluff, the famous bend and falls in the James River. In a short while, we located placid Gettysburg Hill, a green knoll that drops gracefully into a vale dappled by sun and shade. In tidy rows, Confederate marble gravestones—shaped as an oblong with a slight chevron at the top—have been erected by family members who believe their ancestors might be buried there. There's no marker for John Oates, although it is certain he was buried in the mass grave of Confederates who fell at Gettysburg and were reinterred here in 1872.

Donna and I were the only tourists there that day, and we spent a long time contemplating the solemnity of the spot and paying our respects to John Oates. As the day turned into early evening, we watched dark thunderheads appear overhead, signaling that it was time for us to get back on the road. Dusk fell over Richmond and brought an autumn chill to the air, now that the sun was gone.

That was a day to remember. Little did we know that down the road of years, an east wind was coming to change everything we held dear. Last year, Donna died, and I can't quite comprehend her absence or the fact that she is now forever gone. We did so much together over our forty-two years of marriage. She was, as I've hinted, my Muse, among so many other things. I now feel lonely in crowds of people, and empty inside the shell of my body. I search for words of comfort, but I find none. What I find is a line from a letter written by Edna St. Vincent Millay, the American poet: "Where you used to be, there is a hole in the world, which I find myself constantly walking around in the daytime, and falling in at night. I miss you like hell."[19]

Now I know what the two Oates brothers felt when they lost each other at Gettysburg.

D. A. Rock

Gettysburg's First Headstone

TIMOTHY J. ORR

On a rainy Independence Day 1863, Capt. Thomas Henry of Company F, 140th Pennsylvania, gathered a squad of four men to help bury a fallen soldier. They searched for the body of twenty-two-year-old Capt. David Acheson, a resident of Washington, Pennsylvania, who had been killed on George Rose's farm outside of Gettysburg.

Captain Henry's squad found Acheson's corpse on rocky ground near where their regiment had fought two days earlier. Like most corpses left on the battlefield, it was not in great condition. It had been robbed of clothing and a few personal items, and, quite likely, it was bloated and blackened. Nevertheless, it was identifiable. Captain Henry's men carried Acheson's remains to a nearby field hospital—the John T. Weikert farm—and on the north side of it, near an old rail fence, they dug a shallow pit.[1] After covering the body with a few inches of dirt, one of the men—no one ever recorded who—produced a nail and a hatchet and began to chisel two letters—"D" and "A"—into a three-foot-high boulder to mark the head of Acheson's grave. After a few quick words, the soldiers went back to their business, hunting up other fallen comrades to be laid to rest.

Likely, none of Captain Henry's team realized the significance of what they had just done. They had created Gettysburg's first headstone.

I first became aware of "D. A. Rock" in 1999, the year I began working as a seasonal ranger at Gettysburg National Military Park. Not long after joining the Park Service, I stumbled across

CAPT. DAVID ACHESON.
Boulder on Gettysburg Battlefield where Capt. David Acheson was buried.
The Wheatfield—"Whirlpool of the Battle"—where more than 6,000 were killed or wounded.

Capt. David Acheson, the D. A. Rock at Gettysburg, and the Wheatfield. From Robert Laird Stewart, *History of the One Hundred and Fortieth Regiment Pennsylvania Volunteers* (n.p., 1912).

an internet challenge entitled "140 Places Every Guide Should Know." It had been created by Gettysburg's Association of Licensed Battlefield Guides (or LBGs). This list cataloged sites on the battlefield that were particularly hard to find.[2] Near as I can tell, two LBGs formed the list years earlier when they were driving together on a particularly long car ride. They attempted to "one-up" the other by naming a spot the other didn't know. After failing to establish which one of them was the undisputed master of Gettysburg-related minutiae, they put their list on the internet, where it somehow gained legitimacy.

I realized, of course, that finding all 140 locations on the LBG list did not necessarily qualify anyone as an "expert" in Gettysburg history, but I loved the idea of going on a battlefield scavenger hunt—one that would force me to see some of the far-flung, untrammeled areas of the park. I vowed to find them all.

Number 41 intrigued me. "D. A. Rock." For a time, I could not determine what it meant. There are thousands of boulders strewn across the battlefield, some conspicuous, others less so. Who or what was "D. A."? Frustrated, I approached one of my friends in the National Park Service and asked him for help.

"Coke," I asked, using his nickname, "have you ever heard of 'D. A. Rock'?" Strategically, I asked Coke because he had once been an LBG. I figured he might be willing to share their secrets.

Leaning back in his chair, he replied laconically, "Oh, yeah, that's the fellow in Zook's brigade, right?"

"So you know it?"

Coke smiled smugly, proud to possess an inconsequential detail about the battle that I did not. After only a few weeks at the park, I had acquired a reputation for knowing useless trivia, possibly to the point that it became an annoyance to my coworkers.

Coke replied, "Yeah, there's a book about it, in fact." He catapulted out of his chair and went into the stacks of Gettysburg National Military Park's excellent library. In a few seconds, he came back with a book and tossed it in my lap.[3]

"There," he said, "don't ever say that old Coke never did anything for you!"

It surprised me to discover that a whole book could be written about two letters on a rock, but the process of learning the story of the death and burial of Capt. David Acheson became an instructive moment for me. Specifically, it taught me *how* humans learn to appreciate history—how we draw *intangible* conclusions from *tangible* objects.

Here's what I learned.

David Acheson was born January 10, 1841, the third eldest of nine children born to Judge Alexander Wilson Acheson Sr. and Jane Wishart Acheson. The Achesons lived in Washington, Pennsylvania, a borough infamous for being one of the centers of the Whiskey Rebellion of 1794. By 1860, it had grown into a manufacturing hub and was home to two prominent institutions of higher learning. Politically divided, Washington contained a thriving abolitionist society and several popular "Copperhead" (prosouthern, antiwar) newspapers.

At the outbreak of the war, David Acheson was attending Washington College, his hometown's Presbyterian academy. When Abraham Lincoln called up seventy-five thousand militia to suppress the rebellion, he chose to enlist right away. Along with his older brother, John, he joined a company known as "Washington's Invincibles." The Invincibles filled their ranks in under a week, and on April 24, 1861, after journeying to Pittsburgh, Acheson and his seventy-six compatriots mustered in as Company E, 12th Pennsylvania.[4] When his company held elections to choose noncommissioned officers, Acheson received the rank of fourth sergeant.[5]

Acheson's term of service in the 12th Pennsylvania was fairly short. His regiment moved to Camp Scott, an uncomfortable training facility outside of York, Pennsylvania, where it received weapons and uniforms. During June and July, the 12th Pennsylvania performed uneventful guard duty along the Northern Central Railway, preventing Confederate sympathizers in Maryland from attacking the bridges. After several hot, laborious (but uneventful) weeks, the regiment mustered out of federal service on August 5, 1861.[6]

The Acheson brothers returned home from a bloodless campaign, having missed the debacle at Bull Run, and neither seemed content with civilian life. On November 2, John reenlisted in a three-year regiment—the 85th Pennsylvania—and marched off to war a second time.[7] David, meanwhile, returned to his studies at Washington College. He completed one more semester before again answering the war's siren call. In 1862 troubling news arrived from Virginia. Maj. Gen. George McClellan's Army of the Potomac commenced its controversial retreat from the gates of Richmond, and further, 2nd Lt. John Acheson had been wounded at the battle of Seven Pines on May 31, 1862.[8] This news had a telling effect on David. Unable to sit still any longer, he vowed that if the government asked for more troops, he would enlist again—this time for three years.

Providentially, the War Department gave him that chance. On July 2, 1862, President Lincoln called up three hundred thousand volunteers to reinforce McClellan's beleaguered army. Acheson leaped at the chance. Contacting two college friends who had served with him in the 12th Pennsylvania—Isaac Vance and Charles Linton—he proposed to raise a new company out of Washington College's students and alumni. If they recruited a sufficient number, Pennsylvania's governor might commission the three of them as officers.

Acheson executed an intense recruiting drive, spending his personal finances to print broadsides, to hire bands, and to travel to out-of-the-way places. By August 15, he had convinced eighty-five men to join his company, including his younger brother, Alexander Jr. (or "Sandie"). Primarily, his company filled with members of the Republican Party. Indeed, in 1862, the very act of enlisting often became a vote of confidence in the Lincoln administration, and the young Republicans of Washington County wished to show their neighbors that western Pennsylvanians still approved of the war and were ready to die for their country, if need be. One recruit remembered that, above all other concerns, "were the interests, for all time, of the imperilled country, the degradation and dismemberment of its flag, and the clear, unmistakable call to duty."[9]

On August 23, Acheson's company mustered into federal service, becoming Company C, 140th Pennsylvania Volunteer Infantry. Before their muster, the soldiers held an election and chose Acheson as their leader. All commissions required the governor's approval, of course, but Governor Andrew Curtin trusted the choice of the enlisted men, promoting Acheson to the rank of captain. Twelve days after the muster, Company C boarded cars bound for Bee Tree Station, Maryland, where it linked up with the main body of the 140th Pennsylvania.[10]

Even today, more than 156 years after Acheson's death, Acheson's reasons for joining the army are still a bit murky. After his death at Gettysburg, the *Washington Reporter* explained that Acheson's "spirit was again aroused by the President's call for 300,000 fresh troops, after the disasters before Richmond."[11] However, a few of Acheson's letters to his family offer an additional clue about his motivation.

In one cryptic letter to his sister, Acheson hinted that he joined the army to escape an awkward romantic situation. Acheson had had his heart broken by (or had broken the heart of) a neighbor. He wrote,

> There are some recollections connected with Maiden St. [where the Acheson home stood] that I wish I could forget (secrets you know.) A man must act the fool at some time of his life and I have done so. However, the wild oats one sows in his early years may produce the fruit he must eat for the rest of his life. At present I am contented to remain in the army. But I should not talk thus. No one is to blame save myself. Let me once again get free and I assure you for the rest of my life I shall be more circumspect. Please keep mum on this subject Mary. I do not know what induced me to write you thus but know weak minds need sympathy.[12]

Tantalizing as these lines may be—in suggesting that he may have left home to flee a bad breakup—Acheson's decision to fight more likely stemmed from his esoteric devotion to the American republic, now threatened by southern secession. At various points, Acheson's letters clarified his desire to preserve the political ideal established by America's founders. For instance, at Bee Tree Station, Acheson had dinner with his regimental commander, Col. Richard Petit Roberts, the district attorney of Beaver County. Although Roberts was also a Republican, Acheson was not impressed with his commander's cynical depiction of the war's goals. While discussing the state of the country, Roberts casually predicted the nation would never again be reunited. He argued that the "foundations of society" were so broken that "propositions for peace from the North or the South would be gladly received." Shocked by what he heard, Acheson asked his commander if he thought the situation would devolve into a condition equivalent to the French Revolution's "reign of terror." Roberts replied, "The country is ripe for it. The people of the country are dissatisfied. We cannot hold out another year. The influence of Christian education—the boasted morality of our people—will not be sufficient to restrain us."

Unamused, Acheson told Colonel Roberts that he must be "the wrong man in the wrong place." Writing to his father, Acheson wondered how his commander could think so little of American democracy. "Do you believe this?" Acheson wrote angrily, unable to comprehend his commander's negativity. Acheson contended that the southern Democrats would have "caused all of this"—that is, if Roberts's prediction of a reign of terror came to pass.[13]

Like many soldiers, Acheson believed that young men of his generation needed to put their lives on the line to protect the fragile republic. It vexed him to learn that members of the Democratic Party openly discussed establishing peaceful negotiations with the Confederacy. These Peace Democrats—the Copperheads—infuriated Acheson more than any Confederates he had yet to face. Writing to his father, Acheson commented, "I wonder how those Democrats at home can have the assurance to act as they do. Their hearts are certainly dead to every feeling that characterizes a patriot. Could they know how soldiers hate and despise them, would it not have some influence in turning them from their evil ways? Or have they become so besotted in treason to have forgotten those who are not exposing themselves to protect them at home?"[14]

More than anything, Acheson had faith that the Union army would restore the nation through victory. He continued, "The Army of the Potomac is the most democratic army we have, and yet were it called upon to give an opinion concerning the copperheads of the north it would give forth such a cry of hatred and disgust as would make the traitors tremble." Vowing to stamp out treasonous language in the North as harshly as treasonous activities in the South, Acheson threatened, "There were tories at the time of the Revolution. These are the tories now. May they meet with like execration and sink into the same oblivion as with those whom Washington had to contend."[15]

Acheson did not have long to wait to satisfy his eagerness to make the nation's traitors pay. The spring and summer of 1863 took the 140th Pennsylvania into two of the war's bloodiest campaigns. On May 3, 1863, the regiment engaged Confederate forces at Chancellorsville, losing forty-four killed and wounded.[16] Then, two months later—on July 2, 1863—the regiment found itself embroiled at Gettysburg. Taking 515 officers and men into the fray, the 140th Pennsylvania fought atop a small rocky knob (since known as the Stony Hill), just west of George Rose's twenty-acre wheatfield.

Advancing in line-of-battle, the 140th Pennsylvania entered into a fight that was in full swing. The regiment halted atop the Stony Hill, with its four right companies stationed in an open meadow. At 5:40 p.m., a brigade of South Carolina troops—about 1,460-strong—emerged from a cloud of smoke around the Rose farm buildings and engaged the Pennsylvanians. (According to a Confederate brigade commander, the shooting started at about two hundred yards, and it drifted closer until the opposing lines were about thirty yards apart.) After forty minutes, the Confederate line gave way.

Even so, the 140th Pennsylvania suffered heavily. Just as the Pennsylvanians made contact with the enemy, they lost their commander, Colonel Roberts, shot dead by the first volley.

Roberts was not the only officer to fall. During the height of the attack, a bullet struck Acheson in the chest. While being helped to the rear, he was hit by a second bullet that entered his body only a few inches from the first. As the battle raged, a helpful soldier assisted him, but somewhere along the way, Acheson died. No one ever recorded his last words.

At the time of his death, Acheson's comrades lacked any opportunity to evacuate his corpse. At 6:20 p.m., two fresh Confederate brigades swept in from the west, routing the 140th Pennsylvania and the other nearby regiments. Outnumbered and low on ammunition, the Pennsylvanians fell back in disorder. In his diary, 1st Sgt. Benjamin Powelson of Company K described the retreat as "all running for dear life."[17] At dusk, Union reinforcements reclaimed the area around the Wheatfield, which brought an end to the day's fighting. When the survivors of the 140th counted up their casualties, they tallied a horrendous butcher's bill: fifty-nine killed, thirty-seven captured, and one hundred forty-five wounded. Acheson's Company C—which held the far right of the 140th's line (and was thus not linked with any supporting regiment)—suffered the heaviest loss of any company in the regiment, losing seven killed, twenty-two wounded, and three captured out of thirty-eight officers and men.[18]

The Acheson family first learned of David's death when one of his comrades returned home after the battle. 1st Lt. Isaac Vance, who had helped recruit Company C, had been wounded in the left hand, which had to be amputated. He reached his hometown, Amity, on a mission to convince residents to raise funds to help care for the wounded men left on the field. While there, he conveyed the sad story of Acheson's death.

Acheson's father dispatched two of his first cousins, John and Todd Baird, and a schoolmate of his eldest son, James Blaine Wilson, to retrieve David's remains. These three men reached Gettysburg on July 13. Although the Army of the Potomac had since left the battlefield in pursuit of the retreating Confederate forces, detachments remained to bury the dead. The 140th Pennsylvania's grave-digging contingent was still there. Its commander, 2nd Lt. James B. Vandyke, met Wilson and the Bairds and directed them to the boulder with the carving. According to Wilson, who recalled the event fifty years later, the large rock served as the head of Acheson's grave, and "on which the initials D. A. were rudely cut with a nail or some such article." As a memento, Wilson cut a geranium from the Weikert garden to give to Acheson's father.

Collecting Acheson's corpse was no easy feat. The rented carriage moved slowly. The horses that pulled it often struck unexploded shells, but providentially, none of them burst. The weather was hot and muggy, and the smell of thousands of unburied horses filled the party's nostrils "to saturation." In fact, Todd Baird contracted typhoid fever due to his brief exposure to the battlefield. After only a few minutes of excavating, Wilson and the Bairds found Acheson's body. They placed it in

Judge Alexander W. Acheson, father of David Acheson, dispatched three young men to Gettysburg to recover his son's remains. Courtesy of Charles Joyce.

Grave of David Acheson, Washington Cemetery, Washington, Pennsylvania. Photograph by Mark Marietta.

a zinc-lined coffin and began an overland trek to Harrisburg, with Wilson sitting atop the coffin to keep it closed. According to Wilson, "rain poured in torrents almost every mile of the way over the rough mountain road. The lightning flashes were our only light, though part of the way, the driver had a dim lantern which he carried as he walked beside the wagon, being afraid to ride with a corpse after dark."[19]

The exhumation party reached Harrisburg after midnight on July 14 and put the coffin on a train, which arrived at Pittsburgh by midnight, July 15. Via open wagon, Wilson and the Bairds took the coffin to the Acheson residence on Maiden Street, arriving there by 10 a.m., July 15. Later that day, after the funeral service, the Achesons interred David's remains in the family plot in Washington Cemetery.

Although communities everywhere were grieving from the tragic losses at Gettysburg, Captain Acheson's death hit hard because he had become Washington's local hero. On the day of his interment, the *Washington Reporter* described his contribution to the Union's cause this way: "His name shall live in hallowed association with the blood-stained field upon which his country's liberty and fame were redeemed in triumph."[20]

Such proud words undoubtedly suited the public nature of the funeral, but they described inadequately the grief felt by the family. Months later, Acheson's father still felt downtrodden by the memory of his fallen son. On November 8 he wrote: "I can look nowhere about our grounds without being reminded of the son whose taste ran in the same channel and whom I finally hoped, if God spared my life to old age, would take charge of the garden and grounds and make them a source of profit and pleasure to us. That hope has been dashed and broken."[21]

Back in Gettysburg, the boulder remained, unspoiled, except for the scar carved into it by a well-meaning Union soldier. In fact, over the years, the makeshift headstone improved in quality. At some point before 1869, someone—probably a veteran—hired a professional stonecutter, refining the quality of the chiseling. The boulder now read:

D. A.
140
P. V.

Eventually, the veterans of the 140th raised money to fund two monuments on the battlefield—one dedicated in 1885 and the other in 1889—but they never forgot the boulder. Frequent visitation kept the rock and its initials alive in the minds of Gettysburg residents. Eventually, a local photographer, William H. Tipton, took a photograph of the boulder in the 1880s, which is perhaps the earliest known image of it. For a time, D. A. Rock became as well known as any monument on the field, but when the National Park Service developed new touring roads in the 1930s, the boulder became isolated from the main track, and in consequence, it was rarely visited. Only the most dedicated enthusiasts knew of its location.

But in late August 1999, I finally found my way to D. A. Rock. I had to trudge through knee-high, tick-infested grass to get there. A few tiny, faded American flags—likely placed by a reenactor unit—helped mark the spot.

The rock's relative isolation was, nonetheless, welcome. Removed from the crush of visitors who usually filled the battlefield every summer, I was, for a few minutes, alone.

D. A. Rock. Photograph by Melissa Winn.

Naturally, I felt the need to commune with the boulder, to contemplate my reason for seeing it. For whatever reason, I felt as if I had to learn a lesson from this experience. At first, I thought hard about courage, the trait that brought Acheson to Gettysburg. At the time, I wasn't sure what constituted valor in battle, but as a form of praise or flattery, I believed (and still believe) it should be given to those who gave their last full measure of devotion. War's dead can, and should, always be heroic.

But these thoughts didn't satisfy me. Next, I thought at length about death. As a young person, I felt as if I could understand Acheson better than most of Gettysburg's visitors. At the time, I was twenty years old, only two years younger than Acheson when he died. I wondered if he would be comfortable with his legacy—"D.A. 140 P.V."—four letters and three numbers chiseled into a desolate stone. Abstractly, it didn't seem right. I couldn't imagine dying tomorrow and leaving the letters "T. O." notched into an unadorned slab of concrete.

I also thought about Acheson's life. Had he lived it to the fullest? For as much as I now knew about him, he seemed tragically unknowable. I thought about the emotions swirling in the minds of his friends and family: his parents, his schoolmates, his brothers and sisters, his fellow soldiers, and the nameless heartbreak from his hometown.

Finally, I thought about the path that brought me to the boulder: my discovery of the "140 Places Every Guide Should Know,"

Memorial *carte de visite* produced following Acheson's death. Courtesy of Charles Joyce.

my friend Coke's assistance in the NPS library, and Sara G. Walter's helpful book. They were the final steps in a path that started when Captain Henry's four-man squad chiseled their inscription on July 4, 1863. In just two letters, they had created something permanent, a mark upon the battlefield, the battle's first headstone.

But it was more than just a headstone. It was an unhealable scar upon the land, a message left to future generations. D. A. Rock is a memorial to war's ferocity—an epitaph to its sadness, the price paid by the courageous, those who died at Gettysburg.

Unlike so many other memorials that celebrate the grandeur of war, D. A. Rock is beautifully, simplistically sad. My time at the rock forced me to imagine the men who carried Acheson's remains to this spot and, with nothing else but a nail and hatchet, created a permanent signature for his resting place.

Moreover, my experience warned me never to trivialize a piece of Gettysburg's history ever again. D. A. Rock was the tale of a man's life. A tale of his death. A tale of his sacrifice. Traditionally, America's soldiers have given their lives freely. Knowing that, we, the nation's citizens, should make a concerted effort to reflect upon all the forces that have made it so.

As I departed, my opinion of Gettysburg's battlefield—and the raw emotions it stirred—was forever changed.

Graves Forgotten and Found

EDWARD L. AYERS

During a visit to my late grandparents' farm in Burnsville, western North Carolina, several years ago, a flash of color caught my eye in the small family graveyard at the top of the hill. I had been fascinated by that cemetery as a child, sadly noting the rough blank slabs that marked some graves, the ornate memorials of others, and a photograph of a woman embedded in glass on her tombstone.

At the hill's crest, I found a small North Carolina Confederate flag. It bore the twinned dates of North Carolina's commitment to the American Revolution and then to secession in 1861. The tombstone attested that James H. Roland had been born in 1832 and lived until 1920, so I knew he had not died in the war. The headstone itself made no mention of the Confederacy; instead, it bore an engraving of a church and the admonition to "weep not for he is at rest."

Attached to the bottom of the flag was a detachable tag bearing a web address for the Sons of Confederate Veterans. I wrote them an email to ask about the unexpected appearance of the flag in our remote cemetery. A representative promptly replied that my ancestor had been a member of the home guard for the Confederacy, serving his community by traveling to Saltville, Virginia, in 1864 to procure supplies for his neighbors from the only reliable salt mine in the Confederacy, traversing western North Carolina, East Tennessee, and southwestern Virginia, a terrain not only mountainous but teeming with guerrillas, bushwhackers, thieves, and enemy armies.[1]

If he had been a bit younger, Roland would probably have fought in the Confederate army: Yancey County, despite its low numbers of enslaved people, had sent many men to the southern cause. Yancey men had rallied in defiance of abolitionists as early as 1859, in the wake of John Brown's raid; its first volunteers, the "Black Mountain Boys," were mustered into Confederate service in Raleigh in June 1861. Yancey supplied so many men, in fact, that the county court declared in December 1862 that no more could be spared. In June 1863 Governor Zebulon Vance formed the home guard as unionists and the disaffected grew stronger, as the chaos in nearby East Tennessee threatened to spill over the state line. Despite the home guard, in April 1864 the commander of the unit wrote the governor to admit that "the county is gone up." Forty or fifty women had "marched in a body to a store-house" and "carried off" sixty bushels of "Government wheat." The next day, a group of seventy-five unionist men, led by a former Confederate soldier, killed the enrolling officer for the southern army, took or destroyed about a hundred guns, and confiscated five hundred pounds of bacon. The Confederate command sent two hundred fifty men with artillery to confront the four hundred insurgents. The Confederates succeeded in driving out the "tories," as they called the unionists, but by the spring the United States army openly recruited in Yancey.[2]

What I learned about James Roland and Yancey's home guard was news to me, for my family passed on no memories of the Civil War. I once asked my grandfather why we never talked about the war. His answer was simple: "Son, we shot each other." The people of Appalachia were sharply divided. The mountain areas of the South held fewer enslaved people and more unionists than the lowlands, so I liked to imagine that my ancestors had transcended slavery and secession to remain proud American yeomen. But, in reality, I had no idea which way we shot. People learned not to talk too much about the war after war's end, when neighbors had to live among one another. They often voted for generations as their ancestors had fought—Confederates turned into Democrats, unionists into Republicans—even if they forgot the origins of their loyalties. The memory of the Civil War faded in the mountains because people wanted it to, needed it to.

As a social historian, I spent years plowing through censuses, letters, diaries, receipts, military records, and memoirs of people I did not know, whose families I would never meet. I wove entire books out of such materials, treasuring glimpses into people's private motivations and thoughts. I helped build a website that presented an array of genealogical materials for two counties in the years surrounding the Civil War, years before Ancestry.com made such sources commonplace—and profitable. Preoccupied with writing histories of other people's families, I had never explored my own genealogy. Fortunately, a great-uncle sent my mother a brief xeroxed report about our family's background. He had been inspired to examine our family's history when another person with the same last name asked my uncle to take a DNA test to see if they were related. He joined Ancestry.com and paid another company for a DNA test that showed he was, as expected, of British ancestry. Intrigued, he gathered "hard data" from many other family members and "traveled all over Yancey County looking at graveyards."

After his research, my uncle concluded that "We are a God-fearing, hard-working, Scotch-Irish family who loves their country and who have been and continue to be willing to pay the price for the freedom that we all enjoy. I think it is important for us to know where we came from to better understand just who we really are." As with so many southern families, the pride of fighting for our "country" and paying the price of freedom transferred directly to and from the Confederacy. Two of our ancestors had fought for the Black Mountain Boys. One soldier, Robert King, fought at Chattanooga and Chickamauga before being taken prisoner and shipped to Camp Morton in Indiana, where he died of pneumonia.

The other Confederate soldier from my mother's side of our family was a young man named Ansel Randolph. Ansel's family treasured a letter his brother, Thomas L. Randolph, had written home in July 1862 from Richmond. "Dear wife father and mother brothers and sisters with a sad heart and tearful eyes I seat myself this morning to inform you that our beloved brother and son Ansel is dead," it began. The young brother had been wounded in the battle of Mechanicsville, the first of what would become known as the Seven Days battles of the Peninsula Campaign, the battle in which Robert E. Lee took command after Joseph Johnston's wounding. The Confederates lost the battle after suffering twice as many casualties as the United States, but George McClellan dropped back in the face of Lee's unexpected aggressiveness. The southern forces lost 1,400 men to death or wounds, and Ansel Randolph was one of those causalities.

Hit in the leg by a ball, Ansel was taken to a hospital—perhaps the immense new Chimborazo facility in Richmond. Thomas worried over the wounded men who surrounded Ansel in the hospital, noting that "the weather is so hot that it seems all most impossible for them to exist." Though Ansel's "wounds were doing finely until 4 days ago," infection set in and "he commenced getting worse and remained so till he died." Thomas assured his family, and himself, that "I have done all that I could for him for I have stood right by him all the time knight and days without sleeping or ceasing."

Most of Thomas's letter focused on the heavenly glory that awaited Ansel, for "he has been true and punctual to his duties as a Christian soldier. he has been faithful in reading his Bible all of the time he could and has at no time ever disgraced the name of Christianity by following any bad example or using any profane language. He has been mild and sober and faithful to his duties." Thomas told his family that "I hope you will not grieve after him but rather rejoice that he is in a world of bliss and happiness while we are in a world of trouble."

Ansel Randolph received a warm obituary in the Yancey County newspaper, which noted that Randolph had been "among the first to lay his life on his country's alter." He had just turned twenty-one when he enlisted with the Black Mountain Boys, and "when he went into the service of his country he took his Bible of which he made a companion, and on its promises he founded his hope of future bliss; and he died as he had lived—a Christian." In his final moments Ansel "praised God for dying grace, said he was not afraid to die, and left an especial request to all his friends and relatives to meet him in a better world, where there would be no war and bloodshed, but all will be peace and joy. After commending his soul to God, he fell asleep in Jesus."[3]

Thomas wanted to send Ansel's body back to Yancey County for burial but discovered that "the law requires a metal coffin made air tight befour they can be transported by railroad" and such a coffin cost $115, an impossible amount. Instead, Ansel would "be buried here in the large grave yard near this place and his grave will be marked so that if I can have a chance of bringing him home here after I will know where to find him." Ansel was buried in what became Oakwood Cemetery, where many of those who died in Chimborazo or other hospitals on the eastern side of Richmond were taken by wagon. Burial crews tried to put only one man in each grave, though in times of emergency

Graves of Confederate soldiers marked with board markers, in Oakwood Cemetery, Richmond, Virginia, ca. April–June 1865. Photographed by John Reekie. Courtesy of the Library of Congress.

more might be laid in together; Ansel's grave contained three young men. By September of the year Ansel died, 5,483 men had already been interred in Oakwood; by the end of the war, the number had reached about 12,000 and the cemetery had fallen into disarray.

White women took Oakwood Cemetery under their care soon after the war, raising money for headboards. By 1867, one report said, all the graves had been identified by name, regiment, and state on thick planks of wood, black letters on white paint. Twenty years later, however, those planks had rotted beyond use or been taken for firewood. The graves remained unmarked for another fifteen years. While efforts to install marble blocks began early in the twentieth century, the process struggled. In the late twentieth century the Sons of Confederate Veterans assumed responsibility for the care of the Confederate portion of the cemetery, including the installation of new markers, one of which marks the grave of Ansel Randolph.

This was where a neat essay was supposed to end, with a satisfying conclusion: two forgotten graves, forgotten no longer thanks to those who kept the letters, researched the genealogy, and shared their knowledge. Jon White and I planned to contrast a photograph of James Roland's gravesite in the beautiful mountain cemetery with Ansel Randolph's cold bureaucratic marker in the mass burial site of Richmond.

Erected by the Oakwood Confederate Cemetery Trust in 2007, this monument is "Dedicated to the Memory of the Thousands of Confederate Soldiers Who Gave Their All and Who Repose Here Known But to God." Ansel Randolph is buried on the hill behind and across the street from this marker. Photograph by Jonathan W. White.

But the essay could not end with that conclusion after all. Jon, commissioning a photographer and demonstrating a devotion to telling the full story, asked if I could contact my cousin who owns the land where James Roland is buried. I did so, but my kinsman told me that he had removed the Confederate flag and did not want a photographer to visit because he didn't want to risk "protesters" showing up on the farm. I assured him that we would not identify the location of the graveyard and that there was nothing to protest, but the images he had seen of controversies over Confederate monuments had alarmed him. I could not persuade him, despite our close boyhood friendship. The photo of Roland's headstone I had taken several years before on my phone was not suitable for publication, so my hope of juxtaposing the lonely marker in Oakwood Cemetery with the lovely gravesite in the family cemetery disappeared.

In the meantime, Jon had located Ansel Randolph on Ancestry.com, with a photograph of a man standing at the young soldier's grave at Oakwood Cemetery. The small stone marker had been knocked off-kilter by a mower, but the digital marker on the Ancestry site read clearly: Lot CQ, 112. A small clutch of plastic

Grave of Ansel Randolph, Confederate Section, section C, row Q, grave 112, Oakwood Cemetery, Richmond, Virginia. Photograph by Jonathan W. White.

flowers lay on his grave. The man in the photo would not talk with Jon when he called the number online, his academic credentials inadequate reassurance of his purity of motive. My family, on both sides, proved steadfastly resistant to historical inquiry.

The story took yet another turn when Jon discovered, again online, a puzzling gravesite for Ansel Randolph in Yancey County. This time, Jon established a relationship with a man responsible for the graveyard at the church who, in turn, reached out to another Randolph, an elderly caretaker of the cemetery records. Our new ally reported that "Ansel Randolph is not buried in our cemetery. He is buried there in Virginia. Mr. Randolph believes he was killed at Mechanicsburg, Virginia." Referring, it seems, to the same letter I had seen, the Randolph descendant reported that "Ansel's brother Thomas sent the folks here in Green Mountain a letter telling them that he could not afford to send Ansel's body back to Green Mountain so he had him buried there in Virginia. The folks here in Green Mountain had the stone placed in our cemetery so that he would not be forgotten." A North Carolina Confederate flag stands near the tombstone of the empty gravesite, mirrored by that of a brother. Ansel Randolph's body lies hundreds of miles to the north, but his memory lives in the mountains of Yancey County.

Despite its twists and turns, then, the moral of the story remains the same: things once forgotten can be recalled. Though

Headstone for Ansel Randolph, Pleasant Grove Cemetery, Burnsville, Yancey County, North Carolina. Photograph by Johnny Hewett.

we grow farther from the war each day, new means of memory and renewed determination can connect us to events and people long past. Through the improbable means of electronic networks, long-silent places murmur their messages once again. Our understanding of the war, and of ourselves, can grow rather than fade.

A Life on His Own Terms

Albert D. J. Cashier, 95th Illinois Infantry

DEANNE BLANTON

On October 10, 1915, Union veteran Albert D. J. Cashier died at the Watertown State Hospital in Illinois at the age of seventy-one. The local chapter of the Grand Army of the Republic (GAR) arranged his funeral in the Sunnyslope Cemetery in Saunemin. Cashier was buried with full military honors, dressed in his uniform. His grave was marked with the standard government headstone provided to those who had served their country.

Born on Christmas Day 1843 in Clogherhead, Ireland, Cashier immigrated to the United States prior to 1860. By 1861, he had journeyed from New York City to Illinois and was employed as a farmhand. On August 3, 1862, at the age of nineteen, Cashier enlisted in the 95th Illinois Infantry. Cashier stood 5'4" and was described as "a short well built man." With his light complexion, blue eyes, and auburn hair, he resembled the many other Irish Americans serving in the Union army. But unlike many of his peers, Cashier was illiterate. He could not read, and he signed his enlistment papers with an X.

During his service, Cashier was present at approximately forty battles and skirmishes. He was held in esteem by the men in his company and maintained a reputation as a reliable soldier. He was a hardy soldier as well and made it through the war without illness or injury, except for the ever-present chronic diarrhea that plagued nearly every combatant. Cashier mustered out with his regiment on August 17, 1865, having served his full three-year commitment.

After the war, Cashier lived in four Illinois towns, working as a laborer and briefly owning a plant nursery with a friend from his regiment, before settling permanently in Saunemin in 1869. He held a variety of jobs over the next forty years, including farmhand, handyman, day laborer, child sitter, janitor, property caretaker, and town lamplighter. Cashier never married. His social life largely revolved around the local chapter of the GAR, in which he was a long-standing member. From all accounts, Cashier was well liked by his neighbors and employers. In 1890, with the help of a local attorney, Cashier applied for and received a veteran's pension.

In early 1911, while doing odd jobs for Illinois state senator Ira Lish, Cashier's leg was fractured when Lish accidentally backed over him with his automobile. This marked a turning point in Cashier's life. Although treated by a local physician, the leg never properly healed, and Cashier was permanently disabled at the age of sixty-six. Unable to support himself through manual labor, Cashier was admitted on April 11, 1911, to the Illinois Soldiers' and Sailors' Home in Quincy.

Although bedridden some of the time, Cashier reportedly enjoyed the nearly three years he lived at the home. He was amongst his peers and friends. Unfortunately, his mental health declined, and by 1913 the home physicians concurred that Cashier was senile. The Illinois Soldiers' and Sailors' Home was not equipped to care for soldiers with dementia, and on March 27, 1914, in the Adams County Court, Albert Cashier and seven other veterans were judged "distracted" and insane, and committed to the Watertown State Hospital. The last year and a half of Cashier's life was spent in the asylum. It was reported that both his mental and physical health failed rapidly after his arrival.

The life story of Albert Cashier reads very much like the life story of thousands of Union soldiers and veterans. He was an immigrant, working-class man living in a small town who heeded the call to war, and afterward was a proud veteran who accepted the honors and privileges due him as such. It's the common story of the common soldier. Except Albert Cashier was not very common at all. Albert Cashier was assigned female at birth and given the name Jennie Hodgers.

The transformation of Jennie into Albert is not documented; there are no substantiated facts about the time, place, and circumstances. But by the age of eighteen, Albert Cashier had shed a female identity and opted to live his life as a male. Those who

Woman Soldier in 95th Ill.

ALBERT D. J. CASHIER
OF
COMPANY G, 95TH ILLINOIS REGIMENT
Photographed November, 1864

ALBERT D. J. CASHIER
OF
COMPANY G, 95TH ILLINOIS REGIMENT
Photographed July, 1913

"Woman Soldier in 95th Ill." Courtesy of the Abraham Lincoln Presidential Library and Museum.

knew Cashier throughout his adult life never suspected that he was not a man. When Cashier's biological secret was finally divulged, it was met with shock and disbelief among his neighbors, employers, and brothers-in-arms. But when the shock wore off, it was replaced by singular kindness toward Cashier, who was, after all, a respected member of his community. That respect did not wane in the face of Cashier's eschewing of gender norms.

If Senator Lish had not run over him, Cashier's sex might never have been publicized. It was the town doctor, called to set the leg, who made the discovery. He and the senator agreed to keep quiet their knowledge, and carefully selected two others with whom to discuss the situation: two sisters who employed Cashier and who agreed to care for him during his convalescence. All four individuals believed that Cashier should continue living his life as he always had, and they had no wish to violate his privacy.

When it became apparent that Cashier would never work again, Senator Lish arranged for Cashier's entrance into the Soldiers' and Sailors' Home. As a disabled veteran of the Union army, Cashier qualified to live at the home, but it was certainly due to the influence of the senator that the superintendent of the home agreed to accept Cashier and keep the secret. Doctors and nurses employed at the home were also informed of Cashier's sex and also sworn to secrecy. Again, those involved in Cashier's care seemed committed to allowing him to live as he always had.

But by 1914, nearly a dozen people knew that Cashier was a biological woman, and it was perhaps inevitable that someone divulged his secret. It is unclear who initially broke the vow of silence, but sensationalized newspaper stories about Albert Cashier hit the stands. The other residents of the home, the people of Saunemin, the veterans of the 95th Illinois Infantry, and, indeed, the rest of the country read about Cashier's "deception" in local, state, and national papers. When word reached the Pension Bureau, they appointed a special examiner to investigate the case, convinced that Cashier had defrauded the government for the past twenty-four years.

As news of Cashier's sex reached his friends and comrades, he received more frequent visitors. Some went of their own volition, and others were sent at the behest of the Pension Bureau. Newspaper reporters also descended on him. Cashier had no idea that his life story was available for public consumption, and the realization that everyone knew his secret made him feel vulnerable and afraid. In the midst of all the publicity, Cashier was remanded to the state hospital. Cashier's sex was not mentioned in the court proceedings, as all eight of the veterans were referred to as male.

Officials at Watertown State Hospital were well aware of Cashier's sex, and when he arrived at the facility, he was separated from the other veterans, placed in the women's wing, and forced to wear women's clothing, despite his protests. Forcing Cashier to wear long skirts had tragic consequences. He was a frail seventy-year-old who did not know how to walk in such apparel. He tripped, fell, broke his hip, and spent the rest of his life confined to his bed.

The actions of hospital personnel greatly incensed Cashier's fellow veterans, who could hardly bear to witness the humiliation of one who had once been so "brave and fearless." His friends from the 95th Illinois rallied around him, and although their protests over his treatment fell on deaf ears, their support and visits were undoubtedly a comfort to Cashier in his lucid moments. His most frequent visitor was his former commanding officer, Charles W. Ives. As far as the veterans of the 95th Illinois Infantry were concerned, Cashier's sex was not important. After the shock of learning that Cashier was biologically female, they became protective and solicitous. Cashier was one of their own, and sexual identity and gender propriety paled in comparison to their fellowship, to the permanent bonds they had forged in war.

Meanwhile, the Pension Bureau continued its investigation, with the special examiner contacting former employers, neighbors in Saunemin, and veterans of Cashier's regiment. The examiner especially wanted to know if the old soldiers of the 95th Illinois could positively identify the old woman at the asylum as being the same young person who enlisted in 1862. The universal response was yes. Those men deposed by the examiner also consistently praised Cashier's performance as a soldier and swore that no one ever knew he was female during or after the war. The investigation ultimately determined, in February 1915, that "the evidence secured in this case shows beyond any possible doubt that the pensioner is the person who rendered the service. . . . Identity may be accepted."

Cashier was laid to rest more than a century ago, but his story lives on in historical narratives and popular culture. The warm regard that neighbors and employers in his adopted hometown felt toward him in life continue to this day. The town of Saunemin seems very proud of Cashier and has restored his modest one-room home as a museum.

On Memorial Day 1977, the citizens of Saunemin held a ceremony at Cashier's grave and unveiled a second headstone, one that includes his birth name. More recently, a fresh government headstone has replaced the damaged original.[1]

The dual headstones are representative of the duality of Albert Cashier. The government stone presents Cashier as he wanted to be known, and it is significant that this is the stone requested by the GAR. The stone erected by the town presents the broader legacy of Cashier. Largely due to the efforts of the Pension Bureau, Albert Cashier's life is fairly well documented. What is not truly known, however, are his motivations and inner thoughts. Why did Jennie Hodgers become Albert Cashier?

Albert Cashier is certainly not the only woman to pass as a man in nineteenth-century America. Among working- and

Gravestones of Albert D. J. Cashier, Sunny Slope Cemetery, East Moline, Illinois. Photograph by David Wiegers.

immigrant-class women, living as a man gave them a plethora of legal, social, and economic opportunities denied to them as women. Living as men allowed them to bypass the barriers preventing them from having a good-paying job and an independent life. Living as a man meant they were not forced into marriages. Living as a man meant they were free to keep their own money and handle their own finances. Enough nineteenth-century women were passing as men that towns and states enacted ordinances against cross-dressing, hoping that a night in jail and a hefty fine would send those women back to their designated place in society.

Albert Cashier is also not the only woman to serve as a soldier during the Civil War. Hundreds, if not thousands, of women passed as men in order to enlist in the armies of the Union and the Confederacy. Distaff soldiers fought on battlefields from First Manassas to Appomattox Court House. About a third of women soldiers went to war with their husbands. Others enlisted because they wanted to serve their country. Still others enlisted because they wanted for themselves the prerogatives reserved for men.[2]

Available documentation of nineteenth-century women who passed as men, whether in military service or civilian life, indicates that the majority returned to their assigned gender role, either by choice or coercion. Albert Cashier decided to live his entire adult life as a man. From an economic and social viewpoint, such a decision made pragmatic sense. Cashier's illiteracy guaranteed that he would make his living from his labor, and having lived as a man prior to and during the Civil War, Cashier was well acquainted with all the privileges bestowed upon men, and even more so upon Union veterans.

Of course, it is entirely possible that economic possibility and personal security were not the reasons that Jennie Hodgers became Albert D. J. Cashier. Albert Cashier may be a historical example of a transgender man. Cashier was assigned female at birth and given the name Jennie, but perhaps this was not the correct gender identity and expression for this individual. Perhaps Jennie left Ireland so that he could be Albert; so that he could live the identity that was right for him.

The historical record gives us no definitive answers. By the time individuals began interviewing Cashier and pressing him for answers, he was already suffering from dementia. He gave different stories to different people, and some sensed he was just trying to tell them what he thought they wanted to hear. What is obvious from the historical record is that Albert Cashier was exactly as his brothers-in-arms described him. He lived a life that was authentic for him. He lived his life on his own terms. Brave and fearless, indeed.

Encounters with the *Monitor* Boys

ANNA GIBSON HOLLOWAY

I first visited with the two "*Monitor* Boys" when they were still 240 feet below me, resting in the one-mile column of water that defines the Monitor National Marine Sanctuary, which is under the auspices of the National Oceanic and Atmospheric Administration (NOAA). The sanctuary, located sixteen miles off Cape Hatteras, North Carolina, is located in an area that rightfully bears the epithet "Graveyard of the Atlantic." Countless ships in times of war and peace have met their doom here. In that sense, the *Monitor*'s men were not alone in their watery tomb.

It was late July 2002. The presence of the two bodies had just been made known the day before when navy divers encountered smooth bone inside the turret. In the span of a few hours, an archaeological object that had been the subject of years of planning and millions of dollars of funding had suddenly become a grave. Work necessarily slowed. It became a more delicate operation with this new discovery. Salvage divers, used to handling big hunks of metal and (with *Monitor*) interminable hunks of coal, now had to move with surgical precision.

We had known that this might be the case. Being the only means of egress from the vessel on the fateful night of her sinking, it was a logical guess that some of the sixteen who had gone down with *Monitor* that night might be found within the twenty-one-foot diameter cylinder. It was purely happenstance that my visit would occur just twenty-four hours after this major discovery. Departing from Hatteras Village on a resupply vessel, I made the sixteen-mile trek out to the sanctuary in the wake of a

"Loss of the 'Monitor' in a Storm Off Cape Hatteras, December 30th, 1862." Courtesy of Naval History and Heritage Command.

tropical storm. Swells of green water gave way to electric blue as we entered the Gulf Stream. Flying fish whirred beside us, and the smell of diesel was ever-present (and diesel has ever been my kryptonite while on the water). Soon, the barge *Wotan* began to rise up like a misty dream from the horizon—a small village in the middle of the ocean. As the transport vessel wallowed while we began to make the ship-to-barge transfer, off-duty divers and scientists lined the sides of the *Wotan* to see who was coming to visit. And to find out who was hopelessly seasick.

As I whirled over the Atlantic on a Billy Pugh dangling from the massive crane, I wondered how I would feel (besides seasick—I had obliged them on that count). I had been named the curator of the nascent USS *Monitor* Center the previous November. I had been living with *Monitor*'s men as cyphers—two-dimensional beings who existed as ink on paper, emulsion on glass. And now I would be the closest to both ship and men as I had yet been.

The mood on the *Wotan* was electric—and the action unceasing. This was a twenty-four-hour training operation for the navy, and the prize for NOAA would be the successful recovery of the iconic cheese box and its contents. Capt. (select) Barbara Scholley of Mobile Diving and Salvage Unit-2 (MDSU-2) took the time to briefly discuss her thoughts with me. Though the mission's original purpose had been to recover the turret, she now understood that their new mission was to bring these two shipmates home.

A NOAA diver surveys the USS *Monitor* wreck site on August 10, 2011. Courtesy of NOAA.

The "spider" lifts the turret of the *Monitor* from the seafloor off Cape Hatteras, North Carolina, in August 2002. Courtesy of the NOAA Monitor Collection.

Or three—or maybe more. At this point, the turret still held its secrets. I watched footage from the operation below and listened to the comically high voices of the saturation divers as they worked—their bodies saturated with mixed gas for their long-term work at pressure.

A little over a week later, on August 5, 2002, the turret rose from the depths—a precious prize held securely in the claws of the "spider"—a device invented specifically for recovering the iconic artifact. Back at The Mariners' Museum that day, I recall sending out silent entreaties to the universe—to anything or anyone that might be listening—to bring everyone, both the living recovery crew and the two ironclad sailors, home safely. We were all rewarded when the turret broke the surface of the Atlantic—intact and strangely beautiful as water sluiced down in an epic fountain before the turret was gently placed on the deck of the *Wotan* by Bubba, the crane operator. Archaeologists then took over from the divers and began the meticulous work of removing the remains while still at sea. Soon they and the turret would be brought to The Mariners' Museum and be under our care for a time.

I first saw the turret as the *Wotan* arrived at the shipyard in Newport News, Virginia. The turret would be loaded onto a smaller barge and would travel up the James River to a landing point at The Mariners' Museum Park. Invited aboard, I was able to inspect this iconic piece of history up close. I was invited to touch it. It is hard to describe the cacophony of emotions I experienced at that moment. This abstract idea of a gun turret was suddenly very real—and it had returned to the waters that made her famous on March 9, 1862, when *Monitor* met her nemesis *Virginia* (née *Merrimack*) in what would be the first battle between ironclad warships.

Finally, the day came for the turret to arrive at the museum. August 10, 2002, was long, hot, full of skirling bagpipes and the intensely wonderful smell of black powder, and was, quite frankly, one of the best days of my professional life.

The turret came home that day—near to the scene of its former glory—traversing the same waters it cruised 140 years before, along with some of that same crew. As the barge slowly made its way upriver, you could almost believe for a little while that it was really 1862 and that *Monitor* was on her way up the James. The barge that carried the turret was perhaps a bit too short and had a bit too much freeboard, but I don't think that the comparison was lost on anyone.

As the turret stood there at the intersection of Museum Drive and Museum Parkway, the reality of what it was hit several people very hard. There were many eyes filled with tears when Gregg Vaughan read the names of the sixteen men who had perished and when the Chesapeake Sheriff's Pipe Band played "Amazing Grace." There really was nothing gratuitous or maudlin about it. When all the reenactors and spectators fell in around and behind the trailer to escort the turret to its new home, again, the response was spontaneous and genuine. So many people came up to us and thanked us for allowing them to be a part of the day. I in turn thanked Capt. Chris Murray and Capt. Bobbie Scholley of MDSU-2 and Dr. John Broadwater of NOAA for making it all possible when I saw them later. Bear hugs from so many of the master divers were also a highlight of the day!

And so I encountered the *Monitor* boys a second time as we continued the excavation work in our makeshift lab behind the museum. It wasn't unusual to see staff roaming around wearing trash bags to keep the water (and the smell of 140 years of sea life) out of our clothing. Of necessity, our team of curators, conservators, educators, and administrators at the museum became versed in the Geneva Conventions and other things we never imagined learning. As the two fully articulated skeletons were removed from their first resting place, they found a new home in our photographic cold storage until they could be sent to the Department of Defense's Central Identification Laboratory in Hawaii (CILHI) for hopeful identification. So, for a time they shared space with us—though separated by padlock, guard, and protocol. Each of us working on the project was affected in different ways. Gallows humor mixed with spontaneous tears in the hallways as we each grappled with the reality that they were here. With us. But only temporarily.[1]

In time, they left us for their next temporary home at CILHI (now the Defense POW/MIA Accounting Agency or DPAA) in Hawaii. We waited to hear the results. Would we find out who they were? Was one of them Jacob Nicklis, perhaps? He was the young man whose letters I had acquired for the museum during a Bronze Door Society competition, a cutthroat curatorial competition in which the curators present their objects or projects to this donor group in creative ways, all the while insulting or pranking their fellow curators, much to the delight of the crowd.[2] (Despite everyone's best attempts, I won that night.)

We received the initial reports from the forensics lab. Though still nameless, their bones began to share their secrets. One individual was between thirty and forty years of age, a heavy smoker with a slight limp, and stood at about 5'6". The other was younger—between eighteen and twenty-four, and slightly taller. Both had broken but healing noses—perhaps the result of

The turret of the USS *Monitor* in conservation at The Mariners' Museum in Newport News, Virginia. Courtesy of The Mariners' Museum.

a Christmas shore-leave brawl with the crew of a British ship in port in Hampton Roads. One wore a gold band on his right hand. What clothing was left indicated they were enlisted, though, in the chaos of the sinking, clothing was tossed about as men heading to the rescue boats thought better of wearing their heavy wool coats as they leapt across the roiling water. Also indicative of the chaos was the fact that one of the men was wearing mismatched shoes. Mismatched silverware also lay strewn about them in the turret—though by whose agency it came to be there could not be ascertained. Some utensils bore initials: SAL for 3rd Assistant Engineer Samuel Auge Lewis; JN for Seaman Jacob Nicklis; NKA for Acting Ensign Norman Knox Atwater; and Acting Ensign George Frederickson's spoon bore his full name. All names that were known to me, and all names of men who had perished with the vessel. We knew Nicklis through his letters, but we knew George by sight as he glowered in the Virginia summer heat from the image taken by photographer James Gibson in July 1862. These men were all too real to us, despite being separated by 140 years.

Years passed. Work on the artifacts and on the center continued, with the turret, engine, and smaller objects revealing their secrets under the careful hands of our conservators. When we opened our doors to the public on March 9, 2007, we honored the men of *Monitor*, but we were still no closer to knowing who the two from the turret were. What we did know was that we wanted to see these two men buried at Arlington—known or unknown. As work began on the Monitor National Marine Sanctuary's new management plan, the advisory council of whom I was a part made this a priority. I was assigned this section of the plan. I compiled a list of all known *Monitor* graves and monuments and worked with historians and military personnel to craft a plan. But sometimes it takes having the right group of people in a room for a plan to morph into possibility. Bringing together military veterans, federal employees, and museum staff, we struck the right balance, and it was decided that they would be honored in the Hampton National Cemetery in Virginia with a marker—a tribute to a place that was witness to *Monitor*'s most famous day. But the two sailors would be interred at Arlington National Cemetery, with the names of all sixteen hands lost on December 31, 1862, engraved on the marker as it was likely these two men would remain unknown.

Over the years, the men and women who discovered the wreck, the navy divers who recovered portions of the vessel, staff of The Mariners' Museum and NOAA's Monitor National Marine Sanctuary, and a host of friends who had been infected with "*Monitor* Fever" became extended family members to these two nameless men. Each year in early March, as the Battle of Hampton Roads Weekend was held in Newport News, we held a family reunion of sorts. In the absence of identified blood kin, we became their brothers and sisters as we worked to keep their stories alive. However, we were happy to cede our relationships to the actual families that began coming forward thanks to the efforts of the museum, NOAA, and the U.S. Navy.

The NOAA team led off with an effort to bring more attention to the two *Monitor* boys. In 2012 they partnered with the Forensic Anthropology and Computer Enhancement Services (FACES) lab at Louisiana State University. Their forensic anthropologists used casts of the skulls and hip bones (to help determine age) of the two men to create both clay and digital reconstructions of the faces of the two sailors. We all knew that this would make the news and perhaps bring some more descendants to light.

The faces were to be revealed at a press conference held at the Navy Memorial in Washington, DC, on March 6, 2012, just days before the 150th anniversary of the battle of Hampton Roads. The facial reconstructions, as well as the genealogical work done by the brilliant Lisa Stansbury Morgan, had indeed brought new family members to light, many of whom provided DNA samples. Unfortunately, there were no positive matches. The hope with the reconstructions was that someone new would spot a family resemblance. When they were unveiled, there were audible gasps in the room. The two men whom we had only known as bone had now become flesh, of sorts. We eagerly compared them to the images we had, yet their names still remained elusive. But the publicity did spur more relatives to contact the navy and offer DNA.

A year later, they still remained nameless. But we moved forward—first by honoring the sixteen men at Hampton National Cemetery with a marker. Then, we planned to travel north. But first, the *Monitor* boys had to be released to their families for burial. What to do? With no next of kin identified, the navy stepped in to fulfill that role. As of February 2013, these two men became everyone's shipmate and were brothers to everyone who served. As the two made their journey from Hawaii to Arlington, their remains were afforded the same respect and courtesy as a modern casualty, with proper military escort. NOAA also had a presence, and it was thanks to Marine Sanctuary superintendent

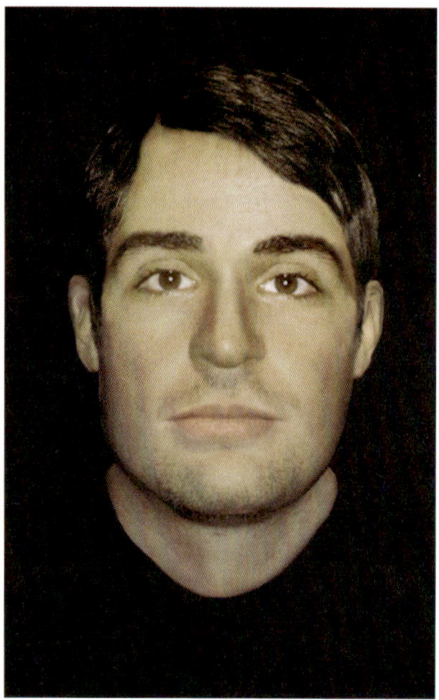
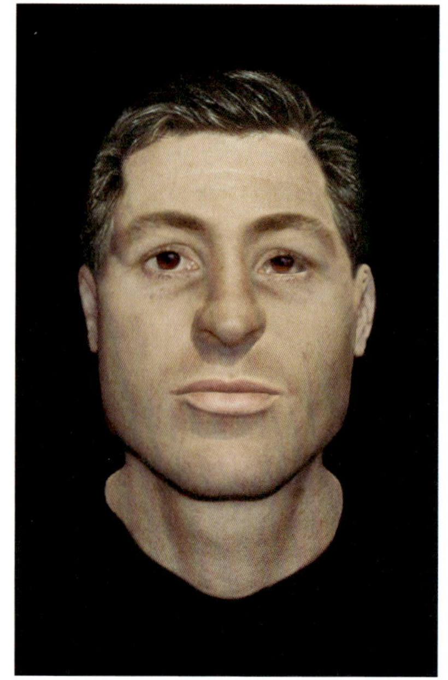

Forensic facial reconstructions of the two sailors whose remains were discovered in the turret of the *Monitor*, created by the Forensic Anthropology and Computer Enhanced (FACES) Laboratory at Louisiana State University. The younger man (*left*) is possibly Landsman William H. Eagan or Seaman Jacob Nicklis; the older man (*right*) may be Yeoman William Bryan or First Class Fireman Robert Williams. Courtesy of NOAA's *Monitor* National Marine Sanctuary.

David Alberg's texts to me throughout the trip that I got to experience some of it, albeit vicariously. His running descriptions of the Delta Honor Guard's welcome in Atlanta brought me to tears.

The day for interment was set for March 8, 2013. I arrived two days early to do press appearances. A cherished memory was sitting across from NPR's Scott Simon telling the story of the *Monitor* boys for *Weekend Edition*, which we recorded on Friday. But that would only be the start of several cherished memories from that day, which included seeing so many friends from our extended *Monitor* family—navy divers, the Newton family, the *Monitor* descendants we had come to know over the years. But perhaps the highlight for me was handing Jacob Nicklis's relatives the very spoon that bore his initials. In that moment, the past called out to them, and though Jacob might not be one of the two being buried, he was suddenly very present and their tears were for him—a young man they would never know.

The entire *Monitor* family was escorted to Fort Myer, where Secretary of the Navy Ray Mabus, NOAA Administrator Kathryn

Sullivan, historian James M. McPherson, Director of the Navy History and Heritage Command Capt. Henry "Jerry" Hendrix, and Navy Chaplain Gary Clore made remarks during a private ceremony. Secretary Mabus remarked, "While Naval tradition holds the site of a shipwreck as hallowed ground and a proper final resting place for sailors who perish at sea, this ceremony pays tribute not only to the two sailors being interred, but to all who died when *Monitor* sank so many years ago during the Civil War. Little is certain in military service, but we can guarantee the Navy will always remain committed to honoring those who pay the ultimate price defending our nation." A beautiful painting of the *Monitor*'s final moments, done for the occasion by the late Tom Freeman, stood at the front of the chapel in tribute to that hallowed ground still off the coast.

The service was a particularly poignant moment for me, having just lost my father a few weeks before. My mother's health was such that we had not been able to have a memorial service yet. Surrounded by so many chosen "family" members, I felt as though I was honoring my dad by being there. He had served in the navy during World War II. The *Monitor* boys were as much his shipmates as anyone. I managed to sing "Eternal Father, Strong to Save" through the tears that began to cascade down

Burial at Arlington National Cemetery, March 8, 2013. Photograph by David Hall. Courtesy of NOAA.

Military funeral for two USS *Monitor* sailors, March 8, 2013, Arlington National Cemetery, Arlington, Virginia. Courtesy of the U.S. Navy. Photograph by Petty Officer 2nd Class Todd Frantom.

my face. Here my two worlds were colliding, and the moment was cathartic. A colleague leaned over and said, "This is for your father too."

The two caskets were then placed on their flag-draped caissons for their brief journey to Arlington National Cemetery. *Monitor* descendants, navy divers, NOAA and Mariners' Museum staff all formed the "family" who would follow behind the caissons. We wound our way through the cemetery to a spot just outside of the amphitheater. What a sight met us! Hundreds of people were there to honor these two men. There in section 46, near the *Challenger* and *Columbia* space shuttle memorials, and in the shadow of the towering mast of USS *Maine*, the military laid them to rest. Under a ragged sky, the precision that is a military funeral played out, as it does countless times a day there. This was, as Secretary Mabus said during his remarks, possibly the

last Civil War burial in history, but it joined in the endless line of military funerals that punctuate our nation's history.

My husband and I chose to spend the next two days in the DC area, returning to Arlington National Cemetery on Saturday to visit the gravesite and to visit with other friends also buried there. In 2014 we moved to the DC area for exciting professional opportunities, so I am now able to regularly visit the final resting place for the two *Monitor* boys—having followed them for part of their epic journey from 240 feet below the Atlantic to six feet below the hallowed soil of Arlington. They rest now in the company of other heroes and wait for their families to find them. But for now, I am honored to still be a part of their extended family, stopping to say hello from time to time, and determined to keep their story alive for as long as I can.

6

Twenty Men, Dead in the Stono

MICHAEL VORENBERG

Charleston, South Carolina, the birthplace of the American Civil War, rests uneasily on swamps and buried bodies. On May 1, 1865, 257 U.S. soldiers interred at the city's old racetrack, all former POWs, were honored with the first "Decoration Day," a ceremony presided over by local African Americans.[1] Since then, Civil War memorials have come to cover the city like an invasive weed. Consider the park at the Battery, a mash-up of markers to the dead. The most infamous memorial is the statue to the "Defenders of Charleston," dedicated in 1932 and still standing, despite repeated protests and defacements in recent years. A stone's throw away from the statue is a sign honoring Robert Smalls, the former slave and eventual congressman who escaped in 1862 by piloting the *Planter* to U.S. ships outside the harbor. Smalls's body lies in Beaufort, but it was in Charleston where he first gained fame. Closer still to the "Confederate Defenders" is a plaque to the 54th Massachusetts, the African American regiment that lost nearly three hundred men in the assault on nearby Ft. Wagner in 1863. A former city planner explained that Charleston should not take down objectionable monuments like the "Confederate Defenders." Rather, it should put up more monuments, ones that tell different or even competing stories of the Civil War dead.[2] At the current rate, obelisks, plaques, and headstones might well sink the city. It's hard to believe that there are any notable Civil War deaths in Charleston left to commemorate—with one possible exception.[3]

On July 2, 1864, in a span of just a few minutes, twenty African American U.S. soldiers, almost all of them South Carolinians, died

Site of the drowning of twenty men of the 21st U.S. Colored Infantry, Stono River, near Legareville, taken at approximately the same time of day of the drownings. Photograph by Ruthie Cohen.

in the Stono River on the outskirts of Charleston. The episode received scant attention at the time and was eventually forgotten altogether. There is no grave marker at the site. Nor, perhaps, should there be. The dead men deserve to be remembered. But a simple sign, a wordy plaque, even an ornate sculpture cannot begin to convey all that their lives and deaths stood for.

This essay is an outlier. In a book about Civil War graves, it is about a death-site unmarked and barely known. It offers no plea for a memorial. Instead, it suggests that the dead, at least in this instance, might be more appropriately honored without one. This, then, is an essay about, and an argument for, an *un*memorial.

The deaths in question occurred on the evening of Saturday, July 2, 1864, about half a mile upriver from the inlet where the Stono meets the Kiawah. The 21st U.S. Colored Infantry (USCI) participated in a coordinated assault on Charleston. Federals had attempted something similar the summer before, an attack that included the heroic storming of Battery Wagner by the 54th Massachusetts. The 21st USCI had a chance to succeed where the 54th Massachusetts had failed. As dusk approached on July 2, 1864, they arrived at the western bank of the Stono. The plan was to cross the river, make camp, and then join with other regiments the next day in the assault on Charleston. The sun was still above the horizon when the first 150 of the 200 troops crossed the river. As the sky darkened, the fifty or so remaining soldiers boarded two pontoon boats and began paddling eastward to join their comrades.

One of the boats didn't make it. Twenty soldiers aboard the vessel, all of them African Americans, drowned in the Stono.

James Seabrook and Cuffey Stoney, two surviving enlisted men of the regiment, later reported that the boat was sunk by the enemy. Seabrook and Stoney had crossed the Stono already. When they looked back, they saw that the two pontoon boats had come under fire from Battery Pringle, also known as Horse Shoe Battery, a Confederate redoubt on the east side of the river, just north of the crossing. One of the boats was shot up so quickly and severely that it sank immediately, dragging most of the men down with it. A few made it out and were able to swim to the eastern shore. The other pontoon boat, still under fire, made a few sweeps across the site of the sinking to look for survivors. A bright moon lit up the river, but no bodies were visible. In the account offered by Seabrook and Stoney, the soldiers were the valiant victims of combat.[4]

Here is a story at once unknown, because the specifics of the event were later forgotten, yet familiar, because similar episodes of Black soldiers' sacrifice to the cause of freedom and Union have become legendary. Anyone lobbying for a memorial to these men would have an excellent case.

First, one could point to the heroism of enslaved people seizing freedom for themselves and then fighting for the freedom of all. The enlisted men of the 21st USCI had all grown up enslaved in the Lowcountry between Charleston and Savannah. Some escaped their masters in early 1861, as soon as they learned that the war had begun. But the major exodus began in November 1861, when they heard U.S. gunships had seized Hilton Head Island: "the gun shoot," as Edward Friday later called the taking of Hilton Head.

Friday, one of the soldiers of the 21st, had been christened "Friday Edwards" by his former master, George Edwards, who owned a plantation on Spring Island, not far from Hilton Head. When Friday heard about "the gun shoot," he stole away to the U.S. encampment at Hilton Head. He also changed his name. The move was less about evading his master—the reversal of first and last name would fool no one—than about claiming his life as his own. Many other future members of the 21st dropped their masters' names entirely. When Jeffrey Tillinghast arrived at Hilton Head after escaping from Bluffton, South Carolina, he discovered several former slaves on the island named Jenkins. He took the name Jeffrey Jenkins, an act both of self-possession and kinship-creation.

The nature of the death of the twenty soldiers—a mass drowning—offers another reason for some sort of commemoration. This was an extraordinary episode of collective death. It was not the only mass drowning during the Civil War, however. Many a sinking of a navy vessel was an episode of mass drowning. Army men, too, sometimes drowned en masse. On April 11, 1862, for example, fifty-one men of the 75th Pennsylvania Volunteers drowned in the Shenandoah River when the vessel ferrying them across capsized.[5] Three years later, on April 27, 1865, came the infamous *Sultana* disaster, just above Memphis on the Mississippi. The steamboat conveyed more than 2,000 U.S. troops, most of them former prisoners-of-war, when a boiler on board exploded. Somewhere between 1,100 and 1,200 men perished. There were Confederate mass drownings, too. By far the most famous was the death of the eight crewmen of the CSS *Hunley*, the submarine that went down in Charleston Harbor on February 17, 1864, after spearing the USS *Housatonic* with a deadly torpedo.[6]

Mass drownings during the Civil War have been cause for commemoration, but not always. Nothing marks the ground near the Shenandoah River where the fifty-one men of the 75th Pennsylvania drowned. The site where the *Sultana* sank is a different matter, no doubt because more than twenty times as many men died. There are two different commemorative markers on either bank of the Mississippi where the *Sultana* went down. Nearby, in Marion, Arkansas, stands the small, privately run Sultana Disaster Museum. This is a quaint shrine compared to the *Hunley* museum next to Charleston's commercial docks. Visitors to the elaborate museum can see the remains of the submarine, which was raised and feted in 2004. They also can see replicas of the faces of the eight dead crewmen. Some are bearded, some clean-shaven. All are white.

The twenty U.S. soldiers who drowned in the Stono were all Black. This fact, more than any other, might stir a sense that some sort of grave marker is demanded. The men were heroes twice over: once for escaping enslavement, once for dying "in the line of duty."[7] Theirs seems a story worth honoring. Yet any grave marker erected to them would run the risk of reducing the men simply to war heroes. Their deaths deserve a deeper reckoning. The men of the 21st, it turns out, did not die honorably. They drowned because of the incompetence of a white man who was supposed to be on their side.

The story told by Seabrook and Stoney of the 21st coming under enemy fire, told more than four years after the episode, was an embellishment. The true story was buried in the unpublished record of a court-martial that took place just a few months after the drowning. The accounts given during the trial all agree with one another. They reveal deaths that were pointless—that is, even more pointless than typical war deaths.[8]

The drowned men of the 21st did not come under enemy fire when they tried to cross the Stono. They left the western shore just before sunset. They were paddling two heavy pontoon boats. It was slow-going, but they were going to make the far shore before nightfall. Then, from downstream, appeared the *Isis*, a U.S. navy tugboat. Acting Ensign Israel Halstead, the boat's pilot, had been ordered to steam up the river, locate two scows left on the western bank, and tow them back to Folly Island at the mouth of the river. When Halstead saw the two pontoon boats crossing the river, he decided they were the crafts that he was meant to fetch.

A scow is broad and boxy, with a deck on one or both of its ends; a pontoon boat is narrower with no decks, each end at an angle to the waterline. Any tug pilot—any child growing up near a river, in fact—would know the difference. Halstead was under orders to transport empty scows. Why he instead decided to tow manned pontoon boats is a mystery. Whatever the reason, he drew near the two pontoon boats and told the men to fasten their bowlines to the stern of the *Isis*. The officers of the 21st at first refused. They were simply paddling across the river, they explained. Halstead countered that he was supposed to take them downriver. The men assumed that Halstead knew something they didn't. They tied onto the *Isis*. Halstead then turned the tug downstream and accelerated to ten knots, about twice the speed of the current. The two pontoon boats carrying fifty men of the 21st were pulled hard downstream.

It is amazing that only twenty men died. When a boat is pointed down a river, the force of the current lifts the stern and drives the bow downward. Experienced river runners compensate by shifting their weight toward the stern when heading downstream. The men of the 21st, long enslaved on landlocked farms and plantations, would not have known to move toward the rear. Even if they had, they were packed too tightly to shift quickly. Halstead, an experienced river pilot, should have known what would happen. As soon as he accelerated, the bow of one of the pontoon boats went below the waterline. The river rushed in over the deck and gunnels. Cramped together, the panicked soldiers struggled to break free. Meanwhile, the *Isis* chugged along at speed, dragging the boat deeper below the surface. Soldiers who managed to get out had to swim across a decent current, weighed down by waterlogged uniforms and packs. A few made it. The white officers, positioned at the very front and very back of the boat, had the easiest time slipping out of the sinking boat. No white men died that evening.

Halstead eventually heard the commotion and turned down the steam. The men aboard the one pontoon boat that had miraculously stayed afloat unhitched from the *Isis* and paddled in circles looking for survivors. But night had fallen on the Stono. No bodies, alive or dead, could be seen.

Had Halstead simply been careless, or was there some darker motive—a racial animus, perhaps—at work? Would he have been more attentive had the soldiers been white? Such questions, which surely would arise under similar circumstances today, were left unasked during the court-martial. The court chided Halstead for his mistake but declared that it fell short of "neglect of duty." As for the charge that he had caused the death of the twenty men, the court rendered a verdict of "not guilty." Halstead was fully acquitted.[9]

Admiral John A. Dahlgren, in command of the entire squadron of the region, was disgusted by the verdict. He was the officer who drafted and signed the charges against Halstead for a court-martial. Dahlgren had found out about the drowning long before the court-martial, and in the most gruesome of ways. On the night of July 4, 1864, two days after the drownings, the admiral had presided over an impromptu Independence Day celebration on the Stono. Gunboats lined their rails with torches and set off flares and fireworks. Under the illuminated night sky, sailors saw bloated bodies floating on the surface. About a dozen of the dead were pulled from the river.[10] They were all men of the 21st. Dahlgren wanted the tug pilot Halstead punished. When the navy court ruled to acquit, the admiral marked the proceedings "disapproved." Dahlgren wanted a new trial, conducted by the army. But it never took place. Halstead was reassigned to the port of Philadelphia and mustered out in the summer of 1865. No mention of the incident on the Stono ever appeared in his service record.[11]

Had Halstead been held to account for the deaths, the episode might have gained some publicity. Instead, the deaths, like many in the Civil War, were registered with barely a notice. The official cause of death was "accidental drowning."[12] An accident, in law and in life, removes culpability. The dead may be deemed as responsible as anyone else for their demise.

Lack of awareness about what had happened on the Stono created a vacuum in public memory. When asked how the men had died, friends and family—even former comrades—usually said they had simply drowned. At least two members of the 21st USCI reported years after the event that the men had drowned after slipping off a pontoon *bridge*, not that they had gone down in a pontoon *boat*.[13] Then there was the story told by James Seabrook and Cuffey Stoney, also former members of the regiment, that the pontoon boat had been shot up by Confederates during battle.

Why did Seabrook and Stoney turn the tragedy into a heroic war story? In part, they were honoring their comrades. Better that they be remembered as fighters to the last, they reckoned, than as victims of gross negligence. Mostly, though, they were trying to help the widow of one of the dead men in particular, Cpl. Charles Miller. Miller's wife, Julia Anna, had applied for a widow's pension in June 1865. When she applied, she was living in Hilton Head on the old "Seabrook plantation." Seabrook and Stoney, along with others from the old regiment, were living there too. The pension investigator was reluctant to accept Julia's application. He found some small errors in detail. For example, she reported that her husband was in Company A of the 21st; he had been in Company E. She also reported the date of death as July 1, 1864, not July 2, and that he was one of fifteen who died, not twenty. Most troubling to the investigator, Julia could provide no written proof of her marriage to the dead man. It was a common problem facing widows of African American soldiers, as marriages among the enslaved were not always carefully recorded. The injustice of antebellum laws prohibiting slave marriages laid the groundwork for further injustice once the war was over and marriages between formerly enslaved African Americans were legalized. In the absence of records, pension investigators questioned whether marriages had in fact been performed. The glitches in the record allowed the investigator to drag out Julia's case for three years. Finally, Charles Miller's former comrades stepped in to speed the process along, perhaps at Julia's request. First, Isaac Seabrook, a possible relative of James Seabrook, testified along with another member of the unit, James Brown, that Miller had drowned "while on an expedition around James Island."[14] The next month, James Seabrook and Cuffey Stoney told the investigator their tale about the men coming under Confederate fire. They likely assumed that the agent would be more inclined to grant the pension if the deceased had died in combat. Fortunately for them, and for Julia Miller, the pension agent did not know about the account of what really happened contained in the court-martial of Israel Halstead four years earlier. Six months after receiving the new testimony about Corporal Miller, the agent awarded Julia Miller a monthly pension of eight dollars, equal to about one hundred fifty dollars today.

The pension investigators were not done with Julia Miller, however. They may have been moved by the stories of her husband's death in combat, but they kept on looking for ways to reverse the award and save the government some money. The easiest way to annul the pension was to marshal evidence that Julia had remarried after Charles's death. Pension policy denied awards to widows who remarried or had reputations for "taking up" with other men. The system rested on the patriarchal principle that the government subsidy was merely a temporary replacement for a husband's salary, and that widows had a moral duty to stay chaste until a formal marriage was arranged. Eventually, investigators learned that soon after Charles's death, Julia had met and married William Holmes, another veteran of the 21st USCI. A pension agent showed up at Julia's door and ordered her to pay a sum equal to all the pension money that she had ever collected: $856.27. The agent marched her to the local branch of the Freedman's Bank so he could collect. Only $425.28 was in her account—her life savings. The agent took it all. A memorial to Charles Miller could never capture the futility of his death; nor could it convey the indignity suffered by his widow.[15]

The relationship between the U.S. government on one side and Black soldiers and their families on the other was fraught with tensions belying the oft-told narrative, contained in many a memorial, of patriotic African Americans earning their nation's respect and citizenship through heroic military service. At least some of the soldiers of the 21st who died in the Stono had a rocky relationship with the nation they served. Esau Fox deserted the first regiment that he had joined. We do not know why. Whatever the reason, U.S. authorities did not hold it against him and allowed him to muster into the 21st.[16] Another of the dead, Jacob Smith, had mutinied along with the rest of his company for reasons never recorded. Threats from their superiors of court-martial and execution brought the men back in line. That the men were not summarily punished suggests that authorities regarded the soldiers' grievances, whatever they might have been, as legitimate.[17] On the day of the mutiny, November 19, 1863, Abraham Lincoln delivered his speech at Gettysburg memorializing the fallen U.S. soldiers for their "last full measure of devotion." What do we really know about the measure of devotion given by the men who drowned in the Stono—or the respect for that devotion offered by their commanders?

Wasn't the very death of the twenty men proof enough of their devotion? If so, do they, like the dead at Gettysburg, deserve headstones befitting heroes? More than three thousand white U.S. soldiers perished at Gettysburg. That scale of death assured, as Lincoln vowed, that the world would never forget them. Twenty Black U.S. soldiers died in the Stono a year later. They *were* forgotten. Were there too few of them? Were they the wrong race? Maybe, on balance, they *did* die in vain.

Not every soldier who dies in war is a hero. And even the heroes can't all be memorialized. When it comes to the dead of the Civil War—America's most heroic war, the one most worth fighting—these truths sit uneasily. Certainly, it seems a heresy to suggest that the African Americans who transformed themselves from southern slaves to U.S. soldiers and then died in a war for emancipation were anything less than heroic. Their deaths, more than any others, must have counted for something. Yet the twenty men who drowned in the Stono disrupt this calculus. They confront us with the inescapable reality that at least some Civil War deaths were needless. They challenge the shibboleth, already under assault in recent years, that the war must have been worth fighting.[18] They unveil the inadequacy of the categories "victim" and "hero," the only two descriptors typically allowed for the African American dead.[19] History has been enriched with more than fifty years of scholarship on the activism, service, and sacrifice of African Americans during the war. The attention came too late, and there's always the risk that it will wither. But for now at least, the reputation of African American Civil War soldiers seems sturdy enough to withstand the proposition that it is "fitting and proper," if we may twist Lincoln's words, that at least some of them be *un*memorialized. I do not mean the dead who are unknown, the ones who might get their due in some memorial to "The Unknown Soldier." Rather, I mean the dead who are known but whose deaths defy memorialization, like those who drowned in the Stono.

The dead of the 21st USCI died as many soldiers die: in a fog of war where there are no victims or heroes. Painful as it may be to concede, they were more the objects than the subjects of history. The historian Jim Downs has written, in a somewhat different context, that it is wrongheaded, albeit right-hearted, to assume in all instances "that freedpeople were all-but unsinkable political actors."[20] He is right. The twenty dead of the 21st USCI, alas, were sinkable, and tragically so. Perhaps, then, the absence of a memorial, an *un*memorial, best represents the meaning, and the meaninglessness, of what happened here. A century after the Civil War and a world away from the Stono, the Japanese novelist and peace activist Makoto Oda mused that he wished that his country would keep its sites of mass death from the Second World War free of patriotic monuments such as those he had seen on European battlefields. Let the land stay unmarked, he mused: "The only way to let these unmemorialized dead rest in peace is to never again produce such dead."[21]

Still, if earnest memorial-makers demand some sort of marker at the site of the Stono disaster, let them have their way. Among many challenges they will face is finding an appropriate spot for it. Should it be placed on the riverbank from which the men departed or on the one where they never arrived? I might suggest tying it to some sort of anchor, perhaps a sunken pontoon boat, and keeping it below the river's surface. Let it stay submerged from view like the men who died there. Let time and the tides decide when the tether will break and the names will surface.

"Durable Stone"

Veterans' Headstones and the Legacy of the Civil War

BARBARA A. GANNON

The last Memorial Day before the long wars of the twenty-first century found me in Elgin, Illinois, the leafy city that sprawls along the Fox River about thirty-five miles northwest of Chicago. In the city's old cemetery, local veterans dutifully gathered for the annual ceremonies. As the observance began, a young African American boy recited the lyrical words of the Gettysburg Address. Then, carrying Lincoln's message of "a new birth of freedom" into the twentieth century, a Black veteran of the Korean War—the first war fought by integrated units—spoke movingly of his service. At the end of the program, an elderly white veteran struggled to his feet for a last salute. A Black woman held him by the arm as a bugler sounded the haunting notes of taps. Nearby in honored memory, Civil War veterans—white and Black—lay together, side by side, for all eternity.

In the late nineteenth century, African Americans were segregated in death no less than in life. Grand Army of the Republic plots were rare exceptions to the rules of Jim Crow—spaces where white men and Black men were buried together in a remarkable recognition of racial equality. In Elgin as elsewhere, Black Union veterans rested beneath uniform, government-issued headstones: the very same headstones erected for their white comrades. On these simple markers, only the record of their wartime units—United States Colored Troops—supplied any indication of race. Made powerfully manifest by the durable stones standing sentinel over their graves, the bonds of interracial comradeship—forged under fire at places like New Market Heights and Plymouth, Olustee and Appomattox—survived the war intact.[1]

The graves of David Smales, 5th Pennsylvania Cavalry, and Andrew Radford, 13th U.S. Colored Infantry, rest next to each other in the Grand Army of the Republic section of Bluff City Cemetery, Elgin, Illinois. Photograph by David Wiegers.

Though historians still dispute the exact numbers (recent estimates have upwardly revised the total casualty count, with some fixing the number at a staggering 750,000), the Civil War was, by any reckoning, America's deadliest conflict. As the historian Drew Gilpin Faust has pointed out, death on gruesome battlefields away from the comforts of family and friends violated cherished, nineteenth-century notions of a "Good Death." Officials struggled to bury the wartime dead and mark final resting places scattered across the continent. Amid the exigencies of war, burial crews deposited the dead in shallow graves on the fields where they fell; however, soil erosion quickly revealed soldiers remains. Before the war ended, practical no less than public health concerns prodded the federal armies to begin the process of permanently interring the wartime dead. The most famous effort was the Soldiers' National Cemetery at Gettysburg, sacralized by Lincoln's 272 words on November 19, 1863. These "cities of the dead" became evocative sites of mourning and commemoration. Historian John R. Neff contends that loyal northerners articulated the Union Cause—or what he called the "Cause Victorious"—at final resting places. In contrast, former Confederates—particularly women—took the lead in locating, collecting, and honoring the Confederate dead. In *Burying the Dead but Not the Past* (2008), Caroline E. Janney identifies the work of Ladies' Memorial Associations in both burying the dead and communicating the Lost Cause.[2]

Headstones were central to this work. The wartime dead and those who were buried later, of course, needed grave markers. During the war, burial crews identified graves with crude wooden headboards. But before long, the cost of replacing weather-beaten, windswept markers prompted Congress to allocate $1 million for a permanent marker "of durable stone, and of such design and weight as shall keep them in place when set."[3] The final design reflected a desire for uniformity. Officers and enlisted men would rest beneath the same headstones, though engravings sometimes denoted rank. Headstones that marked African American soldiers' graves looked identical to white soldiers. The power of the national cemetery as a landscape of collective memory rests as much on uniform headstones as on neatly manicured grounds or greenery.[4]

After the war, the government extended its network of national cemeteries for the wartime dead across the continent. From Alexandria, Louisiana, to Yorktown, Virginia, national cemeteries became distinctive locations on the civic landscape. Burial trenches on battlefields were opened and their contents exhumed; the bones of those obliterated by artillery or rendered "unknown" collected in mass graves. From the beginning, national cemeteries also welcomed indigent veterans who died in local almshouses or poor asylums. Only eight years after Appomattox, the government extended eligibility for burial in national cemeteries to all honorably discharged Union veterans. These burying grounds supplied a powerful, visual representation of the war's staggering cost in human life. Six years later, in 1879, Congress directed the secretary of war to "erect headstones over the graves of soldiers who served in the Regular or Volunteer Army of the United States during the war for the Union, and who have been buried in private village or city cemeteries." Soon, government-issued headstones began to crowd local graveyards no less than national cemeteries. Immediately recognizable, the upright stone slabs created an iconic landscape of democracy and citizenship based on shared military service to the nation. They became "sites of memory." Americans, prompted by these individual Civil War memorials to their neighbors and community members, organized Memorial Day exercises at thousands of graveyards and burying places around the nation—programs such as the one I attended in Elgin.[5]

Eventually, the United States government welcomed Confederate veterans to the community of American veterans—perhaps in part because so many of their sons and daughters, grandsons and granddaughters had served in subsequent wars and earned the privilege.[6] In 1906, as the drumbeats of sectional reconciliation grew louder, the government agreed to provide headstones to Confederates buried in national cemeteries. (Only Confederates who had died in U.S. custody, in wartime prisons or hospitals, rested in national cemeteries.) In 1929, after a world war that made another generation of Americans eligible for these headstones, Confederate soldiers buried in private graveyards received the same benefit—though these slabs had pointed edges. Some speculated that this design prevented Yankees from sitting on these headstones. More likely, the design prompted observers to recognize that there was something different about the veterans interred beneath these markers. Even in an age of sectional reconciliation, sectional differences lingered.[7]

Americans' treatment of the Civil War dead shaped commemorative efforts in subsequent wars. Veterans of the Spanish-American and Philippine-American Wars came to rest under the same type of simple headstone, though shields were added around the deceased's name and unit information. As the decades went on, of course, and Americans engaged in new and distant wars, engravers inscribed more and more headstones. Officials added birthdates and death dates to the markers; stone slabs became either granite or marble. Flat, bronze markers joined the more familiar upright slabs. Engravers included the deceased veterans' awards, including Bronze and Silver Stars, Purple Hearts and Air Medals, Navy and Air Force Crosses. Other changes—the introduction of Latin crosses or Stars of David—reflected the diversity of the dead. Adherents of various Protestant denominations, too, came to rest under their own symbols—Mormons distinguished from Methodists, the Church of God's adherents made distinct from followers of the Church of the Nazarene. Since the rolls of the dead included Wiccans and nonbelievers, their own symbols were also etched. There are now over sixty different emblems of faith. Capt. Humayun Saqib Khan, killed in Iraq while saving his fellow soldiers in 2004, rests beneath a Muslim crescent in Arlington National Cemetery, as does Cpl. Kareem Sultan Khan, another casualty of Operation Iraqi Freedom.[8]

I first pondered the power of headstones—the relationship between the local and the national, the collective and the individual—at that poignant ceremony in Elgin, which I attended not long after my mother's death. She passed away unexpectedly as I was researching the Grand Army of the Republic, the largest fraternal organization for federal veterans—and the only nonsegregated fraternal society in Gilded Age America. As a scholar, I thoroughly understood Memorial Day as a collective commemoration of wartime sacrifice; now, as a grief-stricken survivor myself, I came to understand that individual memorials mattered. Families of old soldiers and seventy-seven-year-old mothers desperately need comfort—the reassurance that their loved ones' lives meant something.

Years later, I found myself at Arlington for the interment of a colleague's father, a Vietnam veteran who died decades after the war from Agent Orange–related cancer. Nineteenth-century people knew that long after war, soldiers died from the effects of diseases or injuries—physical or mental—acquired on the battlefield. In the twentieth and twenty-first centuries, we relearned that lesson as a nation. I drove down to Arlington from Gettysburg, where I had been discussing my research on the Grand Army of the Republic. As the ceremony ended, the squad fired its final salute. I looked out over the rows and rows of headstones and remembered that day in Elgin. The link between all those who passed before—and all those who will rest here in the future—is yet made tangible by those durable stones that stand silent sentinel over their graves.

The Bones of Morris and Folly

DOUGLAS R. EGERTON

Strolling along the coast of Folly Island, South Carolina, today, it is hard to imagine what the men of the Massachusetts 54th and 55th Infantries saw as they gazed out of their tents each morning. Battery Wagner is long since eroded, its sandy footprint visible only from the sky and approachable only by private launch, while much of Folly is packed with expensive beach homes and shops and restaurants that cater to the tourist crowd. Folly Beach Road and a modern bridge connect Folly with Oak Island. But as historian Laurel Thatcher Ulrich once observed, "Some people leave only their bones, though bones too make history when somebody notices." In May 1987 someone did. Developers were bulldozing a crude road through a forested portion of Folly south of Center Street, and two local relic hunters, Robert Borhn and Erik Croen, arrived with metal detectors in search of Civil War–era bullets or belt buckles. A storm the previous night had washed away some of the soil, and Croen spied what he first thought was a root. Looking closer, Croen guessed it was a human femur. Digging a hole for reburial of what the two supposed was an early settler or a Native American, they uncovered six vertebrae and a button from a Union jacket. Borhn left the bodies there and telephoned the University of South Carolina's Institute of Archeology and Anthropology. A skeptical voice on the other end of the line wondered whether the treasure hunters had stumbled across cow bones. Borhn replied that he had never known a cow to wear an army uniform.[1]

This bird's-eye-view of Charleston's defenses published in *Harper's Weekly* on August 15, 1863, reveals the formidable task faced by the U.S. Army. In the foreground, Morris Island's Battery Wagner (numbered 13) and Battery Gregg (numbered 12) guarded Fort Sumter and the southern side of the harbor. The soldiers of the 54th who died in the assault of July 18, 1863, were buried in a sandy ditch below the battery's front wall. At bottom left (numbered 17) is Folly Island, where the 55th made camp and where their dead were interred.

Parallel on Wagner, Morris Island, South Carolina, ca. 1863–65. Courtesy of the Library of Congress.

The university directed the excavation, digging up a two-acre area. Their team discovered the bodies of nineteen Union soldiers. Some had been buried in simple wooden coffins, while others had merely been wrapped in rubber-coated blankets. All but one of those interred lay on their backs, their arms neatly folded across their chests. Analysis of the bones indicated that the deceased had ranged from sixteen to forty years of age. Strangely, however, only two of the bodies formed complete skeletons; the other seventeen lacked skulls. As the bodies had been buried deeply enough to protect against the waves and animals—unlike those tossed into pits just below Wagner—the most likely scenario was that the cemetery had been discovered in later years and looted, perhaps for ghastly souvenirs.[2]

The 54th is famous today for its courageous July 18, 1863, assault on Wagner. But the lull after the battle could be just as deadly as the fight itself. While Union ironclads floating just outside of Charleston harbor bombarded Fort Sumter and Battery Wagner, fatigue parties of Black soldiers began to construct trenches toward Wagner's front wall. In the weeks after the disastrous attack on the Morris Island Confederate position, Union general Quincy Adams Gillmore decided against any further frontal attacks and instead chose to reduce the battery with shelling and trenches. Initially the 54th Infantry was assigned the task, but after it became clear how slow and arduous the chore would be, their sister regiment, the 55th, picked up their shovels and joined in. Maj. George Brooks typically placed three companies in each fatigue unit, who would then dig in eight-hour shifts. Brooks hoped to work around-the-clock, with one unit starting at 4:00 a.m., the second relieving them at noon, and the third picking up their shovels at 8:00 p.m. But "the enemy's sharpshooters were quite annoying during the day," one officer reported, "and it seemed impossible to drive them from the shelter." Instead, Capt. Luis Emilio grumbled, "most of the work had to be done at night." During the day, some soldiers remained in the unfinished trenches, standing guard to repel any potential counterattacks. Each morning at sunup, the weary Black soldiers stumbled back into camp and fell onto their blankets, their grim expressions showing "plainly at what cost this labor was done." Within days, their uniforms "were in rags, [with] shoes worn out, and haversacks full of holes."[3]

While the crews dug, other companies cut and dragged timber for the trenches' sides and floors. Soldiers from both regiments

"Storming Fort Wagner," Kurz and Allison, ca. 1890. Courtesy of the Library of Congress.

hauled the heavy siege guns forward as the parallels advanced, their labors made more difficult as the "sling carts" that carried the guns sank into the sand. When not digging, the soldiers of the 55th stood picket on Folly Island. "All details for fatigue were made from the colored troops," Lt. Col. Charles Fox noted sourly. "If there were any exceptions to this rule, they did not come to [his] notice." Lt. George Garrison, son of the Boston abolitionist, was pleased that the men of the two regiments at least got to see one another as the fatigue companies came on and off duty, and a sort of friendly regimental competition emerged over who had moved the most sand. One soldier in the 55th bragged that most of the digging was "done under fire of the enemy, and the men, more or less of the time, are obliged to dodge the shot of the enemy." But the pressure was "good experience for them," he thought, for they learn to "keep cool" under fire.[4]

The Black soldiers at work in the trenches understood that Charleston's fall was hardly imminent. As the correspondent for the *New York Herald* reported, the Confederates still controlled shore batteries on James Island as well as Battery Bee and

Fort Moultrie on Sullivan's Island north of the harbor's mouth. "Around Castle Pinckney [Confederates] have built up huge barricades of sand extending to the very parapet," the journalist noted, "and have thus rendered that work capable of a strong defense." While riding along the beach, Col. Edward Needles "Ned" Hallowell, who had replaced the martyred Robert Gould Shaw as the commander of the 54th, had his horse shot from beneath him; the shell fragments miraculously missed him. Confederate guns and sharpshooters were not the only peril. As the maze of trenches crept toward Wagner, shells fired from Union ironclads also endangered the diggers. Malaria, typhoid, and dysentery carried off others. Some of the dead were buried on the southern edge of Folly Island, not far from where a crude bridge connected Folly to Oak Island. Others were buried in the southern portions of Morris captured just before the July assault on Wagner, while still more, including Shaw, had been dumped by Confederates into a shallow mass grave in the sands just below Wagner's protective moat.[5]

Complicating matters for both grieving loved ones back home and army bureaucrats was the lack of documentation for those soldiers newly arrived in freedom. Most of the men of the 54th and 55th had been born free in the North, but enough had been antebellum runaways, or the sons of runaways, to pose problems for military bookkeepers. Sarah Dorsey, for instance, was the mother of Isaac Dorsey Jr., who died on Morris Island during the fall of 1863, and the widow of Isaac Sr., whom she had married in Washington, DC, in 1837. But "her husband being at that time a slave, no records [of the marriage were] made or kept." Pvt. Wesley Ryal died on Folly Island during the fall of 1863, leaving two young children behind in Sandusky, Ohio. Ryal had married Julia Rice in 1856, but after he enlisted she vanished, leaving the children in the care of neighbor John Mackey. Acting as their guardian, Mackey applied for a pension for Ryal's children, although he conceded that he possessed no evidence of a legal marriage for the deceased private, nor he did know "the exact day" of either child's birth.[6]

When in the predawn hours of September 7, 1863, Confederates inside the shattered Wagner spiked their guns and boarded barges for Sumter, the entirety of Morris Island came under Union control, and relatives of some of the white soldiers who perished at Wagner begged the army to retrieve their loved ones' bodies. The family of Augustine Webb, a lieutenant in the

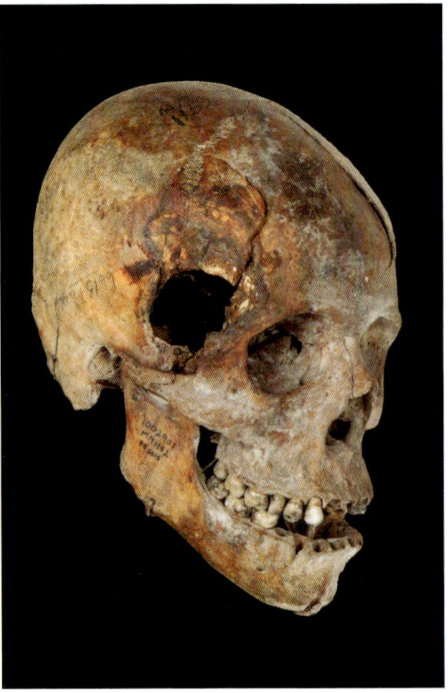

"The skull of a black Union soldier of the 54th Massachusetts found in 1876 on Morris Island, South Carolina, showing the exit wound of an iron projectile (AFIP 10029070)" (Photo ID: 130117-A-MP902-006). Courtesy of the Otis Historical Archives, National Museum of Health and Medicine.

48th New York, requested "permission to disinter [his] remains and send them" home. Ignoring Frank Shaw's public letter of August 24, in which the grieving father had insisted that his son's body belonged beside those of his men, the army began to search for Rob's corpse. Writing again to General Gillmore, Shaw demanded that "such efforts are not authorized by me, or any of my family, and they are not approved by us." Gillmore deferred to the family and ordered that Rob's grave not be disturbed. The army could not control the waves, however, and for months afterward the tide disclosed the soldiers' final resting places on Morris. Susie King Taylor, a former slave turned nurse who assisted the 1st South Carolina Infantry, routinely noticed "many skulls lying about" as she walked along the shore. "They were a gruesome sight," she remembered, "those fleshless heads and grinning jaws."[7]

In May 1989 the bodies, now resting in black pine coffins draped with American flags, were reburied in Beaufort's National Cemetery. Reenactors in blue Civil War uniforms played "Amazing Grace" and then taps before raising their muzzle-loaded muskets to fire in salute. Then-Massachusetts governor Michael Dukakis spoke at the ceremony. "For unlike the men and boys who fought and died for a way of life they believed in," Dukakis observed, these Black soldiers fought for their own liberty, to grasp their own freedom; and to ensure "both for others of their race." Among the two thousand spectators was retired major George Coblyn, a decorated veteran of World War II and Korea. Coblyn's grandfather, Eli George Biddle, had been a Boston sign painter who enlisted in the 54th at the age of seventeen. Wounded at Wagner, Biddle had fought on until the war's end and died at ninety-four just before the attack on Pearl Harbor. "He was an inspiration to me," Coblyn remembered. "We used to march together in Memorial Day parades in Boston until I was 12 or 13. He'd always say, 'Stick your chest out! Be proud, be proud!'"[8]

Today visitors to Beaufort can find the graves and a commemorative marker toward the back of the graveyard, shaded by enormous oak trees. Although State Law Enforcement Division forensic artist Roy Paschal created facial reconstructions from the two skulls, the nineteen soldiers remain unidentified. The Civil War had more than its share of unknowns, and Black regiments particularly so. Despite the state designation of the two Massachusetts regiments, Ohio provided the third-largest contingent for the first unit and gave the second an additional 222 men. Pennsylvania was second in the 55th with 139 recruits. But as few northern states were interested in raising Black regiments in 1863, Black volunteers for both regiments came from

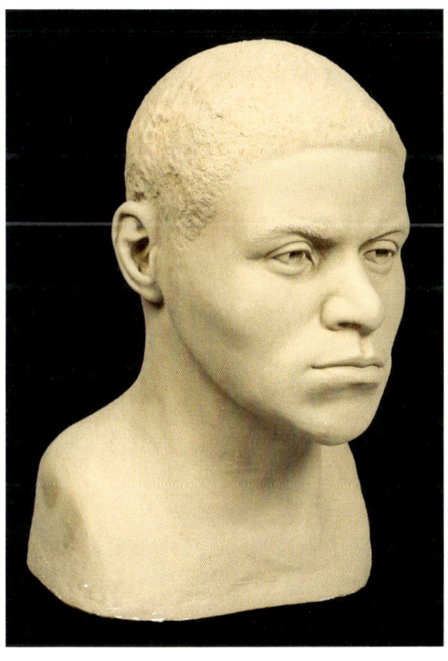

"The facial reconstruction produced from the skull of a 54th Massachusetts Volunteer by visual information specialist Lisa Bailey at the FBI Laboratory in Quantico, Virginia" (Photo ID 190718-D-MP902-0001). Courtesy of the Otis Historical Archives, National Museum of Health and Medicine.

all over. Among those who died on Folly was Arthella Lyles, a twenty-two-year-old farmer from Indiana, carried away by typhoid in August 1863. William Jackson of Elizabeth, New Jersey, died of consumption in May 1864. Tinkerer William Hebert, who had been living, perhaps as a runaway, in Nova Scotia, was only nineteen when he died on Folly four days before Christmas of 1863. Pvt. Edward Mayhew was one of the few in the 55th to enlist in Massachusetts, but he too died on Folly in September 1864 of congestive chills.

At the time of the 1989 ceremony, journalists speculated that the bones *all* belonged to the soldiers of the 55th, but there is no reason to believe that to be exclusively so. Both Massachusetts regiments spent time camped on Folly, and at least three soldiers of the 54th died there. William Brown, a mariner from Michigan, survived Wagner only to perish of fever in December 1864, while Lewis Smith, a laborer from Philadelphia, drowned on Folly's beaches in December 1864. And because some men from the first unit transferred to the newer regiment, sometimes to serve alongside friends or family, John Davis, a cook from Niagara, New York, fought with the 54th at Wagner but

Graves of Massachusetts soldiers interred at Beaufort National Cemetery, Beaufort, South Carolina. Photograph by Chloe Baker.

Unmarked graves of Massachusetts soldiers at Beaufort National Cemetery, Beaufort, South Carolina. Photograph by Chloe Baker.

died a member of the 55th on Folly in June 1864. When possible, well-to-do white officers, such as George Crockett Strong, who died of tetanus from wounds received as his men retreated from Wagner, were shipped home for formal burial—in Strong's case, with a stately monument in Brooklyn—but working-class Black soldiers were invariably laid to rest close to where they breathed their last.[9]

"It's a final endorsement of Black soldiers everywhere in the struggle to be recognized," George Coblyn reflected at the Beaufort service. "I feel like my grandfather is watching this from somewhere." So too, perhaps, were the nineteen soldiers reinterred with proper honors. Yet in a sadly poetic fashion, those fallen soldiers, like Rob Shaw, perhaps truly belonged in unmarked and forgotten graves on Folly and Morris rather than in graveyards in northern states. The Black men who enlisted from Salmon Chase's Ohio, from Abraham Lincoln's Illinois, and from Thaddeus Stevens's Pennsylvania did so even though those states denied them the ballot, and would continue to do so until the Fifteenth Amendment forced their hand. They fought for a nation whose Supreme Court, just seven years before their enlistments, had ruled them not to be citizens in the land of their birth. Their country had not wanted them and for two years denied them the right to enlist. "As soon as the government would take me I came to fight," Maryland runaway Charles Reason assured his doctor as he lay dying in a makeshift hospital in Beaufort, having lost an arm at Wagner. "*Not* for my country, [as] I never had one," he added, "but to gain one." The fellow soldiers of those buried in the sands in 1863 and 1864 knew their names. They thought of them like brothers as they carefully folded their dead arms across their chest, dusted off their worn uniforms as best they could, and said a simple prayer as they lowered them into the ground.[10]

Granite Remnants Left along the Delaware

The Shohola Railroad Calamity

MICHAEL P. GRAY

Winding through the thickly forested Pocono Mountains, several roads lead to the sleepy village of Shohola, Pennsylvania, named by Indigenous peoples for the slow-moving stream that flows into the more powerful upper Delaware River. Nestled in these mountains, outdoor enthusiasts thrive. Since childhood, I have visited the area many times in pursuit of its fisheries—a passion that eventually caused me to enter college as an environmental studies major. My ambitions for a career with the Fish and Wildlife Service, however, eventually met with my shortcomings in mathematics; the only numbers I study now deal in our past.

Although the Civil War era is my mainstay at East Stroudsburg University of Pennsylvania, I also teach frontier history and westward expansion. In these courses, I lecture to my students on Indigenous peoples, the environment, and conservation movements. These are relevant subjects at a university situated on the base of the Pocono plateau, an idyllic region that has cultivated a thriving tourism industry. The outdoors and history have always intertwined for me. I sometimes camp near historical sites. I also give tours of prison sites, cemeteries, and battlegrounds. Being in nature, near where an event actually took place, affords the advantages of deeper insight, enhanced perspective, and sharper focus. Indeed, history and nature thrive in this small corner where Pennsylvania, New York, and New Jersey meet. This region also attracts encroaching crowds from the urban sprawl of nearby cities, whose laughter and conversations while floating down the river on rafts, canoes, and kayaks sometimes thwart anglers' solitude and casts.

After partaking in such outdoor pursuits, enthusiasts can quench their thirst at a local tavern in Shohola, now named Rohman's Pub. Built in 1849 and known during the Civil War as the Shohola Hotel, it was one of the main meeting places for visitors in this region. Near Rohman's entrance is a gravel road flanked by railroad tracks. When I first came to this place more than a quarter century ago, I was working on a master's thesis on Andersonville and Elmira prisons. Little has changed with the place from that time. Customers can enjoy food delivered by a hand elevator from a second-floor kitchen, play darts, or even venture upstairs to a single-lane bowling alley, all while enjoying a Pennsylvania staple—Yuengling lager ("America's Oldest Brewery"). Upon exiting the bar, the customer might not even notice a small plaque on the wall, which reads:

TO THIS HOTEL
WERE BROUGHT
UNION & CONFEDERATE SOLDIERS
VICTIMS OF A TRAGIC TRAIN WRECK
JULY 15, 1864

The sign, as well as a nearby historical marker, begin to unravel a story ostensibly lost in time, when the quietude of this village, surrounded by the peaceful currents of nature, was abruptly awakened on that summer day. Indeed, the country was already tragically disrupted in civil strife, but that was at faraway battlefields. But when two locomotives fought over a single track near Shohola, the wounds of battle literally came to Shohola's front door, and specifically to Rohman's Pub.[1]

On July 6, 1864, Confederate prisoners were being transferred from the overcrowded Point Lookout Prison in Maryland to the newly opened Elmira Prison in upstate New York. It was the fourth contingent being processed to their new confines, and the men were tired from the long maritime voyage on the *Crescent*, a passage that took them around the Chesapeake Bay to New York Harbor, finally boarding freight cars on the Erie Railway in Jersey City. All told, it was the largest group being moved to Elmira, numbering 833, along with 125 guards and 3 officers of the 11th and 20th Veteran Reserve Corps. As the men climbed aboard the cars of the Erie Railroad, the officers realized that three Confederates were missing, hiding on the steamer. It delayed the entourage more than an hour. They finally left at 6:00 a.m., but an opened drawbridge prolonged their delay two additional hours. Locomotive 171, operated by William Ingram and assisted by Daniel Tuttle, pulled eighteen cars behind the tender as they moved slowly onward. Upon reaching Port Jervis, New York, at 1:00 p.m. in the early afternoon, the train took on water and wood before steaming ahead. At this juncture in the trip, the next twenty-three miles of the Erie Railroad's dual rails converged into one single track in order to hug the limited ground forged by railroad builders so they could gouge into the rocky earth.[2]

As the train proceeded behind schedule, it crossed into Pennsylvania and followed the Delaware River's twisting course. The train nudged precariously along the steep ledges of the scenic Poconos. Travelers could do little but admire the beauty, brace for curves, and rely on the skill of those who worked the iron horse. Trying to make up for lost time, Ingram and Tuttle pushed at a pace of twenty-five miles an hour until they reached Shohola station. There, they were given permission to proceed on the lone track.

Chugging from Shohola toward Lackawaxen on the sun-drenched afternoon of July 15, 1864, the prisoner train approached King and Fuller's Cut, a halfway point between the junctions. The cut was named after the contractors who hollowed out rock-filled ground around a ridge for rails, which resulted in a tricky bend that could limit vision to fifty feet when cornering. In this turn, another locomotive suddenly appeared. For some reason, at the Hawley connection in Lackawaxen, a heavily laden coal train pulling fifty cars had been admitted to the already occupied rails. The coal train rolled down the grade at twelve miles per hour, each swaying car loaded with twelve tons. William Ingram frantically reversed his engines, while the engineer of the coal train dove out of his cab. About 2:45 that Friday afternoon, a tremendous crash shook the ground, the screech of metal resonating over the natural quietude of the upper valley. An eerily silent moment preceded the heartrending cries, moans, shouts, and screams of the wounded and dying.[3]

When the smoke dissipated and the debris cleared, it revealed a grim spectacle. Both locomotives were elevated high against the other, and cars down the line were crushed, overturned, ripped in half, or on top of one another. A guard, Frank Evans, described the two locomotives as "raised high in the air, face to

Railroad tracks at King and Fuller's Cut, the crash site near Shohola, Pennsylvania. Photograph by Jonathan W. White.

face against each other, like giants grappling." All but one man in the first boxcar perished, thrown to safety before the impact smashed the car to a length less than six feet. Soldiers in the leading cars, the majority being prisoners, bore the brunt of the accident.[4]

The echoing sounds of the eighteen-car train full of human freight striking the heavily loaded fifty-car coal train reached about a mile and a half west of Shohola, and it brought villagers rushing in. They followed the tracks as shrieks of releasing steam from boilers and screams for help competed against each other, all growing louder as they neared the calamity. What it revealed was nearly indescribable. Bodies were strewn on or around the track; victims still living pleaded for help. Maimed and mangled body parts were tossed about. As afternoon passed into evening, more than a hundred injured soldiers were taken to the village. A relief train arrived at the station from Port Jervis with doctors and railroad employees. Union guards, Confederate prisoners, and local citizens were already helping in the aftermath, a task that went into the next morning. Corpses were moved closer to the river as the property owner where the crash occurred preferred a mass grave dug off his property. Discarded arms, legs, and trunks were collected, and at least two bodies were found decapitated. Some bodies were so disfigured that they were unrecognizable. Five prisoners who allegedly escaped during the mayhem might have been among them. Even so, uninjured guards encircled the scene to prevent any captives from attempting to flee.[5]

By 11:00 p.m. the digging of a trench, seventy feet long, eight feet wide, and the customary six feet deep had begun on the west bank of the Delaware. Men were identified as best as possible and placed in hastily built coffins from battered boxcars until some pine wood was hauled in. The majority of dead Confederates—around forty-nine—were placed four to a box and interred at one end of the grave. Each of the seventeen Union dead was placed in a single casket at the other end. At this spot, between rail and river, they would rest for nearly six decades.[6]

Coverage by the local press likened the crash to battle. The *Honesdale Republic* wrote that it was "most appalling," with the track covered "with debris, car piled upon car in the most indescribable confusion, the bodies of those thrown from them covering the road at every step, the flying dust . . . blinding smoke . . . quenching fires . . . noise of the escaping steam," and "above all, the fearful groans and heart-rending cries of the injured and expiring will never be forgotten." The *Wayne County Herald* continued, "Some of the corpses were shockingly mutilated, heads were completely crushed, bodies transfixed, impaled in timbers or iron rods, or smashed." The *Port Jervis Tri-States Union* concluded, "Here death did its horrid work. Men were jammed between cars, under the cars, under the tender; cut, maimed, mangled, and killed. The groans of the dying and shouts of those able to call for relief were heartrending indeed." More sobering facts came as "bodies were found without an arm, others without a leg, some with neither arms nor legs, and one or two decapitated trunks," yet there was still hope for some as "injured men, both Union and rebel, were tenderly taken to Shohola."[7]

Some of the wounded were being crowded onto the depot platform, into the freight house, and flooded through the waiting room. If they could be moved to the Shohola House, they were taken there. By nightfall word spread to surrounding communities, and help continued to come, including from across the river in Barryville and Port Jervis, New York. Six doctors mustered into service and deserved "great praise," according to a newspaper correspondent, yet they were prohibited by the commanding officer from performing amputations. An onlooker noticed that the "surgeons were powerless" due to orders stopping them from using surgical tools; their work was literally cut short,

Shohola Glen Hotel. Courtesy of the Pike County Historical Society.

while patients made incessant requests to have their painful limbs removed. Despite this, the *Wayne Herald* revealed how "the ladies of the vicinity" were "unwearied in rendering those kind offices which tenderness alone knows how to bestow." A reporter from the *Tri-States Union* was more specific, writing, "By their side, ever ready to minister to the parched lips of the distressed and console the afflicted men, as angels only can, we must mention the ladies of Shohola and Barryville. . . . They were early on the scene, coming from all quarters and by the dozens." Hot coffee and tea, cold milk and water, crackers, bread, different cakes and pies, and meats were brought in, one reporter noting that "every sort of edible was bestowed by these ladies with a lavish hand. And oh! How grateful were these half-famished men." Allegiance had no boundaries, as "Rebels though they were, they received from these noble women food and comforting words, cooling drinks, and sympathy in their truly pitiable condition." Finally, southerners "seemed to feel it, to know that, though they were prisoners of war whose principles as rebels these women despised, as unfortunate cripples they were their friends and ministering angels."[8] Among the "ministering angels" who crossed over the river from Barryville to the Shohola station were Miss Minerva Drake, Mrs. William Hickok, and Mrs. Benjamin Austin.

As the events unfolded and the gravity of the situation set in, an informal triage-like system had been employed and seemed to be working. Those strong enough to travel would board a relief train sent by the Erie Railroad to bring them to Elmira, where more medical care awaited. Those who were not expected to survive remained in Shohola, where they would eventually be buried in the mass trench at King and Fuller's Cut. And still others, whose conditions were nebulous, were nursed locally. At least six men were left behind in hope that they would survive. Among them were two privates, John D. Johnson of the 31st North Carolina and Michael Johnson of the 8th North Carolina, both too fragile to travel a long distance. John had enlisted early in the war, in October 1861; Michael had signed up only recently, at Petersburg, Virginia, in April 1864. Both men had been captured at Cold Harbor on June 1. It was decided that these two southerners should be taken on the shorter trip, across the river to neighboring Barryville, while their comrades left in Shohola remained at the hotel. Although the Johnsons were not related, they would be forever tied to the wreck. As both men clung to life, too risky to travel a far distance on iron rails, they were transferred to the Hickok house, neighbors to the Drakes.[9]

As the southerners were being treated by local ladies, back in Lackawaxen, men were tasked with bringing justice as a jury quickly met to investigate the cause of the crash. At an impromptu court that was convened the next day, engineer Samuel Hoitt and conductor John Martin both testified that the dispatcher in Lackawaxen, Douglas "Duff" Kent, made a fatal mistake in giving them the rails. The Erie's policy was that all first-class trains westward-bound superseded other first-class trains traveling east, as well as second-class trains hauling coal. A jury found Kent negligent, believing that his mind was clouded as a result of his well-known "intemperate habits." Apparently, he had been imbibing at a dance in nearby Hawley the night before the accident and was still feeling the effects of his binge. Still inebriated, according to reports, he forgot that he had admitted the coal train on the already occupied rails. The guilty verdict mattered little, however, as allegedly Kent fled on a westward train the day after the collision. His station log—the written proof of his dereliction—vanished with him.[10]

Although unrelated, John D. Johnson and Michael Johnson share a single headstone in the old Barryville Congregational Church cemetery, Barryville, New York. The church is now a private residence. Photograph by Jonathan W. White.

The aftermath of the fatal mistake was still being felt back in Shohola and Barryville. By the time it was reported that Kent made his getaway, those who had been well enough to ride to Elmira were taken aboard the Erie relief train. At least four prisoners had already died at the Shohola Hotel, and their corpses transferred down the railroad tracks and interred in the mass trench. Across the river in Barryville, the Johnsons were being nursed by Hickok and Drake. Minerva, being single, took a special hand in their care, but despite doing her best, they both succumbed. Michael had resided in Alamance County, and John in Anson County, a little more than one hundred miles apart from each other in North Carolina, but it was too far to inform their families. It was also suggested to bring the Tar Heel soldiers to rest in the mass grave at King and Fuller's Cut, but the North Carolinians were ultimately buried in New York state, side by side, at the nearby Congregational Church cemetery. John was about twenty-six years old when he died. He left behind a wife and two little daughters in Anson County, one five, the other not yet two. Michael was only seventeen.[11]

Not until the next century was any concerted effort made to remember the Shohola victims. In the early part of the twentieth century, a movement emerged to better mark the graves of Confederates who had died in Union hands at northern prisons as an important gesture of sectional reconciliation. In 1906 Congress approved an act "To provide for the appropriate marking of the graves of the soldiers and sailors of the Confederate army and navy who died in Northern prisons and were buried near the prisons where they died."[12] Commissioner William Elliot was tasked with the work, which brought him to Shohola and the mass trench at the cut. From 1906 to 1910, he and his colleagues tracked the bodies down at the burial site. When Commissioner William Oates took over the project, his investigation was made easier with newspaper reports of old soldiers' bodies being washed out of the site and into the Delaware during floods. Oates worked with local funeral home services and supervised the arduous but careful task of exhuming the bodies and moving them to Elmira.[13]

The Shohola victims now rest with some three thousand comrades who perished at Elmira, a prison that had the reprehensible distinction of having the highest mortality rate of all northern pens at nearly 25 percent. A special "Shohola Monument" was dedicated in 1911, and although the ceremony was rained out—seemingly another way for their story to be forgotten—the large stone stands above the forty-nine prisoners and seventeen guards killed in the crash. The exact number of victims of the Shohola train wreck may never be known due to the mutilated conditions of bodies and possible escapes. The Erie Railroad also paid an undisclosed amount to the families of injured Union guards in an attempt to silence indignation and bring closure to controversies and ambiguities in a shrouded mishap.[14]

Eventually, William Oates, the commissioner for marking graves, stumbled onto Barryville's Congregational Church where he finally found the Johnsons. In his report, he stated "that at least two prisoners were cared for in private homes where they died and were buried in a cemetery." But even these bodies could not entirely escape controversy. Some have questioned why John and Michael Johnson were not brought to the mass trench by the crash site and interred with their brethren, which would have ultimately led to their reinterment at Woodlawn Cemetery in Elmira. Explanations for why they remained in Barryville include a July heat with decomposing bodies or the cost of crossing a toll bridge from New York into Pennsylvania. Others suggest that the Hickocks and Drakes grew to have affection for the dead Confederates and wanted to afford them a proper "Christian burial." Some sources even suggest that when

Monument for the Shohola Dead, Woodlawn National Cemetery, Elmira, New York. Courtesy of the Chemung County Historical Society.

Close-up of monument for the Shohola Dead, Woodlawn National Cemetery, Elmira, New York. Courtesy of the Chemung County Historical Society.

the grave commissioners came looking for the two Johnsons, locals purposely misguided them, not wanting to disclose the graves' whereabouts. "Despite many years of visits from Union officials," according to one report, "they never told the location of the graves."[15]

I tell my students that the Civil War seeps into our countryside, far from the traditional Civil War battlegrounds. One of the reasons I became interested in Civil War prisons is how the great conflict touched the far reaches of the home front. Death and tragedy can be found in unexpected and remote places. Perhaps this chapter can illuminate a forgotten moment in the past, at a place where tourists already flock. Explorations into the Pocono's historical resources also lay in wait, bringing the adventurous to Rohman's Pub, to the crash site (where a boulder monument with a plaque has been placed next to the railroad tracks within the last four years), and finally to the Johnsons' graves across the Delaware River. The graveyard looks over the now-closed church and sits alongside a bed-and-breakfast, named the Stickett Inn. The vacationer pursuing nature's bounty in the upper Delaware, from casts to paddles, can also see what history had wrought on the area, witnessing firsthand the granite remnants left in their backyard.

“That Derogatory Rock”

The Contested Memory of the 1862 Hanging of Thirty-Eight Dakota in Mankato, Minnesota

MELODIE ANDREWS

In the fall of 1990, while browsing through a Mankato, Minnesota, antique shop, I came across an old postcard displaying a photographic image so arresting that it helped inspire a search to uncover the larger meaning of a tragic episode of the Civil War long shrouded in controversy, myth, and mystery. The image that caught my eye was of a young woman smartly dressed in clothing that dated the photo to the early twentieth century. She wore a broad-brimmed hat and even wider grin. And she was standing next to a large tombstone-looking stone marker engraved with the words: “Here were hanged 38 Sioux Indians Dec. 26th 1862.” The jarring contrast between the woman’s smiling face and the monument’s grim text immediately brought to mind photographs of the happy crowds that gathered during the same era to witness the public lynchings of African Americans. Why would anyone want to put up a monument to a mass hanging, I wondered. I had recently moved to the community from the Northeast, and as I gazed at the postcard, I had no idea that the “here” of the stone’s text was Mankato or that the hanging to which it referred was, in fact, the largest government-sponsored execution in American history. Feeling somewhat disconcerted, I set the postcard down and walked away, but the image lingered in my mind. I eventually returned to the shop in hopes of finding the postcard again but it was gone. Ironically, the monument it depicted, long removed from public view, would soon disappear as well—under very mysterious circumstances.

"Little Crow, Sioux Chief and Leader of the Indian Massacre of 1862, in Minnesota." Courtesy of the Library of Congress.

The execution that took place in Mankato brought to a dramatic close one of the most controversial events in Minnesota history: the U.S.-Dakota War of 1862. This conflict was rooted in long-simmering tensions between the Dakota and non-Native settlers over land and tribal sovereignty. The outbreak of the Civil War helped bring these tensions to a head when U.S. government officials delayed food and cash payments owed to the Dakota in exchange for the lands they had been forced to cede in earlier treaties. By the spring of 1862, after a poor harvest the previous fall, the Dakota were starving. When white traders refused to allow the Dakota to buy food on credit (one merchant going so far as to tell them to "eat grass"), some of the desperate Indians, led by Chief Little Crow, declared war. After six weeks of bloody fighting throughout southwestern Minnesota, the

Dakota were defeated by troops under the command of former governor Henry Sibley.

The warriors believed they would be treated as prisoners of war, but military tribunals sentenced 303 Dakota men to death for participating in the fighting. The trials were brief, most lasting less than five minutes each. The defendants had no legal counsel and the proceedings were conducted in English, which many of the Dakota did not understand. In response to an appeal from Episcopal bishop Henry Whipple emphasizing the many injustices the Indians had previously suffered, President Abraham Lincoln personally reviewed the trial records and granted clemency to all but thirty-nine Dakota. One warrior was later pardoned. The remaining thirty-eight died together on one scaffold before thousands of onlookers in Mankato on the day after Christmas. The Dakota were buried in a mass grave not far from the place of their deaths, but only for a few hours after the execution. Doctors from Mankato and the surrounding area spirited the bodies away in the middle of the night to

“Execution of the thirty-eight Sioux Indians at Mankato, Minnesota, December 26, 1862,” Hayes Litho. Co., 1883, was commissioned by Mankato newspaper owner John C. Wise. Courtesy of the Library of Congress.

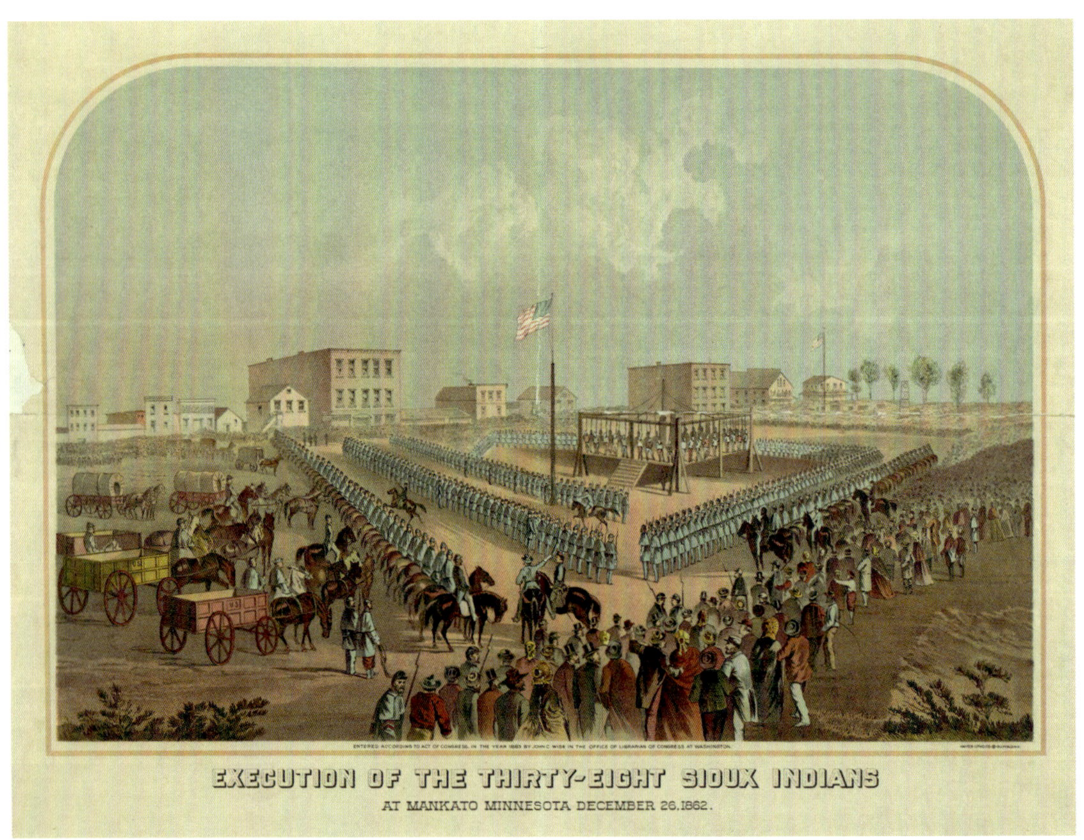

use for anatomical studies. And in the months that followed, the military rounded up every Native American they could find, whether they participated in the war or not, and forcibly exiled them from the state.

The events of 1862 have received considerable scholarly attention in recent years, especially as Minnesota approached the conflict's sesquicentennial in 2012. It is the aftermath of this story—the public memory of these events—that remains largely unexplored. My purpose here is to examine how the community of Mankato and the Native American peoples of the region have chosen to remember the war and attempted to come to terms with their turbulent history through the construction of public monuments, memorials, and new commemorative ceremonies at the Mankato hanging site. This process is complicated by the fact that members of the Native American and non-Native communities view their shared past in profoundly divergent ways. Descendants of white settlers often remember the bravery of their ancestors or the brutality of their killings. The descendants of Dakota people remember the mistreatment of their ancestors by the U.S. government, the hanging of the thirty-eight, and the suffering caused by forced exile. As a consequence, the hanging location has always been contested ground for public memories of the war.

Monuments are history sites that select, legitimize, and interpret the past for the public. Their purpose is to summarize and synthesize the past into a coherent narrative, but when the past being interpreted is a disputed one, monuments often open new chapters of struggle over the meaning and significance of the past. In Mankato, the addition of memorials at the hanging site sparked public debate, reinvigorated competing narratives about the past, and played an integral role in continuing struggles to reshape cultural and community identities. More recently, however, new monuments have been erected to help heal the wounds of the past and to facilitate an ongoing process of reconciliation between the Mankato community and the Native American peoples of the region.

The hanging monument that I first saw on an old postcard was erected by prominent citizens of Mankato and gifted to the city to mark the fiftieth anniversary of the execution in 1912. The city's aging founders realized that public memory of the most significant event in the town's history was fading. And as a result of half a century of construction, even the exact location of

Postcard of the original monument near the execution site. Courtesy of the Blue Earth County Historical Society.

the hanging was now in some doubt. Strangers coming to town wanted to know where the hanging took place. But according to the local newspaper, "Even many of the older settlers of the city cannot accurately describe the spot," while "the younger generation has no definite knowledge of the place."[1]

Judge Lorin Cray and Gen. James Baker, both local participants in the U.S.-Dakota War, led the campaign for a monument. Their objective was to perpetuate community memory of an event that had played an important role in their own lives. Historical interpretation was less important and perhaps deliberately avoided. Unlike the state's other conflict-related monuments, which were paid for by the Minnesota legislature, the Mankato project was privately funded. Cray and his brother paid for the six-foot high, four-and-a-half-foot wide, four-ton granite monument. Local businesses donated the services required for its installation.[2] The monument's tombstone-looking appearance was sadly ironic given the fact that the bodies of the thirty-eight Dakota never had a final resting place after their burial and surreptitious removal just hours after the execution. The stone's stark text, "Here were hanged 38 Sioux Indians," was unique not only because of the singular event that it recorded but because of what it omitted—any mention of the war itself.

So what larger meaning can we derive from these few words etched in granite? And what might the text suggest about the community's attitudes toward the history it represented? The first word of the monument's text is "HERE" in extra-large letters. It emphasized the desire of Mankato's elderly veterans to precisely mark the spot of an event that represented their definitive victory over the Dakota. In actuality, however, they did not place the monument at the exact place of the execution but rather at a more prominent location on the edge of the hanging site at the intersection of Mankato's two main streets.

The next line of the monument, "WERE HANGED," is awkwardly phrased but, more importantly, makes use of the passive voice, meaning the text has no clear subject. This omission leaves viewers of the monument with some important unanswered questions. Who carried out this hanging? Who were these Indians and why were they hanged? With no reference to the war, the larger historical events that led to the execution remain unknown. This absence of context is particularly interesting because even the briefest of the many state-sponsored monuments mention the "Sioux Uprising" or the "Indian Massacre." On the next line of monument text, by itself and in the largest type, is the number "38," which gives the hanging in Mankato its unique significance as the largest government-sponsored execution in American history.

"SIOUX INDIANS" is chiseled on the next line and employs the term of derision first used by the Ojibwe, and later adopted by whites, to describe the Dakota as "snakes" or "enemies." Many Dakota see this term as dehumanizing and emblematic of the mind-set of most white Minnesotans at the time of the war and long afterward. Concluding the inscription on the last line, and in the smallest type, is the date of the hanging, "DEC. 26th 1862." Could the smaller type be indicative of the community's discomfort with the fact that the hanging, however justified, took place the day after Christmas?

If the men who erected the monument hoped that their brief text would allow them to avoid confronting the history that preceded the hanging, they soon learned otherwise. Public controversy over the monument erupted shortly after its dedication, as visitors and local observers constructed their own interpretations of its seemingly straightforward words. Lorin Cray always argued that the monument was nothing more than an accurate marker of a historical event and not a boastful memorial to the defeat of the Dakota.[3] Some members of the community clearly did not share his view, however. In the 1920s they presented the governor with a petition calling for the removal of the monument, even though the hanging site had become a popular tourist destination widely publicized by postcard images like the one I had found. The execution itself had long been commemorated in prints, on souvenir silver spoons, and on beer trays promoting a Mankato brewery.[4]

Some of the harshest criticism of the hanging monument came from out-of-state visitors. Nationally known attorney Clarence Darrow found the monument shocking when he toured Mankato in 1927. "I would never believe that the people of a civilized community would want to commemorate such an atrocious crime," he declared. When Chicago financier George Ackerman visited the site in 1936, he described the hanging as "legalized butchery" and declared that people "ought to forget the incident and attempt to keep it from the minds of children."[5] Newspaper accounts of the lynching of African Americans in the 1920s and 1930s may have contributed to the discomfort felt by some who viewed Mankato's granite proclamation of the mass execution of Native Americans.

Until the early 1950s the monument was displayed in a spacious, ornately fenced grassy plot. Then it was moved about one hundred feet to the front of a Standard service station parking lot. Some older residents still remember when the station owner put up a pole in the parking lot and hung thirty-eight tires on it with a sign declaring "Here lies 38 red skins." In 1965 the monument was moved again to the other side of the service station right next to the street. In spite of its unattractive location, the monument faced the main bridge into town and was the first thing that many visitors saw as they drove into the community. The hanging monument was now a neglected-looking reminder of an uncomfortable past many in Mankato and elsewhere wanted to forget. While the Dakota kept their memories alive through private ceremonies and tribal traditions, public memory of the U.S.-Dakota War began to fade.

After decades at its prominent, ornamentally fenced location, the hanging monument was moved to the front of a nearby service station parking lot in the early 1950s, in a dismal change of scene that reflected changing public attitudes as well. Courtesy of the Blue Earth County Historical Society.

But in the 1970s, as political and social turmoil roiled the nation, in Mankato the hanging monument once again incited public rancor. Mankato State College (MSC) students began protesting the Vietnam War in 1971, and their marches from the campus ended on the street directly in front of the monument. Some students drew parallels between American imperialism abroad and American imperialism at home against Native Americans and demanded that the monument be removed. They also joined the small number of Native American students on campus in calling for an end to another lingering legacy of the U.S.-Dakota War, the college's cartoonish Indian mascot.[6]

In February 1971 Mankato City Council member Dave Commisky asked the council to remove the monument. While he did not oppose the installation of a different historical marker at the site, he did note that "every Indian I've ever talked to is offended by the monument." The question of who owned the land where the monument stood delayed council action at that time.[7] Several months later, MSC theatre students staged a play dramatizing the long history of "white man's mistreatment of the Indians." It ended with a replica of the hanging monument brought on stage to remind the audience of Mankato's part in the tragic saga of Native American suffering. The play seems to have had a powerful impact on those who saw it. As one attendee told the student newspaper, "We are all sick and tired and sad . . . and I felt along with the rest of the audience that we also should fight no more forever."[8] Nonetheless, tensions continued to escalate. Protestors threw red paint on the marker to symbolize blood, and one man, probably inebriated, tried to set fire to the stone "to drive out all of the evil spirits," he told arresting police officers.[9] In the local newspaper, community members once again wrestled with the meaning of their past history. Were the thirty-eight Dakota heroic defenders of their starving people and threatened way of life, and victims of a terrible injustice born out of racial hatred and a desire for revenge? Or were they brutal criminals and murderers who deserved their fate? The continuing presence of the hanging monument seemed to galvanize opinions on both sides of the debate.[10]

During this same period, Native Americans in Minnesota and across the country assumed a more active role in developing and interpreting their own history as an integral part of their movement for greater political, legal, and cultural rights. In the first century after the U.S.-Dakota War, white Minnesotans had controlled public memory of the conflict by erecting monuments to the fallen, marking the anniversary of their victory over the Dakota, and promoting tourism to sites associated with the war. Native Americans, long denied the right to honor their fallen ancestors in any of the state's public spaces, now insisted that the time had come to tell their side of the story. They argued that only through "truth telling" could they counter the narrative of white triumphalism they saw in the writing of most American history books and inscribed in the state's commemorative landscape. In Minneapolis, activists founded the American Indian Movement (AIM) to work for Native American rights and political empowerment. The Mankato hanging monument became a particular target of their ire.

In October 1971, as Native Americans became more politicized and antiwar protests intensified, a combination of factors finally led to the removal of the controversial monument. The city planned a large urban-renewal project at the site, and some community members were disconcerted by the growing militancy of AIM. Would anger over the monument bring even more protests to the embattled town? In spite of these concerns, the original plan was to re-erect the monument in "a more dignified parkette" after the completion of municipal construction.[11] When both the local and state historical societies declined to take temporary possession of the monument, it ended up in a city maintenance garage, half buried under a sand pile, where it remained for the next twenty years. It appeared to some that the city was literally trying to bury part of its controversial past. A group of Dakota made the same point when they visited the storage facility in November 1974 and prayed over the partially uncovered stone. "You can't bury the past like that under gravel," one of the Dakota declared.[12]

The last publicly known photograph of the monument was taken at the city garage in November 1993. Two years later, the notorious stone simply "disappeared"—never to be seen again. As time passed, the ultimate fate of the monument became something of an urban legend, cloaked in a miasma of contradictory stories and enduring mystery. I was intrigued by the many tales I heard around town and decided to try to determine the monument's final disposition with the assistance of a class of dedicated history students.

My interest in the hanging monument had increased steadily through the years. In the spring of 2006, as I prepared to teach my first public history class, I decided that the missing monument would make a great local history project for my students. They enthusiastically embraced the opportunity to become history detectives. After their research revealed that the monument was last seen on city property, the students appeared before the Mankato City Council and formally requested that the council ascertain the monument's current location. Several weeks later, a city official responded to our query with an explanation that surprised the entire community. Who was responsible for the monument vanishing in 1995? It was none other than Stan Christ, the man serving as mayor at the time. He had hauled the monument away from the city maintenance garage with the help of several city employees. Four years later, in the middle of his third term, Christ had abruptly resigned and left the state. Our efforts to contact him were unsuccessful. But the students did track down one of the maintenance workers mentioned in the city's official account. He was retired but clearly remembered helping load the monument into a large truck and watching Christ drive it away. "That's the last time anyone is going to see that thing," he remembered someone remarking.

So where did Christ take this controversial piece of Mankato's history? The idea floated at the time was that he gave it to the Dakota, but the tribal members contacted by local reporters firmly denied this. They had no interest in possessing "that derogatory rock," as one Dakota called it. My students' search for the monument was front-page news in the Mankato newspaper and stirred up plenty of talk, but not from Christ, who refused to confirm that he had taken the stone. Nor were city officials able to provide a satisfactory explanation for why the mayor had been able to abscond with city property. The city attorney at the time of Christ's heist later said that she did not prosecute the mayor because she was never asked to investigate what happened to the monument.[13]

The mystery surrounding the monument's disappearance remained unsolved until 2012, when Minnesota marked the U.S.-Dakota War sesquicentennial. In April of that year I gave a public lecture on the missing monument. Two days later Christ finally broke his long silence in a newspaper interview. "I got rid of it," he admitted. But he refused to reveal the monument's whereabouts, stating, "There's only three people in the world who know, and two of them may be dead."[14] Christ's revelation earned him a "thumbs down" from the editorial board of the local newspaper: "Maybe the marker was an embarrassment and maybe it was an unfortunate monument to a dark moment in history, but it's not the prerogative of small town politicians to rewrite history or 'delete' it," they declared.[15]

For the next four years it appeared that Christ had uttered his last public words on the subject of the missing monument. But in February 2016 he agreed to a telephone interview with the television station in Mankato and opened up about why he had taken the controversial marker. Christ, who is part Native American, said his grandfather took him to see the monument by the service station when he was a child. "He'd stand there with tears in his eyes and I didn't understand when I was small what it meant," he recalled. By 1995 efforts were underway to expand interpretation of the hanging site, and although the old monument was now in storage, "very negative" feelings about it remained. When Christ heard talk that the monument might be re-erected, he decided he needed to prevent that from happening. He was convinced that if the monument disappeared, the strong emotions associated with it would disappear as well. Subsequent events have proved him wrong, but he remained satisfied that he did the right thing at the time. The three men he had told about the monument's disposal were now dead, he revealed, and he vowed that he would take the secret of the stone's location to his grave.[16]

By the time that Christ decided to permanently remove the most evocative symbol of Mankato's difficult past, the hanging site was undergoing a significant transformation that would finally add a Dakota perspective to the events of 1862 and allow the Dakota to honor their thirty-eight executed ancestors. The addition of new monuments became essential to ongoing efforts to bring reconciliation between the Mankato community and the Native American population of the region. This challenging process started shortly after the hanging monument came down in 1971 and grew out of a friendship between local businessman Lewis "Bud" Lawrence; Amos Owen, a Dakota spiritual leader and chairman of the Prairie Island Reservation; and James Buckley, Mankato YMCA director. In 1972 the three men helped organize the first Mankato Wacipi or Powwow. This three-day event, held annually ever since, brought Dakota people back to the city for the first time in 110 years. It is part of a larger effort to reintroduce knowledge of Dakota culture in Mankato and heal the wounds of the past.[17] Another purpose of the early powwows was to raise funds for a Dakota memorial at the hanging site.

In subsequent years, as fundraising efforts for a monument continued, the Dakota worked with the Minnesota Historical Society on a plaque that would include the Dakota perspective in the historical context of the war and Mankato hanging. The plaque was installed in 1980 in front of the library that now occupied part of the hanging site. The creation of a more balanced and inclusive view of the events of 1862 had begun. These efforts continued in 1987 when Governor Rudy Perpich declared a "Year of Reconciliation" in the state. To commemorate this event, a local sculptor, Thomas Miller, created a monument entitled *The Winter Warrior*. It was placed near the historical plaque in front of the library and dedicated on December 26, 1987, the 125th anniversary of the hangings. The execution site was beginning to assume an unmistakably Native American identity, but across Minnesota markers and monuments commemorating white victims of the U.S.-Dakota War continued to vastly overshadow the few that memorialized the war's Native American victims.

An important step in redressing this disparity occurred in 1997 when Bud Lawrence facilitated the acquisition of a small plot of land directly across the street from the library that ultimately became Reconciliation Park. It is the setting for a massive statue of a buffalo carved from a six-ton block of local stone by Thomas Miller. The Dakota chose the buffalo as an iconic representation of their culture, strength, and resilience. On a large boulder nearby is inscribed one of Amos Owens's prayers for peace and understanding. The Dakota also wanted the names of the

Located across the street from the site of the 1862 hanging, Reconciliation Park is dedicated to promoting reflection and healing between Dakota and non-Dakota peoples. A large memorial scroll inscribed with the Dakota names of the thirty-eight executed is the closest thing to a tombstone that they have. Courtesy of the Blue Earth County Historical Society.

executed included at the site, but this proved too controversial for some community members, while others expressed fears of vandalism. This addition to the park was deferred until 2012, when a buckskin-looking scroll monument listing the names of the thirty-eight Dakota was finally erected.[18]

For the Dakota, Reconciliation Park is sacred ground where they gather to honor the memory of their executed ancestors and strengthen their emotional, spiritual, and familial connections to the past. It is a place of healing and reflection, and the site of ceremonies that help the Dakota build a bridge between the traditions of the past and the life of their people today. The old hanging monument that once stood nearby symbolized one version of Minnesota's remembered past that dominated the historical record for over one hundred years after the U.S.-Dakota War. The monuments that have replaced it suggest that the Mankato community and the Dakota are involved in an ongoing process of reconciling different versions of their history. As a result, a more diverse, multivocal narrative is now part of

Mankato's public memory. But it remains a contested narrative to be sure.

The original hanging monument may have disappeared, but the past it represented is neither dead nor buried. On December 26, 2018, a Native American protest group known as "Anti-Colonial Land Defense" descended on Sibley Park in Mankato, named for Henry Sibley, the man who had defeated the Dakota in 1862. The protesters installed a tripod with a noose around a dummy symbolizing Lincoln and unfurled a banner reading "Hangman's Park" over the park entrance. They also demanded that the park be renamed.[19] And so the struggle over the meaning and significance of Mankato's troubled past continues. Which returns us, in conclusion, to the enduring mystery of the missing hanging monument.

Christ always said there were three people who knew his secret. Back in 2006, in the course of my class's search for the missing monument, one of my students identified a man whom we had many reasons to believe was one of those three people. When contacted, he readily admitted that Christ had told him what he did with the monument. The story he told made a lot of sense, but without confirmation from Christ, it remains impossible to verify. And our informant has subsequently died. The most persistent rumor around Mankato is that the monument is with the Dakota, in spite of their denials and clear animosity toward the "derogatory rock" and all it symbolizes. Several years ago, a friend of mine inquired about the monument's location when he visited Dakota friends at the Standing Rock Reservation. "Look to the place where the eagles circle over the river in Mankato," they told him. This answer may be the best we have at the moment and, in my view, comes close to the ultimate truth of the matter.

Confederate Tombs on Brazilian Soil

A Trip, a Cemetery, and a Nexus of Confusion

VITOR IZECKSOHN

In April 1972 Jimmy Carter, then governor of Georgia, went on a tour through Latin America sponsored by the Lockheed Aircraft Corporation. The trip took Carter to five Latin American countries: Mexico, Argentina, Colombia, Costa Rica, and Brazil. His wife, Rosalynn, and a small group of advisers joined him on his first international mission. By that time, Latin America appealed to the U.S. as both a lost tropical paradise and a region with trade potential. The trip was undertaken at a strategic moment so that the governor could avoid involvement in the troubled Democratic presidential primaries and in the relentless debates over the Vietnam War and civil rights that engulfed his divided party. The Latin American tour helped project Carter as an international leader and a viable contender in the 1976 presidential primaries. Two years of language studies and readings on the peculiarities of each country preceded the trip. As a young governor from an influential southern state, Carter's agenda combined a search for southern heritage with his future commitment to human rights. But business opportunities still figured as the paramount objective.

April 19, 1972, was sunny in the state of São Paulo, Brazil. Carter's entourage left the industrial city of São Paulo, the state capital, for the town of Americana, which had been founded by southern slaveowners soon after the Civil War. There, his visit included a short helicopter trip to the Field Confederate Cemetery at nearby Santa Bárbara D'Oeste. The mayor of Santa Bárbara had improvised a heliport to receive the important visitor.

Georgia governor Jimmy Carter visiting the graves of Confederados in 1972. Courtesy Wikimedia Commons.

However, for reasons not exactly clear, Carter and his associates came by car, a forty-minute journey over dusty roads from Americana to the Confederate cemetery. The governor laid the cornerstone of what was to have been a museum of American emigration. An audience of about thirty Confederate descendants welcomed the visitor. As he was introduced to the descendants, he received an honorary membership in the Fraternidade Descendência Americana (Fraternity of American Descendants). Carter's speech was short. He talked about "familiar faces" and "a recognizable accent." He underscored the way the colonists had persevered to build their home in Brazil. He told listeners that "all of this makes me remember my home," and "it does not matter where we are in the world, we share a common heritage," finally emphasizing that "[i]t makes me feel at home in Georgia, seeing so many familiar names and faces."[1] As the Carters toured the cemetery, Rosalynn Carter stopped by the tomb of William Wise and murmured, "My grandmother was a Wise." After they went back to the United States, Carter told journalists from the *Atlanta Constitution* about his impressions: "My primary feeling was one of appreciation for their preserving in an almost unblemished way, in names, inflections and voices of their ancestors, their obvious love for the United States."[2]

Brazilian Confederate descendants provided an appropriate audience for the Georgian politician because their grandfathers had migrated from the U.S. South before the major conflicts of southern Reconstruction took place. Consequently, Carter could pay tribute to the emigrants' determination to remake their lives in Brazil without apology to racially oriented extremism, a position appropriate for a region of the U.S. where Democrats faced renewed challenges from conflicts between civil rights activists and white supremacists. Consequently, Carter's discourse with Confederate descendants at "Campo" did not compromise his position in the Democratic Party as a future national leader on a liberal ticket.

Within six years Carter would return to Brazil as president of the United States and a champion of human rights. Four decades later, his first visit is still remembered by the colonists' descendants. It was documented in pictures and articles reproduced in newspapers in Brazil and in the U.S. South. In general, the press showed astonishment at this "lost colony." Thus, Carter was able to call attention to the peculiarities of southern emigration as well as to his evolution as a southern Democratic leader. Yet, despite its political resonance, no evidence suggests that William Wise was actually related to Rosalynn Carter, as some reports intimated. That potential link looks like wishful thinking, an attempt to enhance the meaning of the visit in terms that would appeal to southern audiences back in the U.S.

Emigration, an unusual decision for inhabitants of the U.S. territory, was undertaken by some five thousand southerners during the mid-1860s. During a period of three to five years, these former Confederates tried to reestablish themselves outside the U.S. by taking advantage of commercial networks already established by traders and politicians who dealt with Brazilians and other Latin American countries such as Mexico. For the Confederate descendants, Carter's visit marked a recognition of their elders' efforts to persevere in a place they considered to be a new frontier: an agrarian empire that had used diplomacy to protect blockade runners, while at the same time recognizing the state of belligerence existing between the Union and the Confederacy. Taking chances in one of the last slaveholding nations gave meaning to an adventure that connected these settlers to their lands and was consecrated in history by means of a burial ground that became a reference point for supporters of the Lost Cause.

In the western reaches of Brazil's southwestern province of São Paulo, this small cemetery sometimes attracts visitors from the United States. Ninety-six of its graves belong to U.S. Civil War veterans from the former Confederate States. After 1865, Confederate combatants and their families immigrated to Mexico, England, Canada, and Brazil in different waves, fleeing the destruction of their racially oriented hierarchy. These immigrants did not envision a new world but instead sought a society with at least some similarity to the vanished Confederacy and its agrarian ways of life.

Many southerners rejected Yankee dominion and Reconstruction. Some, like Matthew Fontaine Maury, tried to establish a colony in northern Mexico, which perpetuated slavery under the guise of "apprentices."[3] Others migrated to the northern states, searching for better economic opportunities. A large group went to Brazil, the largest remaining slave society, an empire struggling to find alternatives to slave work. Their motivations for leaving the U.S. varied, but their general impetus was to be as far away as possible from the reach of the Union army and the social and economic transformations taking place in the American South after the Civil War. At the end of the sectional conflict, the shock of military defeat, social and political transformation, destitution, and a willingness to emigrate contributed to decisions to take risks in other countries. The emancipation of four million Black slaves, the destruction of the secessionist impulse, and the implementation of procedures privileging market rules in social relations were seen by many Confederates as unacceptable modifications of their social landscape. Even some nonslaveholders refused to abide by the new rules.[4]

This singular diaspora, and its tentative attempt to recreate part of the Confederate way of life abroad, is one of the least studied aspects of the Civil War. Many ex-Confederates arrived in São Paulo after frustrating experiences in other parts of the Brazilian Empire, such as in the provinces of Pará and Espírito Santo where lack of support, bad roads, internal divisions, or epidemics contributed to the failure of the enterprise. Others came after trying their chances in Mexico or Venezuela. A considerable number would return to the U.S. after some years.[5]

Col. William Hutchinson Norris, a Mexican American veteran and former Alabama senator as well as grand master of Alabama's Masonic lodges, founded a colony at the town of Santa Bárbara D'Oeste, near the city of Campinas.[6] There, the red land, with its vast plantations of coffee and sugarcane, reminded colonists of parts of the South. The province was thriving with emigration and agricultural innovations. A railroad network was being built to connect interior lands to the city port of Santos. The region around Campinas was a natural magnet for those interested in investing in land.[7]

Norris succeeded in his endeavors, building a farm he called "Sitio da Serra," acquiring farmstock and around fifteen slaves who worked in cotton and sugarcane fields. He brought his family, consisting of his wife and three children, a boy and two girls. We can wonder about the difficulties of the sea voyage between the U.S. and Rio de Janeiro, of railroad travel from Brazil's capital to the city of São Paulo, and finally days on a wagon train between the provincial capital and Santa Bárbara D'Oeste, a frontier region where slave labor and free labor coalesced in the expansion of coffee farms.

By the mid-1860s, Brazil was the only independent country in the Americas that maintained Black slavery as the basis of export agriculture. A monarchy organized around conservative political elements that brought some constancy to its political regime, the empire had been a stable polity since the 1850s. No separatist movements or internal civil wars threatened the country. Unlike most of its neighbors, Brazil was able to maintain its territorial unity.[8] Most political factions respected the emperor as an arbiter in disputes over different projects and agendas. Compared to Mexico and other Latin American countries, the Brazilian Empire's future seemed more predictable, at least for the time being. Cuba, still a Spanish colony, also kept slaves at work on its sugarcane plantations. However, the island's political instability, its independence movements, and its proximity to the U.S. made Cuba a complicated choice for prospective emigrants. Mexico formed the southern border of the U.S. Nevertheless, recurrent civil wars between conservative defenders of Emperor Maximilian I's empire and republican liberals compounded the risks for those willing to emigrate there.[9]

With a more stable political system controlled by a centralized state, featuring bipartisan competition in its parliamentary system, Brazil provided better prospects for agricultural enterprises. The empire's business community was well connected to European centers of commerce, and links with the U.S. associated coffee and flour in a stable commercial network featuring strong commercial relations with Baltimore enterprises. Life seemed more promising and less uncertain there than in other areas of the western hemisphere. And because Brazil was almost as large as the United States, persons could move freely around a similarly vast and diverse territory.

However, not all prospects were positive. Despite the optimism of Confederate slaveholders, it was clear to many Brazilian leaders that the institution was doomed. The defeat of the Confederacy in the American Civil War terminated their last illusions concerning the survival of slavery in the long term. For those better acquainted with the international scenario, emancipation was only a question of time. British diplomacy had forced an end to international slave traffic, isolating Brazilian slaveholders in a world less willing to tolerate slavery. Low birth rates could not replace population losses due to death and manumission. Unlike in the U.S. South, there was no natural increase in the slave population without the arrival of new captives, and the end of the traffic in slaves tremendously increased the cost of slave labor. Slaves were becoming too expensive for farmers to buy, rent, and maintain: a reserve of free men provided additional workers to help on plantations.[10] Commenting on the issue of the rising prices of slaves a few years before, American diplomat James Watson Webb observed:

> The simple truth is, when the slave trade was permitted and was active, a negro [was] sold for from $50 to $200, and his master was glad to hire him out for four dollars per month, being an interest of from twenty-five to thirty-five per cent per annum on the investment. Now the same negro is worth from $1000 to $1500 and is readily hired out at $20 per month. Of course, slavery and negro labor degrade white labor; and hence the whites do not, and will not work, sooner or later, the price of labor in a country regulates the price of all the necessaries of life, because they are the product of labor; and consequently, the price of labor in Brazil having advanced in thirteen years five hundred per cent, it is not strange that the cost of living should have doubled and trebled.[11]

Brazil's emperor, Pedro II, intended to bring European immigrants to the country to help substitute free workers for slaves in the fields. This project was as old as the nation, but in the

1860s it was propelled by an urgent need for fresh arms to work in lands recently opened to agriculture. Pedro II also understood that, with the end of the Civil War, the U.S. cotton supply would dwindle, opening an opportunity for Brazilian exports. American agricultural techniques could improve soil productivity and diversify and modernize farming practices, even via simple tasks such as butter making and the use of superior plows, which had already appeared in the country but were not widespread. Mechanization was particularly important because the importation of new slaves had been forbidden since 1850. The agricultural expertise of U.S. whites could help improve farm productivity in Brazil, and the possibility of productivity increases made them welcome. A reputation for hard work reinforced the emperor's resolve to support and facilitate immigration from the Confederate states and give settlers access to land. During the U.S. Civil War, despite Brazil's recognition of the state of belligerence between the two parties, the imperial government had given safe harbor in its ports to some Confederate vessels. This circumstance created a connection that helped propel transhemispheric migration and provided an easy path for negotiations between Brazilian bureaucrats and former Confederate agents.[12] According to a Brazilian colonization agent:

> The emigration of real planters from the American South, currently leaving their country due to political dissentions, and coming with their capitals, their machines, their industries and their intelligent work, enemy of routine would provide a great, an enormous benefit to Brazil, even if their intention is to buy slaves and work with them.[13]

The unpretentious cemetery was established on land belonging to Col. Asa Thompson Oliver. A few tombstones are embellished with more sophisticated decorations, but flat marble and cement markers predominate in this field of graves scattered among tropical flowers and trees. Most of the inscriptions are in English, and many of the tombs are marked with Masonic symbols, a common affiliation among the colonists. Although the place contains the bodies of many former Confederate soldiers, it is not a military cemetery.

Most of the immigrants were Baptists, Presbyterians, and Methodists. At that time, Catholicism was Brazil's official religion, and Protestants could not be buried in Catholic cemeteries.

Obelisk monument at Cemitério do Campo, Santa Bárbara d'Oeste, 2017. Photograph by Alan P. Marcus.

The church had been united with the imperial state since independence, a situation that changed only with the coming of Brazil's Republican regime in 1889. When Colonel Oliver's wife, Beatrice, died in 1868, Oliver committed the land of one of his fields for a cemetery since there were no Protestant cemeteries nearby. Beatrice Oliver was the first American to be buried in that place, at the back of her husband's farm. In the following decades, as many others joined Beatrice in their final rest, the field became the official cemetery for Confederates, called the "Cemitério do Campo" (or Field Cemetery).

Colonel Oliver, dreadfully murdered on July 27, 1873, was also buried there.[14] Initially, Lourenço, a twenty-year-old migrant from the state of Rio de Janeiro and one of Oliver's fifteen slaves, was accused by another captive of executing the crime. Lourenço was a rebellious slave who liked to spend time wandering around off the farm. Oliver did not tolerate his servant's behavior and had already punished him. Oliver's body was found the next day. There were no witnesses to the crime and no knowledge of its perpetrators. The situation prompted accusations against Lourenço. The young slave was indicted by a citizens' jury, but, amazingly, he was unanimously acquitted at his trial for lack of proof and subsequently sold to another master. Colonel Oliver's murder remains a mystery to this day.[15]

Cemitério do Campo, Santa Bárbara d'Oeste. Photograph by Alan P. Marcus.

Currently, a foundation made up of the descendants of these first colonists, Fraternidade Descendência Americana (Fraternity of American Descendants), supports the maintenance of the area. A Confederate flag, the Stars and Bars, flutters atop a white obelisk stamped with ninety-six names. At present, the place is surrounded by sugarcane and cotton plantations and can only be reached by a short dirt lane off the main road that connects the towns of Santa Bárbara D'Oeste and Americana. This still-prosperous region is located at the heart of what was a new agricultural frontier during the second half of the nineteenth century. The region used both slave and free labor to expand cotton, peanuts, and sugarcane as well as coffee cultivation. With the coming of the railroad, the city of Americana developed as a new urban center, the name of which became a tribute to those colonists. Four times each year Confederate descendants organize to pay homage to their ancestry.

Ironically, by the time the colonists settled in the region, the Brazilian Empire had become involved in a relentless war against Paraguay. Although war with that nation had been expected for some time, its outbreak took Brazilian elites by surprise. The empire needed to organize an army quickly, provide for recruits, and buy weapons. Those measures increased the national debt and diverted resources originally destined for infrastructure.[16] The campaign was long and costly. War efforts consumed the nation's revenue and resources, including much of its free workforce. The Brazilian government obtained loans to maintain war efforts at full tilt, even as escalating inflation helped compromise the empire's capacity for economic development. Lacking expected support from the national state, the new colonists had to improvise. Many returned to the U.S. Others, mostly liberal professionals, left the rural colony to practice their vocations in larger towns, developing a network of Baptist schools that is still a reference for technical education. Notwithstanding these hardships, a group of five hundred families stayed in Santa Bárbara D'Oeste, becoming the nucleus of a community that would thrive in subsequent decades. Despite difficulties in learning the Portuguese language and adapting to a different cultural environment, many of those colonists adjusted well to local circumstances and customs. Their productive farms became integrated into the national economy. In addition to cotton, sugarcane, and peanuts, these immigrants introduced the cultivation of watermelon, which in the following decades become a popular commodity in Brazilian markets.

For four decades, the descendants of the Confederate migrants, known as Confederados, have hosted a festival called Festa Confederada (Confederate Party) on this giant, painted concrete slab at the cemetery. In recent years, antiracism activists have protested the festival and its use of Confederate symbols, and in 2023 the festival was canceled on account of the protests. Photograph by Vitor Izecksohn.

Within this cemetery, a careful search takes the visitor to the grave of William S. Wise, a South Carolinian who enrolled in the Confederate army in October 1861. His record of service states that he joined an artillery unit and remained a private for the duration of the war. We do not know how this man got to Santa Bárbara D'Oeste or how he paid the cost of the long trip. It is not clear which of the immigrant waves brought him to Brazil. His name does not figure among the colony's famous leaders. The Norrises, Dodsons, Joneses, and the MacNights each commanded tens of families in their search for new lands in the southern hemisphere. They negotiated the acquisition of these lands with Brazilian authorities, searched for the best options, and planned the settlement. Wise's fame is a postmortem phenomenon related to a supposed connection to former First Lady Rosalynn Carter. Her grandmother's family name was Wise, and William could have been a great-uncle who left the South after the Civil War was over. As for his life in Brazil, nothing is known.

The cemetery has gained new tenants since that visit. For Brazilians passing through and occasional U.S. visitors, it remains a tourist attraction as well as a meeting place for Brazilian descendants of Confederates: a lost nexus between two former slaveholding societies.[17]

The University of Virginia Cemetery

CAROLINE E. JANNEY

As an undergraduate at the University of Virginia (UVA), in the spring of 1998 I enrolled in an English course titled "Civil War Culture" taught by Franny Nudelman. Although I was a politics major planning a career in law, the course sparked my interest. The capstone project asked us to choose an aspect of Civil War culture—poetry, music, painting, monumentation—and write a major research paper. I elected to write about the university's cemetery, specifically why it held the remains of more than one thousand Confederate soldiers. Little did I expect that the project would lead me to graduate school in history (rather than law school), to write a book on the topic, and, eventually, back to the University of Virginia where the cemetery would become part of my classroom. Both personally and professionally, the cemetery serves to remind me of the many layers of history to be uncovered even in a small plot of ground. But more importantly, its ever-changing meaning and aesthetic underscores the dynamic nature of memory and memorialization.

The university cemetery dates to 1828 when a typhus epidemic claimed the lives of several students and city residents. At least one of the students, John Temple, was buried in a tract of land between the Rotunda and Observatory Hill next to the remains of Henry William Tucker, brother to a professor. Soon, other victims reposed among them, and a cemetery was born. During the subsequent decades, the graves of more students were added to the small burial ground. Among the deceased rested Alabamian John A. Glover, murdered in 1846 at a performance

Although UVA students called for a monument in the Confederate section of the cemetery as early as 1866, the monument would not be dedicated until 1893 under the direction of the local Ladies' Memorial Association. Courtesy of the Albert and Shirley Small Special Collections Library at the University of Virginia.

by a traveling menagerie. Glover and several other students had pressed too closely to a lion cage with a trainer inside. In the uproar that followed, an elephant rushed into the ring, throwing his tusks in the air, causing the crowd to flee in terror. In a rage, the elephant trainer struck the students with a stick, killing Glover and injuring two others.[1]

The university reserved the cemetery for those with ties to the school and, not surprisingly, limited it to white people. Enslaved and free African Americans were to be buried just north of the wooden enclosure. Perhaps more importantly, the plots of African Americans proved vulnerable to grave-robbing by medical students. Completed by the fall of 1827, the university's Anatomical Theater offered a state-of-the art space where professors performed cadaver dissections in front of students (but with high, small windows preventing the outside world from observing the operations). In medical schools both north and south, students needed cadavers to hone their skills, and at UVA, according to university records, "grave-robbing squads were a normal element of undergraduate activity." Chief among the targets: the graves of free and enslaved African Americans throughout the region—including those just outside the university cemetery. Charles C. Wertenbaker, an 1853 alumnus, recalled that "fear of having their dead taken up by the medical class . . . caused the negroes to inter their dead secretly, and hold their usual ceremonies over the dummy" graves containing only "log or wood or stones."[2] Even in death, African Americans often found it difficult to escape the grasp of white brutality.

From 1828 through the 1850s, the official cemetery expanded slowly by adding students, professors, and members of the Board of Visitors. But during the Civil War a new category of occupants would come to inhabit the ground, redefining its meaning and purpose.

Charlottesville quickly became a vast hospital complex after the battle of Manassas (Bull Run) on July 21, 1861. Along with the city's General Hospital, the Rotunda, Lawn, the East and West Ranges, and Dawson's Row were soon overflowing with some 1,200 to 1,400 Confederate casualties. More than 100 wounded still lingered on grounds the following month when an outbreak of typhoid fever swept the area. During the spring of 1862, another 1,400 wounded from Stonewall Jackson's Valley Campaign arrived via the Virginia Central Railroad, while still more trickled in after the battle of Second Manassas.[3]

The exigencies of war meant that many if not most soldiers who died in hospital complexes would not be returned to their homes but buried in close proximity to their place of death. The same held true in Charlottesville. Between July and November 1861, 220 soldiers died in the hospital. Of these, 180 were buried adjacent to and just west of the university cemetery. African Americans, both enslaved and free, likely conducted the burials just as they performed other types of hospital labor, including cleaning facilities, building fires, preparing meals, and bathing patients.[4] As the number of dead continued to increase, officials extended the boundaries of the soldier burial grounds and eventually created an entire section for the war dead. The university's Confederate burial grounds, therefore, did not begin as a memorial; rather, it offered a practical solution for interring the ever-growing number of dead.

By 1865, enslaved and free hospital workers had buried 1,097 Confederate soldiers in the new section. Soldiers from the Army of Northern Virginia hailed from nine Confederate states, with Georgia (224), North Carolina (200), and Virginia (192) claiming the highest numbers. As with other Confederate burial grounds, this was a *national* Confederate cemetery—not a memorial to local men. Indeed, unlike those buried in the university's original cemetery, these men were not students or faculty. The only former student buried in the cemetery during the war was Brig. Gen. Carnot Posey, a Mississippi native who had attended the law school. Posey was wounded in the thigh at Bristoe Station on October 14, 1863, and brought to Charlottesville where he died in Professor John S. Davis's pavilion on the Lawn a month later. Rather than placing his remains in the soldiers' section, Davis had Posey interred in his family plot—leaving the Confederate portion of the cemetery to those who had no connection to the school other than as the site of their death.[5]

At least one of the soldiers who slumbered in the cemetery had not died in the local hospital. For several years, cavalry general Turner Ashby rested among the dead. Although he hailed from Fauquier County, following his death at Harrisonburg on June 7, 1862, his body was brought to Charlottesville along with many of the wounded from Jackson's Valley Campaign. His funeral would be among the most elaborate the town ever witnessed. A large body of his cavalry led a procession including townspeople in carriages and on foot as well as Ashby's famous black horse attired in all its equipment, draped in black crepe, and led by two enslaved men.[6]

Approximately ten Union soldiers likewise found themselves temporarily reposing in the university cemetery.[7] Among them rested Lt. Col. Henry Burton Stone of the 5th Connecticut Infantry. Severely wounded at the battle of Cedar Mountain in August 1862, he was captured and taken to Charlottesville's Delevan Hospital. "I am lying here on my back, suffering continual pain, patiently waiting for my wounds to heal," he wrote in September. But such was not to be. After his leg developed an infection, he succumbed on January 20, 1863. Initially buried in Charlottesville, at some point between 1866 and 1867 the United States Burial Corps reinterred his remains in the Culpeper National Cemetery.[8]

After the war ended in the spring of 1865, locals initiated efforts to transform the burial grounds into hallowed spaces that would honor the Confederacy and the men who died for it. In May 1866 a group of men led by Professor J. L. Cabell formed the Albemarle Confederate Memorial Association, dedicated "to enclosing, beautifying, and caring for the cemetery, and erecting a suitable monument to the memory of our fallen braves."[9] Their efforts appear to have been motivated by the city's first Confederate Memorial Day, held on May 10, the anniversary of Stonewall Jackson's death in 1863. As in other communities throughout the commonwealth that spring, this was to be a day of mourning under the direction of local women—not men.[10] With the city's shops closed and businesses suspended, hundreds of townspeople, students, and faculty assembled at the Baptist Church at three o'clock that afternoon. After listening to fiery addresses by Thomas Wood and Rev. Mr. Ware, the procession marched to the university cemetery where they strewed flowers, wreaths, and evergreens over the graves of the dead. "It was a solemn scene; the vast concourse of loving friends assembled to honour the memory of the dead," twenty-year-old Sallie Strickler recorded in her diary that evening. "I almost wish I was dead, & in the grave with them, when I think of our state of degradation," she concluded.[11]

During the summer of 1866, the literary societies at the university resolved to erect a monument in the Confederate portion of the cemetery. To finance the memorial, the students proposed appropriating any surplus funds each group might have at year's end. But taking a cue from the Ladies' Memorial Associations (LMAs) across the state, they likewise asked communities in the entire state to aid their endeavor. "We now appeal to you, the people of Virginia, to help us in our effort to preserve the names and memory of your sons."[12] This would be a collective effort—a means of memorializing and enshrining the Confederate cause.

Neither of the men's efforts bore fruit. Instead, women came to control the memorial landscape. By December 1866, Charlottesville women had followed the lead of like-minded female associations in nearby Winchester, Fredericksburg, Lynchburg, Richmond, Harrisonburg, and Staunton in forming a Confederate Memorial Association.[13] Perhaps their formal organization had been spawned by the Winchester LMA's efforts to reinter Turner Ashby and his brother Richard in its newly established Stonewall Cemetery. Despite objections by those in Charlottesville, Ashby's sisters consented to both brothers' reinternment in Winchester during an elaborate cemetery dedication in October 1866.[14] Or perhaps the Charlottesville women, many of whom had supported the Confederate war effort by sewing uniforms or nursing in the university's hospitals, had been motivated by the flurry of LMAs that sprang up across the state in 1865–66. Regardless of their reason, the Charlottesville LMA took over the initial efforts of the men's association, pledging to protect and beautify the graves of their Confederate dead. Their work included copying the hospital register, thereby recording the name, state, regiment, death date, and grave location of each soldier in the cemetery. Eventually, they raised money to build a brick wall enclosing the grounds.[15]

Gendered ideas about mourning, politics, and nationalism proved crucial to the story of Confederate memorialization. Women took the lead in establishing and protecting Confederate burial grounds not only because the nineteenth-century Victorian mourning culture encouraged them to do so, but also because it was politically expedient. Viewed by society as "nonpolitical" beings, they and their male supporters claimed that women's efforts to enshrine the Lost Cause would not threaten political reunification or sectional reconciliation. They claimed their work was *merely* an expression of grief. In fact, their work was not nearly so benign. Through cemeteries and Memorial Day remembrances, the Ladies' Associations helped initiate and perpetuate the Lost Cause. The LMAs, and not the United Confederate Veterans nor the United Daughters of the Confederacy, were responsible for remaking military defeat into a political, social, and cultural victory for the white South.

In my exploration of the LMAs during graduate school and in my first book, I left the Charlottesville LMA and UVA cemetery behind as I ventured into other parts of Virginia. But the story of Confederate memorialization in Charlottesville, which began with a cemetery conceived out of necessity and transformed into a shrine, mirrored that of other locales. As the strictures of Reconstruction gave way in the 1870s, Confederate men began to play a more active role in perpetuating the Lost Cause. In July 1876 the 19th Virginia Regiment held the first Confederate reunion in Charlottesville, which began with a parade up Main Street to UVA and "on to the Soldiers' cemetery near the University" where ladies had decorated the graves with flowers and evergreens.[16] Even as tributes to the Lost Cause continued to grow in the late 1880s with the formation of groups such as the United Confederate Veterans, by 1890 the soldiers' section of the cemetery had fallen into disrepair, prompting an editorial in the *Jefferson Republican* to ask whether the Charlottesville Ladies might reorganize. During the next three years, the sixty women composing the LMA (many of whom were the wives and daughters of university professors) raised funds to restore the cemetery by removing the decaying wooden headboards and planting a field of grass.[17]

The Charlottesville women identified as their principal goal the erection of a monument to the dead. Although calls for the memorial had emerged as early as 1866, the poor condition of Confederate cemeteries in the closing decades of the century compared to those of their former foes spurred them into action. "The United States Government spends great sums in protecting and beautifying the graves of the Federal dead," the Ladies' appeal read, observing that "Our dead are as sacred to us." While they could not build "such beautiful cemeteries or splendid monuments" as the victorious unionists, they could "at least keep their graves green and rescue their names from oblivion."[18] By 1890, the monument was as much about honoring the Confederate dead as it was about ensuring that a Confederate memory was not overwhelmed by the growing number of Union monuments dotting northern cities and battlefields such as Gettysburg. The Ladies thus turned one of the tenets of the Lost Cause—defeat by overwhelming manpower and material—into a rationale for memorializing the Confederacy.

On June 7, 1893, an immense crowd gathered to witness the unveiling of an eight-foot-tall bronze figure of a "youthful Confederate soldier." In pageantry that had become the mainstay of Confederate memorialization by the 1890s, former Virginia

Only one Confederate soldier who died during the war, Brig. Gen. Carnot Posey, is buried in the main university cemetery (pictured here). The 1,097 soldiers buried in the Confederate section were neither students nor faculty, but soldiers who died in the vast wartime hospital complex. Photograph by Rufus W. Holsinger, February 28, 1916. Courtesy of the Albert and Shirley Small Special Collections Library at the University of Virginia, Charlottesville.

governor and Confederate general Fitzhugh Lee served as chief marshal, leading a procession of veterans from across the region and local civilians. After the usual speeches glorifying the Confederate soldier and his cause, a band struck up "Dixie" as the Ladies unveiled the monument, which bore the names of all those buried in the section and the inscription "Fate denied them victory, but crowned them with glorious immortality," a fundamental tenet of Lost Cause ideology.[19]

The former Confederates who crafted UVA's memorial landscape assumed their tributes—and their meaning—would endure indefinitely. Accepting two bronze tablets on the south portico of the Rotunda in 1906 that listed the names of more than five hundred alumni who had died fighting for the Confederacy, university president Edwin Alderman observed that the "endless procession of youth" who passed the school's most visible landmark would "gaze with awe upon these names." (The names of students, faculty, and formerly enslaved men who died for the Union Cause were not included.)[20]

Memory, commemoration, and meaning have never been static—even at a place so awash in "tradition" as UVA. In the wake of the white-nationalist rally in August 2017 prompted by the city of Charlottesville's decision to remove statues of Robert E. Lee and Stonewall Jackson, the university removed the Confederate plaques from the Rotunda. Well before the events of that summer, the cemetery had witnessed constant change both in meaning and in form, so it should come as no surprise that it continued to evolve. In 2012, an archaeological survey of land adjacent to the cemetery revealed sixty-seven mostly unmarked grave shafts determined to be those of enslaved and newly freed African Americans (many might have been sites of the earlier grave robbing). The President's Commission on Slavery at UVA initiated efforts to preserve the African American cemetery, subsequently enclosing it and adding interpretive plaques. Although not nearly as well attended as the Confederate memorial dedication in 1893, in October 2014 the commission held a ceremony to honor those buried at the site. A reminder of the centrality of slavery to the university, the section offered a countermemory to the Confederate memorial atop the hill.[21] And in April 2020 the university unveiled an even grander and bolder acknowledgment of the school's legacy of slavery with the dedication of the Memorial to Enslaved Laborers, acknowledging and honoring the four thousand or more individuals who built and maintained the university for more than four decades.[22]

Returning to UVA as a professor in the fall of 2018, I recognized the teaching possibilities the cemetery offered. In my class on Civil War memory, we pondered the meaning and evolution of the burial grounds. Amid national discussions of removing Confederate monuments, we discussed whether place mattered—did a Confederate statue in a cemetery mean something different from one in front of a courthouse? Some students suggested that as a memorial to the dead, the monument was a fitting tribute in the cemetery as opposed to on a courthouse lawn. Others believed that any tribute to the Confederacy in any place might be deemed offensive. We likewise addressed the discrepancies between the marked graves of Confederate soldiers and the unmarked graves of the enslaved men and women, a topic that enlivened more than a few. Many found this fact disgraceful, but they acknowledged that the efforts by the university to honor the lives of the enslaved laborers even without their names was a step in the right direction. Above all, we asked

Even before the first Confederate memorials were removed from the university landscape following the Unite the Right Rally in August 2017, efforts had begun to acknowledge the university's history of enslavement. In April 2020 UVA unveiled the Memorial to Enslaved Laborers. Photograph by Sanjay Suchak, University of Virginia.

questions about the social, cultural, and political purposes of memorials to individuals and groups.

A night view of the Memorial to Enslaved Laborers, which pays tribute to the four thousand or more enslaved individuals who labored at the institution. Photograph by Sanjay Suchak, University of Virginia.

Perhaps it is trite for a historian to suggest that cemeteries are more than tributes to the dead—that they are educational in nature. Yet that is the case. UVA's cemetery was an entry point into my own examination of Confederate memorialization, and all these years later, it continues to serve as my classroom—as a place to learn and to teach, to question both history and the construction of memory, and the ever-changing nature of both.

"A Martyr in the Cause of Liberty"

The Death and Burial of John Rodgers Meigs

BARTON A. MYERS

Scouting within the Union lines near Harrisonburg, Virginia, three Confederate soldiers wore rubber raincoats over their uniforms to shield themselves from the drizzling rain of an autumn evening in the Shenandoah Valley. One of the men, Benjamin Franklin Shaver, a private in the 1st Virginia Cavalry and a local resident of the area, guided the southern soldiers as they observed the Union army positions of Gen. Philip Sheridan's command then making its way up the valley, focused on destroying the agricultural lifeline of Robert E. Lee's Army of Northern Virginia (ANV). That same evening, October 3, 1864, John Rodgers Meigs, chief engineer of the Middle Military Division serving under Sheridan, was leading two Union army orderlies along Swift Run Gap road on a similar scouting mission to obtain information about the topography and local landscape when the two enemy parties encountered each other. In the confusing moments that followed, there was an exchange of gunfire, and while the accounts differ on the precise sequence of events, one fact remains clear. Meigs, first in the West Point Class of 1863 and the eldest son of Union army quartermaster general Montgomery Meigs, was killed. As the frightened orderlies scattered to relay the story back at Union headquarters, his body was left in the road. The corpse would not be recovered by Union soldiers until the following morning. When orderlies recounted the story, they reported that they had been waylaid by Confederate "bushwhackers."[1]

In retaliation for what the general believed was an extralegal guerrilla or bushwhacker assault on unsuspecting troops,

John Rodgers Meigs. Courtesy of the Library of Congress.

415.

Rock Ribbed lateral road. From Sketch I made of the locality after the War. Hamlet of Dayton – Round Hill – Cooks Run – Bridgewater Pike

Death of Major John R. Meigs, as described by Ben Franklin Shaver, who fired the fatal Shot
Scene looking South – time dusk –

J. E. Taylor

Seemingly there was no fight in the dead mans companion, who having halted at the little run (Cooks) beyond pistol range, who upon seeing the brave man fall, turned tail, and gaining the Pike speeds to Harrisonburg after his companion.

A hasty inspection of the dead soldiers papers revealed him to be Major Meigs, Sheridans Chief Engineer, and realizing that in a very brief time a merciless pursuit, and a short shrift if we were caught, would follow, we hastened away – leaving the body undisturbed where it lay, and made good our escape" –

Shaver thus supplements his statement: "These are the facts, and by the same I am willing to stand committed before my Maker and Man, and when the true history of the Campaign, compiled from the Official Records, is given to the public, it will be shown that it was not, as has been reported, the deadly murderous work of bushwhackers, but the outcome of a fair open stand up fight that was not our seeking".

"Death of Major John R. Meigs, as described by Ben Franklin Shaver, who fired the fatal shot. Scene looking south—time dusk." Sketch by J. E. Taylor. Courtesy of the Western Reserve Historical Society.

blustery Philip Sheridan ordered his trusted and zealous subordinate, Brig. Gen. George Custer, to execute a draconian retaliation against the civilians and property in the region near the killing. Eventually the order was rescinded, but not before approximately thirty buildings were destroyed and hundreds of refugees, many of them antislavery and unionist Dunkards and Mennonites living in the region in and around Dayton, Virginia, were displaced. The area of the valley where the destruction occurred became known as the "Burnt District."[2]

The high impact of fear among Union soldiers over Confederate "guerrillas," a term often assigned by these soldiers to all types of irregular units—authorized and unauthorized—is evident in this sequence of events. By this point in the war, Confederate partisan ranger units under John Singleton Mosby and John H. McNeill had successfully harassed Union invading forces in Virginia enough to create both animosity and dread about surprise death at the hands of Confederate irregulars—death that might spring from behind any bush, tree, or rocky outcropping. The difficulty of identifying the precise circumstances of the Meigs killing demonstrates the acute impact on one family but also the loss of a nation, who mourned the sudden death of a rising star among the Union army's officer corps. Ultimately, his father's decision to bury his son in the former rose garden of the Custis-Lee family at Arlington plantation in northern Virginia was a punitive act of retaliation as well as one of mourning on the personal level and on the national stage.[3]

Labeling John Rodgers's death "an act of murder," his father, Montgomery, called him "a martyr in the cause of liberty." A few days after his death on October 7, his mother wrote in John Rodgers Meigs's diary that he "Was brought home this day the sacred remains of my noble precious son." The following day his parents held a funeral at Oak Hill Cemetery in Georgetown attended by President Abraham Lincoln, Secretary of War Edwin Stanton, Secretary of State William H. Seward, and Gen. Henry Wager Halleck. The Meigses lost their firstborn son and the Union "a noble boy, gallant, generous, gifted." The depth of the family's despair was palpable.[4]

Editors reported the story and events of the young Lieutenant Meigs's death widely in the northern and southern states. His prominence as first in the West Point graduating class of 1863 and son of one of the Union army's highest-ranking officers captured the public's attention. "His examination at the Academy was brilliant beyond all competition. We never knew a more promising young man. He came here to enter upon his military life—stopped a few days in the city, and after having acquired all that it was possible for him to learn by inquiry touching the country, reported for duty," described the *Wheeling Daily Intelligencer* in an obituary published on October 8, 1864. "His whole soul was in the war. He loved his country and her service, and had the highest appreciation of all that was becoming a soldier. The army and the country have sustained a great loss in his death, not so much for what he has done, but for what he might have done. Honor to his memory." The editor of the newspaper, who knew Meigs prior to his death, had published several articles by the precocious engineer on West Virginia campaign activities.[5]

Early reports of John Rodgers Meigs's death outraged the Union officer corps. Meigs was shot under the right eye and left breast. He died immediately. There was no chance for a last goodbye or a "good death" surrounded by those who cared for him. He was snatched away by death suddenly, abruptly. That was terrifying and difficult to reconcile for his friends. The chief of staff of the Army of the Shenandoah, James W. Forsyth, reported on October 4, 1864, that Meigs "was killed by guerrillas about 8 p.m. yesterday, between Bridgewater and Harrisonburg. His body has just been found, and will be forwarded today to Martinsburg."[6]

Sheridan's Army of the Shenandoah faced considerable resistance from self-constituted guerrilla bands during the course of the 1864 Valley Campaign. Governor John Letcher of Virginia encouraged a general use of guerrilla warfare by the citizens of the valley when regular Confederate army resistance waned. Sanctioned partisan rangers under John "Hanse" McNeill and John Singleton Mosby active in Virginia were frequently interpreted as "bushwhackers" and unlawful "guerrillas" by the Union army because of the partisans' use of concealment, ambush, and hit-and-run tactics against their more numerous foe. In theory, the method of guerrilla warfare could be adopted by anyone among the Confederate populace, making discernment in the field difficult. While "partisan rangers" as a lawful category were sanctioned officially under Francis Lieber's code in 1863 and issued as General Orders No. 100 to Union armies, the code was not always deployed with legal exactitude by Union officers facing units like Mosby's. Though Mosby was a sanctioned

The body of John Rodgers Meigs discovered by Union soldiers. Sketch by J. E. Taylor. Courtesy of the Western Reserve Historical Society.

partisan ranger—a protected legal category—he was frequently referred to as commander of "Mosby guerrillas" in Union army valley correspondence, and since they believed he was the only organized opposition in the valley in early October 1864, it created conditions for Meigs's death to be interpreted as a murder by bushwhackers.[7]

Union secretary of war Edwin Stanton had given wide latitude to Union army commanders in the valley to deal with "the guerrilla problem." In a letter on October 6, Stanton communicated to Brig. Gen. William H. Seward Jr., commanding at Martinsburg, Virginia, that he "suggest[ed] that after providing suitable guards any surplus force that you may have should be used in routing out and destroying any gangs of guerrillas or robbers that may infest your vicinity." Stanton believed that "It may be possible that after you have become sufficiently acquainted with the personnel of your command, you can organize a small but efficient corps that may accomplish much in destroying the robbers and murderers that make it a business to plunder our trains and transportation and kill our soldiers in ambush." Perhaps most startling was Stanton's final admonishment: "If you can do so, you are at liberty to employ any means that may be within your power to accomplish that object, and when persons guilty of such transactions come within your power, you may deal with them as their crimes merit, without making any report upon the subject."[8]

Secretary of War Stanton was clearly aware of the problem of "guerrilla parties" disrupting supply and communication lines around Sheridan's force. Yet Meigs's death struck very close within the family circles of the Union high command, and he recognized this in his correspondence. Stanton wrote his own account, seemingly to come to grips with the event himself. "In the death of this gallant young officer the Department has occasion to deplore no ordinary loss. Last year he graduated at the Military Academy at West Point with the highest honors, at the head of his class; was commissioned as a lieutenant of engineers, and immediately sent to the field," Stanton lamented. "He performed meritorious and distinguished services during the campaigns of the last year on the fortifications at Baltimore, at Harper's Ferry, and at Cumberland. . . . In every position he gave proof of great professional skill, personal courage, and devoted patriotism. One of the youngest and brightest of the military profession, he has fallen an early victim to murderous rebel warfare." Stanton's use of the word "murder" and his belief that the talented Meigs had been gunned down by bushwhackers in cold blood drove his anger. Clearly, Meigs was "no ordinary loss" to the Union military's senior leadership.[9]

Philip Sheridan's October 7 report of the incident to Lt. Gen. Ulysses S. Grant detailed his punitive operations. "I have destroyed over 2000 barns filled with wheat and hay and farming implements, over seven mills, filled with flour and wheat, have driven in from the army over four herd of stock, and killed not less than 30,000 sheep," Sheridan recounted. "Lieutenant John R. Meigs, of the New York engineers, was murdered beyond Harrisonburg near Dayton. For this atrocious offence all the houses within an area of five miles were burned. Since I came in the valley from Harper's Ferry, every train, every small party and every straggler has been bushwhacked by the people, many of whom have protection papers from commanders who have been hitherto in that valley." Sheridan ended on a triumphal note: "[Confederate partisan John H.] McNeil was mortally wounded, and fell into our hands. This was fortunate, as he was the most daring and dangerous of all the bushwhackers in this section of the country."[10]

Sheridan's *Memoirs* offer another version of events based upon the relatively vague account of one of the Union orderlies who quickly escaped the incident. "Meigs was murdered within my lines. He had gone out with two topographical assistants to plot the country, and late in the evening, while riding along the public road on his return to camp, he overtook three men dressed in our uniform," Sheridan remembered. This was not accurate. It is likely that Union soldiers could not see the uniforms of the Confederates because they were under raincoats. "Meigs was killed without resistance of any kind whatever, and without even the chance to give himself up," the general related. Sheridan believed, at least initially, that Meigs did not have a chance to discharge his revolver in the exchange of gunfire. He appeared to have been killed instantly. "The fact that the murder has been committed inside our lines was evidence that the perpetrators of the crime, having their homes in the vicinity, had been clandestinely visiting them, and been secretly harbored by some of the neighboring residents. Determining to teach a lesson to these abettors of the foul deed—a lesson they would never forget—I ordered all the houses within an area of five miles to be burned." Many were burned, but after Sheridan learned of his error, that it had been a fair if confusing exchange of gunfire, he rescinded the order. George Custer was given the command of the destruction. According to Sheridan, "when a few houses in the immediate neighborhood of the scene of the murder had been burned, Custer was directed to cease his desolating work, but to fetch away all the able-bodied males as prisoners." In short, Sheridan's account in his *Memoirs* makes sense as a defense and rationalization for his subsequent orders to Custer, but is less specific than other accounts of the death.[11]

Confederate accounts of the incident provide another dimension to understanding the confusion of John Rodgers Meigs's death. There was also some confusion in the Confederate accounts of the incident, though these accounts are more detailed on the specific events. F. M. Campbell and George W. Martin were scouts from Company H, "Black Horse Troop" of the 4th Virginia Cavalry, Wickham's Brigade, Fitzhugh Lee's Division, ANV, and Benjamin Franklin Shaver, a member of Company I, 1st Virginia Cavalry, was a scout who lived in the local area. In the fall of 1865, Martin claimed responsibility for shooting

Meigs in a detailed affidavit about the confusing incident. The sun had nearly "gone down, and the evening cloudy and rainy. We were wearing oil-cloths over our uniforms." "Riding slowly along until the foremost man came up by my side I immediately presented my pistol, which I had drawn under my oil-cloth; each of my companions did the same, dropping back to the side of the man they selected. I ordered my man to surrender; his response, which was an immediate one, was the discharge of his pistol, which he must have had drawn and under his overcoat cape, wounding me severely through the body," Martin recalled. "I fired almost simultaneously, killing my adversary dead. One of the other men surrendered without resistance, the other sprang from his horse and, under cover of the woods on the right of the road, escaped. I succeeded in avoiding capture with a great deal of difficulty, owing to my wounded condition and proximity to the enemy." The Confederates captured one prisoner, who shared that he had shot Lt. Meigs, of Gen. Sheridan's staff. Martin's own wound from the affair was so severe that he did not return to "service for three or four months." From the collateral accounts of the incident, it appears as though both Martin and Shaver believed they fired the fatal shot(s). The exact responsibility is difficult to discern given the postwar accounts of the incident. While Martin's affidavit about the affair is the closest to the actual death and is highly detailed, Shaver claimed after the war that he had actually fired the fatal shot(s), and his explanation convinced his family, some Union veterans, and many ex-Confederates after the war. Given the location of John R. Meigs's wounds, this would mean that Shaver fired two pistol shots in rapid succession that both hit Meigs's body. Shaver's claim rested on the specific detail that he had taken the wounded Martin's pistol and belt back to camp after Meigs's death and inspected the weapon. The pistol and belt had been placed on the back of Meigs's captured whiteface horse. Shaver claimed Martin's pistol must have misfired when they both aimed at Meigs, since all of the loads remained in Martin's pistol but that the percussion caps had all burst. If Shaver's account is accurate, then it was he, not Martin, who fired the fatal volley(s). The third Confederate, F. M. Campbell, had fired at the orderlies with Meigs. Benjamin Franklin Shaver believed that Martin did not know the information about his pistol until 1877. Regardless, the Confederate eyewitness accounts again demonstrate the confusion at the base of the incident.[12]

After the war, Montgomery Meigs received an account of the night from one of the Union orderlies. He determined that the man had seen little and fled almost upon the first shots. The level of detail in the Confederate accounts from both George W. Martin and Benjamin Franklin Shaver, however, leave little doubt about their specific motives on the evening of Meigs's death. Confederates had attempted to capture Meigs's party, and Meigs was killed in the attempt. Sheridan's account was clearly a stilted defense of his own somewhat rash reaction after receiving a false report that bushwhackers had attacked Meigs's party. It was understandable that the escaped Union soldier believed the men might have been bushwhackers, but they clearly were not—only cavalry scouts from a regular regiment on patrol. Sheridan's actions fit within his overall strategic goal of crippling the valley's economic and agricultural support for the Confederacy and punishing irregulars and their supporters. It is almost impossible to know if Montgomery Meigs ever made a final determination in his own mind about the exact events leading to his son's death, but after receiving this Union account, he appears to have been satisfied with his search for truth.[13]

The entire incident of mistaken guerrilla identity demonstrates a central conundrum for both the North and South as they waged an increasingly deadly civil war in which political divisions and the use of ambush, deception, and hit-and-run tactics became common across every seceding state. Identifying the regular enlisted man versus the self-directed bushwhacker was not always possible in the often chaotic, happenstance conditions of the field. And emotion frequently drove the punitive responses of both Union and Confederate commanders as a result.

Meigs was clearly not killed by bushwhackers, but the fear of Mosby's partisan rangers and self-constituted bushwhackers in the Shenandoah Valley and northern Virginia created conditions where some Union soldiers saw a guerrilla around every tree and bush. Mosby used this to his own advantage time and again, but on balance, the guerrilla conflicts during the Civil War frequently led to less restraint by military officers on both sides, pushing the war's violence to new levels and greater inhumanity toward innocents. After the funeral, Montgomery Meigs worked with an intelligence agent to discern who had killed his son. At first, Meigs suspected McNeill's rangers, Elijah White's partisans, and then Mosby's men. Nevertheless, after careful investigation, he eliminated all of these sanctioned ranger commands as possibilities, based primarily on these Confederate units' proximity to Dayton at the time of his son's death. In the end, Montgomery Meigs's leads circled somewhat frustratingly back to the regular Confederate scouts who actually killed his son. A clearer picture of the night would eventually emerge when Confederate accounts of the incident became available.[14]

In the interim, the Meigs family began a memorialization process that used their son's remains as a weapon against the Confederacy, even after the surrender of its regular armies in 1865. An article in the *National Republican* from 1868 described the monument that the Meigs family placed over John's initial burial site in the Georgetown neighborhood of Washington, DC: "Upon an oblong variegated marble block in the portion of the cemetery near Rock Creek, is a bronze figure, recumbent and in uniform, of Lieutenant John R. Meigs (son of Major General Meigs), who was killed by guerrillas while in service as chief engineer of the army of the Shenandoah."[15] More than a decade later, his father, as quartermaster general, who was principally responsible for the effort to turn Arlington plantation into a cemetery for Union war dead, had the body of his son moved and reinterred in what is now section one of Arlington National Cemetery on November 23, 1880. This followed the interment of his wife, Louisa, in the same section in 1879.[16]

The cenotaph of John Rodgers Meigs sculpted by T. Fisk Mills in 1865 is a startling reminder of the human cost of the American Civil War. Sitting upon a green marble base, the cenotaph depicts Meigs's body as it was found in the road by Union troops following his ill-fated reconnaissance mission. In the cenotaph, Meigs is accoutered in full Union army uniform and tied around his neck is a new cape, one of his father's final gifts to him that came during a visit to West Point, a moment described in one of John's journals.[17] His sword and sword belt still firmly affixed, the Union officer's ubiquitous eagle belt plate shining in the light. His binocular case is slung across his body. Meigs's pistol, a Colt Army Model 1863, lay in the mud beside his body, dropped at his death; his boots look freshly polished, his hair boyish and tousled. Perhaps most striking is the size of the monument. The cenotaph is not a full-scale model. Meigs, a grown man of twenty-two years at the time of his death, is re-created in the size of a small boy, which is no doubt how his parents saw him. Etched into the bronze are the imprints of horse hooves representing the act of Confederates on

Graves of John Rodgers Meigs, Montgomery Meigs, and Louisa Meigs, Arlington National Cemetery, Arlington, Virginia. Meigs's parents are buried next to him. Photograph by Melissa Winn.

Grave of John Rodgers Meigs, Arlington National Cemetery, Arlington, Virginia. Photograph by Melissa Winn.

horseback driving the body into the muddy Shenandoah Valley road where he died. Around the base of the bronze is the text: "Lt. John Rodgers Meigs, U.S. Eng'rs., Chief Engineer Army of the Shenandoah. Born 9th February, 1842. Killed 3d October, 1864."[18] Next to the John Rodgers Meigs burial site is the much larger grave marker of his parents, Montgomery Cunningham Meigs and Louisa Rodgers Meigs.[19]

In the John Rodgers Meigs grave marker, one can see the expression of sorrow of two parents who lost their promising firstborn son in a war that Montgomery Meigs blamed, at least in large part, on Robert E. Lee, a former commander of Montgomery Meigs in the antebellum U.S. Army. Meigs, a Georgian by birth, believed the Lee family were criminals and traitors to the United States, and Lee one of the most important commanders of rebellion. The exhumation and placement of Meigs was also a continuation of his father's earlier political statement of having the unknown dead of First Bull Run reburied in a large pit in the rose garden that was next to Arlington during Mary Custis Lee and R. E. Lee's time on the property. It is, along with many, many other Union Civil War grave markers placed within yards of Arlington House, a political statement, a powerful form of vengeance and retaliation toward Lee and his family, a permanent reminder of their guilt and punishment for their part in America's most costly war. The act of turning Arlington into a cemetery stripped the Lee family of its tangible family homeplace and part of its long history and attachment to the nation. It symbolically forced them to atone for their leadership role in the rebellion that led to hundreds of thousands of deaths by forcing them to own those deaths by turning up the soil at Arlington with the loyal Union dead. Clearly, men like Sheridan, John Rodgers Meigs's superior, as well as a long list of Union officers including Daniel Sickles, David Dixon Porter, William S. Rosecrans, Abner Doubleday, George Crook, John Gibbon, and Nelson A. Miles, had their own graves placed there as a final act of guarding the Union. The large number of soldiers' graves on the property ensured that Arlington would never fully be restored to the Lee family as a working plantation, even after a U.S. Supreme Court decision returned the property to the Lee family in 1882. After extensive negotiations, Lee's son Custis subsequently sold the property back to the U.S. government for $150,000 in 1883.[20]

In the end, the John Rodgers Meigs story, the story behind his grave marker, is one of punitive warfare on several levels, punishment of R. E. Lee for his role in leading a secessionist rebellion, but also punishment of the Confederates who killed Meigs by a father powerfully positioned to make Confederate leaders feel his pain as personally as he possibly could: retaliation for guerrilla violence and sudden, unexpected death in the field at the hands of regular soldiers, mistakenly identified as bushwhackers. In microcosm, Meigs's death offers a mixture of personal and national atonement and retribution for how violent the war became as Confederates sought independence through the use of irregular warfare, and Union soldiers sought restoration of the Union through a war of retributive destruction.[21]

2

Generals and Their Steeds

The Grave of Robert E. Lee, Lexington, Virginia

ALLEN C. GUELZO

Robert Edward Lee was sixty-three years old when he died on October 12, 1870, in Lexington, Virginia, although he looked much older.[1] Photographs taken of him that summer by Michael Miley of Lexington capture a stooped posture, deep, exhausted facial lines, and an utter absence of light in his eyes. And no wonder. Lee had begun suffering the first evidences of heart disease as early as June 1860, when he complained of "rheumatism." "I am sure," he told his wife, Mary Custis Lee, "I am not getting young." And as if he needed a reinforcement of that, his "rheumatism" struck again in August. The attack "was a slight one," he assured his family.[2] But his health was not improved by the stress of command during the Civil War. Lee suffered what was clearly a major heart attack in March 1863. He called it a "heavy cold," mostly to allay his wife's anxieties. But in fact he experienced "a good deal of pain in my chest, back, & arms . . . in Paroxysms . . . quite sharp," and required several weeks of bed-rest. In the medical vocabulary of the 1860s, he had developed a "rheumatic inflammation of the sac enclosing the heart."[3] He recovered sufficiently to direct an invasion of Pennsylvania that summer. But he probably suffered at least one more episode of heart trouble in September 1863.

For Lee, the war ended on April 9, 1865, when he surrendered the Army of Northern Virginia to Ulysses S. Grant. There was no prospect of returning to his prewar home at Arlington, since the Arlington property had been sold for taxes to the United States government, turned into a "freedmen's village," and was in the process of being converted into a national cemetery for the Union war dead. He lived briefly in rented quarters in Richmond, but after he was indicted for treason by a federal jury in Norfolk, he was anxious to put as much distance as possible between himself and any possible legal pursuit, and in August he accepted the invitation of the trustees of Washington College in far-off Lexington to become the college's president. He arrived in Lexington in September and on October 2 was officially sworn into the office of president. He was no longer wearing his uniform, only "a military coat divested of all marks of rank; even the military buttons had been removed."[4]

Lee was an unlikely choice as a college president. He had served for three years as superintendent of his alma mater, the U.S. Military Academy at West Point, but that position had involved little more than executing the orders of the U.S. Army's chief engineer in Washington. He frankly told the Washington College trustees that "I do not feel able to undergo the labour of conducting classes in regular courses of instruction," and they would have to take him or leave him on that basis. But the glamor of his name sufficed for them. Surprisingly, Lee provided much more than glamor. He undertook a major overhaul of the college's classical curriculum, insisting that it must now embrace the kind of practical and vocational subjects that would help the South to rebuild. "The fundamental principle of the Collegiate System should be to give to the Commercial, Agricultural & mechanical Classes the advantages of an education but adapted to their wants." By 1867, he had grown the college's minuscule endowment to $234,207. In another year, the student body had swelled to 411, almost the equal of the University of Virginia. Lee, declared the *Richmond Times*, had become the college's "second founder."

> The radical changes which have taken place in this college have given it prodigious popularity. The course of studies has been enlarged, the corps of professors increased, and General Lee now presides over the destinies of a well endowed and most prosperous college.[5]

But all this came at a cost to Lee's precarious health. As early as the summer of 1867, Lee was so oppressed by fatigue that, having "done all the good I can for the college," he proposed to "retire to some quiet spot, east of the mountains" where (as he told his youngest son, Robert) he "might prepare a home for your mother and sisters after my death." His visit to the White Sulphur Springs spa that summer produced little improvement, and he notified the college faculty that he was "so feeble that the Dr is reluctant for me to make the journey" back to Lexington for the opening of the new academic year. It is entirely possible that he had suffered a third heart attack, especially since he admitted that "it seems to me if all the sickness I ever had in all my life was put together, it would not equal the attack I experienced." By October, he was finally back in Lexington. But there he suffered what was probably another heart attack. "The affection in my chest under which I labour, adhesion of the lungs & pleura or whatever it is, incapacitates me from exertion & as yet I cannot walk farther than from my house to the College without pain, & I have to proceed carefully at that."[6]

Lee's physical decline was becoming noticeable to the faculty, the trustees, and even to the students of the college. "I don't think I ever saw a man break down more rapidly than he has in the last year," one student wrote. In March, a faculty committee took matters into its own hands and proposed that he "take at once a journey and a couple of months' relaxation," and allow "a professor to attend to his duties during his absence."[7] The vacation, which sent him south that spring to warm weather as far as Florida, appeared at first to restore him. At the opening faculty meeting in September, he looked so much better that one professor was elated "at the increased prospect that long years of usefulness and honor would yet be added to his glorious life." But the photographs taken by Michael Miley during the summer were not so reassuring. Lee suffered a stroke on September 28, and though he showed signs of improvement by October 4, his weakened heart could not support a recovery, and he died on the morning of October 12.[8]

Both the former Confederate capital in Richmond and Lee's own hometown of Alexandria claimed the body for burial. The state legislature and the Richmond city council wanted Lee buried "in the State section" of Richmond's Hollywood Cemetery, which was already filled with Virginia's Civil War dead; in Alexandria, it was hoped "that his remains would be brought here for interment." But neither Lexington nor Mary Custis Lee had any intention of allowing Lee's burial to occur anywhere far afield, and Lee's oldest son, George Washington Custis Lee, firmly informed the legislature that "the remains have been committed to the authorities of Washington College."

Lee's body was dressed in a "simple suit of black," and since furious rains through the weeks before had made shipment of a coffin from Richmond impossible, a slightly undersized one had to be retrieved for use. The coffined body was carried to the college chapel (which Lee had designed and where he kept his office) by an "escort of honor, consisting of officers and soldiers of the late Confederate army," followed by Traveller (Lee's "old gray war horse . . . with saddle and bridle covered with crepe"), and by the trustees, faculty, and students of both Washington College and the nearby Virginia Military Institute. There, the body was watched over by "a students' guard of honor," with the coffin "open, allowing mourners to gaze upon the face of their friend, general, and president one last time." On October 14 an Episcopal service was conducted by William Nelson Pendleton, the rector of Lee's parish church in Lexington, who preached from verses of Psalm 37: "The steps of a good man are ordered by the Lord: and he delighteth in his way. Though he fall, he shall not be utterly cast down: for the Lord upholdeth him with his hand."[9]

Lee was buried the next day "in a brick vault" in the basement of the chapel, after a public procession that wound from the chapel through the streets of Lexington, "down Washington street and up Jefferson street to Franklin Hall, thence to Main street" and VMI, and finally back to the chapel. "Every class, young and old, rich and poor, white and black, turned out to do him honor, for he was the friend of all." Throughout the town, "the buildings were all appropriately draped, and crowds gathered on corners and in the balconies to see the procession pass." In a quiet nod to the political realities of Reconstruction, no Confederate flags were in view, and "the old soldiers" in the procession "wore their ordinary citizens' dress, with a simple black ribbon in the lapel of their coats." At the chapel, Pendleton read the Episcopal burial service, but "No sermon was preached, it having been the desire of General Lee that there should be none." As a hymn was sung, the coffin, "literally strewed with flowers, which had to be removed separately," was interred in the center of the chapel's basement, under a slab that bore only the inscription: "Gen. Robert Edward Lee, Born Jan 11, 1807 Died Oct 12, 1870."[10] A week later, the Richmond newspapers delicately acknowledged that the inscription was wrong: Lee's birthday was January 19.[11]

Lee's horse, Traveller, survived him by less than a year. He developed tetanus and was euthanized in June 1871, and was at

Scenes from the funeral of Robert E. Lee, *Frank Leslie's Illustrated Newspaper*, November 5, 1870. Courtesy of Special Collections and Archives, James G. Leyburn Library, Washington and Lee University.

first buried behind the main college buildings. His bones were exhumed for exhibition in the college's museum and then in the chapel. But by 1971, they had deteriorated so badly that what remained was placed in a wooden box and buried just outside the entrance door of the chapel.[12]

The trustees were aware of how much the college stood to lose by Lee's death, and in order to keep Lee's association with the college as prominent as possible, they met on the day of Lee's funeral to rename the college as "Washington and Lee University," and began deliberating on a "suitable monument" to act as a visible marker for Lee's remains. Even before Lee was buried, a Lee Memorial Association had been called into being in Lexington to supervise the monument, and within days, Mary Lee had given her approval to a plan to rebuild the apse of the college chapel (which would also be rebaptized the "Lee Chapel") as a mausoleum for her husband's coffin, with a new crypt on the basement level and an honorific space for the monument on the level above, opening out into the chapel itself. (All of the members of Lee's immediate family, including his father, the Revolutionary War general "Light-Horse Harry" Lee, would eventually be buried there, too).

FRANK LESLIE'S ILLUSTRATED NEWSPAPER

Entered according to the Act of Congress, in the year 1870, by Frank Leslie, in the office of the Librarian of Congress, at Washington.

No. 788—Vol. XXXI.] NEW YORK, NOVEMBER 5, 1870. [Price 10 Cents. $4 00 Yearly. 13 Weeks, $1 00.

PREPARATIONS FOR A PERMANENT "WORLD'S FAIR."

Interest and duty combine in stimulating cities to render their respective localities pleasant to visitors as well as to the inhabitants. Attractions for both classes usually "pay well"—directly or indirectly—and the "paying" qualities are, of course, among the essential considerations in this utilitarian age, among a matter-of-fact people.

One of the most prominent public improvements in New York is now in process of accomplishment by a chartered company, which aims at organizing an institution that will attract attention from multitudinous strangers, while forming a constant resort for the inhabitants of this commercial metropolis. The enterprise, when completed, will furnish one of the greatest attractions possessed by any city in the world.

The company is chartered with a seven-million capital, and with ample powers for constructing and managing the concern. The edifice will be built chiefly of iron and glass—to serve as a permanent "Industrial Exposition"—resembling the structure erected in 1851 for the "World's Fair" in London, and which was afterward removed piece by piece, and reconstructed at Sydenham, convenient for the resident London millions and the additional millions usually visiting that mighty city.

LEXINGTON, VA.—SCENE IN THE INTERIOR OF THE CHAPEL OF WASHINGTON-LEE COLLEGE—LADIES DECORATING THE CASKET OF GENERAL ROBERT E. LEE WITH IMMORTELLES.—From a Sketch by our Special Artist.—See Page 119

"Ladies Decorating the Casket of General Robert E. Lee with Immortelles," *Frank Leslie's Illustrated Newspaper*, November 5, 1870. Courtesy of Special Collections and Archives, James G. Leyburn Library, Washington and Lee University.

Traveller's Grave. Courtesy of Special Collections and Archives, James G. Leyburn Library, Washington and Lee University.

The upper level of the new apse would feature a recumbent sculpture of Lee, "lying asleep on his field cot during the campaigns of the war," in the fashion of a royal medieval tomb. The model for this medieval Lee would be based on a bust of Lee made by a Richmond sculptor, Edward Virginius Valentine, back in the spring of 1870. Valentine met with the association in November 1870 to discuss preliminary ideas, but it took another four and a half years before Valentine completed the commission, in marble. It took eight years more for sufficient funds to be raised by the association to have J. Crawford Nielson make the alterations needed in the chapel, and not until 1883 could Lee be reburied in the new crypt and Valentine's memorial be appropriately installed on the level above, flanked by portraits (of Lee, Washington, Jefferson, and other southern worthies) rescued from Arlington. Despite Lee's refusal, in the postwar years, to encourage displays of southern military nostalgia, Valentine's recumbent Lee appears in full Confederate uniform, resting his left hand on a half-hidden sword, and in 1930 twelve Confederate battle flags (reminiscent of the flags displayed at Napoleon's tomb in Les Invalides) were ranged around Valentine's sculpture.[13]

The dedication ceremonies, in June 1883, praised Lee as the knight-errant of the Lost Cause. In the principal oration, Confederate veteran and historian John Warwick Daniel declared that, even though an unforgiving northern government had made Reconstruction into an intolerable burden, Lee had benignly and "thoroughly understood and accepted the situation." Resigned to defeat, Lee had "realized fully that the war

Lee Chapel with the Army of Northern Virginia flags loaned by the Museum of the Confederacy. Courtesy of Special Collections and Archives, James G. Leyburn Library, Washington and Lee University.

had settled . . . the peculiar issues which had embroiled it." Nevertheless, the general was nobly determined to share the South's "humiliation," and even though he was "indicted for treason . . . never word of bitterness escaped from him; but, on the contrary, only counsels of forbearance, patience and diligent attention to works of restoration." Lee became the South's Christ figure, bearing the South's cross (for whose "issues" he had done nothing himself to acquire guilt) and urging nothing afterward but forgiveness for the madmen who had inflicted his, and the South's, pain.[14]

Not everyone, however, was inclined to lay tributes at Lee's grave. Frederick Douglass complained, after wading through endless newspaper obituaries for Lee, that "we can scarcely take up a newspaper . . . that is not filled with *nauseating* flatteries of the late Robert E. Lee" and his "bad cause." Douglass was not surprised that many of these tributes came "from the

South," but he was amazed that "many Northern journals also join in these undeserved tributes to his name." With a touch of sarcasm, Douglass allowed that "if Lee has gone to heaven, we are sincerely glad of it," but Lee did so in spite of "the liberation of four millions of slaves and their elevation to manhood." "I think it safe to say," declared Vermont's U.S. senator George F. Edmunds, that no one "has committed the crime of treason against more light, against better opportunities of knowing he was committing it" than Lee. In Atlanta, James Fitzpatrick—"a degenerate son of the 'Emerald Isle'"—stood up in the middle of a mass meeting honoring Lee and read a "protest" against memorializing "a man who, more than all the others, attempted to destroy the best government under the sun."[15]

Although the Lee Memorial Association hoped that the Lee Chapel would remake Lexington into a "Mecca, visited by caravans of Summer wanderers, who come to do honor" to Lee, the authority of Lexington's Lee was quickly usurped by a far more dramatic equestrian Lee statue, designed by Antonin Mercié (professor of sculpture at the École des Beaux-Arts and the creator of massive statues of Lafayette and Francis Scott Key) and erected in 1890 in Richmond by the rival Lee Monument Association. For more than a century thereafter, controversy over Lee monuments (and other Confederate statuary) foamed around the Richmond statue, leaving Valentine's Lee and the Lee Chapel mostly untouched. But on August 12, 2017, fanatical factions of Ku Klux Klan and neo-Nazi thugs clashed in the streets of Charlottesville, in a "unite the Right" rally, with black-clad partisans of the "Antifa" left. One woman was killed, and the entire nation was stunned into silence. Much of the violence in Charlottesville swirled around a twenty-six-foot-high equestrian statue of Lee in one of the city's parks, and almost as if Lee had become a symbol of a reenergized white-supremacy movement, Lee statues in Dallas, Baltimore, New Orleans, and at the University of Texas and Duke University were removed or defaced. And Lee, at Washington and Lee, would enjoy no exemption.[16]

After all, Lee had fought for the Confederacy—fought, in other words, for a cause dedicated to the perpetuation of African American slavery—and fought with sufficient skill to prolong the contest to four years and an estimated 750,000 deaths on both sides. He had, moreover, been a slaveowner, and the manager of slaves, both for the United States government (before the war) and for the Confederacy (during the war), not to mention serving occasionally as a manager of the slaves of his father-in-law. Yet the record of Lee the slavemaster is not a straightforward one: in the prewar years, he condemned slavery as "a moral & political evil in any country," even though he never lifted a finger to protest it publicly; he only actually owned one enslaved family in his lifetime (inherited from his mother) and voluntarily emancipated them in 1862; in that same year, he supervised the emancipation of his father-in-law's slaves, in accordance with the old man's will; and he advocated the recruitment and emancipation of slaves for service in the Confederate army.[17]

Although he made no gesture as president of Washington College to integrate the school, he also reproved white students who planned to terrorize freed Blacks in Lexington. Yet, in a fit of rage, he presided over the flogging of three slaves in 1859 who attempted to flee Arlington, and may even have taken the whip in hand himself.[18] His attitude toward African Americans in the postwar years was politely disdainful, and he preferred the imposition of some kind of racial segregation as a safeguard against Black retaliation for the injuries of slavery. "You will never prosper with the blacks," he warned his youngest son in 1868. "I wish them no evil in the world—on the contrary, will do them every good in my power." But it remained "abhorrent to a reflecting mind to be supporting and cherishing those" whom Lee would always suspect of "plotting and working for your injury, and all of whose sympathies and associations are antagonistic to yours."[19]

Once Washington and Lee began to be integrated in the 1960s, the abundant Lee imagery on the campus increasingly grated on African American sensibilities. In August 2014 students successfully pressed the university to remove the displays of Confederate battle flags from the chapel. Three years later, the echoes of the Charlottesville riot had hardly died away before Washington and Lee's president, William C. Dudley, announced that, because of the university's "complex history," it would be necessary to review how Confederate symbols were displayed there. A yearlong self-study made it clear that "Lee, our former president and one of our namesakes, has become a particularly polarizing figure," and although the recommendations of a twelve-member commission pulled shy of erasing Lee's name from the institution entirely, they did propose moving official functions away from the chapel and converting it

Lee Chapel after the removal of the Confederate flags. Courtesy of Special Collections and Archives, James G. Leyburn Library, Washington and Lee University.

into a museum, changing all references to Lee from "General" to "President," and replacing portraits of Lee in uniform with portraits in civilian dress, or else replacing Lee portraits entirely with others "who represent the university's complete history." But only two years later, in the wake of the George Floyd killing and the nationwide protests over it, a renewed surge of calls from the faculty demanded the removal of both Lee's and George Washington's names from the university, and a special faculty meeting in July 2020 voted by a resounding 79 percent in favor of the Lee removal motion (although not for a similar motion to remove Washington's name).[20]

Despite the faculty vote and faculty op-eds in support of dropping Lee's name, the trustees of the university felt otherwise, and on June 4, 2021, they announced that they had voted by an equally resounding twenty-two to six to keep Washington and Lee as the university's name. "We have listened carefully and are grateful for the thoughtful manner in which you have shared your views and experiences with us," the university announced, but the trustees had "found no consensus about whether changing the name of our university is consistent with our shared values." Still, the faculty repudiation of Lee had clearly had its effect: the trustees also announced that Lee's name would be stripped from the chapel (it would henceforth be known simply as the University Chapel) and the interior redesigned to separate the apse with the Valentine sculpture from the rest of the building; the university's "Founders Day" would no longer be celebrated on Lee's birthday; and a portrait of Lee that usually appeared on student diplomas would now be excised.[21]

No one appeared entirely pleased with the decision. An anti-removal coalition known as "The General's Redoubt" was satisfied that the "reaffirmation of the name of the college was the correct and responsible decision" but disagreed with "the proposed changes to campus symbols, buildings, and practices," including "the newly-designed diploma."[22] Black alumni of the university expressed a sense of weary impatience. "I'm not surprised. I didn't think they were going to change," said Robert Ford, a 1970 graduate, and one law professor, Carliss Chapman, complained that the trustees "seemed to be very concerned of being accused of being a part of cancel culture, of erasing history." Another law professor, Brandon Hasbrouck, frankly declared that the decision "signaled that Washington and Lee University will continue to shine as a beacon of racism, hate, and privilege."[23]

In the face of such unresolved polarization, it is unclear what the future of the Lee name will be at the university. What this, in turn, will mean for Valentine's Lee is even more unpredictable. Although antiracist protests have involved numerous incidents of statue-toppling and statue defacement, protest gestures have not, at least to this point, involved the removal of tomb statuary or grave desecration. Yet it will be difficult to see how the Valentine memorial can remain as a nagging reminder of the Lee presence at the university, even partitioned off from the rest of the structure, or even whether the Lee family in the crypt may be the object of removal. Even in their graves, the figures of the Civil War continue to stir us uneasily.

Ulysses S. Grant

A Monumental Undertaking

KATHERINE REYNOLDS CHADDOCK

During a muggy summer afternoon in 2007, I took off early from archival research I was undertaking at Columbia University's Butler Library. I walked toward the Hudson River to enjoy a growing breeze and found myself at the General Grant National Memorial on Riverside Drive. Suddenly, I was staring at a display about the life and work of Richard Greener. I recognized the name, at that time known to me only as the first Black professor at the University of South Carolina, where I was a professor. I thought, *Who knew?* Certainly, in South Carolina, only archivists and historians were familiar with his name; and many of those knew little of Greener's history beyond his accomplishment as the first Black graduate of Harvard College. He was a figure of Reconstruction, an era that the South pushed under the rug for many years.

I learned what I could from helpful National Park Service professionals at the memorial, and I was happy to now have a few new factoids about Reconstruction on our campus—then called the "Radical University"—to share with students in my history of higher education classes. But my research was then concentrated on figures of the early twentieth century, so it would be some time before I thought more about Greener's work with the Grant Monument Association. Still, I had a copy of a detailed booklet developed for a 1980 exhibit sponsored by the National Park Service and the National Park Foundation, "Richard T. Greener: His Life and Work."[1] Slowly, I was able to add to that information.

Richard Greener (3A, olvwork361109). Courtesy of Harvard University Archives.

President Ulysses S. Grant (1822–1885) led a roller-coaster life marked by great military triumphs, personal financial disasters, presidential successes and scandals, a strong marriage, and satisfying friendships. It was perhaps fitting, then, that the man who led the effort to honor his legacy with New York City's monumental "Grant's Tomb" also lived a life of extremes. Richard Theodore Greener, a light-skinned Black born to free parents in 1844, was by age eleven a kid on the Boston streets with a widowed mother. Yet he was smart enough to attract a benefactor who helped him become the first Black graduate of Harvard College. From there, he gained and lost a succession of jobs, depending on the effects of changing U.S. policy and local largesse regarding opportunities for Black citizens.

By the time of Grant's death in July 1885, Richard Greener had been a teacher at a Black high school in Philadelphia; a professor at the University of South Carolina during Reconstruction; a law school graduate from the same university; a clerk at the Treasury Department in Washington, DC; a Howard University Law School instructor and dean; a husband and a father; and a naïve investor in several failed businesses. His professional endeavors typically lasted only from one to three years. In between, he had time for speaking, writing, and lobbying for racial justice. He even managed to meet President Grant on several occasions while serving on delegations pushing for congressional efforts to grant civil rights.[2]

New York City mayor William R. Grace knew of Richard Greener. More importantly, he knew that when President Grant died, his final resting place must be in New York City. In fact, since he realized that other locales might argue for Grant's burial site, he contacted Grant's son, Frederick, a full week before his father's death to invite him to Manhattan to confer about specific locations. On the day of Grant's death, he sent a representative to offer the family burial options in one of the city parks. He was elated when Frederick telegraphed: "Mother takes Riverside; temporary tomb had better be at the same place."[3] Grace then wasted no time calling a meeting of nearly a hundred wealthy and influential New Yorkers—including names like Vanderbilt, Morgan, Cornell, Steinway, and Pulitzer—to launch the Grant Monument Association (GMA). Richard Greener immediately headed from Washington, DC, to New York City when Grace asked him to join the group as its only Black representative. At the first meeting of the GMA, Greener was elected secretary of the association, its only full-time paid executive, and later was elected a trustee.[4]

By the time of Grant's funeral, held on August 8, 1885, the GMA, with former president Chester A. Arthur as its chairman, was fully committed to plans for building "a national monument in the city of New York worthy of the illustrious dead soldier and patriot and worthy of the city itself."[5] Forty-one-year-old Richard Greener, charged with the organization and administration that would make such a lofty goal a reality, immediately moved from Washington, DC, to New York, leaving behind his wife, Genevieve, and four children ages four to eight years old. He quickly became immersed in setting up the GMA office at 146 Broadway, managing correspondence, drafting fundraising materials, and interacting with committee members and other interested citizens. Grant's funeral gave him welcomed time off. In the largest U.S. ceremonial parade to date, sixty thousand marchers, mostly participants in military campaigns, processed by an estimated one million spectators to accompany the coffin to Riverside Drive and 122nd Street, where it would rest in a brick vault to await the monument construction.[6]

"Day of Entombment of General Grant at Riverside Park." Courtesy of the Bultema-Williams Photograph and Print Collection and the Ulysses S. Grant Presidential Library, Mississippi State University.

"First Floral Decoration of the Tomb of General Grant." Courtesy of the Bultema-Williams Photograph and Print Collection and the Ulysses S. Grant Presidential Library, Mississippi State University.

"The Resting Place of General Grant." Courtesy of the Bultema-Williams Photograph and Print Collection and the Ulysses S. Grant Presidential Library, Mississippi State University.

The most immediate and time-consuming task at hand for Greener was fundraising. The GMA set a goal of $1 million for design, site planning, construction, and related expenses, with $100,000 milepost goals at various dates. To Greener's relief, the first of those was met just three months after Grant's funeral. However, after initial enthusiasm from New Yorkers with deep pockets, fundraising became much more difficult. Unexpectedly, the great nationwide affection for the revered general and former president became an impediment, inspiring many other locations to mount their own costly efforts for sculptures and other public works to honor their hero. The city of Chicago began planning a statue near Lake Michigan; Leland Stanford made a generous contribution to a Grant monument effort in San Francisco; a committee formed in Fort Leavenworth, Kansas, to initiate a local Grant memorial; and the city of Brooklyn began fundraising for a "Soldiers' and Sailors' Monument" to include figures of both Lincoln and Grant. Additionally, nationwide concerns that found citizens contributing elsewhere included a devastating earthquake in Charleston, South Carolina, and the great flood of Johnstown, Pennsylvania.

Greener continued to draft and distribute press releases, leaflets, church bulletins, progress reports, and even appeals to U.S. consular officers who might be able to attract contributions from Americans living abroad. He also fielded correspondence and visits from individuals whose desires to help included ideas ranging from impressive to impossible. Writers and editors came up with ideas for mail-in contests with entry fees to be turned over to GMA. A puzzle maker wanted investment money to produce a puzzle with Grant's profile, with some profits later going to the Grant Monument effort. Eventually, some funds beyond individual contributions came from activities such as the sale of souvenir items from Grant's funeral, installation of collection boxes at the state capitol in Albany, and benefit concerts at Madison Square Amphitheater and the Metropolitan Opera House. However, Greener's lobbying efforts urging state legislators to appropriate nearly half the estimated cost of the monument proved futile.[7]

Greener's wife and children moved to New York City two years after his arrival and seemed to enjoy their new location immediately. Although Greener continued a bit of essay writing on issues of racial justice, his active participation declined. All his associates at GMA were white, and not even 2 percent of the city's

Black residents were classified as "professionals."[8] Some family friends and commentators in the Black press began to criticize Greener's relative silence on race issues and questioned whether he and his family might be fostering assumptions that they were white. Encouraged by a longtime white friend, Greener joined the Commonwealth Club, founded by a group of influential white New Yorkers. He ceased his usual public support of political candidates liberal on race issues. His separation from direct support for racial justice, perhaps combined with his light skin and his "white man's" education, would soon leave him seeming both too Black for the whites and too white for the Blacks.

Monument siting and design proved as daunting as fundraising, with a steady stream of local architects and landscapers writing the GMA or visiting its office to argue for various specific ideas. Although some funding goals had been missed, by 1888 the GMA trustees decided to push ahead to get a design in hand that might give impetus to next steps and a renewed spirit of contribution. With Greener getting the word out and fielding questions, an open competition netted sixty-five design submissions—including many equestrian statues and even a mausoleum of red, white, and blue glass columns. A panel of judges presented their top five designs to the GMA executive committee, but none were deemed suitable. In an effort to regroup, a second competition was limited to only five well-known East Coast architects and included more explicit guidelines about cost and deadlines. At Greener's urging, in late 1890, New York architect John H. Duncan won the final round with a neoclassical design calling for granite from Maine, marble from Massachusetts, and glass from Tiffany.[9]

While Greener and GMA members were optimistic that the architectural design would reinvigorate fundraising, they first had to stave off an effort in the U.S. Congress to pass a resolution that would have Grant exhumed and moved to Washington, DC. Greener and Grace reminded Congress that the Riverside spot was approved by Grant and his family. Finally, New York representative John Raines carried the day when he noted, "You cannot break into a graveyard with a joint resolution of Congress. . . . It is a ghastly, and I had almost said a ghostly, impertinence."[10]

With plans in hand, Greener began in 1891 busily organizing a spring groundbreaking ceremony for the monument. An estimated ten thousand onlookers attended the occasion and were treated to salutes from navy ships on the Hudson River as well as military formations, song, prayer, and oratory. Within a week, another $50,000 had been raised. Work on the foundation started shortly after, giving hope that the effort was truly underway. However, the donations soon slowed to a trickle, and more complications were waiting on the horizon.

The GMA membership always represented a fragile balance of various factions, with ongoing issues about who sided with whom. The representatives of the Grand Army of the Republic, particularly eager for more authority, managed to elect two of their faction to the executive committee and tip the balance toward the more politically conservative. Impatient with the ongoing political maneuvering and its results, Mayor Grace resigned from the GMA in late 1891. Others followed, including GMA vice president Hamilton Fish, Columbia University president (and future New York City mayor) Seth Low, and New York governor Roswell Flower. The newly influential members elected as their president Brig. Gen. Horace Porter, a heroic Civil War figure and vice president of the Pullman Company. Determined to cut costs and work only with volunteers, they announced the termination of Greener's salary by February 1892. As Greener moved on to begin a legal practice and undertake some student tutoring, he could take some solace in a *New York Age* article that praised him as "one of the most eloquent Afro-Americans . . . and one of the best critical scholars the race has produced."[11]

Porter quickly expanded the GMA trustee group to include more wealthy and influential citizens such as Andrew Carnegie, Augustus Juilliard, Elihu Root, and Charles Tiffany. More importantly, he designed a new fundraising approach that proved immediately successful in assuring that building could begin later in 1892. Porter and other GMA members met with hundreds of mercantile, trade, and professional entities throughout the city and developed a committee system that established their responsibility for reaching specific groups for contributions. Listed among groups for outreach at meetings and conferences were millinery workers, perfumers, telegraph operators, electricians, gold pen manufacturers, opticians, stevedores, lawyers, pharmacists, diamond importers, insurance agents, and produce sellers. GMA members met regularly with representatives from each group to receive contributions and hand out printed materials and lists of new members. A cornerstone laying ceremony, on Grant's seventieth birthday in April 1892,

"Dedication of Gen. Grant's Tomb, Riverside, New York." Courtesy of the Library of Congress.

netted more new funds. Contributions soon nearly doubled the funds previously available for the Grant Monument.[12] Not at all unlike the vicissitudes of the life they honored, the endeavors of the various individuals pursuing a Grant Monument had included a roller-coaster of soaring successes punctuated by serious doubts and downturns. In the end, honor prevailed.

Richard Greener remained on the GMA board of trustees throughout his lifetime, although he was not mentioned among the many individuals thanked by General Porter at the dedication of the completed monument in 1897.[13] After several years of limited employment, lecturing, writing, and ongoing job seeking in New York City, Greener went to the Midwest as assistant manager of the Colored Bureau for the William McKinley presidential campaign. His family stayed in New York. In 1898 the new president appointed him as a consular officer to Vladivostok, Russia, where he served until 1906 as the first Black U.S. diplomat to a majority-white country. His family, still in New York City, took new names and passed as white citizens. The children went on to become educated at places like Barnard College, Columbia University, and the University of Tennessee. Upon his return from Russia, Greener retired and lived with distant cousins in Chicago while continuing some writing and speaking for the Black cause. He attended and spoke at the Harpers Ferry meeting of the Niagara Movement. Yet, when he died in 1922, his death certificate from the Chicago coroner's office identified him as "white." He was interred in Chicago's Graceland Cemetery, joining such luminaries as Marshall Field, Cyrus McCormick, and Joseph Medill.[14]

In the fall of 2010, during a trip to Cambridge, Massachusetts, I found myself near the Harvard Book Store staring at a large, descriptive plaque dedicated to "Richard T. Greener, Educator, Lawyer, Diplomat." My surprise, and likely the expression on my face, was exactly what I had felt three years earlier at the Grant Monument: *Who knew?* Although I was now familiar with Greener, the plaque, placed by the Cambridge Historical Commission, contained four hundred words of detail about his boyhood, his father's disappearance, his education at Oberlin and Phillips Andover, his various professional endeavors, and more.

When I returned to South Carolina and shared this discovery with a class of graduate students, they immediately wondered why there was nothing on our campus in remembrance of its first Black professor whose work, from 1873 to 1877, included not only teaching but also serving as acting university librarian and leading efforts to recruit and prepare Black youngsters for college. What to do about it? Start a committee, of course. With two faculty colleagues, I co-chaired an ad hoc group (informally referred to as the Greener committee) without any official university sanction but with a revolving door of members—faculty, students, alumni, and administrators. During the next seven years, our work seemed eerily reminiscent of what I knew of the challenges that had faced the GMA. I frequently found myself remarking to colleagues, "This is exactly what Greener went through trying to get a monument to Grant!" Like the GMA, we had suggestions galore about what to do and where to put whatever we did. Someone suggested that a grassy area near the library be renamed "Greener Pastures." Someone else suggested a sound and light show across a central fountain. A particularly popular idea was to change the name of the main library from Thomas Cooper Library to Richard Greener Library. This would have the advantage of removing the name of an unpopular early nineteenth-century college president and vocal secessionist.

The committee finally launched an "Ideas Competition" that netted initial proposals from students, faculty, and others. It became apparent that the favored ideas related to statuary, possibly combined with fountains, arches, or horses. To move on to a design competition, we needed a site as well as specifics about timing, cost, and materials. Involvement in the issue grew, now to include committees of the Board of Trustees, the office of the university architect, several deans, and the development office. Predictably, not everyone agreed on everything; but the national design competition somehow occurred, with expert sculptor Jon Hair selected for his design of an immensely impressive statue. With design in hand, the committee was able to move through several layers of official approval and on to fundraising. Just as the GMA had stalled in the fundraising effort, the Greener committee proved to be less than expert at the task. There was competition for donors who might open their wallets. The university was, as was almost always the case, amid a capital campaign. The university's law school, where we could emphasize Greener's alumni status, was seeking donations for a new building. A small statue of "Cocky," the university's gamecock mascot, was to be placed on a central bench where fans could snuggle up for a photo. But Cocky needed donors too.

Fortunately, just as the Grant Monument was reinvigorated by new funds from new directions, so too was the Greener statue. The university president, Harris Pastides, and many trustees saw great goodness in the effort. Amid controversies about removing statues of Civil War–era figures representing unsavory historical realities, why not raise a statue to celebrate a quite different side of the struggle? What funds the Greener committee was unable to raise (which was most of them), a university foundation managed to contribute. During a community-wide ceremony in early 2018, the Greener statue, twice life-size and with a descriptive plaque on the base, was unveiled in a central location between the main campus library and the student union building. Among those doing the unveiling were three of the students from the 2010 class that started the conversation about why we had no Richard Greener remembrance on campus.

Burial monuments, plaques, and statues are public history. If my experience with them is any indicator, public history is

Statue of Richard Greener on the campus of the University of South Carolina. Photograph by Kim Truett. Courtesy of the University of South Carolina.

every bit as much of an educational tool as written history in books and articles. It stirs curiosity and reminds us of important events, issues, and people that have shaped our current lives. The Grant Monument, impressive in its size, art, and sight, reminds its constant stream of visitors not only of the man it honors but also of the history of an important era. And, hopefully, as it did for me, it will inspire future visitors to delve deeper and learn more.

Gabriel and Nannie Wharton

WILLIAM C. DAVIS

It is something of a cliché, the image of a famous man's grave lying forgotten and neglected in some remote field. For Brig. Gen. Gabriel Colvin Wharton, the situation is rather the reverse—a once-noted man now largely forgotten, lying in an until-recently neglected grave in the middle of a thriving city. Every day thousands of Virginians pass within a few blocks of it in Radford, and on several Friday evenings and Saturday afternoons in the fall, hundreds of yelling and cheering high school football and track and field fans sit within fifty feet of him, most completely unaware that he is looking down on them.

Born in Culpeper, Virginia, in 1824, Wharton graduated second in his class from the Virginia Military Institute in 1847. He first worked as a civil engineer on Virginia railroads and then accompanied a surveying expedition from Memphis to southern California, ostensibly to locate a wagon road but, in reality, to find a route for a transcontinental railroad across the southern United States. A happy-go-lucky fellow, much beloved by his closest friends like future Confederate generals A. P. Hill, Robert Rodes, and William Mahone, he was a typical southern Whig, diffident toward slavery and averse to disunion until Virginia seceded.[1]

Wharton spent the first three years of the war in backwaters, seeing minor action in western and southwestern Virginia and East Tennessee from 1861 through early 1864. Only when he was sent west to Fort Donelson, Tennessee, early in 1862 did he experience a truly important engagement. That all changed for him

Gen. Gabriel Wharton. Courtesy of Sue Bell.

in the spring of 1864, when federal threats to the Shenandoah Valley sucked him out of the southwestern part of the state to play significant roles as a brigade and division commander at New Market, Cold Harbor, Jubal Early's raid on Washington, Winchester, Fisher's Hill, Cedar Creek, Waynesboro, and more.

But for Wharton, surely the most memorable moment of his war took place off the battlefield with his May 1863 marriage to Anne Rebecca "Nannie" Radford of Central Depot, Virginia. She was the daughter of Dr. John B. Radford, Central Depot's leading citizen. High-spirited, opinionated, and rather spoiled by her father, she was also well educated, intelligent, well read, and anxious to converse on topics from current politics to romantic literature. She was also nineteen years younger than Wharton and, at age eighteen, had already accepted that she might never find a man equal to her expectations to wed.[2]

Theirs was a romance seemingly without parallel among other officers of his class—or at least a romance vastly better illuminated thanks to their correspondence. It began immediately after they became engaged and continued through to the end of the war. While a few of their letters and telegrams have

Nannie Wharton.
Courtesy of Sue Bell.

been lost, 524 survive, a wartime correspondence virtually without parallel among Confederate generals. They wrote almost every day—sometimes two and three times a day—and about everything from politics and literature to economics and the war.

But more than anything else, they wrote about their growing love for each other. They were little more than acquaintances at their betrothal. It was in their letters that they gradually came to know each other. Wharton was obviously smitten from the outset, while she freely admitted that she did not love her "Gabe" at first, but thought him a good match, a man destined to rise, and whose ambition matched her own. More than that, their correspondence is striking because it reveals them to be remarkably twenty-first-century people in many respects. Gabe was all about "feelings." He could not stop himself from pouring out his every thought and emotion to Nannie, over and over. His love for her overpowered virtually every other thought and emotion, even his commitment to the Confederacy.

Nannie, meanwhile, was all business at first, refreshingly frank about her desire for a notoriety and prestige befitting the daughter of the leading family in her community, and her ambition for him to rise in rank. Only gradually did she fall more and more in love with her husband, until she confessed that all ambition had fled her. In time, both of them wrote as if the catastrophe engulfing North and South was an inconvenience deliberately put in the way of their being together. They would even speak of him resigning so they could leave the failing Confederacy and go abroad to some isolated place where they might live with and for each other, both repeatedly echoing one of their favorite poems, Alexander Pope's *Eloisa to Abelard*, in which he wrote of living in "the world forgetting, by the world forgot."[3]

There was a lot of war for Gabe and Nannie to weather before they could hope for that. It had already touched her tragically in 1862 when her brother Lt. William Moseley Radford was killed during the Peninsula Campaign. It touched her again in November 1864 when her brother Lt. Col. John Taylor Radford was killed in the Shenandoah. Gabe was able to bring "Johnnie's" body home to the family, to be the first burial in the family plot where they all rest now. After the war, the family retrieved "Willie's" remains and brought them home to be buried beside his brother.

In their letters, Gabe and Nannie got each other through those and other tragedies, but their long separation for months at a time preyed on their minds and emotions. Both came to judge his commanders almost solely on the basis of whether or not they would grant him leave to go home to her. Emotionally high-strung, Nannie sometimes almost feared she had been abandoned by a husband who repeatedly told her everything would work out for the best, but who never seemed to appear on her doorstep. There is something almost naïvely heartwarming about their romance, and their unrealistically self-centered outlook on the war and the Confederacy. Whenever I see or think of their graves side-by-side on the hilltop, I cannot help but be moved by the fact that this is what they always wanted, just to be together and out of the way of the world's worries.

Another stone nearby is a constant reminder of one of the most difficult times of the war for them. Nannie was tiny. The thought of going through childbirth terrified her, and not unreasonably considering how many women lost their lives during delivery in that era. When she mistakenly thought she was pregnant in the summer of 1863, she became morose and fatalistic, and her relief at finding it not so made her almost giddy. But then in September she did conceive, and during the months leading up to the birth of their son, William Radford Wharton, she became increasingly despondent, made worse by Gabe's constant absence. Her letters communicated her fear and panic, and his constantly tried to soothe and balm her apprehensions. When their "Willie" was born in June 1864, they both immediately doted on him and did so for the rest of their lives. He lies buried near them, surrounded by his own family. All of them there together seem to represent the war and its aftermath. The tragedy of those killed in battle. The hope for the future of those born during the cataclysm. And the love of two people that sustained them through it all.

With the war over, the Whartons set out to rebuild themselves and southwestern Virginia. He farmed for a time, but it did not suit him. He returned to engineering, working for new railroad building projects, and later trying to capitalize and build his own. He looked for ways to get coal out of the mountains to new factories, including industrial facilities that he envisioned for Central Depot. He opened a hotel for railroad traffic, and Nannie even edited and published a weekly newspaper. After her father's death, she inherited much of the land immediately west of Central Depot, which she set about developing into lots for residential and commercial sale. Three years later the town changed its name to Radford.

During those years, Gabe was also a civic leader, especially interested in promoting industry and education. Elected to the Virginia House of Delegates in 1871, he partnered with his VMI roommate William Mahone to accomplish legislation allocating Virginia's proceeds from the 1862 Morrill Land Grant College Act to the Preston and Olin Institute in Blacksburg—later to become Virginia Tech, where Wharton was rector of the board of visitors—and the Virginia Normal and Collegiate Institute, later to become Virginia State University, the nation's first state-supported, four-year university for Black students.

Times were often hard. Gabe was a soft touch for a hard-luck story and often loaned money that was never repaid. Financial

Confederate veterans at the Wharton grave. Courtesy of Sue Bell.

recessions after the war stymied most of his railroad and industrial projects. Debts mounted to the point that he had to take a job with the Department of the Interior as a land inspector and surveyor in the Southwest, while Nannie ran their affairs at home. The separation they had vowed never to endure again after the war kept them apart for months at a time, but still their letters bridged the distances, and as their son, Willie, grew to manhood, they somehow remained a family until 1890 when Nannie, aged only forty-six, joined her parents and brothers on the hill. That was a distance even their letters could not traverse.

Before the lots laid out by Nannie sold to sprout houses and trees, the view from Wharton's grave looked northwestward less than a thousand yards to the New River, the vital artery that powered the region he so loved. Beside it ran the railroad that he helped build to bring the raw resources out of the mountains to waiting factories to the east, and along its tracks sat the local industry that he and Nannie encouraged to revitalize southwestern Virginia after the ravages of war. Due eastward atop a low knoll overlooking the river, he might have seen "Glencoe," the home he built for his Nannie, where both of them died, and which is today Radford's city museum and gallery. Ironically, while his own business and development endeavors almost all came to nothing, others took his visions and made them work.

The small town of Central Depot had grown into the city of Radford. It bore Nannie's family name, but its growth and success were largely testimony to the foresight and effort of her husband.

There is for me a wonderful, coincidental, and personal dimension to Gen. Wharton's grave. My great-great-grandfather served in and died as a private in the 45th Virginia Infantry, Wharton's first regiment. My second book was about the May 15, 1864, battle of New Market, where Wharton was one of two Confederate brigade commanders. More to the point, for thirteen years I was a professor of history at Virginia Tech, a great university with origins in Wharton's efforts to promote education. More personal still, the woman I married on coming there had built a property management business in Blacksburg and Radford. Some of her properties were actually on the old Radford family property, while in Blacksburg one of her buildings sits on Wharton Street. In a not-too-exaggerated sense, General Wharton played a role in the chain of events that brought my wife and me together. It can't get much more personal than that.

After his death, family burials continued occasionally in the Radford family cemetery. Gabe and Nannie's son, William, was buried near them in 1918, and his grandson and granddaughter after them. Nannie's three sisters are there, as are a few other cousins. At some point the property left family hands, but to this day, as is often the case with such small private cemeteries, neither the city nor the high school acknowledges ownership. Only by turning from Walker Street into a private drive can it be reached, where it sits behind a residential home's private swimming pool, on one side, and immediately overlooking the Radford High School track and football field on the other. For years it sat neglected and overgrown until recently, and is now maintained by two of the general's great-great-grandchildren.

Following Nannie's death in 1890, Gabe patiently waited until he could rejoin her, ever confident that one day they would be together again. When he died in 1906, the next to last of Virginia's living Confederate generals, his funeral brought one of the largest crowds yet seen in Radford. For two days people white and Black filed through Glencoe's main hallway to pay their respects. Then with all the public ceremony done, he made his last journey up the hill to Nannie, to rest beside her and realize at last their wartime dream to be together, "the world forgetting, by the world forgot."

"A Wonderful Tenacity of Life"

Old Baldy, George Meade's Veteran Warhorse

JENNIFER M. MURRAY

Visitors to the Grand Army of the Republic Library and Museum in Philadelphia, Pennsylvania, are afforded a unique opportunity to stand face-to-face, or fittingly eyeball-to-eyeball, with a rare relic of the American Civil War. Prominently displayed in a glass case is the head and neck of Old Baldy, the famous warhorse of Gen. George Gordon Meade, the "Victor of Gettysburg," and Philadelphia's cherished son. While other Civil War generals' horses may garner more acclaim—most notably Robert E. Lee's gray steed Traveller—arguably no Civil War mount accumulated a record of service as distinguished as Baldy. Wounded at least five times during the war, and once described by Meade as having a "wonderful tenacity of life," Baldy served the general more than three years before being retired in the spring of 1864. Ultimately, the warhorse outlived Meade by a decade. Baldy's life, but as importantly his death and subsequent commemoration, provides an opportunity to highlight the faithful service of one of the "greatest of all chargers."[1] Efforts to preserve Baldy underscore more than sentimentality; they reflect a desire to honor the horse's wartime service, while also offering an opportunity to memorialize the man whom he served, George Meade.

Little is known about Baldy prior to the time that Meade acquired the steed. Most accounts indicate that Baldy was raised on the "western frontier" and, at the outbreak of the Civil War, was transported east to be used as a cavalry horse.[2] Baldy's Civil War service began in the summer of 1861, and his baptism of fire came on July 21 at the battle of Bull Run. While carrying

Col. David Hunter into battle, Hunter was wounded in the neck and the cheek, while his horse suffered two wounds, one in the nose and the other to his flank.[3] Thereafter, the wounded horse was sent to the Quartermaster Department in Washington, DC, becoming government property. The summer offered a respite and the steed recovered. In September, Meade purchased the horse, who was approximately eight years old, for $150. Writing to his son, John Sergeant, recounting his new purchase, Meade described Baldy as an "excellent horse in his day" but noted that the horse had been wounded at Bull Run.[4]

Old Baldy—or Baldy, as Meade commonly called him—boasted a full white or "bald" nose. Once described as a "handsome brown horse," Baldy had four white feet, a "small, well-shaped head," and "truly formed legs" that carried him gloriously into battle. Aside from his defining physical features, Baldy possessed an awkward gait, something between a trot and a canter. Baldy's peculiar gait became a source of frustration for Meade's staffers, who struggled to keep pace with the general and his horse.[5]

Old Baldy. Courtesy of the Civil War Museum of Philadelphia and the Union League Legacy Foundation.

Countless numbers of horses were requisitioned into service for Union and Confederate armies. The "hard hand of war" fell heavily upon these animals, and generals commonly owned multiple horses. Indeed, in the war's early months Meade searched for quality mounts. Two months after purchasing Baldy, and perhaps initially dissatisfied with the horse, the general wrote, "I am very badly off for horses." Meade claimed no special knowledge of equines, lamented his poor fortune with horses, and anticipated that he would have to continue with his "old hacks."[6] Of Meade's horses, Baldy undoubtedly became the most trusted and carried the general into battle for the next three years.

Meade rode Baldy through the grueling campaigns of 1862 and 1863. In August 1862 Baldy suffered his third battle wound when he was shot in the right hind leg at the battle of Second Bull Run.[7] Again, the horse recovered and later carried Meade into battle at Antietam on September 17, 1862. As Meade led his division into the fray, both the general and his steed were wounded in the fight. Meade's wound was minor; a slight contusion to his right thigh. Baldy, however, sustained a serious injury when he was shot through the neck.[8] With his bridle and saddle taken off of him, presuming the wound mortal, Baldy was left among the carnage on the bloody fields of Antietam. The following day, Meade's groom, John Marley, approached the area where Baldy had been left to die and found the horse standing, quietly grazing upon the field. The spirited horse had yet again survived.[9] Less than a week after the battle that claimed twenty-three thousand casualties, Meade penned encouraging words home. "Old Baldy is doing well," he cheerfully wrote, "and is good for lots of fights yet."[10]

Baldy's fifth and final wound occurred during the battle of Gettysburg. The white-nosed horse now carried the commanding general of the Army of the Potomac. On July 2, 1863, the second day of the battle, Confederate assaults targeted the Union flanks. As waves of Confederate soldiers assailed the Union army, Meade hurriedly positioned reinforcements to secure his line along Cemetery Ridge. While directing Union reinforcements along the southern end of Cemetery Ridge, a shell exploded in front of Meade, showering the general with dirt. Without wavering, the general continued to order units into position, exposing himself to small arms fire.[11] Amidst this chaos, a bullet nicked Meade's pant leg, passing through the saddle and a blanket that had been doubled and folded lengthwise to prevent chafing of the horse's back. Passing between the ribs, the bullet then lodged into Baldy's stomach. Upon being hit, the charger staggered slightly but then steadied himself. The general encouraged Baldy onward, but the warhorse refused. Meade reportedly remarked, "Baldy is done for this time. This is the first time he ever refused to go under fire." As the fight raged around him, Meade promptly received another horse, and Baldy was then escorted to the rear of the Union line. For Baldy, his fight at Gettysburg was over. It would be his last.[12]

Indeed, approximately five thousand horses and mules died during the three-day battle. Once again, Meade expected that Baldy would be among the carnage. Four days after the battle's closing salvos, the general happily reported that Baldy's condition was improving. "I did not think he would live," Meade reported to his wife, yet "the old fellow has such a wonderful tenacity of life that I am in the hopes he will."[13]

Baldy remained with Meade during the winter of 1863–64. The general hoped that he would recover and be serviceable again, but Baldy's Gettysburg wound had not completely healed. Thus, as the federal army prepared to cross the Rapidan River, Meade, fearing that his old steed would be a hindrance during the ensuing Overland Campaign, sent Baldy to Pennsylvania. On April 23, 1864, George Melloy, Meade's orderly, boarded a train with Baldy to Philadelphia. The general wrote his wife the following day, remarking, "I thought he was entitled to better care than could be given to him on the march."[14]

Although Baldy would never be "fit again for hard service," Meade ensured that the veteran warhorse would be well cared for after his service for the Union had ended. When Baldy arrived in Pennsylvania, he spent the duration of the Civil War on a farm owned by Capt. Samuel Ringwalt in Downingtown, located about thirty miles west of Philadelphia. Meade paid Ringwalt for Baldy's care.[15] The general eagerly awaited news from home on the condition of his steed. "I am glad to hear the good news about Baldy," Meade wrote three months after Baldy's departure from camp, "as I am very much attached to the old brute."[16] Indeed, for a man famed for his temper and irascibility, the general clearly had developed a bond of affection with his warhorse.

Many accounts, both from the pens of Civil War veterans and later generations of historians, inaccurately note that Baldy continued with Meade through the duration of the war. Indeed, some authors ascribe as many as fourteen wounds to the warhorse. In doing so, such claims deviate from the historical record, namely Meade's own words, but also blend fact with fiction, further weaving the legend of Baldy. More than likely, these observers have confused Baldy with one of Meade's other horses, perhaps his brown Morgan.[17]

Fortunately, by the end of the war, Baldy's health had improved, and although his body bore the scars of battle, he once again became Meade's trusted steed. The general stabled his old warhorse, under the care of John J. Davis, a blacksmith who lived close to Meade's summer home in Jenkintown.[18] Baldy garnered the attention of the neighbors and the blacksmith's children. One day, when Baldy arrived to be shod, Davis's daughters created a floral wreath and draped it around the neck of the brown warhorse. Meade often rode Baldy through Fairmount Park.[19] Inevitably, old age and war wounds made Baldy unsafe to ride. Meade bequeathed Baldy to Davis, stipulating that the caretaker would not sell the horse and, when the time came that old age gripped the steed, Davis would end his suffering.[20]

In Baldy's final years, the warhorse participated in two grand parades. First, on November 6, 1872, after four decades of service to his nation, George Gordon Meade died at the age of fifty-six. Five days later, pallbearers carried Meade's casket from St. Mark's Church, placed it on a caisson drawn by six horses, and began the procession to Laurel Hill Cemetery. Baldy marched with the procession, riderless, following the casket to Meade's final resting place.[21] The warhorse's final public appearance occurred on December 16, 1879, when Philadelphia hosted former President Ulysses S. Grant. Baldy, now approximately twenty-six years old, marched behind veterans of the Army of the Potomac. Decorated "with all the trappings of war," and reported to have attracted much acclaim, this parade would be the last for the aging veteran.[22]

Nearing thirty years of age, the old charger would increasingly be seen lying in his stable at Davis's farm, struggling to stand. Owing to his promise to Meade, Davis determined that the end had come for the old warhorse. On December 16, 1882, he summoned the neighborhood veterinarian, Dr. Benjamin Davis, and together the two men led Old Baldy across the pasture to an apple tree, where they had dug the horse's grave earlier that day. Baldy, ever faithful, stood bracing the cold December weather while Dr. Davis poured two ounces of cyanide, followed by a dose of vinegar to activate the fatal concoction, into the horse's mouth. Baldy convulsed, shuddered, and within moments fell to the ground. Old Baldy, bearing multiple battle scars and wounds, had fulfilled his duty to the nation.[23]

Baldy had outlived his master by a decade. Four days later, Meade's daughter wrote Davis expressing her gratitude for his efforts in caring for her father's horse. Baldy's interment, however, proved temporary. News of the death of General Meade's warhorse spread quickly throughout Philadelphia. Indeed, two days later, when the commander of the George G. Meade Post No. 1 announced Baldy's death, some members urged that a portion of the remains be secured to honor the warhorse, and by extension a means to honor the "Victor of Gettysburg." And so unfolded one of the most unique commemorative tributes of the American Civil War.[24]

On Christmas Eve, two members of the post, Albert C. Johnston and H. W. Hervey, traveled to Davis's farm in Jenkintown. They explained the desire to acquire a part of Baldy for commemorative purposes. Davis agreed. He offered to exhume Baldy's body and invited the two men back to his farm the following day. Thus, on Christmas Day, Johnston and Hervey returned "equipped with a knife, hatchet, and overalls" to secure their relic. Fortunately, the cold winter weather had helped preserve the carcass, which had only been buried nine days. When Johnston and Hervey arrived, Davis had already unearthed the dead horse. Davis then proceeded to decapitate Baldy, walked his head to a nearby pump to wash it off, and then helped the two veterans wrap it in a bag before loading it in their carriage. With Baldy's head in the back, they returned to the city.[25]

Johnston and Hervey transported Baldy's head to a local taxidermist. Nearly two months later, the work was complete. The horse's head was mounted on an ebony shield, with his record of service emblazoned in gold letters framing the mounted head. On February 26, 1883, the two veterans presented Baldy to their fellow GAR members. Pleased with their commemorative efforts, a week later, members passed a resolution that Baldy's head would be prominently displayed on the east wall of the meeting room, as a "tribute to the dead war horse" and as a tangible symbol of their esteem for Old Baldy as well as their "veneration" for General Meade.[26]

In the months to follow, Baldy's wartime heroism and the circumstances of his death received coverage in newspapers across the nation. Far removed from Philadelphia, the *Washington*

Standard, the local newspaper for Olympia, Washington, offered a fitting tribute to the veteran charger. "No roll of musketry pealed forth over his newly made grave, no clang of arms or roll of cannon announced that the brave old war horse had been laid to rest beneath the gnarled apple tree," eulogized the February 9, 1883, article announcing Baldy's death. Back in Pennsylvania, children in Jenkintown regularly decorated the horse's grave on Memorial Day, spelling out "Old Baldy" with daisies.[27]

Death engenders fond reminiscences, some undoubtedly exaggerated. Baldy's death proved no different. One recollection described an aging Baldy found one morning alert and standing in his stable. It was the Fourth of July. When Baldy emerged from his stable and looked around, the old charger identified a billowing American flag. As reported, when Baldy saw the flag that "he had followed so long, floating over him, he sprang like a colt from his halter and for some minutes pranced up and down the lane, only to lie down with exhaustion at the end of his gallop."[28] Perhaps cloaked in hyperbole, it offers a warming image of an aging horse that had so nobly served General Meade and the Union army.

The latter part of the twentieth century witnessed controversy over the ownership of Baldy, culminating in a legal dispute, and further underscored the symbolic importance of the warhorse and the man whom he served. As the last of the war's veterans died and the Meade Post No. 1 closed, the Grand Army of the Republic Museum opened and inherited its building. By the late 1970s, Meade's horse exhibited visible signs of deterioration, as did the facility that housed him. Desiring a restoration for Old Baldy and the ability to showcase him in a modern facility that attracted more visitors to see the warhorse, the GAR board members loaned Old Baldy to the city's Civil War Museum. This museum, located on Pine Street, prominently situated in Center City, managed an extensive collection of Civil War relics from a veterans' organization of Union officers, the Military Order of the Loyal Legion of the United States (MOLLUS). Under the care of the Civil War Museum, Old Baldy received a much-needed restoration and took his rightful prominent place in their exhibits. In the early 2000s, however, the Civil War Museum experienced financial troubles and considered loaning some of its artifacts, including Old Baldy, to the Tredegar National Civil War Museum in Richmond, Virginia. Because the original agreement held that the artifacts, including Old Baldy, would not

Old Baldy at the GAR Museum in Philadelphia. Photograph by Jonathan W. White.

leave Philadelphia, a legal battle ensued over ownership of these Civil War relics. In 2008 the Civil War Museum, after becoming a casualty of funding, closed its doors. Its artifacts, including Old Baldy, were moved into storage.[29]

And so began a legal dispute over the ownership of Meade's trusted steed. With the Civil War Museum closed, discussions ensued over new locations for the museum's artifacts. Among the potential repositories included Gettysburg National Military Park. Meanwhile, GAR board members resolved to regain possession of Old Baldy. After years of legal wrangling, the Orphan's Court ruled that Old Baldy would remain in Philadelphia. The horse's head returned to his original home, the Grand Army of the Republic Museum and Library, in March 2010. The museum houses a treasure trove of Civil War relics and a substantial library and archives. Prominently displayed in the main room is a glass enclosure with Old Baldy's mounted head.[30] In addition to this tangible "last bivouac," a local Civil War roundtable honors Baldy in naming their organization the Old Baldy Civil War Roundtable.

To be sure, animals have been accessories to war for millennia. Countless numbers of horses, mules, dogs, pigeons, oxen, and elephants have performed essential work for soldiers and armies across continents and across conflicts. While there is no precise count for the number of horses used and killed during the Civil War, historians estimate that approximately 1.5 million horses and mules died in the four-year struggle. Recently, Civil War historians have drawn attention to animals' contributions to the war effort. Whether used as mascots or companions, or requisitioned for artillery or cavalry use, or used in logistics to draw wagons and ambulances, horses were fundamental to the conflict.[31]

While tens of thousands of equines earned no special recognition, a few garnered distinction for the men whom they served. Indeed, the names of General Lee's Traveller, or Grant's Cincinnati, or Stonewall Jackson's Little Sorrell, have become iconic names within the Civil War lexicon. Upon the death of a general's warhorse, which often occurred after the general's own death, both Union and Confederate veterans sought to honor the horse. In doing so, their efforts commemorated not only the animal but, by extension, the man associated with the horse. Drew Gilpin Faust described this commemorative process, concluding, "As vestigial remnants of the great men they had carried, they were less horses in their own right than extensions of their masters."[32]

To that end, Baldy's death, and subsequent decapitation as a tribute, was not particularly unique. After Traveller's death in 1871, a year after Lee's death, Traveller was buried on the campus of Washington College. Like Baldy, this also proved temporary. A few years later, Traveller's body was disinterred, and eventually his skeletal remains were displayed in the college's chapel. In 1971 Traveller's remains were buried outside of the Lee Chapel. Confederate general Thomas "Stonewall" Jackson's Little Sorrell experienced a commemorative trajectory similar to Baldy. Upon Sorrell's death, he was taken to a taxidermist and then put on display at the Soldiers Home in Richmond. In 1950 Little Sorrell was transferred to the Virginia Military Institute in Lexington, Virginia, where Jackson had taught before the war. His hide mounted, Little Sorrell is on display for interested visitors.[33]

Indeed, for the veterans of the George G. Meade Post, the most "fitting and proper" tribute to Baldy, and in turn General Meade, was to secure and preserve a portion of the body of the warhorse. Baldy had indeed accumulated a distinguished war record and earned all the accolades and tributes upon his death. Wounded twice at Bull Run, shot in the hind leg at Second Bull

Run, left for dead on the fields of Antietam after being shot in the neck, and suffering his final wound in the stomach at Gettysburg, Baldy served Meade, and, indeed, the Union war effort, admirably. Through the desire of a group of Union veterans to honor the old charger, Old Baldy's "final resting place" is more than a nondescript grave in Jenkintown, lost to time and urban sprawl. Instead, generations of Civil War scholars and enthusiasts can travel to Philadelphia's GAR Museum and stand at eye level with a Civil War veteran. We are presented the opportunity to admire Baldy's defining white nose, one that bears the scars of battle, and reflect on Baldy valiantly carrying George Meade into battle, enduring some of the bloodiest days of the American Civil War.

Joshua Lawrence Chamberlain

"Hero of Little Round Top"

RONALD C. WHITE

The grave of Joshua Lawrence Chamberlain at the Pine Grove Cemetery in Brunswick, Maine, has become a place of pilgrimage in recent decades. I joined visitors in the summer of 2018 at the beginning of research for a new biography of Chamberlain. Entering, I encountered a three-foot-square polished red granite gravestone. The simple engraving read:

Joshua Lawrence Chamberlain
1828–1914

I was surprised. Having viewed gravestones of Civil War veterans at numerous cemeteries, I knew most included rank, and often honors, to identify the veteran. At Pine Grove Cemetery, I expected the Chamberlain gravestone might include:

Bowdoin College Professor
Hero of Little Round Top
Congressional Medal of Honor Recipient
Governor of Maine
President of Bowdoin College

It included none of these. I wondered why not. I knew there had to be a story lurking behind the polished gravestone.

But there is a second gravestone in the Chamberlain family plot. This one, unlike all the others, is flush to the ground. It was probably erected in the 1960s during the centennial remembrances of the Civil War.[1] It includes all the identifications missing from the original 1914 gravestone.

Joshua Lawrence Chamberlain. Courtesy of the Library of Congress.

Joshua L Chamberlain
Medal of Honor
BVT MAJ GEN 20 MAINE INF
CIVIL WAR
SEP 8 1828 FEB 24 1914

I learned that Chamberlain designed the 1914 gravestone. As gravestones are guides to interpreting the past, I wondered what these absences might mean about this Civil War hero. Most visitors to the cemetery know that Chamberlain, on the afternoon of July 2, 1863, was assigned to defend the far left Union line at Gettysburg. At a hill called Little Round Top, when the men of his 20th Maine Infantry ran out of ammunition, Chamberlain led a charge that defeated a larger Confederate force. From that moment forward, whatever his later accomplishments, and they were many, he would be known as the hero of Little Round Top.

The initial visit to Chamberlain's grave became a catalyst in my research and writing about a remarkable and complex American leader. Chamberlain was largely forgotten for sixty years after his death. His star has risen in recent years thanks to Michael Shaara's Pulitzer Prize–winning historical novel, *The Killer Angels* (1974); Ken Burns's documentary, *The Civil War* (1990); and the portrayal of Chamberlain by actor Jeff Daniels

Grave of Joshua Lawrence Chamberlain, Pine Grove Cemetery, Brunswick, Maine. Photograph by Niles Singer.

in the movie *Gettysburg* (1993), written and directed by Ronald Maxwell. This trifecta has produced a huge contemporary following, especially among Civil War enthusiasts.

In deciding to write a biography of Chamberlain, I was struck immediately by the passion of the praise of early biographers and the intensity of recent pushback from writers who believe Chamberlain exaggerated his role in the Civil War. One historian accused him of "a penchant for self-promotion."[2] The story is told that in the 1990s, National Park Service staff at Gettysburg wore T-shirts beneath their official uniforms embroidered with the question: "Joshua Who?" Today, thanks to Chamberlain's fame, Little Round Top is the most visited place at Gettysburg,

One year after Gettysburg, on July 18, 1864, a Minié ball tore through his right hip on the battlefield at Petersburg, scraping his bladder and urethra before coming to rest just under his skin by his left hip. Suffering these grievous wounds, two physicians told him he would die.[3] When Gen. Ulysses S. Grant received a report that Chamberlain was mortally wounded, he issued Special Order No. 39. "Colonel Joshua L. Chamberlain . . . is, for meritorious services on the field of battle, and especially for gallant

Marker to the rear of Chamberlain's gravestone, installed at an unknown time in the mid-twentieth century. Photograph by Niles Singer.

conduct in leading his Brigade against the enemy at Petersburg, Virginia, appointed Brigadier General of Volunteers, in rank as such from the 18th of June, 1864."[4]

Chamberlain, believing he would die, wrote a letter to his wife, Fanny.

> My darling wife, I am lying mortally wounded the doctors think, but my mind & heart are at peace. Jesus Christ is my all-sufficient savior. I go to him. God Bless & keep & comfort you, precious one, you have been a precious wife to me. To know & love you makes life & death beautiful.[5]

Abner O. Shaw and Morris W. Townsend, skilled physicians, found the bullet and removed it. They cut away dead tissue and tied off blood vessels. They inserted a urinary catheter, which allowed them to try to repair the urethra. Catheters used at this time were made of metal, thus not soft and pliable. If left in too long, a catheter could cause a stricture of the urethra.[6]

For the rest of his life, even with undergoing several surgeries, Chamberlain lived in constant pain from his wounds. Concealed beneath his blue uniform, or later his civilian clothing, were the invisible but terrible wounds incurred at Petersburg.[7] Because Chamberlain soldiered on, seldom speaking about his wounds, biographers have devoted little space to them; the visible wounds of amputation are what are usually discussed in stories of the staggering human toll of the casualties incurred in the Civil War. The continuing effects of his wounds produced continual infections.[8] He also experienced the emotional pain of coming to terms with the knowledge that he would never be well for the rest of his life.

My angle of vision for this essay springs from Chamberlain's unadorned gravestone. I have come to believe that throughout his life, he sought to balance a teeter-totter between ambition on one side, where he felt pride in his accomplishments, and self-effacement on the other, where his Christian formation instilled within him as a youth taught him not to toot his own horn.

Modern biographers skip too quickly over the early years of their subject's life. Born in Brewer, Maine, young Chamberlain was raised with the values passed down from New England Puritanism. Puritanism has too often been mischaracterized as a repressive religious movement, but young Lawrence did not experience it that way. Both nurture from his parents, and the influence of Brewer's First Parish congregation, encouraged a life of the mind.

His intellectual curiosity grew when he entered Bowdoin College in 1848. Mastering Greek and Latin as part of the college's entrance requirements, at Bowdoin he learned five more languages: French, German, Hebrew, Spanish, and Italian. He believed languages were the pathways to understanding cultures far beyond his New England home. After graduating in 1852, he enrolled at Bangor Theological Seminary. His father wanted him to be a soldier; his mother wanted him to be a minister or missionary. At Bangor, believing he might become a missionary, he learned two more languages: Arabic and Syriac.

His three years at Bangor Theological Seminary receive mere sentences in Chamberlain biographies. Wanting to understand the growth of his values, I have been mining the papers of the seminary—closed in 2013—at the Maine Historical Society in Portland. In the weeks before his seminary graduation in 1855, he received invitations from three Congregational churches to serve as their minister. At the same time, Bowdoin invited him to offer a master of arts address at their 1855 commencement. In response to his outstanding address, the next day he received an invitation to teach at Bowdoin.[9]

In July 1862, at a moment of northern despair about the course of the Civil War, Chamberlain made a life-changing decision. In that month President Abraham Lincoln issued a call for 300,000 more men for three years' service. Believing this war should not be fought alone by the boys in his classes, on July 14 he wrote Maine governor Israel Washburn offering his services to Maine and the Union. "I have always been interested in military matters." He wrote decisively, "What I do not know in that line, *I know how to learn*."[10]

Chamberlain knew that his age, thirty-three—the average age of enlistment for Union soldiers was twenty-three and a half—meant that he would not be condemned for staying home.[11] He had a wife and two young children. Bowdoin had just elected him to the prestigious faculty position of professor of modern languages. With this position, once held by Henry Wadsworth Longfellow, it granted him a two-year leave to study modern languages in Europe. Aware of all these mitigating factors, Chamberlain told the governor, "But, I fear this war, so costly of blood and treasure, will not cease until the men of the north are willing to leave good positions, and sacrifice the dearest personal interests."[12]

Over the next three years, Chamberlain would fight in twenty-six skirmishes and battles. He would be wounded six times. Twice he was recommended for general, but refusing to pull the military's political levers—one side of his teeter-totter—he was denied this advancement until his deathbed promotion by Grant at Petersburg. At the end of the war, at Appomattox, he was given the honor of commanding the Union troops receiving the surrender of the largest group of Confederates commanded by Gen. John B. Gordon. As the downcast Confederates approached, Chamberlain offered a "marching salute"—a signal of respect for the bravery of his former foes. Chamberlain's gracious gesture surprised both Gordon and his own men.[13] The truth of Chamberlain's initiative has been challenged in recent years—part of the pushback—but I have become convinced of the veracity of the account.[14]

After the Civil War, in 1866 Chamberlain was elected to the first of four one-year terms as Republican governor of Maine. He would serve three more terms. Of the previous thirty-one Maine governors, only two had been elected to more than three terms. In 1871 Chamberlain was elected president of Bowdoin College. Heeding the winds of change blowing through American colleges after the Civil War, he upgraded and enlarged the curriculum. In his inaugural address, he surprised his audience when he declared, "Woman too should have part in this high calling. Because in this sphere of things her 'rights,' her capacities, her offices, her destiny, are equal to those of man."[15] He did not elaborate about how he envisioned women becoming part of the college. He did admit women to a two-year experiment with a summer school but later turned down a female applicant to the medical school. He established a science department that won him praise from students but elicited fears among his more conservative constituents.

Mirroring initiatives in at least twenty colleges, in 1872 he put in place military drill for all students, believing America had been unprepared for the recent war. Initially popular with students, it soon became unpopular, producing a "Drill Rebellion" in 1874. Under pressure from students, faculty, and trustees, Chamberlain was forced to withdraw military drill.[16] After twelve years, he resigned as president in 1883.

A largely unexplored aspect of Chamberlain's biography is his long participation in a second civil war. This second war began shortly after the first when veterans began speaking and writing about their experiences in the war's battles. He became a popular speaker at encampments and reunion gatherings, not only in Maine but in Boston, New York, and Philadelphia. The former professor of rhetoric offered eloquent speeches that were received with standing applause. His speeches were altogether different in kind from those of William T. Sherman, Philip Sheridan, and other Civil War heroes. Greece and Rome took their place alongside Gettysburg and Petersburg. He included examples and metaphors from European cultures.

Some have charged that Chamberlain puffed up his role in the battles he described in his speeches. Comparing them to Sherman and Sheridan, I do not find them self-serving. Balancing his teeter-totter, Chamberlain claimed his important role but was always generous in crediting the contributions of others. The speeches went beyond detailed descriptions of particular battles to lift up the meaning of the Civil War and the preservation of the Union.

By the early twentieth century, Chamberlain became "The Grand Old Man of Maine." In 1905 Fanny, his wife of fifty years, died. Her body was laid to rest at the family plot at Pine Grove Cemetery. He traveled to Gettysburg to participate in the planning for the 1913 fiftieth-anniversary battlefield encampment at Gettysburg but was too ill to attend the event itself.

Chamberlain died in Portland on February 24, 1914. At eighty-five, his death occurred fifty years from 1864 when a minié ball ripped through his body at Petersburg. News that "the hero of Little Round Top" had died spread rapidly. By order of the governor, all American flags flew at half-staff across Maine.[17] He planned a simple funeral service. On February 27, 2,500 hundred people gathered at Portland's City Hall. Chamberlain's sword lay atop his casket. A lover of music, he chose Frédéric Chopin's funeral march and Grieg's *Peer Gynt* suite to be played on the large organ.[18]

When the special train carrying his body arrived in Brunswick, all businesses had closed and all classes at Bowdoin College cancelled. More than a thousand people, including the entire Bowdoin student body, formed a walkway as the casket was carried from the train station to the sanctuary at First Parish. Chamberlain chose the hymns: "Abide with Me" and "Nearer My God to Thee." The president of Bowdoin College, Dr. William DeWitt Hyde, offered a eulogy to Chamberlain as student, professor, soldier, governor, president, and memoirist.[19]

At the conclusion of the service, a procession formed and started east on the Old Bath Road, the same road the nineteen-year-old Lawrence had traveled from the opposite direction to enroll at Bowdoin sixty-six years before in 1848. Chamberlain's grave lay in the family plot beside the grave of Fanny in the Pine Grove Cemetery.

On that day, in death, a life of enormous accomplishments might have been memorialized, yet his simple gravestone spoke of a man comfortable in his life and trusting in an eternal life to come. He could not know that more than one hundred years after his death, the story of his remarkable life would receive growing and widespread interest.

3

Civilians

"I Stood before His Silent Grave"

John Albion Andrew, the Soul of a Champion

STEPHEN D. ENGLE

Soldiers' graves cast a hallowedness over cemeteries like none other. They remind us of our troubled past, and their enduring shadows challenge us to find meaning in the present. Because I grew up in Charles Town, West Virginia, in the Lower Shenandoah Valley, a place known for such graves, I was reminded of the past as a young boy, especially when I walked through the town cemetery Edge Hill, where many Civil War soldiers are buried. Having grown up in the storied Valley of Virginia, it seems as though the entire region is a vast gravesite to fallen soldiers, as headstones are scattered across the landscape. Knowing that my grandparents owned the house behind the alley where John Brown died on the gallows, then known as Rebecca Hunter's farm, and as my grandfather regaled me with stories of old man Brown, I developed a fascination with the Civil War.

My connection to John Brown, the Shenandoah Valley, and the Civil War ironically led me to John Albion Andrew, the Massachusetts Civil War governor, known for raising several of the Union's most famous all-Black regiments. Andrew, however, dedicated his life to peaceful, lawful, and democratic means to unshackling bondsmen, and he lived to see the consummation of his and Brown's life's work. Although it remains unclear if Andrew and Brown were anything more than acquaintances through mutual friends, their paths intersected in a profound way. Following Brown's incarceration, Andrew helped raise funds for his defense, but conviction came sooner than the monies. He may have met

Brown's wife in Boston when she passed through on her way to Virginia to see her husband for the last time. For his efforts, Brown died on a scaffold in an obscure Virginia hamlet and was transported to his farm in North Elba, New York, where he was buried in the family graveyard. There is nothing majestic about his cemetery, and yet his life's work, for better or worse, lives on prominently in America's antislavery narrative.[1]

In contrast, for his efforts in pressing President Abraham Lincoln for emancipation of southern slaves, and in raising African American regiments to fight the Confederacy, Andrew hardly registers in the Civil War's master narrative. Yet, for his obscurity, Andrew's gravesite is adorned with a marble statue of the governor that towers over the Hingham, Massachusetts, cemetery. In an almost metaphorical sense, Thomas R. Gould, the Boston sculptor chosen to carve his marble likeness, understood Andrew's profound significance, found meaning in his contributions to humanity, and cast his statue larger than the man himself to remind visitors of his remarkable accomplishments. Perhaps Gould foresaw that historians would also appreciate Andrew's larger-than-life contributions and chronicle his deeds.[2]

By advancing the abolitionist front, it could be argued that Andrew helped complete the revolution that Brown commenced at Harpers Ferry that fateful night in mid-October 1859. Not long after the raid, Andrew remarked at a meeting held in Boston's Tremont Temple that Brown and his companions were victims or martyrs to an idea. "There is an irresistible conflict between freedom and slavery," Andrew said, "as old and as immortal as the irrepressible conflict between right and wrong." And while he refused to say whether the "enterprise of Brown's actions at Harpers Ferry were wise or foolish, right or wrong," he declared emphatically that "John Brown himself is right."[3]

A far cry from the ominous circumstances and gallows where Brown was executed, John Albion Andrew died quietly of apoplexy at his Boston home on Charles Street on the evening of October 30, 1867. While he lay dying, local African Americans gathered in the street in front of his house. The very next day Mayor Otis Norcross called board members together to plan for a ceremony to mourn the forty-nine-year-old former governor. A memorial service was held in Music Hall on the morning of November 26. It was fitting that a marble bust of Andrew was flanked by a bust of John Brown and John Rogers's statue, *Uncle Ned's School*, representing a freedman receiving instruction

Postcard of John Albion Andrew grave. Courtesy of the Hingham Public Library.

from a young girl. Methodist minister Edward Thompson Taylor, affectionately known as Father Taylor, the iconic Seaman's Friend, gave the benediction. It was a solemn day in Boston, as all businesses were closed and as mourners crowded into the galleries and side pews. African Americans sat humbly in the back of the church, stood outside, lined the streets, and walked in the mile-long procession that escorted the hearse to Mount Vernon. Andrew was laid to rest in Cambridge's Mount Auburn Cemetery, the first rural cemetery in the United States. Frederic Henry Hedge, New England minister, Harvard divinity professor, and transcendentalist, characterized the death of so young a statesman as "a national calamity."[4]

Two years later, on the anniversary of his death, Andrew's remains were disinterred and transferred to the Hingham Cemetery in Hingham, Massachusetts. In December 1871, at the annual reunion of the officers of the 32nd Massachusetts Volunteers, members decided to mark Andrew's gravesite with a statue and formed the John A. Andrew Monument Association. Brig. Gen. Luther Stephenson Jr., a member of the Grand Army of the Republic who had been an officer in Hingham's prewar militia and ultimately commander of the 32nd Massachusetts Volunteer Infantry, headed the monument drive. Stephenson considered it essential that Massachusetts veterans build a memorial to Governor Andrew "to testify their gratitude to the Executive, who in the great struggle for the nation's life, had been their constant friend and supporter, who had sent them forward with words of cheer and inspiration, and received them on their return with welcome and congratulations such as could emanate only from a heart inspired by the truest friendship, and an earnest conviction of the justice and glory of the cause for which they had fought."[5]

By 1873, the Hingham Cemetery Commission contracted Gould to sculpt a statue of Andrew to place at his gravesite. Gould was a well-known Boston sculptor, acquainted with Andrew, but, having lost his fortune in the war, moved to Florence, Italy. Gould took great care to select an Italian Carrara marble that could endure the New England weather.[6] He returned to the U.S. with the statue in October 1875 to see that it was properly transported and situated for the dedication ceremony. Commission members placed the imposing statue beneath the town's Soldier's and Sailor's Monument overlooking Hingham Harbor. Leaden cases containing twenty-five documents were deposited in its cavities. Perhaps in a gesture representative of the promise of a new era, Andrew's face was turned toward the rising sun. Stephenson predicted that "the people of this land shall come here to revive the fires of patriotism, to reflect upon their duties to God and their country, to learn that the noblest impulses of life demand sacrifice." Perhaps most significant, "the soldier of the Union will come, and, beside this marble form, live over again the deeds of the past . . . the dark-skinned child of Ethiopia shall come, and kneeling at the feet of him whose philanthropy and love was limited by no distinction of race or color, class or condition, shall drop a tear of gratitude and affection."[7]

Veterans came by the thousands to pay their respects to the war governor and reflect on his role in preserving the Union. Arthur Beale, adjutant of the Hingham GAR Hall, wrote at the turn of the century that the "town is particularly pleased with the fact that not only did Governor Andrew spend many of his living years here, but in death the town has custody of his body." Now, more than 150 years after the war, as people wander the Hingham Cemetery, known for its beautiful memorials, perhaps they look up at the marble statue, the base of which simply reads "Andrew," and wonder who he was.[8] As I gazed at the statue of the man whose biography I was writing, it appeared just as a correspondent described it in *Appleton's Journal* on the cold October day it was unveiled:

> The statue of the great war governor is of slightly-gray carrara marble, a color in the full light of day superior to white marble, which often appears sheeny and dazzling under such conditions . . . and it is rather larger than life. It represents the governor standing, dressed in a double-breasted frock-coat, and with a long military-cloak hanging from his shoulders, and fastened across his chest by a cord and tassels. Upon the collar is carved the star of the Commonwealth's escutcheon. Governor Andrew, as all will recollect him, was a short stout man with a firm, broad-shouldered figure, well knitted and determined. But his beauty lay in his fine and well-poised head. No subject could be better adapted for the sculptor than his clean-cut Roman nose, with nostrils flexible and energetic, his well-marked handsome mouth, with full lips and rounded chin, dimpled in the middle, and his large eyes, and forehead crowned by closely-curling hair. A face mobile and brilliant, it afforded every advantage to the artist. At first sight the statue looks a little under-sized, though it is really larger than life, but a further impression dispels this feeling, and, while many persons may regret that it has not a more public situation in Boston or

perhaps Washington, it is, on the whole, well placed on its simple pedestal in the old graveyard at Hingham.[9]

American poet and author Julia Ward Howe knew Andrew and appreciated his dedication to the antislavery cause. Julia and her husband, Dr. Samuel Gridley Howe, were the Andrews' closest friends, involved in promoting abolition, women's rights, and prison reform in the 1840s and 1850s. When the Civil War erupted, Andrew appointed Howe superintendent of the State Sanitary Commission to oversee soldier welfare. The Howes were working in Washington when, in the fall of 1861, Andrew arranged for them to accompany him and his wife, Eliza, to meet President Abraham Lincoln at the White House. Afterward, they attended a military review of Maj. Gen. George B. McClellan's army, and while traveling back through the Virginia woods, the marching regiments surrounded and delayed them. The visitors passed the time in the carriage watching the troops and singing marching songs, concluding with "John's Brown's Body." The soldiers seemed to like that and shouted back "Good for you," whereupon Rev. Freeman Clarke, who was accompanying the party, suggested to Julia that she write new verses that explained the purpose of the war. "Mrs. Howe, why do you not write some good words for that stirring tune?" That night she was divinely inspired to compose the *Battle Hymn of the Republic* by candlelight in her room at the Willard Hotel.[10]

Andrew's death also inspired Howe as she lionized him for his character, dedication, and resolve by composing a poem entitled "I Stood before His Silent Grave." In Europe at the time of his death, she wanted to return but, unable to do so, instead sent Rev. Clarke the poem for him to recite at the funeral service. It read:

I stood before his silent grave,
And heard a record long and low,
How he was merciful and brave,
How his swift help sped to and fro. . . .

A champion in our hour of need,
A prophet armed with forethought wise,
He flung our banner on the lead,
He gave our watchword to the skies.

Poorly our blended efforts try
To set his image in his room;
We lift the Poet's laurel high
To lay it on the Patriot's tomb.

And this I said when, laid in earth,
His funeral song was asked of me:
"The world has few to match his worth,
And none to praise it perfectly."[11]

Howe's tribute to Andrew reflected the life's work of a tireless reformer, abolitionist, and war governor who was a "champion in our hour of need."[12]

Over the 143 years since Andrew's statue was unveiled, the harsh New England weather has taken its toll on the impressive features and eroded the stone's exterior. In May 2010, celebrating the 375th anniversary of Hingham's settlement, the Hingham Cemetery Corporation with help from Andrew's descendants raised funds to restore the statue.[13] Although Andrew's statue towers majestically over the town of Hingham, its long shadow stretches to the State House, so much so that when Deval Patrick became Massachusetts's first African American governor in 2006, he connected with Andrew's significance. Following the customary tradition of hanging a former governor's portrait in the executive chambers from which to draw inspiration, he chose Andrew's portrait. His decision to select Andrew provided a fitting tribute to a crusader in national, as well as Massachusetts, political and racial history. "I chose the portrait of Governor John Andrew," wrote Patrick in his State of the Commonwealth Address, "who came to office just before the outbreak of the Civil War and who, among other things, gave freed Black men their first opportunity to serve their country as soldiers. It was not a popular thing for Governor Andrew to do, or for legislators then to support, but it showed political courage. And that act of courage meant something to those men, to this Nation, and to future generations." "At a time of great divide in America," remarked Patrick, Andrew "demonstrated a willingness to change the status quo and encouraged others to do the same." "I am proud to display his portrait . . . and hope that I may govern with the same compassion and foresight that he demonstrated."[14] Perhaps he also drew inspiration from Andrew's often quoted remarks spoken in 1862 in an address at Martha's Vineyard: "*I know not what record of sin awaits me in the other world—but this I know, that I was never mean enough to despise any man because he was ignorant, or because he was poor, or because he was black.*"[15]

As much as Andrew was central to the antislavery story of the mid-nineteenth century and to the enlistment of African

American regiments in the Civil War, it was providential that Patrick drew inspiration from the governor's exploits as much as his contemporaries did. Harriet Beecher Stowe predicted as much in 1872, when she included Andrew in her work entitled *The Lives and Deeds of Our Self-Made Men*, a work dedicated to providing sketches of leaders who helped preserve the Union and define America's national character. Of Andrew, she wrote that in the same way Abraham Lincoln offered "to the world a new type of pure, Christian statesmanship . . . John A. Andrew . . . presents a type of consistently Christian State Governor."[16] Unlike his statue, Andrew was not tall in stature, but as Julia Ward Howe and Harriet Beecher Stowe acknowledged, he towers over our past in a memorable way.

"For His Father's Sake"

The Grave of Joseph Evan Davis

JOHN M. COSKI

In the narrative of the American Civil War, the deaths of several prominent innocent children provide poignant counterpoint to the hundreds of thousands of deaths that occurred on battlefields and in hospitals and prison camps. In early 1862, three of Mary Louisa and James Longstreet's four children died of scarlet fever in Richmond, Virginia. Weeks later, William Wallace "Willie" Lincoln, son of Mary and Abraham, died in Washington of typhoid. In another of the ironic coincidences in the lives of the two native Kentuckians who led opposing sides in the Civil War, Confederate President Jefferson Davis's son, Joseph Evan, died from a fall on April 30, 1864. He was five years old.

Apparently, Joseph fell from a porch railing a distance of fifteen to twenty feet. Both parents were absent, and there were no witnesses. Bleeding and gravely injured, Joseph lived only a short while before expiring. "What an awful blow to his parents, who dote with great fondness on their children, of whom the little one just taken was probably the brightest and most attentive," wrote Virginia politician William C. Rives of the accident to his wife. Constance Cary, who later married Davis's private secretary, Burton Harrison, recalled hearing of "the mother's passionate grief and the terrible self-control of the president, who, shutting himself in his own room, had walked the floor without ceasing all of the first night."[1]

The most heart-wrenching account came from Varina Davis's 1890 memoir of her husband. "The most beautiful and brightest of my children," Joseph "was Mr. Davis's hope, and greatest joy in life. At intervals, he ejaculated, 'Not mine, oh, Lord, but thine.'" Interrupted in his grief by a courier, Davis tried to maintain his famous workaholic ways, but "then called out, in a heart broken tone, 'I must have this day with my little child.'"[2]

It is tempting to conclude that Varina made her description of Joseph and his relationship with his father conform to a tragic narrative that magnifies its emotional impact. But, by the time she wrote it, all four of their sons had predeceased their father, so there was little need to embroider the facts to establish the image of Jefferson Davis as the "Tragic Father." Several contemporary accounts suggest a special relationship between Jefferson and Joseph. In December 1863 Mary Chesnut recounted in her diary sitting down for evening tea with the Davises. "Just then little Joe rushed in and insisted on saying his prayers at his father's knee, then and there. He was in his nightclothes."[3]

The day after he died, Joseph Davis was buried in section Q of Richmond's Hollywood Cemetery. Established in 1848 on the western edge of the city on a hillside overlooking the James River, Hollywood was a parklike rural cemetery inspired by Boston's Mount Auburn. After a financially shaky first decade, it became—and remains—the fashionable address for Richmond's dead, thanks to the presence of former presidents James Monroe and John Tyler.[4] It was one of two Richmond cemeteries that each became the burial ground for more than fifteen thousand Confederate soldiers' bodies, including such prominent generals as J. E. B. Stuart.

"Immense crowds at the funeral," wrote Mary Chesnut, who delayed her departure for South Carolina to attend. "Sympathetic but shoving and pushing rudely, thousands of children. Each child had a green bough or a bunch of flowers to throw on little Joe's grave, which was already a mass of white flowers, crosses, &c, &c." "The morning I came away from Mrs. Davis, early as it was," she recounted in another passage, "I met a little child with a handful of snowdrops. 'Put these on little Joe,' she said. 'I knew him so well,' and she turned and fled without another word. I do not know who she was, then or now." Constance Cary Harrison recalled that "To the bier of the little lad, it seemed that every child in Richmond brought flowers and green leaves."[5]

A month after the funeral, on June 3, 1864 (coincidentally the president's fifty-sixth birthday), Hollywood Cemetery Company's board of directors wrote Davis to express their sympathies and to "tender for your acceptance, without cost, the lot in which your son, Joseph is buried, and to say, that if there be any other unsold lot in the Cemetery which you would prefer to the one selected under the trying circumstances of your late bereavement, you are at liberty to exchange the one for the other."[6] That gesture of kindness proved to be of vital importance to the story of Joseph Davis's grave.

The grave apparently lacked a permanent marker for two years. In May 1866, on the eve of the first specially designated day to decorate the graves of Confederate soldiers at Hollywood, a movement began to change that situation. "The little boys and girls of Richmond have, within a few days past, raised a sum of money sufficient to erect a neat and appropriate monument over the remains of little Joseph Davis," reported the *Alexandria Gazette* on May 17.[7] On such short notice, it was funded, engraved, and placed in time for the May 31 ceremony.

"The monument is chaste and elegant in design, and was elaborately decked on yesterday with rare and beautiful flowers and evergreens," reported the *Richmond Dispatch*. "It bears the following inscription: Joseph / Son of our Beloved President, / *Jefferson Davis*. / Erected by the Little Boys and Girls of the / SOUTHERN CAPITAL."

The headstone on Joseph's grave was erected *too* hastily, containing an unspecified error in the inscription. When the stone disappeared in July 1866, the *Richmond Dispatch* assured readers that, contrary to rumors that had circulated days earlier, Joseph Davis's monument had not been "desecrated" but taken to the stone yard of Rogers & Miller to be corrected.[8]

From the time it was placed, Joseph Davis's headstone was a focus of attention at the annual Memorial Day events, but it was Joseph's father who occupied the thoughts of many visitors. "He who would with tender care have guarded zealously the spot where lie the remains of his darling child is a prisoner," the *Daily Dispatch* reminded its readers shortly after the war, while Jefferson Davis sat imprisoned at Fort Monroe. "To him, in his dreary incarceration, it will be a consolation beyond all price to know that he is beloved and remembered by those whom he still represents, and it will bring a thrill of pleasure to his aching heart, and to that of the noble partner of his sorrows and joys, to feel that the people of Virginia have taken under their own protection the last resting-place of that son whose voice is now pleading before the throne of God for that mercy to his earthly father which vindictive fanatical men are not willing to bestow."

A child looking at Joseph Davis's grave, ca. 1890–1920. Courtesy of the Library of Congress.

Davis was released from prison on May 10, 1867, in Richmond. After the bail hearing, he and Varina visited Joseph's grave at Hollywood.[9]

At the Memorial Day ceremony three weeks later, the children dropped their flowers by what the *Dispatch* described as "a beautiful cross of heart's-ease and evergreens, leaning against the head-board, [bearing] the inscription: "LITTLE JOE DAVIS. / FOR HIS FATHER'S SAKE." Judge Robert Ould, formerly the Confederacy's commissioner for prisoner exchange, forwarded to Jefferson and Varina Davis a message about the ceremonies: "Hollywood was glorified with flowers. The little one who sleeps there was not forgotten. Garland upon garland covered every inch of turf and festooned the marble that bore the beloved name, some with the touching words, 'for his Father's sake.'"[10]

Joseph Davis's grave quickly achieved marquee status. In 1868, at its twentieth annual meeting, the Hollywood Cemetery Company issued a report to the stockholders and to the community at large calling attention to its natural beauty and to its important residents (and appealing funds for a proper enclosure). "On the slope of the hill washed by the waters of the river, whose ever-passing sound mingles so soothingly with the spirit of the place, stands a simple monument, of chaste and appropriate design, bearing this inscription: 'Joseph, Son of our Beloved President, Jefferson Davis, Erected by the Little Boys and Girls of the Southern Capital.'"[11]

At the annual Memorial Day observation later that year, the grave "seemed to possess a peculiar attraction for the children," reported a Richmond newspaper. Children from a local orphanage and from a Sunday-school class decorated the grave with masses of flowers and crosses placed at the head and foot of the grave with inscriptions reading "To Little Joe Davis" and "We Love to Honor his Memory."[12]

As years accumulated into decades, paying tribute to the grave of Joseph Davis continued to be a ritual for Richmond and for the family. "The little boys and girls placed their usual tribute upon the grave of the little son of President Davis who met his death by accident here during the war," observed the *Daily Dispatch* in 1875. When business brought Jefferson Davis to Richmond in 1873, he visited Hollywood and sent Varina "some sprigs of grass gathered on the spot."[13] In late 1880 Davis arranged for some unspecified "necessary repairs" to the grave.[14]

By the late 1880s, public pressure mounted to make Joseph Davis's gravesite more visually prominent. An unnamed local doctor had taken an interest in the grave, and the *Dispatch* suggested that mounding up the grave and ensuring perpetual care for it would be a worthy project for a new generation of Richmond children. The Hollywood Cemetery Company took the hint and resolved to "take charge of the grave," proposing to raise the headstone higher "and make a bed of roses around it, and repaint the iron fence enclosing the section."[15]

Two years after those improvements were made, Jefferson Davis died in New Orleans.

A special correspondent from the *Birmingham Age-Herald* published an open letter from Richmond describing Joseph's "little tomb" at Hollywood and declaring that "in this section it is hoped by all Virginians, and perhaps a very large portion if not majority of all southerners, that the remains of that 'beloved President' shall find their last resting place."[16] The same thought occurred already to local officials, who proved willing and able to leverage Joseph Davis's grave to win for Richmond the Confederate president's remains.

However unpopular Jefferson Davis had been in 1865—in the South as well as the North—his alleged mistreatment at the hands of his captors shrouded him in the martyr's mantle, and his determined defense of the principles he believed to be the foundation of his failed nation's existence resurrected his image among white southerners (and even won the admiration of some northerners). Thus, when he died on a visit to New Orleans, southern cities entered into a sometimes-unseemly sweepstakes to be the final resting place of his body.[17]

Ten days after Davis's death, Mayor J. Taylor Ellyson wrote Varina Davis, laying out Richmond's official case why her husband's body should rest in the former Confederate capital. He apparently emphasized the association with Robert E. Lee and other Virginia Confederate heroes. The Hollywood Cemetery Company board followed up with a January 1, 1890, letter tendering to Mrs. Davis "any lot" she wanted as the burial place for her "Honored husband and family." There they would rest among "those who then knew and honored him," and he would be in the same cemetery where "lies the little form of the Son he loved so well and whose grave is so frequently decorated by the willing hands impelled by the loving hearts of those who delight to honor Our President by thus remembering his child." To both letters Varina Davis replied that other cities were making strong cases, and that she would need a year or more to reach a decision.[18]

Richmond continued to press its case (prompting other cities to cry foul). Joseph Reid Anderson, a former Confederate general and owner of Richmond's Tredegar Iron Works, led a delegation to New York in June 1891 and won over Mrs. Davis. She made her decision official in a July 1891 open letter to the "Veterans and the People of the Southern States." In November 1891 Mrs. Davis traveled to Richmond to discuss details and "expressed her wish that the body of Mr. Davis should be interred in Hollywood Cemetery, and that burial places should be left in the lot for herself and other members of the Family."[19]

Over the next eighteen months, Varina Davis and Mayor Ellyson met and communicated frequently about the details. In February 1893 Ellyson visited Mrs. Davis in New York "to secure her approval of the action so far taken with respect to the removal of the remains of Mr. Davis from New Orleans to Richmond, and that she had approved the same, and was willing to leave the arrangements of all the details to this Board. And that she also desired to have interred in the section chosen by her in Hollywood and by the side of Mr. Davis the remains of her children now buried in other places."[20]

After much planning and politicking among officials from various southern cities, a funeral train—reminiscent of that which took the remains of Abraham Lincoln from Washington, DC, to Springfield, Illinois, in 1865—carried Jefferson Davis's remains from New Orleans via Biloxi, Montgomery, Atlanta, Greenville, South Carolina, Greensboro and Raleigh, North Carolina, to Richmond. There, tens of thousands gathered for what was essentially a state funeral on May 31, 1893.[21]

In subsequent days, with no ceremony and so little attention that the exact date is not certain, four more bodies were laid to rest in what became known as Davis Circle: son Samuel, brought from a cemetery in Washington, DC; son William and grandson Jefferson Davis Hayes, from a cemetery in Memphis, Tennessee; and son Joseph, transferred from his original grave in Hollywood's section Q. In accordance with laws and practice involving yellow fever victims, son Jefferson's body was transferred from Memphis months later, after the passing of the fever season.[22]

Davis Circle today is one of Hollywood Cemetery's highlights, boasting a dramatic view of the falls of the James River and

Jefferson Davis Circle, Hollywood Cemetery, Richmond, Virginia. Photograph by Jonathan W. White.

featuring a life-size statue of Jefferson Davis and richly symbolic monuments to his two daughters, Varina Anne "Winnie" Davis and Margaret Davis Hayes, all sculpted by George Julian Zolnay, as well as the little grave of Joseph Davis, its simple headstone often obscured by the relentless English ivy.[23]

Fourteen years after the reinterment of the several male Davis bodies, as many as two hundred thousand people gathered again in Richmond—this time on Monument Avenue—to dedicate the South's monument to Jefferson Davis. It was one of the largest celebrations of the Confederacy during the so-called "Lost Cause" era. As J. Taylor Ellyson had promised Varina Davis in 1889, her Kentucky-born, Mississippi-bred husband was enshrined in the pantheon of Virginia's Confederate heroes.[24]

One hundred and thirteen years later, a new generation of Richmonders not only expelled Jefferson Davis from that pantheon but rejected the pantheon itself. The monuments that were a source of civic pride in earlier decades became a source of embarrassment and objects of hostility for a younger, more diverse population. In June 2020, after groups of protesters pulled down several of Richmond's Confederate monuments, city authorities preemptively removed several others—including the statue of Jefferson Davis.[25]

The fate of the Jefferson Davis monument throws an obviously ironic twist into the story of Joseph Davis's grave, which Richmonders had tended so faithfully "For His Father's Sake." If the body of his reputedly favorite son had not rested in Hollywood Cemetery, it seems unlikely that Varina Davis would have chosen Richmond as the final resting place for the Confederate president. And, although the former Confederate capital certainly would have honored Jefferson Davis in some way (as cities throughout the South did), Davis may not have achieved the symbolic prominence that he did in Richmond had his body not been moved there to rest beside his son. If the grave of little Joe had led only to the reuniting of the Davis family in death on a hill overlooking the falls of the James River and not to an aggressively defensive monument to Davis as leader of the Confederate cause, would the human appeal of Davis's tragic family life have softened the edges of Jefferson Davis for future generations?

A Lost Child

James Hutchison Stanton

WALTER STAHR

For many years I lived less than a mile from the gravesite of James Hutchison Stanton. Jamie and his parents, Edwin and Ellen Stanton, are buried in Oak Hill Cemetery, on the eastern edge of Georgetown. As a young lawyer living in that part of Washington, I would see the cemetery almost every day, as I jogged or cycled in Rock Creek Park. But I only entered the cemetery a few times, and I am not sure I ever paused at the obelisk that marks the Stanton graves. I cannot claim that the Stantons spoke to me from beyond the grave and asked me to write their life stories.

I came to write the life of Edwin Stanton, and to learn about his son Jamie, through quite a different path. One evening in Hong Kong, another place I lived and worked as a young lawyer, I finished reading a book on some aspect of the Civil War. "That was not very good," I said to myself; "even I could write a better book." And then a voice, it seemed, spoke from a corner of the room. "So, Stahr, if that is what you think, *write a book*." That seemed implausible, impossible: I was a busy lawyer with a wife and two young children. But I started to read books with an eye to finding a topic on which I might write. I eventually settled on John Jay, a lawyer, legislator, judge, and leader who had not been the subject of a full-length biography in decades. We moved back to Washington, where I managed to combine research with a legal career, and published my biography of Jay in 2005.

When I started thinking about a second book, I offered my agent several ideas, from which he selected William Henry

Grave of Edwin M. Stanton, Oak Hill Cemetery, Washington, DC. Photograph by Melissa Winn.

Side view of the grave of Edwin M. Stanton, Oak Hill Cemetery, Washington, DC. Photograph by Melissa Winn.

Seward, the most colorful member of Lincoln's cabinet. Even before the Seward book was published, in 2012, my agent and I were talking about my third book, and I reluctantly brought up the possibility of Edwin McMasters Stanton. I was reluctant because I knew Stanton somewhat from my Seward work, and I did not like Stanton. Yes, he was a brilliant lawyer and secretary of war during the Civil War; yes, he was a central figure in the impeachment of Andrew Johnson; but Stanton was not a pleasant person. Just after Stanton's 1869 death, the New York diarist George Templeton Strong described him in his diary as "honest, patriotic, able, indefatigable, warm-hearted, unselfish, incorruptible, arbitrary, capricious, vindictive, hateful, and cruel."[1] I think Strong had Stanton about right.

I started work on Stanton in 2012, when we were living in New Hampshire, and although I visited Washington often for research, I did not go to Oak Hill to sit by his grave. Few people enter Oak Hill Cemetery, although I gather it has become more popular of late, with the success of George Saunders's novel *Lincoln in the Bardo*. When Lincoln's eleven-year-old son William died in February 1862, William Carroll offered Lincoln a place in the Carroll family vault at the cemetery for his son's coffin. Lincoln visited the cemetery and even reportedly opened the coffin, taking the corpse of his son into his arms. "That image," wrote Saunders, of "Lincoln with his dead son across his lap: a mix of the Lincoln Memorial and the Pieta—rose up in my mind and stayed there for many many years."[2]

The life of Jamie Stanton was brief and painful. He was born in October 1861 and named after an uncle on his mother's side of the family. At the time, his father, Edwin Stanton, was a leading Washington lawyer and Democrat: a former member of the cabinet of James Buchanan but not yet a member of Lincoln's cabinet. Jamie's mother, Ellen, daughter of a prominent Pittsburgh merchant, was Stanton's second wife; his first wife and their first child had died young. Two weeks after Jamie's birth, his father reported to his friend John Dix (another former member of the Buchanan cabinet) that both mother and child were "doing well." But, Stanton continued, Jamie arrived "in the dark period of history that will be known and abhorred as Lincoln's administration."[3]

Reading Stanton's words today, when we almost revere Lincoln, they seem heretical. But at the time Stanton wrote, he had good reason to criticize Lincoln and his administration.

As Stanton noted, the Union armies had suffered disastrous defeats at Manassas and at Ball's Bluff. In Washington, the "War Department swarms with horse contractors railroad agents letter writers," and "no one else has access to the Secretary [Simon Cameron]. Murmurs and discontent are heard on all sides." Stanton almost envied Dix, serving as a general in relative isolation in New York at Fort Lafayette, rather than in the midst of the "discord which prevails around Washington."[4]

In early January 1862 Ellen Stanton wrote to her sister-in-law that "Jamie is the dearest little patient fellow. He is in very nearly as bad a condition as ever [your daughter] was—the result, I think, of having been vaccinated before his skin was perfectly clear." The family doctor had persuaded her to vaccinate the child against smallpox, "there being so much of it about." Now Jamie was "very restless at night" and had a "dreadful condition of the skin." Ellen had already consulted two doctors but, not happy, consulted a third, who prescribed a "wash of lead." But Ellen insisted that, overall, Jamie was a healthy and happy little baby boy.[5]

A few weeks later, in March 1862, Edwin Stanton wrote to his sister in much darker terms. "Our babe, which was hearty and thriving when it was born, was, at the age of two weeks, vaccinated. That was soon followed by a dreadful eruption all over it—for the last six weeks we have not expected it to live—I have no idea that it can do so. Ellen is up day and night, her strength and health is wasted in taking care of the child. Today she took the baby to Baltimore as a last hope that a change of air and change of doctors might do something to save it."[6]

It would seem, from these accounts, that Jamie Stanton contracted smallpox, or something similar, through the vaccination. Doctors managed to eradicate smallpox forty years ago, so that we no longer vaccinate children for smallpox, but the rule of thumb in the twentieth century was to wait to vaccinate a child until its first birthday. There were indeed many doctors in the nineteenth century who argued against smallpox vaccination altogether, insisting that the risks outweighed the benefits, and even those doctors who advocated the vaccine conceded that in some cases it could cause illness and death. Such, it would seem, was the fate of Jamie Stanton, although we do not have a precise medical account of his case.

In early January 1862, in a somewhat surprising move, our first Republican president, Abraham Lincoln, brought the die-hard Democrat Edwin Stanton into his cabinet, as secretary of war. Stanton instantly took charge of the disorganized department and the war effort; among other early changes, Stanton moved the hub of telegraph wires in Washington into the War Department, to rooms right next to his own office. Stanton rarely used the departmental telegraph for personal purposes, but there are a few exceptions in the case of Jamie. At the end of April 1862, for example, Stanton sent a telegram to a doctor in Baltimore, asking him to come as soon as possible to see and treat the child. Stanton added: "I am hopeless of its recovery."[7]

Jamie Stanton also makes an appearance in the Lincoln papers, in the form of a letter from Stanton to Lincoln on June 29, 1862. "A note from Mrs. Stanton calls me to home on account of the increased illness of my child." (This home was a rented summer home near the Maryland border, perhaps in what we now call the Palisades.) Stanton had evidently planned to have breakfast with Lincoln, for he insisted that the president "get your breakfast at my house; it is ordered for nine o'clock." (This house was the permanent Washington home of the Stantons, on the north side of Franklin Square.) "If my child is not dying, I will be in town as early as possible, and would be glad if you would attend to the department in my absence."[8] (Stanton was writing in the midst of the Seven Days battles, so both Lincoln and Stanton were staying close to the War Department telegraph, waiting for word from McClellan.)

On July 10 Stanton sent another telegram to the doctor in Baltimore. "If our child should live until tomorrow it would be a great relief to Mrs. Stanton to have you see it. I would therefore earnestly beg you to come down tomorrow in one of the morning trains unless you get notice from me that it is needless." Then, on the morning of July 11, there is another message: the doctor need not bother to come to Washington, for the child died in the night. And on this same day there are messages to Pittsburgh: "Jamie died last night about one o'clock will be buried Sunday."[9] He was only eight months old.

I have only found one newspaper article about the death of Jamie Stanton: the *New York World* wrote that "While the corpse of his child lay silent in his home, the over-tasked Secretary was toiling on the country's behalf, finding no time to mourn over the little clay."[10] I suspect Stanton was too busy—and too sad—to write a notice about Jamie's death for the Washington papers.

The funeral service was held at the Stanton summer home,

on Sunday, July 13, and attended by President Lincoln and most members of the cabinet, including Secretary of State William Henry Seward, Secretary of the Treasury Salmon Portland Chase, and Secretary of the Navy Gideon Welles.

Weeks or months or years later—I think it was more likely years—Welles wrote that on this day "President Lincoln invited me to accompany him in his carriage to the funeral of an infant child of Mr. Stanton. Secretary Seward and Mrs. Frederick Seward were also in the carriage. Mr. Stanton occupied at that time for a summer residence the house of a naval officer, I think Hazard, some two or three miles west, or northwest, of Georgetown. It was on this occasion and on this ride that he first mentioned to Mr. Seward and myself the subject of emancipating the slaves by proclamation in case the Rebels did not cease to persist in their war on the Government and the Union, of which he saw no evidence. He dwelt earnestly on the gravity, importance, and delicacy of the movement, said he had given it much thought and had about come to the conclusion that it was a military necessity absolutely essential for the salvation of the Union, that we must free the slaves or be ourselves subdued."[11]

This bit of memoir, printed as part of the Gideon Welles diary, has become the basis for many accounts of Lincoln's "carriage ride conversation" with Welles and Seward. I believe there was no such carriage ride conversation about emancipation. Lincoln, Welles, Seward, and Anna Seward were on their way to a funeral, a funeral for a young child. All of them had experienced the death of children: Lincoln most recently, with the death of William, but Seward and Welles and Anna as well. It was not the time or place to discuss a controversial political question. And the tone in which Welles writes is much more like his tone after the war, when he wrote a series of articles and was keen to emphasize his own role in events, rather than his tone during the war, when he was living the confusion and chaos.

Welles wrote another account of this same carriage ride, and of the Jamie Stanton funeral, in a letter to his wife on the very day of the events. He wrote that "Tom [their son] and I were just starting out this morning to go to the Department, when the President, Mr. Seward and Mrs. F. Seward drove up and invited me to go with them to the funeral of Stanton's child. It was a duty in any event, and I could not refuse, so I stopped at once with the carriage, and we drove off. I scarcely knew what to make of it. We drove through Georgetown, over and past the heights, away

Grave of Jamie Stanton, Oak Hill Cemetery, Washington, DC. Photograph by Melissa Winn.

Footstone of Jamie Stanton showing his age, Oak Hill Cemetery, Washington, DC. Photograph by Melissa Winn.

several miles to a fine old place on the high hills between Tenley town and the River. I was not aware that Stanton had removed his family there. It belongs I find to some officer—they, Seward & daughter, said of the Navy but I think it must be of the Army. All the members of the cabinet were there, except [Montgomery] Blair and [Caleb Blood] Smith. Some twenty or thirty others, all I believe officers of the Army or of the naval Duponts. Dr. Pinkney was the officiating clergyman. [William Pinkney was at the time the rector of Ascension Episcopal Church in Washington.] The corpse was then brought to the Georgetown Cemetery."[12]

Which brings us back, full circle, to Jamie's graveside in Georgetown. In addition to the impressive obelisk, there are two much smaller markers, little bricks in the grass. One reads simply "Jamie" and the other "Aged 8 Mo's." These, I believe, were the first markers on the grave, when it was simply the grave of a little boy, not the grave of a famous American leader. But I like to think that, in the midst of all his work on the Civil War and Reconstruction, the famous leader, Edwin Stanton, found time to spend at the gravesite of his son Jamie Stanton. Stanton was not just the tyrant whom Strong described; he was also a warm-hearted, loving father, grieved by the death of his son. Jamie Stanton's grave was and is a beautiful place to remember that there is more to life than the time we spend on this earth.

Not-So-Final Resting Places

Grave Reflections on the Historical Reputation of Elizabeth Keckly

MICHELLE A. KROWL

"To look upon a grave, and not feel certain whose ashes repose beneath the sod, is painful, and the doubt which mystifies you, weakens the force, if not the purity, of the love-offering from the heart." This is how former slave Elizabeth Keckly explained her decision not to visit the final resting place of her beloved mother, buried in an unmarked grave in a public cemetery in Vicksburg, Mississippi. While Keckly moved north after buying her freedom in 1855, her enslaved mother followed the Garland family to Vicksburg, after which Keckly "lost sight of the family for a few years" and the location of her mother's grave as well.[1]

While my connection to Elizabeth Keckly lacks the intimacy of a family member, I understood Keckly's sentiment when I first tried to visit her grave in October 1995. After writing an undergraduate seminar paper on Keckly, the African American modistc and confidante of First Lady Mary Lincoln, I pledged to place flowers on her grave at Harmony Cemetery on a future visit to Washington, DC. That opportunity came in 1995, while conducting dissertation research. I knew from John E. Washington's book *They Knew Lincoln* that Keckly had made arrangements to be buried at Harmony Cemetery, a prominent African American cemetery in northeast Washington, DC, and that a granite headstone marked her tomb.

When ready to fulfill my promise, however, I was confused to find that Harmony Cemetery was now listed as National Harmony Memorial Park in Landover, Maryland.[2] More concerning was discovering that Keckly's grave bore no marker at all, as was the case for many of the graves in the Costin section of the cemetery. Cemetery staff provided me with an approximate location near a section marker where Keckly's remains should be located, but in Keckly's own words, I could "not feel certain whose ashes repose[d] beneath the sod." I paid my respects and left my floral offering as best I could, but the visit felt incomplete. For a woman who loomed large in my own studies, and served as an important witness of the Lincoln White House, to have been forgotten and neglected in death seemed wrong. But as it turned out, the state of Elizabeth Keckly's grave often mirrored her own historical reputation.

Born into slavery in Virginia in 1818, Elizabeth Hobbs Keckly was enslaved by the family of Col. Armistead Burwell, who was also her biological father. Burwell loaned the teenaged Elizabeth to his eldest son, Robert, who in 1835 took her with his family to Hillsborough, North Carolina, where he accepted a church position. Here Elizabeth personally experienced the violence of slavery more than ever before. The Burwells engaged a neighbor to whip her, which Keckly resisted with as much force as she could. Another white man in Hillsborough, Alexander Kirkland, pursued and sexually violated her, leading to the birth of her only child, George. By 1842, she and her son had returned to Virginia, where she was reunited with her mother. In 1847 Colonel Burwell's daughter Anne and her husband, Hugh Garland, moved to St. Louis, Missouri, taking Elizabeth and her immediate family with them. While the Garlands' social standing remained high, their coffers continued to empty, and Hugh Garland contemplated renting out Elizabeth's mother, Agnes. Horrified at the thought of her mother leaving the only family she had ever known, Elizabeth offered to use her skills as a seamstress to generate income. Garland agreed, and Elizabeth successfully "kept bread in the mouths of seventeen persons for two years and five months," including the Garlands, who could "live in comparative comfort, and move in those circles of society to which their birth gave them entrance."[3]

This arrangement changed the course of Elizabeth's life. As a sought-after dressmaker for prominent women in St. Louis, Elizabeth made connections in the white community. After Hugh Garland set $1,200 as the price of freedom for Elizabeth and her son in 1852, several white clients later advanced her the money in 1855. Elizabeth decided to seek a new life in the North in 1860, following the death of her mother in 1857, the failure

Elizabeth Keckly. Courtesy of Moorland-Spingarn Research Center, Howard University.

of her marriage to the dissipated James Keckly, and the enrollment of her son at Wilberforce University. Elizabeth ultimately settled in Washington, DC, where her St. Louis connections provided her entrée with the ladies of political Washington. This included Varina Davis, the wife of then-Senator Jefferson Davis, who offered to take Elizabeth south with them when Jefferson Davis joined the Confederate government.

Keckly's ambition, however, was to work for the ladies of the Union White House. Her chance came in March 1861 when the new first lady, Mary Lincoln, required a dressmaker to replace a gown spoiled in an accident. Keckly's good reputation preceded her, and after assuring Mrs. Lincoln of reasonable rates, she became Mary Lincoln's primary modiste for the next four years. Keckly also became an intimate of the Lincoln family, observing the domestic side of the White House as few did during the Civil War. Mary Lincoln especially came to rely on Keckly's calming presence during many times of trial and tragedy, perhaps finding in the African American Keckly a reminder of the enslaved women in the Todd family home on whom she relied for comfort as a child. "Lizabeth, you are my best and kindest friend," Mary Lincoln told Keckly, "and I love you as my best friend."[4]

Keckly's association with the Lincolns, and other prominent women who formed her clientele in Washington, provided Keckly with an unusual financial and social status for a woman of her race. Beginning in 1862, Keckly used her connections to form and help fund the Contraband Relief Association, of which she served as president for several years. The association provided aid to formerly enslaved people in their transition to freedom during and after the Civil War.

Abraham Lincoln's death on April 15, 1865, not only changed the course of the nation's history but also the life of Elizabeth Keckly. Mary Lincoln suffered "wild, tempestuous outbursts of grief from the soul," and few but Elizabeth could comfort her. She remained with Mrs. Lincoln for weeks after President Lincoln's assassination and was persuaded to leave her own business to help the Lincolns get settled in Chicago. "I had been with her so long," Keckly explained, "that she had acquired great power over me." Mary Lincoln continued to turn to Elizabeth for assistance, disastrously so in 1867. During her time as first lady, Mary Lincoln amassed tens of thousands of dollars in shopping debts. She rashly proposed selling the gowns and jewelry she would no longer wear and trusted agents in New York to manage the scheme. Mary implored Elizabeth to help her in what became known as the "Old Clothes Scandal." The agents mishandled the operation, Mary Lincoln's reputation sunk even lower in public estimation, and Elizabeth Keckly was left in New York to sort out the mess while her own finances suffered.[5]

To assist in Mary Lincoln's public rehabilitation, and to demonstrate her own upright behavior in the relationship, Keckly published *Behind the Scenes: or, Thirty Years a Slave, and Four Years in the White House* in 1868. "My own character, as well as the character of Mrs. Lincoln, is at stake, since I have been intimately associated with that lady in the most eventful periods of her life," Keckly wrote. "To defend myself I must defend the lady that I have served." The book combined elements of a slave narrative, autobiography, and exposé of the Lincoln White House. And it was a disaster for its author. Keckly shared intimate details of the Lincolns' domestic life, and Mary Lincoln's candid opinions on notable public figures. Worse, Keckly entrusted her editor, James Redpath, with many of Mary Lincoln's letters to be consulted for context, and they were instead published as an appendix to the book. Keckly's "literary thunderbolt" drew condemnation as a betrayal of the Lincolns and ruined her friendship with Mary Lincoln, who dismissed Keckly as "*the colored* historian." Mary's son Robert may have had the book suppressed, and it certainly generated no income for Keckly, who lost the trust of many of her former clients. Not only did Elizabeth lose her good name for a time, but for over a century she also lost her name itself. She signed documents using the surname "Keckly," but the book was published under the name "Keckley." While she had been called by many names during her lifetime, and her surname had been misspelled before, *Behind the Scenes* perpetuated the spelling as "Keckley" with an additional "e" for years to come.[6]

Keckly remained a respected figure in Washington's African American community, where she was active in her church and admired for her dignity, intelligence, and fashion sense.[7] And she returned to her sewing for support. In 1892 she accepted a teaching position at Wilberforce University and helped organize its display at the 1893 World's Fair in Chicago. Sometime in the 1890s she returned to Washington, DC, where she lived modestly at the National Home for Destitute Colored Women and Children. She died at the home on May 26, 1907.

Consistent with the self-reliance that characterized her personal life, she made arrangements for her death and burial.

Reflective of the racial segregation of the living in Washington, DC, in 1907, burials in most cemeteries, or sections within cemeteries, in the capital region were segregated by race. Keckly chose to be buried at the Columbian Harmony Cemetery. Established in the 1820s as part of an African American mutual aid society, at the time of Keckly's death Harmony Cemetery had become a prominent burial ground for Black Washingtonians. Keckly's estate paid $304 for the undertaker, her grave at the Columbian Harmony Cemetery, and the monument that marked what she anticipated would be her final resting place. "At the grave, at least, we should be permitted to lay our burdens down," she once wrote.[8] But Keckly could not control events in the living world.

After failing to achieve much circulation in 1868, *Behind the Scenes* was republished in 1931. By 1935, however, not only did Keckly's authorship of *Behind the Scenes* come into question, but journalist David Rankin Barbee also claimed that no such person as Elizabeth Keckly even existed. Amateur historian John E. Washington quickly disputed Barbee's assertion, but the incident inspired him to conduct further research and publish the stories he had heard since childhood of African Americans who personally knew Abraham Lincoln. Elizabeth Keckly assumed a prominent place in Washington's 1942 book *They Knew Lincoln*, which reproduced several documents relating to Keckly's life. Washington also included a photograph of Keckly's grave and tombstone at Harmony Cemetery, plus his description of the spot. "On a beautiful knoll, facing the east beneath a mammoth spreading elm tree rests forever all that remains of Elizabeth Keckley," he wrote. "Mrs. Keckley's name and date of death are carved on the face of her tomb, and she selected these words from Psalm 127, second verse, to be inscribed beneath them: FOR SO HE GIVETH HIS BELOVED SLEEP."[9]

For Elizabeth Keckly and other residents of Harmony Cemetery, "forever" ended in the year 1960, when Harmony Cemetery moved. After having been one of the preeminent African American cemeteries in Washington, DC, at the turn of the century, lack of land for expansion, increasing maintenance costs, and declining revenues plunged the cemetery into financial crisis by the 1930s. By the 1950s, the physical state of the cemetery reflected its disordered finances, ultimately prompting the Columbian Harmony Society to sell the Rhode Island Avenue property to developer Louis N. Bell in 1958. Bell agreed to expand a cemetery in Landover, Maryland, to accommodate the existing Columbian

Harmony Cemetery and to involve the society in the new National Harmony Memorial Park. Bell also agreed to pay for the reinterment in the new cemetery of the 37,000 remains, which included those of Elizabeth Keckly.[10] Part of the old Harmony Cemetery site on Rhode Island Avenue in northwest Washington, DC, was ultimately incorporated into the Rhode Island Avenue Metro subway station, opened in 1976.

While the agreement with Louis Bell specified that he would fund the removal of remains, nothing was said regarding the fate of the existing tombstones and monuments on the graves. Apparently, the markers were either plowed under at the old cemetery or hauled off as debris. In 2009 hikers discovered some old Harmony headstones forming part of a riprap constructed on the shore of the Potomac River in King George County, Virginia. By 1960, no one seems to have been paying attention to Elizabeth Keckly to ensure that her tombstone accompanied her remains. Without direct descendants or other friends to monitor the marking of her grave, Keckly's remains at the new Harmony Cemetery were left unmarked, just as her mother's had been in Vicksburg a century before.[11]

Similarly, Elizabeth Keckly's name largely seemed to fade from public memory apart from the Lincoln scholars who continued to use *Behind the Scenes* as an essential source for the

Bronze sign marking the former site of Columbian Harmony Cemetery, Rhode Island Avenue Metro Station, Washington, DC. Photograph by Melissa Winn.

domestic side of the Lincoln White House. Renewed interest in African American history following the Civil Rights Movement of the 1960s occasionally generated interest in Keckly's memoir.[12] Various publishers reprinted *Behind the Scenes* every twenty or thirty years, but John E. Washington's important *They Knew Lincoln* remained out of print for decades. Keckly continued to serve as a witness, or a source, but rarely a focus of research in her own right. Her unmarked grave in Maryland reflected her status on the periphery.

The new millennium brought a welcome change to Elizabeth Keckly's historical reputation. In 2003 Jennifer Fleischner published the dual biography *Mrs. Lincoln and Mrs. Keckly*, which not only gave Elizabeth equal billing with Mary Lincoln but also prompted a reevaluation of the spelling of Keckly's surname in light of historical evidence. Steven Spielberg's 2012 motion picture *Lincoln* included Elizabeth Keckly as a supporting character, portrayed by actress Gloria Reuben. In 2013 Jennifer Chiaverini published her novel about Elizabeth Keckly, *Mrs. Lincoln's Dressmaker*, and Tazwell Thompson's play *Mary L. & Lizzy K.* ran at Arena Stage in Washington, DC. George Saunders quoted Keckly repeatedly in his 2017 blockbuster novel, *Lincoln in the Bardo*. Kate Masur shepherded a welcome 2018 republication of *They Knew Lincoln*, and later that year the *New York Times* included Keckly in its "Overlooked No More" series of obituaries devoted to historical figures neglected at the time of their death. Academics also increasingly gave Keckly her due with scholarly articles devoted to various aspects of her life, some of which were collected by Sheila Smith McKoy in the two-volume *Elizabeth Keckley Reader*.[13] Tamika Y. Nunley's

Close-up of photograph of Keckly grave in 2011. Photograph by Bruce Guthrie.

Original gravesite of Elizabeth Keckly. From John E. Washington, *They Knew Lincoln* (New York: E. P. Dutton, 1942).

contribution to *New Perspectives on the Union War* (2019) examined Keckly's wartime experiences with barely a reference to Abraham or Mary Lincoln.[14] The proliferation of digitized books in the public domain included *Behind the Scenes*, which is now available to anyone with an internet connection.

This renewed attention on Elizabeth Keckly extended to her final resting place as well. In 2009 researcher Richard Smyth alerted several historical organizations about the unmarked location of Keckly's grave, which prompted an effort to rectify the situation. The Surratt Society, The Lincoln Forum, and other groups raised the funds for a marker, which was dedicated at the National Harmony Memorial Park on May 26, 2010, the 103rd anniversary of Keckly's death.[15] The new marker includes her name and life dates, a photograph, a copy of her signature, a brief history of her life, and describes her as "Enslaved—Modiste—Confidante."

On a sunny Sunday morning in September 2019, just shy of twenty-four years since my first attempt to visit Elizabeth Keckly's grave, I once again journeyed to the National Harmony Memorial Park in Landover, Maryland. Armed with the grave

Flowers placed by Michelle Krowl at Keckly's grave in September 2019. Photograph by Michelle Krowl.

number and a general memory of the location of the Costin section in the park, I easily located Keckly's grave on a gentle slope. Unlike several other markers I passed that honored the memory of unknown "remains found at Columbian Harmony Cemetery" in the early 2000s, Keckly's new marker proclaims her identity and invites contemplation of her extraordinary life. Unlike my 1995 "offering from the heart," this visit felt complete. The marker over Elizabeth Keckly's grave provided a recognized spot at which to pay my respects and leave royal purple flowers, in homage to Mary Lincoln's purple dress at the Smithsonian Institution, credited to Keckly's craftsmanship.[16] All these years later, my pledge to leave flowers on Elizabeth Keckly's grave has been fulfilled at last.

Reflections on the Gravestone of William H. Johnson

MICHAEL BURLINGAME

In the voluminous literature about Abraham Lincoln and race, there has been until recently little written about his interaction with African Americans, how he treated them, and how they regarded him. That was unfortunate, for as Frederick Douglass observed, "It is something to know how a man will deport himself to his admitted equals, but more to know how he will bear himself to those who are recognized as his inferiors."[1] In the past few years, several books have filled that gap and shown that Lincoln was, by the standards of his time, a racial egalitarian.[2] Their examination of Lincoln's interaction with Blacks in Springfield and later in Washington—with servants, with guests at White House receptions, with callers at the executive mansion, with residents of contraband camps, with workers at Washington hospitals, and with others—indicates that Lincoln related to them as he did to Frederick Douglass, who said of Lincoln: "In his company I was never in any way reminded of my humble origin, or of my unpopular color."[3] Douglass also spoke of Lincoln's "kindly disposition towards colored people" in general, not just toward him.[4] As the political journalist Horace White noted, Lincoln "never gave himself any airs of superiority over anybody, old or young, white or black."[5]

A good example of Lincoln's interaction with African Americans is his relationship with William H. Johnson, a servant who accompanied him to Washington in 1861. Little is known about Johnson's time in Springfield other than that he began working at the Lincoln home in early 1860.

Lincoln may not have used Johnson's services regularly. According to Henry C. Whitney, a fellow attorney and political ally, Lincoln had a "disinclination to employ a clerk, errand boy, or servant," a disinclination that "arose from his self-reliance, secretiveness, and absolute desire to be wholly independent." After Lincoln won the Republican presidential nomination, his wife Mary "procured the services of an excellent colored man, but Lincoln dispensed with his services whenever he could." Whitney recalled that in January 1861, as he and Lincoln were preparing for a short rail trip, "the servant tried to carry our hand baggage, but Lincoln could not relish the idea of a servant following him with a slender satchel, so he devised a pretext to get rid of him."[6]

The following month, Johnson did join Lincoln on a much longer journey—the one to Washington. A journalist aboard that train described Johnson as "a very useful member" of the entourage; his "untiring vigilance" as "he took care of the Presidential party" was "entitled to high credit."[7]

Shortly after his arrival in Washington, Johnson began working at the executive mansion as a porter and presidential valet. According to John E. Washington, a Black historian who interviewed African Americans who had been employed at the Lincoln White House, Johnson's appointment "almost caused an open rebellion" because his "color was very dark, and White House servants were always light. He was mistreated in such a way that it became necessary for the president to look elsewhere for employment for him."[8]

The servants' reaction was not uncommon. In 1864 Charles Lenox Remond, a Black abolitionist from Massachusetts, chastised Washington's African Americans: "I am truly sorry to learn that among your people here there exists a degree of prejudice one to another. You speak of the white man's prejudice, but you need not expect the white man to be true to you unless you first learn to be true to your own people. I know you do not like for me to expose your wrongs in this particular before the white portion of your audience, but a wrong is a wrong, and these wrongs the white man knows. And I am also told that if one among you should by his industry or energy rise in position a little above another, he only lives in this degree to gain your prejudice. This indeed is a miserable state of things which should not be."[9] According to a chronicler of intraracial prejudice in Washington, "Before emancipation, the tradition of complexion-based elitism among blacks was formal, well organized, and of dire social consequences in the District."[10]

Such prejudice was hardly confined to the nation's capital. In 1855 the abolitionist preacher Owen Lovejoy introduced into the Illinois state legislature "a remonstrance from the colored people of the State against their colonization in Africa . . . unless separate colonies be assigned to those of different shades of color," for "blacks and mulattoes cannot live in harmony together."[11] Bigotry of this sort has recently been denominated "colorism."[12]

Three days after his inauguration, Lincoln gave Johnson a letter of recommendation: "William Johnson, a colored boy, and bearer of this, has been with me about twelve months; and has been, so far, as I believe, honest, faithful, sober, industrious, and handy as a servant."[13] Soon thereafter, the president wrote to navy secretary Gideon Welles: "The bearer (William) is a servant who has been with me for some time & in whom I have confidence as to his integrity and faithfulness. He wishes to enter your service. The difference of color between him & the other servants is the cause of our seperation. If you can give him employment you will confer a favour on yours truly."[14] When nothing came of that overture, Lincoln appealed to treasury secretary Salmon P. Chase a few months later: "You remember kindly asking me, some time ago whether I really desired you to find a place for William Johnson, a colored boy who came from Illinois with me. If you can find him the place [I] shall really be obliged."[15] In response, Chase promptly appointed Johnson a messenger in the office of the Treasury Department's librarian. Johnson continued working at the White House as Lincoln's barber, valet, and body man, apparently spending mornings at the White House and afternoons in the nearby Treasury building.[16] As Henry C. Whitney recalled, Lincoln "had a servant [doubtless Johnson] who kept him considerably 'slicked up': but he frequently had to reason Lincoln into fashionable attire, by telling him his appearance was 'official.'"[17]

In October 1862 Lincoln again wrote a recommendation for Johnson: "The bearer of this, William Johnson (colored), came with me from Illinois; and is a worthy man, as I believe."[18] Two months later, the president penned a memo in which he referred to the "colored man William Johnson" who "came with me from Illinois."[19]

In November 1863 Lincoln asked Treasury Department officials to grant Johnson time off so that he could accompany him on his trip to Gettysburg. Soon after they had returned to Washington, Johnson, like Lincoln, was laid low by smallpox, which sidelined the president for three weeks and which killed Johnson in January 1864. One day that month, as Johnson lay in his hospital sickbed, a journalist discovered Lincoln counting out greenbacks. He explained that such activity "is something out of my usual line; but a President of the United States has a multiplicity of duties not specified in the Constitution or acts of Congress. This is one of them. This money belongs to a poor negro [Johnson] who is a porter in one of the departments and who is at present very bad with the smallpox." Johnson, then hospitalized, "could not draw his pay because he could not sign his name. I have been at considerable trouble to overcome the difficulty and get it for him, and have at length succeeded in cutting red tape. . . . I am now dividing the money and putting by a portion labeled, in an envelope, with my own hands, according to his wish." The reporter who took down these words concluded that nobody "who witnessed the transaction could fail to appreciate the goodness of heart which would prompt a man who is borne down by the weight of cares unparalleled in the world's history, to turn aside for a time from them to succor one of the humblest of his fellow creatures in sickness and sorrow."[20]

To buy a house, Johnson had borrowed money from the First National Bank of Washington, using Lincoln as an endorser. After Johnson died, the bank's cashier mentioned the outstanding notes to Lincoln:

"The barber who used to shave you, I hear, is dead."

"'Oh, yes,' interrupted the President, with feeling; 'William is gone. I bought a coffin for the poor fellow, and have had to help his family.'"

When the cashier said the bank would forgive the loan, Lincoln replied emphatically: "No you don't. I endorsed the notes, and am bound to pay them; and it is your duty to make me pay them."

"Yes," said the banker, "but it has long been our custom to devote a portion of our profits to charitable objects; and this seems to be a most deserving one."

When the president rejected that argument, the banker said: "Well, Mr. Lincoln, I will tell you how we can arrange this. The loan to William was a joint one between you and the bank. You stand half of the loss, and I will cancel the other."

After thinking it over, Lincoln said: "That sounds fair, but it is insidious; you are going to get ahead of me; you are going to give me the smallest note to pay. There must be a fair divide over poor William. Reckon up the interest on both notes, and chop the whole right straight through the middle, so that my half shall be as big as yours. That's the way we will fix it."

The banker agreed, saying: "After this, Mr. President, you can never deny that you indorse the negro."

"That's a fact!" Lincoln exclaimed with a laugh; "but I don't intend to deny it."[21]

It is not clear just where William Johnson is buried. Some claim that Lincoln had him interred at Arlington Cemetery, but the evidence is inconclusive. A grave there is marked with a headstone labeled "William H. Johnson, Citizen," but it is not certain that Lincoln's servant is the William Johnson (a common name) who is buried there; he could well have been interred in a graveyard, long since destroyed, for Black smallpox victims. Some also assert that Lincoln paid for his headstone, which may be true; as noted above, Lincoln said he bought Johnson's coffin. If in fact the headstone in Arlington Cemetery marks Johnson's final resting place, some have inferred that the designation "Citizen" indicates that Lincoln regarded Blacks as citizens. But the word "Citizen" is found on many gravestones in the area where Johnson is purportedly buried; that word was merely a synonym for "civilian," as opposed to military veteran, so it lacks the larger significance that some attribute to it.[22]

Nevertheless, the story of Lincoln's relationship with William Johnson sheds light on the president's humanity and his racial egalitarianism. Some may object that Lincoln, by twice referring to Johnson in writing as a "boy," demonstrated something less than full respect for his servant. But the president also referred to him twice in writing as a "man," indicating that in his mind "boy" did not have the pejorative meaning we associate with it today.[23] Moreover, as John E. Washington wrote in 1942: "Lincoln's constant interest in William Johnson shows us, even more than do some of his greatest public deeds and much heralded acts, the great heart of this man. He had induced Johnson to leave Springfield and accompany him to Washington on a most perilous journey and thereafter never ceased to be interested in him, but continued to assist him in every manner possible. Lincoln was not like many employers who bring servants to strange cities and then dispense with their services and leave

Grave of William H. Johnson, Arlington National Cemetery, Arlington, Virginia. Photograph by Melissa Winn.

them stranded in a strange place without home or employment. Although he deemed it undiplomatic to force Johnson's presence upon the resentful servants of the White House, Lincoln felt it a bounden duty to look out for him."[24]

When I think of Johnson, I also think of Lincoln's treatment of other African Americans during his presidency, especially those with whom he consulted about public affairs. A most dramatic example is his 1864 meeting with Frederick Douglass, whom he invited to the White House. Douglass thought Lincoln's willingness to host him remarkable: "He knew that he could do nothing which would call down upon him more fiercely the ribaldry of the vulgar than by showing any respect to a colored man," Douglass said. "Some men there are who can face death and dangers, but have not the moral courage to contradict a prejudice or face ridicule. In daring to admit, nay in daring to invite a Negro to an audience at the White House, Mr. Lincoln did that which he knew would be offensive to the crowd and excite their ribaldry. It was saying to the country, I am President of the black people as well as the white, and I mean to respect their rights and feelings as men and as citizens." In Douglass's estimation, Lincoln was "in a sense hitherto without example, emphatically the black man's President: the first to show any respect for their rights as men," the "first American President who . . . rose above the prejudice of his times, and country."

When Douglass was admitted to the president's office, he found Lincoln easy to talk with: "He set me at perfect liberty to state where I differed from him as freely as where I agreed with him. From the first five minutes I seemed to myself to have been acquainted with [him] during all my life." He "was one of the very few white Americans who could converse with a negro without anything like condescension, and without in anywise reminding him of the unpopularity of his color."[25]

Lincoln informed the great Black leader that "slaves are not coming so rapidly and so numerously to us as I had hoped." Douglass "replied that the slaveholders knew how to keep such things from their slaves, and probably very few knew of his Proclamation." With "great earnestness and much solicitude," the president said: "I want you to set about devising some means of making them acquainted with it, and for bringing them into our lines."[26]

After the interview at the White House, Douglass excitedly told Col. John Eaton that the president "treated me as a man; he did not let me feel for a moment that there was any difference in the color of our skins! The President is a most remarkable man. I am satisfied now that he is doing all that circumstances will permit him to do." The admiration was mutual, for Lincoln told Eaton "that considering the conditions from which Douglass rose, and the position to which he had attained he was, in his judgment, one of the most meritorious men in America."[27]

An African American historian noted that during Lincoln's presidency, "political access to the White House had been extended to the black community for the first time in U.S. history." In addition to luminaries like Frederick Douglass and Sojourner Truth, "many lesser-known activists and ordinary African Americans met with him there as well. The significance of these encounters cannot be overstated." The "multiracial space that Lincoln opened would be a critical new element in the ongoing struggle for black freedom and equality."[28]

Though we cannot infer Lincoln's views about Black citizenship from William Johnson's headstone, we may do so from the president's willingness to support Black voting rights. On March 3, 1864, two educated Black men from New Orleans—Jean Baptiste Roudanez and E. Arnold Bertonneau—presented Lincoln a petition signed by several hundred African American property owners in the Crescent City. "We are men," it asserted, and asked the president and Congress to "treat us as such." It called for voting rights to be extended to Louisiana's freeborn Blacks.[29] Roudanez reported that "Lincoln listened attentively to our address" and "sympathized with our object."[30] After reading the document, the president reportedly said: "I regret, gentlemen, that you are not able to secure all your rights, and that circumstances will not permit the [federal] government to confer them upon you. I wish you would amend your petition so as to include several suggestions, which I think will give more effect to your prayer, and after having done so please hand it to me."

When one of his two callers volunteered to rewrite the document on the spot, Lincoln asked: "Are you, then, the author of this eloquent production?"

"Whether eloquent or not, it is my own work," he replied, and incorporated the president's suggestions into the petition. According to a journalist, several people witnessed this scene, including some "Southern gentlemen" who "did not hesitate to admit that their prejudice had just received another shock."[31]

Though Lincoln "received the deputation cordially," he denied their request, explaining that he "must finish the big job he had on his hands of crushing out the rebellion," and that if "the recognition of black men as having a right to vote was necessary to close the war, he would not hesitate" to support such a policy. He added that he "saw no reason why intelligent black men should not vote—but this was not a military question, and he would refer it to a Constitutional Convention in Louisiana."[32]

A few days later, Lincoln wrote to the governor of Louisiana suggesting that the new constitution of his state—to be adopted soon—should enfranchise African American veterans of the Union army and "very intelligent" Blacks, by which he probably meant the literate: "They would probably help, in some trying time to come, to keep the jewel of liberty within the family of freedom."[33]

In a speech delivered on April 11, 1865, Lincoln for the first time publicly called for African American voting rights on the same basis. Frederick Douglass, who heard that speech, thought the president's call for Black suffrage "seemed to mean but little" because of its limited scope. But another member of the audience, John Wilkes Booth, realized its importance; he turned to a companion and declared: "That means nigger citizenship. Now, by God! I'll put him through!"[34] He added: "That is the last speech he will ever make."[35] And so it was. Thus Lincoln should be considered a martyr to Black political rights, as much as Martin Luther King Jr. and other civil rights champions who fell victim to racist violence a century later.

Soon after Lincoln's assassination, Douglass acknowledged that the president's endorsement of limited Black suffrage actually "meant a great deal. It was just like Abraham Lincoln. He never shocked prejudices unnecessarily. Having learned statesmanship while splitting rails, he always used the thin edge of the wedge first—and the fact that he used it at all meant that he would if need be, use the thick as well as the thin."[36] Thus, even though William Johnson's tombstone in Arlington Cemetery cannot be taken as a sign that Lincoln regarded Blacks as citizens, his support of Black voting rights suggests that in fact he did so.

The Slave Cemetery and Apology Marker at the University of Alabama

HILARY GREEN

A small cemetery lies nestled between the biology building and the Transportation Center on the campus of the University of Alabama (UA). This remaining fragment of the original university burial grounds seems out of place. A small marker in front of the iron fencing, however, sheds light on UA's institutional history of race and slavery. The marker notes the names of two enslaved campus laborers and a student who were originally interred here. Moreover, the surviving headstones enshrine the names of a faculty member's widow who regularly hired out her enslaved carpenter to the university for several decades. Together, this cemetery and the recently installed slavery apology marker reveal the foundational role of slavery—and the politics of race, remembrance, and reconciliation—at the University of Alabama.

An African American junior's comment—"But Dr. Green, slavery did not exist on our campus"—revealed the institutional myths and silences embedded in the campus landscape. The innocent comment compelled me to develop an alternate campus tour, "Hallowed Grounds," that ends at the cemetery. As an untenured scholar of post-emancipation African American experiences, I was convinced to be brave, intentional, and willing to range beyond my comfort zone. As a result, I regularly engaged with this historical cemetery and the complicated history of race, slavery, and memory with current university stakeholders and African American communities. By disrupting whitewashed narratives, my new tour shifted campus conversations.

UA community members began asking new questions around building a more diverse, inclusive, and equitable future. The effects of the tour contributed to several reforms, culminating in the 2020 removal of Confederate memorials and a building renaming process. The existence and history of the cemetery and slavery apology marker made these reparative changes possible.

The death of a student, Samuel James, in 1839, initiated the series of events that led to the establishment of the university burial grounds. University president Basil Manly honored James's last request by distributing five dollars to enslaved campus servants and reporting his dying words to his mother.[1] Manly then appealed to Governor Arthur P. Bagby and other university trustees for the creation of a cemetery. They quickly granted his request. James became the first interment on the designated land, "just East of the college enclosure," on October 21, 1839. Desiring to have him closer to home, surviving family members later disinterred James from the campus cemetery.[2]

With the full support of Manly and faculty, the Board of Trustees permanently designated the College Burial Grounds with adequate land for expansion. According to the 1852 hand-drawn university survey, the cemetery was located in section 23, part C. The initial interments occurred in the upper-left portion of the designated forty-nine and a half acres. At the time of the survey, a color line existed where white UA students, faculty, and faculty relatives were buried together in the front half of the cemetery and enslaved campus laborers were interred in the rear. A grass expanse separated the white and enslaved graves. A fence separated the cemetery from the campus community.[3]

Although created out of necessity, the enslaved inhabitants made the cemetery noteworthy. Jack Rudolph became the first documented enslaved person interred. Previously, enslaved campus laborers were either interred in a city cemetery or transported to their enslavers for burial.[4] Since President Manly owned Rudolph, the normal procedures did not apply. Manly extensively documented the elderly enslaved man's death from "bilious Pneumonia" in his May 5, 1843, diary entry: "He was an African, a member of the Methodist Church, honest and faithful, did as much and as well as he knew how." For these reasons, Manly had Jack "buried in the University burial grounds."[5]

William Brown was the second documented enslaved person interred. Unlike Rudolph and the countless other enslaved campus laborers, his death received special attention. Enslaved directly by Manly, the university president noted his arrival to campus as an infant with his mother from Charleston, South Carolina. He labored alongside his mother, Mary, on campus until his death. Affectionately known as "Boysey," Manly held a funeral service at the president's mansion before having "him buried in the University burying ground."[6]

These detailed entries helped in framing the later twentieth- and twenty-first-century reconciliation efforts at the university. Campus narratives and the slavery apology marker maintained Manly's preservation of surnames to denote prior enslavers, as one documents the provenance of art and other cultural artifacts. These later efforts, however, contributed to the silencing of the other enslaved individuals interred on campus. Self-congratulatory narratives, meanwhile, promoted Jack Rudolph and William Boysey Brown as exceptional enslaved laborers.[7]

Subsequent interments solidified the cemetery's color line. The burial ground became a site of reflection for students, faculty, and President Manly following the death of William

"Cemetery's iron gate and fence at the University of Alabama campus," 1890. Courtesy of the University of Alabama Libraries Special Collections, Tuscaloosa, Alabama.

University Cemetery in 1950. Courtesy of the University of Alabama Libraries Special Collections, Tuscaloosa, Alabama.

J. Crawford, a popular student who died on July 4, 1844, after suffering eleven days with typhus fever. Crawford's funeral services were held in the Rotunda, enslaved laborers dug the grave, and his burial in the college cemetery occurred over the next two days. Manly considered him to be "undoubtedly one of the brightest and best boys we have ever had."[8] His death even affected the faculty, who drafted a special letter of condolence to his father.[9]

The Pratt family also used the cemetery. Horace S. Pratt was an early faculty member who regularly hired out enslaved laborers to the university.[10] His widow, Isabel Pratt, maintained a relationship with the university until her death in 1864. She and her sister, Mary Drysdale, continued the practice of hiring out several enslaved laborers, including William, a master carpenter responsible for constructing the dome of present-day Maxwell Hall.[11] Her stepson attended the school and eventually joined the faculty. Her son enrolled at the university but died before completing his degree. He was buried in the campus cemetery.[12] In light of her friendship with Manly, as well as her husband's role at the university, Isabel Pratt requested the title of the land where her relatives were buried from the Board of Trustees in 1854. The board granted the request with a provision of reverting the land back to the university if the Pratt family abandoned the cemetery. Thus, Isabel Pratt, her sister, her son, and her stepdaughter secured prominent places in the burial grounds and cemented it as yet another visible reminder of the university's complicated slave past on the built landscape.[13]

While surviving the April 4, 1865, campus destruction by Gen. John T. Croxton and U.S. Army soldiers, the cemetery shrank as the university expanded into a modern research university.[14] Much of the old cemetery, including the majority of the enslaved people originally interred, lies hidden under concrete parking lots, buildings, and new greenspaces. The Pratt family section survived; however, collective memory of the enslaved inhabitants persisted only in university lore, archives, and a 1953 official campus history, until the 2001 arrival of a UA law professor.[15]

Alfred Brophy, a Harvard University–trained intellectual historian with a law degree from Columbia University, embarked on a multipronged campaign to draw attention to the original slave cemetery inhabitants.[16] Focusing on the archival record left behind by Basil Manly, Brophy publicized his research findings and earned the support of faculty, student groups, and community activists.[17] Opponents also responded. Skeptics felt that the proposed apology dishonored institutional memory, reopened "old wounds," and ultimately served as a publicity stunt.[18] Hostile critics derided Brophy and his allies as part of an "imported intelligentsia" engaged in "the most ridiculous example of political-correctness run amok."[19] Some openly called for a return to the campus's pre-desegregation past where Governor George Wallace would have given "these money-grubbing reparation morons exactly what they deserve."[20] Others likened Brophy to a terrorist who waged "cultural genocide."[21] Media coverage amplified this opposition and generally characterized the movement as a one-man show that railroaded the university into debates over slavery, reparations, and the fate of the cemetery.[22]

Brophy and his coalition pushed forward. He presented a drafted resolution for consideration at the March 16, 2004, meeting. It was referred to the Faculty Life Committee and brought to a final vote at the April 20, 2004, meeting. In a 36-to-1 vote, the Faculty Senate concurred with UA President Robert Witt's April 15, 2004, apology. In approving the resolution, senators ignored the sole dissenter's prepared written statement regarding the futility of apologizing "for something that happened so long ago."[23] The movement achieved a milestone. The final resolution issued the apology and approved a new historical marker yet edited out the creation of a truth-and-reconciliation commission.[24]

Days before the second anniversary of the apology, the university erected a historical marker in front of the cemetery. The plaque text draws directly from Manly's diaries and accepted university histories:

> Buried near this plaque are Jack Rudolph and William "Boysey" Brown, two slaves owned by the University of Alabama, and William J. Crawford, a University student who died in 1844. Rudolph was born in Africa about 1791 and died May 5, 1846, from "bilious pneumonia." Brown was born April 10, 1838, and died November 22, 1844, from "whooping cough."
>
> Jack Rudolph and Boysey Brown were among the slaves owned by the University of Alabama and by Faculty. Their burials were honored and recognized by the University of Alabama on April 15, 2004. The Faculty Senate apologized for their predecessors' role in the institution of slavery on April 20, 2004. This plaque honors those whose labor and legacy of perseverance helped to build the University of Alabama community since its Founding.[25]

The plaque, though, does not include the names of the other known students (Samuel Jones and Horace S. Pratt), the other unnamed enslaved people interred in the burial grounds, or the Pratt family. This rewriting of history, including the apology process, influenced the *Tuscaloosa News* coverage of the dedication. The preservation of the cemetery also never resulted in the desired rebalance of campus history. The marker, though, forever enshrined the site as a slave cemetery marked with the slavery apology marker.[26]

The preserved cemetery and new historical marker did not immediately contribute to reconciliation. "For cleansing identity," as scholars Max Clarke and Gary Alan Fine argue, "apologies, along with material and ideological support for those apologies, are essential." Based on the Clarke and Fine classification, the university completed three of the four essential components of reconciliation apologies with the 2006 historical marker. Yet, the fourth component—"a commitment, explicit or implicit, to reparation"—remained unfulfilled.[27] Rather, the emergence of a "we gave them a marker" culture prevented meaningful conversations and led to a university-wide suppression of this bold acknowledgment. In 2008 Brophy joined the faculty of the University of North Carolina at Chapel Hill. The efforts of a few professors and the occasional *Crimson White* articles on the cemetery proved incapable of moving the campus toward meaningful reconciliation.[28] From 2006 to 2015, the slavery apology marker and cemetery remained hidden in plain sight of the ever-expanding university.

By 2015, rapid demographic change, the emergence of the Universities Studying Slavery consortium, and national events renewed the reconciliation efforts. Applying valuable lessons from the original 2004 movement, this modern movement consisted of archival research, alternate campus tours, public lectures, and the purposeful engagement of various university stakeholders. National events, specifically the 2015 Charleston Massacre and 2017 Charlottesville Riot, changed both national and campus conversations regarding how the built landscape was defined by slavery and the Lost Cause ideology.[29] Moving beyond the problematic building names, the diverse campus community now asked why the university had not done more to acknowledge its slave past after the 2004 apology. They demanded the revision of the official campus tours with content contained in the alternate campus tours developed by myself and other faculty members. Students involved in the UA Honors College's "Why Nott?" movement brought Brophy back for a panel discussion regarding Josiah Nott's contributions to the proslavery argument. They also broached renaming the home of the Honors College for an individual reflecting its current professed values to educate all students irrespective of race, class, gender, and sexuality. Working with faculty members, a new coalition renewed the stalled post-apology efforts. Above all, they demanded a more central role for the slave cemetery and apology marker in defining the campus's present and future.[30]

With the hard work of securing an apology done, the Faculty Senate again played a role after a faculty-developed petition reached the body.[31] Unlike the 2004 process, this petition slowly advanced through the process from a subcommittee to a steering committee to a final vote on a resolution proposing the creation of a Commission on Race, Slavery, and Civil Rights at the University of Alabama. On October 16, 2018, the Senate passed the resolution unanimously, with one abstention. President Stuart R. Bell concurred with the resolution. Headed by the vice president for diversity, equity, and inclusion, the university is moving toward the direction of reconciliation and development of inclusive narratives showcasing the slave cemetery, apology marker, and institutional slave past. To date, the work remains incomplete.[32]

The Hallowed Grounds tour and the almost five thousand individuals reached before the Covid-19 pandemic halted all in-person tours encouraged a shift in campus politics. The tour increased participants' awareness of the cemetery, the slavery apology marker, and the two original enslaved inhabitants' names. By the end of the sixty-minute tour, participants find the cemetery's existence, the marker's text, and the university's bold 2004 leadership striking. Instead of being shamed as the original apology critics feared, these current beneficiaries of the complex slave past leave empowered and better equipped to engage in the ongoing process of reconciliation. Most importantly, they become well versed in the complicated history of slavery embodied in the cemetery at the University of Alabama. They have the necessary language, tools, and historical context.

Following the 2020 murder of George Floyd, the twenty-first-century UA inheritors grappled with the legacy of the Lost Cause campus landscape while contending with previous successful reforms surrounding the cemetery, institutional apology, apology marker, and the conversations generated by the Hallowed Grounds tours. George Floyd's murder, however, conveyed the urgency of the moment. UA activists, like "southern blacks, who had no stake in celebrating the Confederacy, had to share a cultural landscape that did."[33] Students drafted two petitions: one asking for removal of the United Daughters of the Confederacy Boulder as part of their demands for a more equitable and just campus, and a second calling for the renaming of buildings whose namesakes had ties to slavery, the Confederacy, the Ku Klux Klan, and segregation. Despite garnering twenty thousand signatures, few expected administrators to speedily listen to their demands. Delay tactics and gradualism had been the norm. On June 8, 2020, however, UA administrators removed three memorial plaques and announced a UA system commission tasked with reconsidering problematic

Hallowed Ground tour participants at the University of Alabama, 2019. Courtesy of Hilary Green.

building names. The following day, more importantly, a facilities crew hoisted the 110-year-old UDC Boulder off its pedestal and removed it from the centrally located Quad to an undisclosed location.[34] The university has subsequently followed through with the renaming process. The campus is no longer marked by buildings named after two white supremacists and one enslaver. Additional buildings remain under consideration by the task force. While the process has not fully engaged the entire campus community, the Confederate commemorative footprint has lessened while the cemetery, apology marker, and other sites of campus enslavement have become hypervisible.[35]

Without a concerted, five-year public history effort, the post–George Floyd reckoning would not have taken place. Jack Rudolph, William "Boysey" Brown, and countless enslaved men, women, and children are essential to the campus present and future. Honest conversations about these individuals, experiences, and legacies permitted the overcoming of collective amnesia, the revision of campus narratives, and a return to the reconciliation process first promised in 2004. Indeed, this campus cemetery reminds current campus stakeholders of James Baldwin's haunting words: "To accept one's past—one's history—is not the same thing as drowning in it." Instead, it can help build a more diverse, equitable, and inclusive future.[36]

"Let the Son of a Bitch Die"

An Abandoned Graveyard Reveals a Sad Story of Murder

DANA B. SHOAF

It was a beautiful, early November day. Bright sunshine helped offset a chill in the air, and the deep blue sky was a marvel. But my eyes couldn't linger on the sky. My two companions—my wife, Heidi, and *Civil War Times* director of photography Melissa Winn—and I had to focus on every step. We were picking our way through a forgotten, overgrown southern Frederick County, Maryland, graveyard. The small "Otho Thomas Cemetery," named for a prominent early burial, is not far from Point of Rocks and the Potomac River. Our steps had to be carefully chosen. Cloying brambles undid our shoelaces; gnarled roots and tumbled gravestones made heroic attempts to trip us into sunken graves.[1]

Even though the day was bright, it felt gloomy inside the tangled spinney surrounded by close-cropped soybean fields. We frequently gasped at eroded eighteenth- and early nineteenth-century dates and inscriptions on canted gravestones: "In Memory of Mary Thomas Wife of Edward Thomas, Who was Born 17th September 1759, Died the 22nd November 1793, Aged 34 years, 'Why Should we Mourn DeParted Friends or Shake at Death's Alarms. . . ?'"

But we weren't there simply by chance or to admire the craft of long-gone stonecutters. I was walking through this scene from a gothic novel trying to find the grave of Samuel Calvin Lamar, a teenager shot dead by a Union soldier in 1861. I chanced on his story perusing the internet. A dealer of Civil War artifacts was selling unique documents that told of a "murder"

Otho Thomas Cemetery, Point of Rocks, Frederick County, Maryland. Photograph by Melissa Winn.

near Adamstown, Maryland, located not far from my home. The price was reasonable, and my intrigue was up. I bought the documents and was fascinated by their contents. In neat writing by two different hands, the story of Lamar's shooting and death is recorded for history. Below, you will read excerpts of those documents. The testimonies taken from witnesses within hours of the senseless, liquor-fueled shooting bring an immediacy to the incident as only primary sources can. Reading them, it is easy to imagine confused, shocked civilians attempting to process what had happened as well as the earnestness of a young officer trying to make things right by recording the statements.[2]

I had to find Lamar's resting place. Did it still exist? One source indicated that he was buried near the hamlet of Burkittsville. I searched, but no luck. Heidi helped me by digging through Frederick County records, one of which indicated Lamar was buried in Otho Thomas. We headed to Point of Rocks, turned east on Route 464, and located the narrow gravel road that led to the graveyard. But after an hour of creeping through the resting place of farmers, "Wife of," and young children gone far too soon, we could not find his grave.[3]

On the way to the car, Heidi noticed a stone a bit off by itself, covered by brush. And there was the victim, his death date, July 21, 1861, visible under the lichen. A weeping willow forever expressing grief for Lamar carved on the stone's face. Because of a chance purchase and cemetery searching, Lamar's tale could be told.

The sad story played out on a summer Sunday afternoon on the north bank of the Potomac River at Point of Rocks. A group of eight to ten men, including Lamar, had been enjoying a local watering hole. Between five and six o'clock in the afternoon, they commandeered a Baltimore & Ohio Railroad handcar and began laboriously cranking their way north along a spur of the railroad that ran to Frederick and passed by their homes near Adamstown, about six miles north of Point of Rocks.

It was likely a familiar outing for the men. Take a day to go have a few drinks at the end of the week, and then head home and get ready for the Monday workday. But things were far from ordinary in southern Frederick County on this Sunday, July 21, 1861. The battle of Bull Run was raging in Virginia some forty miles to the south, signaling the beginning in earnest of an American bloodbath. And for the past month, federal regiments had been marching into Maryland's Potomac River bottomlands. One of those regiments was the three-month 1st New Hampshire Volunteers, which had been formed in May and was in a brigade commanded by Col. Charles P. Stone.

The 1st was in Maj. Gen. Robert Patterson's 7th Brigade of the Department of Pennsylvania, hastily formed to protect Pennsylvania, Delaware, and Maryland. Sources differ as to who the 1st was brigaded with, but in the *Official Records* and in the regimental history, *The First Regiment New Hampshire Volunteers in the Great Rebellion*, it appears the New Englanders were sent with the 9th New York, the 1st Pennsylvania, elements of the District of Columbia Volunteers, some cavalry, and an artillery battery to keep an eye on the railroad line, the Chesapeake & Ohio Canal, and important river crossings such as Point of Rocks.[4]

To that end, the 1st, outfitted in gray uniforms trimmed in red, complete with swallowtail coats, had been marching back and forth from Rockville, Maryland, to Harpers Ferry, Virginia, leaving detachments scattered along the riverbank at important locations. The men had seen no serious action, and the majority of their contact with Confederates had consisted of taunting rival pickets across the Potomac. By late July, some of the New Hampshire men had established "Camp Berry" at Point of Rocks. Regimental history author Stephen Abbott, the 1st New Hampshire's wartime chaplain, described the riverside hamlet of less than a hundred people as a "dirty secesh village," and recounted how Colonel Stone was refused "entertainment" at Point of Rocks's St. Cloud Hotel. Stone got a company of troops to take over the hotel and help him "run it on his own account."[5]

Frederick County was a divided county in a divided state. The 1st had spent some time in Frederick City, a town of more than eight thousand inhabitants who were largely pro United States. But just fifteen miles south along the Potomac River, where the bluffs of Loudoun County, Virginia, were clearly visible just across the waterway, public sentiment skewed Confederate. The dismissive treatment of the Union troops reflected the southern sympathies found in Point of Rocks and much of southern Frederick County.[6]

Things could get murky along the border of this border state. Overeager and inadequately trained volunteers far from home were quartered among a populace wary of their presence. When that handcar full of Sunday revelers ran into men from the 1st heading home from their own drinking outing in Adamstown, tensions mounted. Hubris and alcohol combine for a volatile cocktail, and when the soldiers stopped the car, a confrontation between them and the civilians ensued, and Sgt. Samuel Webster shot dead Samuel Calvin Lamar.

Though all the soldiers involved in the incident were from Company B, Lt. William F. Greeley of the 1st's Company E was assigned to investigate the matter, perhaps at an attempt at impartiality.

One can imagine the rattled lieutenant trying to make sense of the tragedy. To his credit, he immediately placed Webster under arrest and then collected statements from four of the civilians on the handcar and one soldier. All were taken down on sheets of paper. The accounts are timed to 7:00 p.m. on the 21st and describe a Sunday gone wrong with one theme in common: alcohol. Without question, strong drink helped fuel the oaths and gunplay.[7]

George C. Bready, a twenty-seven-year-old Adamstown farmer, left the most succinct retelling of the altercation:

We started from Pt. of Rocks about 6.00 this afternoon in a handcar to go to Adamstown. There were about ten of us. Had gone about one half mile from here when we were met by a party of two soldiers and four or five citizens.

The soldier ordered [us] to stop and take his party to camp. All of our party got off the car excepting Calvin Lamar & myself. One of the soldiers said he was a Sergeant. He had two stripes on his arm, said we must obey his orders. When the soldier (the Sergeant) ordered us to halt he drew his pistol and threatened to shoot us if we did not obey him. I told him I was ready to obey him. He threatened us again and leveled his pistol, firing at me then at Lamar. Lamar said shoot and be damned. The soldier then fired on Lamar and Lamar fell to the ground. When our men first got off the car the Sergeant threatened to shoot unless they stopped.

After the shooting the soldiers got on the car & we went to the camp with them. Lamar was a farmer and worked for his uncle Jno. B. Thomas. Am satisfied the Sergeant was drunk. Can recognize both of the soldiers. I recognize Chas. S. Davis, Co. B as one of the soldiers. My party all live at Adamstown, had been to Pt. of Rks on a pleasure excursion, had drank there a number of times.

Point of Rocks, Md.
Sunday July 21
7 o'clock P.M

The testimony of handcart passenger John P. Crown, a twenty-two-year-old printer, added some detail to the interaction between Webster and Lamar. Crown remembered that Lamar said to Webster, "I am not under your orders, *fire away*. I remonstrated with Lamar and told him not to say anything. . . . Some of the persons who were on the car started towards Adamstown when the soldiers turned around and bade them halt. After he had said this the soldier pointed his pistol at Lamar when Lamar said he was not afraid of him. The soldier then fired and Lamar fell on the left side of the car. I then said that we must take the car down to camp and get a surgeon, when the soldier said let the son of a bitch die." Crown then concluded: "Previous to his shooting Lamar the soldier pointed his pistol at all of us and fired at a man named Thomas Hardwood and missed him. The soldier who shot Lamar was drunk. I think that Lamar was drunk also."

Curtis Wheeler is the most mysterious of those who gave testimony, as nothing can be found of him in records, at least to this point. His account adds yet more detail to the interchange between Webster and Lamar: "The soldier then drew his revolver upon which Lamar said shoot and be damned. The soldier said I do not want to shoot you. There was some talking among the men and boys who were with the car and the soldier pointed his revolver at one of the men, Thomas Harwood. One of the men spoke when the soldier told him to shut up. Harwood went toward the soldier and the soldier moved his pistol and fired without taking aim at anyone. The ball I think went in the ground. There was some talk again between Lamar and the soldier when the soldier fired at Lamar and he fell. Think that the soldier was drunk. Lamar drank during the two hours before we saw the soldiers. Three times of whiskey and two of beer. We all drank several times of whiskey and beer before we saw the soldiers."

Charles E. Bready, George Bready's seventeen-year-old younger brother, supplied the last civilian testimony. He also recounted, "The soldier told Lamar to hold his mouth or he would shoot him. Lamar said shoot and be damned, you can't scare me. The soldier drew his pistol and fired on him. Lamar fell to the ground. . . . I think the soldier that shot Lamar was intoxicated."

The civilian side of things was well represented by these documents, but I was lacking a military perspective. Incredibly, a year after I made their purchase, I was alerted that an online auction house was selling the testimony of Pvt. Charles B. Davis, the very soldier mentioned by name in George Bready's account.[8] By keeping my nose glued to my computer and finger poised to bid, I managed to purchase Davis's account:

Statement of Charles S. Davis
Private, Company B
1st New Hampshire
I left Adamstown this afternoon to return to camp, in company with Sergeant Webster of Co. B and four or five men belonging to Adamstown. Was on my return to camp from Picket guard—was relieved about 9 O.C. A.M.

We walked along till within a quarter of a mile of the camp when we met a hand car coming towards us on the R. Road. One of the men in our company said he would stop the car and that we would go to the camp with it.

When up with the car he ordered it to stop & told the men on it to get off, they did not get off but moved the car on. He again ordered them to stop, which they would not do. He then said to Sergeant Webster & myself, "Get on the car and we'll go to camp with it." They still contrived to move the car when Webster ordered them to "halt!" One of them said he "wouldn't halt for any northern son of a bitch." The Sergeant again ordered them to halt! I got on the car while moving and had hardly seated myself on it when I heard the report of a Pistol, looked around & saw the man Lamar hit the ground. Did not see who fired the Pistol. My back was turned towards the man shot and did not see him fall.

We had drank a good deal of whiskey during the day. Don't think Webster was drunk. Don't remember what was said or what took place after the shooting. Think I walked to camp with Webster. Did not speak of the shooting while coming to camp. The man who first ordered the car to stop is called O. L. [illegible]. J. O. [illegible] was also one of the party who left Adamstown with us.

News of the murder quickly spread throughout Frederick County, and Frederick City resident and copious diarist Jacob Englebrecht noted the incident in his journal on July 22: "Killed—Calvin Lamar . . . was shot yesterday (Sunday July 21, 1861) near the Point of Rocks by Samuel Webster of Company B, 1st New Hampshire Regiment . . . stationed at the Point of Rocks & along the Potomac. His age was 19." Webster's service record at the National Archives states that he had been placed "Under arrest and detained by civil authority at Frederick City, MD, since July 22, 1861."[9]

War's diaspora scattered the soldiers involved in the incident. Webster remained in jail through the summer and fall until his trial in November. On the 13th of that month, diarist Englebrecht penned, "Acquitted—Samuel Webster of the 3 months New Hampshire Volunteers who shot Calvin Lamar on the 21 of July 1861 near the Point of Rocks had his trial yesterday in Frederick County Court & was 'acquitted.' ('Not Guilty.') The trial lasted all day & the verdict rendered about 8 o'clock PM For the state, John A. Lynch Esquire. For the prisoner, Colonel William P. Maulsby and Grayson Eichelberger Esquire. Wednesday November 13, 1861 8 o'clock AM."[10]

Webster later served as a sergeant in the 7th New Hampshire Infantry when he was twenty-four years old. In October 1863 he transferred to the 1st New Hampshire Heavy Artillery and died of disease in February 1864.[11]

Durham, New Hampshire, native Charles S. Davis also mustered out in August 1861, when his regiment's term expired. From October 1861 until discharged for disability in June 1862, he brandished a saber as a trooper in the 1st Rhode Island Cavalry. Surprisingly, he enlisted for one last hitch, this time as a member of the U.S. Navy aboard the USS *Vandalia*. He left the service for good in April 1865.[12]

William Greeley, who was thirty in 1861, would go on to serve as a lieutenant in the 11th U.S. Infantry. On October 1, 1864, he was shot in the right eye during the battle of Peebles Farm, Virginia. The bullet drove pieces of his skull into his brain. He spent the remainder of the war in hospitals and left the service after Appomattox. The veteran married and raised a family while living in New York City. But his National Archives pension file indicates the wound troubled him the rest of his life, causing him headaches, nerve issues, and sleeplessness.

In January 1879 his story took a sad twist when he walked out of his home at 183 West 135 Street and never returned to his family. His son, William L. Greeley, wrote in the pension file that although he saw his father from time to time, the elder Greeley never saw his wife, Francis, again, though they did not divorce, and the marriage was never annulled. Lieutenant Greeley died in 1914 in Waverly, Massachusetts, and is buried in New Hampshire.[13]

Most of the civilians who witnessed Lamar's shooting also fought in the war, but they crossed the river and wore gray. An August 1863 federal draft roll states that John Crown was "In the Rebel Army" and twenty-six years old. He had joined Capt. Elijah Viers White's 35th Battalion, Virginia Cavalry, often called "White's Comanches." On September 15, 1863, Crown was captured in Loudoun County and spent the rest of the war imprisoned at Fort McHenry in Baltimore. He took the oath of allegiance to the United States in May 1865. The 1870 census lists him living in Frederick City, working as a printer.[14]

At least one of the Bready brothers, Charles, also enlisted and rode with White. A postwar member of the Alexander Young Camp of the United Confederate Veterans, he died in Frederick County at age seventy-two. His older brother George, who had remained on the handcart with Lamar, moved to Baltimore and worked as a railroad conductor after the war.[15]

Thomas Harwood was mentioned in the testimonials as another man at which Webster shot. Harwood also enlisted in the 35th Battalion, Virginia Cavalry, and was captured at the June 9, 1863, battle of Brandy Station.[16]

No information could be found on Curtis Wheeler.

That leaves the man whose grave remains in a tangle of underbrush. Born on September 12, 1842, Samuel Lamar, who seemed to prefer to go by "Calvin," was nineteen years old and working as a merchant when he was killed. He was one of six children of Benoni and Mary Lamar, well-off farmers and one of the 794 slaveowners in Frederick County. They enslaved two people. Benoni died in 1858, when he was struck by lightning, and Mary is listed as a single widow on the 1860 census. Calvin Lamar's sister, Annie, married Charles E. Bready, one of her brother's handcar companions, in 1869.[17]

Stephen Abbott, the 1st New Hampshire historian, mentioned Lamar's shooting in the regimental history. At Point of Rocks, he wrote, "occurred the unfortunate conflict, the only one of the kind during the campaign, in which a young Rebel was killed by a pistol shot fired by a soldier named Webster." It's worth noting that Lamar is referred to as a "Rebel" by Abbott, although he was clearly a civilian when he was shot.[18]

Less than an hour's drive from Point of Rocks, the July 21, 1861, Bull Run battlefield is marked with monuments and cannons that commemorate sacrifice and courage. The only monument to the sad incident that claimed the life of a teenager, the result of a drunken squabble for an easy ride home, is Lamar's eroded, lonely grave in that abandoned cemetery not far from where his life ended.

I've gone back to gaze at Lamar's weeping willow several times. Standing at his headstone, you can hear trains rumble along tracks that have been in the same location since the

Grave of Samuel Calvin Lamar. When Dana Shoaf did a *Civil War Times* "First Monday" Facebook broadcast at Otho Thomas Cemetery in 2019, Lamar's grave was unmarked. When he returned to the site in 2021, he found it decorated with two Confederate first national flags. Photograph by Melissa Winn.

1860s—the tracks on which his murder occurred. Cars zip by on a nearby road, their drivers oblivious to me and my thoughts.

It's impossible to know how much trauma and misery this small, sad incident of the conflict caused. Surely it brought as much grief to the Lamar family as the comparatively titanic battle waged that day delivered to hundreds of domiciles. Did it trouble Webster? Did Greeley's experience with green volunteer troops spark him to join the more structured regular army? What of the civilians who joined the Confederate forces? Did they ride with White to avenge their friend's death, or were they predisposed to join the rebellion?

Lamar's lichened gravestone renders a bit more legible the less than heroic ends that so many people—men and women, soldiers and civilians, free and enslaved—met during the Civil War. Between 1861 and 1865, casualties were not just tallied on battlefields; the "marrow of tragedy" reached between battles and behind the lines. Walt Whitman famously wrote, "The real war will never get in the books." I'm glad I've proven him wrong, at least when it comes to Samuel Calvin Lamar.

Civil War Gothic

The Gravestones of William Barclay Napton and Melinda Williams Napton

CHRISTOPHER PHILLIPS

Marshall, Missouri, takes some work to find. Imagining this now-Midwestern town of about thirteen thousand as a center of southern antebellum political power requires even more work. Perched on a high rolling prairie in the center of the Missouri River's looping northern bend, full of turn-of-the-century four-squares and classical revival homes, the seat of Saline County once served the local planter nabobs of Missouri's slave belt, an area later known as "Little Dixie." In the 1850s they directed the state's fractious, proslavery politics during its thwarted expansion into Kansas Territory. The ensuing violence led directly to the Civil War—and to ruin.

Belying any hint of ruination, past or present, Ridge Park Cemetery, established in 1885, rests quietly on Marshall's eastern edge. Walking the grounds toward its old center, lying together in lot 51, section 10—easily missed among fluttering moths and skippers in the torment known as summer—are two recumbent gravestones, table-flat among family members' vertical headstones. Sharp-eyed visitors will discern from their respective death dates in 1862 and 1883 that both graves predate the cemetery, indicating reinterments from former gravesites. William Barclay Napton's stone, broken in two and later cemented, adumbrates a life irreparably fractured by circumstance. By contrast, his wife Melinda's is pristine, the eye drawn to the Latin inscription carved on her stone's face: *Heu quanto minus est cum reliquis versari quam tui meminisse*: "Alas, how much less it is to mix with those who remain than to remember thee." (To further intimate the engraving, Napton added his initials below it.) Sharper minds will recognize this phrase as having inspired Lord Byron's brooding 1812 poem, "And Thou Art Dead, as Young and Fair." Written after the Romantic poet viewed this inscription on a burial urn at the end of the Lovers' Walk in the garden of the English poet William Shenstone's former estate, Byron dedicated it to a woman whom cruel fate, in this case smallpox, took too young.

Napton's carefully chosen words about undying love were far more than simple testament to a man's grief at the untimely loss of his beloved spouse. Carved in stone and time, they spoke to grievance, bearing restive witness to an uncivil conflict that transgressed his and his family's fragile lives during the American Civil War. The pair of stones serve as a martyr's monument of sorts, common in border states like Missouri to commemorate wartime atrocities against proslavery and Confederate sympathizing families at the hands of occupying federal troops. Their defiant narrative was of suffering, in wartime as inflictions—occupation, dispossession, and exile—and then for subsequent generations as bitter memories of death, destruction, dissent, and alienation. William Barclay Napton saw himself in Byronic terms, his deeply felt war wounds having penned his fallen world as a southern gothic tale. In turn, he had that tale etched on his dead wife's gravestone for all to read.

Ironically, Napton was not to any southern manor born. Born in 1808 the son of a tailor, he was a native New Jerseyan and graduate of the College of New Jersey (soon Princeton University). Named for the famous Scottish jurist and defender of the divine right of kings, perhaps it was inevitable that he would pursue law and, while at the University of Virginia, ingest the conservative "Old Republican" political philosophy that held up slavery and white supremacy as foundational for enlightened national American culture. Moving to Missouri in 1832, as a Jeffersonian Democrat he served as the state's attorney general and became a supreme court judge. In 1849 he also became notorious by authoring a partisan series of legislative resolutions (introduced by Saline County neighbor and then-state senator Claiborne Fox Jackson) instructing Missouri's congressional delegation to vote unfailingly for all bills supporting slavery's territorial extension. In the 1850s, with Jackson (now the prosecession governor) he established the *Marshall Democrat.*

During the winter of 1860–61, Napton had mostly harsh words for northern Republicans, blaming them for the South's

Judge William Barclay Napton. Courtesy of Dora Witten Harvey.

Melinda Napton. Courtesy of Dora Witten Harvey.

secession. "My mind is made up as to what I am for and what I will do," he argued, "and it is useless to argue the matter." The moderate "quietists" of the state "will find me disposed to no half way wishy washy plans. . . . All this is only a *pretext*—the object is to abolish slavery here." At the outbreak of the war, Napton was a well-known proslavery polemicist. Yet wishy washy he was, at least in public, with one foot in the unionist state capital and one in the secessionist countryside. In March 1861 a state convention held in St. Louis voted 98-to-1 against seceding but adopted a position of neutrality, which he privately derided as "submit[ting to the] abolitionization of Missouri." Napton had demurred from being a convention delegate, knowing his vote for secession would cost him his seat on the supreme bench. The overwhelming vote further convinced him to keep silent about his Confederate sympathies. After the firing on Fort Sumter on April 12, followed by Lincoln's subsequent call for seventy-five thousand volunteers to put down the southern rebellion and Virginia's April 17 decision to secede, Napton sent two inflammatory letters to Melinda, avowing his opposition to neutrality and denouncing the Lincoln administration. "Thank God," he exclaimed. "K[entuck]y. and Missouri, I hope, will follow soon. . . . I would rather give up every negro I own and lose them all and my land too, than . . . submit to menaces of this Abolition despotism now ruling the North."[1]

Despite being some 150 miles downriver from his farm, Elkhill, St. Louis was suddenly too near when it saw armed conflict similar to that suffered weeks before in another border slave state city, Baltimore, Maryland. On May 10 the federal commander at the St. Louis arsenal, Nathaniel Lyon, and Republican U.S. congressman Frank P. Blair led a preemptive strike on a state guard encampment (called out to repel all invaders from the state) on the western outskirts of the city. After Confederate cannon arrived by steamer from Baton Rouge and were secreted to the self-styled "Camp Jackson," Lyon and Blair marched some 6,500 mostly German home guardsmen from the arsenal and surrounded the camp, forcing the surrender of 669 openly secessionist militia—two-thirds of the entire muster. Then, in a grandiose display of might, they marched the prisoners under guard nearly the entire six miles from the camp to the arsenal through city streets thronged with hostile residents. A fracas impelled the barely trained home guard units to open fire. Rioting tore through the city for days, resulting in the deaths of twenty-eight and the wounding of as many as seventy-five civilians. Thousands fled the "murdering dutch"—government troops who many believed were "shooting women and children in cold blood." The "coup de tat at St. Louis," as one referred to the Camp Jackson affair, galvanized Missouri's countryside, turning thousands of conditional unionists into southern rights advocates or outright secessionists.[2]

Within hours, rumors arrived of Lyon's troops heading by river for Jefferson City. A special session of the legislature hastily passed Jackson's long-debated military bill, granting the governor sweeping military powers "to repel such invasion or put down such rebellion." Within a week, the legislature authorized Jackson to take possession of the state's railroads and telegraph lines and mobilize the state guard to resist federal intervention. A real coup followed when rumors became fact: Lyon's riverine incursion to Jefferson City ousted and exiled the governor and a number of secessionist state legislators, then easily defeated the state guard's feeble defense at Boonville, only miles from Elkhill. Among the guard's casualties was Napton's eldest son, Billy, who took a slight wound, one of only two in his entire county.

In August, these same troops, along with Confederates from Arkansas, defeated Lyon's force at Wilson's Creek in the Ozarks.

Billy Napton.
Courtesy of Dora
Witten Harvey.

Lyon was killed, and his federal force hastily retreated. Led north by former governor Sterling Price, Missouri's quasi-Confederate state guard briefly gained control of the Missouri River, upending loyalties and forcing new realities and vulnerabilities on residents, white and Black. Outnumbered and outflanked by massed federals at St. Louis and Leavenworth, Price quickly retreated. A new provisional government replaced the deposed one, maintaining loyalty to the federal government. Military commanders began implementing an occupation that subverted civil liberties at the local level as part of a broader strategy to keep order among divided populations, to determine allegiances, and to prosecute the war. An inner war front formed in Missouri, a state that had not seceded but was also not safely behind the lines, hastening the realignment of communities into loyal, disloyal, and dissenting memberships.[3]

That fall, Napton refused to take the "provisional oath" required of all public servants. Because it mandated allegiance to the national government, he argued that he had taken such an oath already. Taking the new oath, he averred, insinuated disloyalty. He lost his seat that December, along with both other justices. As the war deepened, Napton developed a bitter hatred for "Radicals"—unconditional unionists and emancipationist Republicans—and their prosecution of a war that he believed sought the "total extermination and subjugation of the South and the consequent destruction of slavery everywhere within its limits." Fearing his candid daily journals might fall into federal hands, he buried them (and likely much of his private political correspondence) on Elkhill in tin containers. At the war's end when he dug them up, he found that water had destroyed the volume he kept from October 1857 to December 1862.[4]

Despite the lost record of Napton's life during this momentous time, the family's private war record over that period is not entirely a mystery. In spring 1861 whispers about Napton's disloyalty became open talk when the eldest two of his nine sons, Billy and Tom, enlisted in the state guard. After Boonville, Billy went home to recuperate. There, federal militia captured him; he quickly took the oath and received a parole, making him draftable for the local enrolled federal militia, so he headed out west. Tom and the judge's brother and farm manager, Welling, were then both arrested. Each posted a thousand-dollar bond and took the oath, pledging not to give aid or comfort to the Confederacy in any way and to offer information on any person doing so. A year later, rather than submit to the deepening occupation, Tom rode south through the Ozarks and ultimately to Memphis, Tennessee, enlisting there in the 2nd Missouri Cavalry. Serving in the Confederate cavalry for the duration of the war, he rode with Nathan Bedford Forrest before finding his way back to the Trans-Mississippi in the fall of 1862, seeing action at Cane Hill, Prairie Grove, and Helena. He was twice wounded.[5]

Tom's treason likely came to the attention of local federal authorities, who decided to make an example of the family. The militia commander in the state's northwestern district was Benjamin F. Loan, a Radical who would soon be elected to the U.S. House (in Missouri, led by St. Louisans, the Republican Party was officially named "The Radical Party"). Loan might not have been able to prove Napton himself disloyal, but he certainly could exact revenge for his sons' actions by using militia to subject the family to "outrages." In mid-November 1862 a squad of soldiers from the 40th Enrolled Missouri Militia (EMM) headquartered in Sedalia—a unit the state government would soon disband "for evil conduct" and "illegal and outrageous practices"—rode to Elkhill upon a unionist neighbor's tip that Napton was hiding "guns and powder." While Napton was temporarily away from the farm, the German American squad leader barked to Melinda, then seven months pregnant, that if she "did not bring those guns out in ten minutes, he would burn the house." When she could not produce them, the officer ordered everyone out of the house and had his men search it. When the company commander arrived, the Naptons complained of ill treatment, forcing him to reprimand the squad leader "that such talk to a Lady in her fix was out of the question" and to order "that he should wait 'til Napton come." He then rode off. When the former judge finally arrived, he denied having any weapons and "remarked . . . frequently that they was doing wrong." Assured that the soldiers would commit no depredations upon his farm, and having found no weapons, they nonetheless destroyed property and confiscated one of his mules. Then the squad commander cruelly confiscated the family's bedclothes for the use of his men.

A second rousting occurred on Christmas Day. Despite Napton having protective papers from the provisional governor, Hamilton R. Gamble, another squad of the EMM arrived. It claimed intelligence—reputedly from one or more of Napton's forty-five slaves—that weapons were indeed concealed on his property in violation of the state's Militia Enrollment Act. Passed the previous summer, this act created the EMM and required all citizens to report their arms to federal authorities. Provost marshals were also to compile lists of those who refused, declaring them disloyal and liable for assessments to pay unionists for guerrilla property damage. Napton again denied the charge but soon admitted the concealment of four shotguns and a military carbine, which he turned over to the local EMM commander the following day. Embarrassed, he claimed weakly that his overseer had hidden them a year ago to prevent them from being carried off by guerrillas or partisans. The militia confiscated some of Napton's horses.[6]

Despite such treatment, Napton had not yet fully embraced the Confederacy's separatist insurgency. Slavery more than independence framed his views of the conflict. As he indicated in the first entry in his undamaged journal on December 30, 1862, he was privately hopeful for restoration of the Union and offered a proposal for it centered on protections for slavery. Just twenty-four hours later, on New Year's Eve, any feelings of moderation that Napton might once have held were erased forever by the greatest tragedy of his life—the shocking, sudden death of his wife, Melinda.

Early that afternoon, as the family prepared for their New Year's holiday festivities, Melinda went into labor. Then forty-two and carrying her eleventh child in twenty-three years, she quickly showed signs of distress, worrying enough for Napton to summon a physician to their bedroom. Melinda then began hemorrhaging, likely suffering a placenta previa—a premature separation of the placenta from the uterus. Her bleeding soon became uncontrollable. The only surviving record, Napton's emotional journal entry, describes the chaotic scene: "Oh God! fatal day—my dearest wife—'I am not afraid to die, Doctor' cried this excellent woman,—amidst cries for help—addressed to her heavenly father and her 'dear husband,' who stood by miserable whose life and light are now gone." Within an hour of giving birth to a stillborn infant, their tenth son, Melinda died despite the physician's frantic exertions. "'Be good to Mary' [a reference to the couple's only daughter] were her last words to me," Napton wrote that evening, "how faithfully this injunction will be fulfilled time will show—But what will become of me?" Now motherless were six children at home between the ages of two and fourteen, and four older children away at school, their father now suddenly a widower. The following day, after their bondmen dug them a hasty grave, a benumbed Napton buried his wife and infant child together near the orchard at Elkhill. He would never remarry.[7]

These separate tragedies now entwined in family lore, becoming embittered, southernized grievance tales of the Napton family's private Civil War. One telling has it that in late 1862, while Melinda was working in the family garden, a squad of federal soldiers approached her from behind. The commanding officer drew his sword and threatened her so violently that she fainted, never regaining consciousness, and died soon after. Another telling has Napton being dragged from the house by federal troops with a noose around his neck, only to be saved from death by one of the soldiers, a former client, who argued that he was a man of integrity. When the Yankees turned him loose, an unfazed Napton returned to the house to finish his lunch. Neither version is true.[8]

What is true is that within days of Melinda's burial, a squad of the same 40th EMM again arrived at Elkhill. The militia's depredations continued. "[M]y stock is reduced to a few cows, some old horses and a flock of sheep and hogs," Napton lamented, "my gates and fences are down or out of repair—my negroes are seeking their fortunes in Nebraska and in the army, only two women and one man, with some children remaining. . . . This looks like a settled determination to leave me without means and drive me from the state." After a year without work, Napton soon found his finances near collapse. Practicing law was his only viable option. With St. Louis's civil courts in operation (military courts and commissions having largely superseded them elsewhere), in May 1863 Napton reinstated his law license and advertised his services.

Alerted to his presence by the newspaper advertisement, federal authorities quickly arrested and interrogated Napton, accusing him of violating the ordinance that required him to take the convention oath. Desperate, he now took it. The city's federal provost marshal, Franklin A. Dick, Frank Blair's brother-in-law, soon demanded a second interrogation. Politely yet resolutely, Napton declined to answer most questions: his political convictions, his opinion of the right of secession, the Emancipation Proclamation, legitimate bases of loyalty and disloyalty, and whether or not he supported the war and the president. He did state definitively that he opposed emancipation and, using a lawyer's trick, denied having any relatives in the Confederate army "that I know of." Mendaciously, he claimed he had "never received any communication whatever from any person in the rebel army." (In fact, he had passed communications to and from exiled Missouri secessionists in Canada and England.) Asked if he was loyal or disloyal, he answered evasively: "I consider myself loyal to the Constitution, but there are so many interpretations now to the word Loyal, that I must leave it for others to judge whether I am loyal or not as meant."[9]

Surprisingly, the interviewing officer allowed Napton to retain his law practice. But the superheated political environment in the city soon cost him cases and fees. Two of Napton's sons headed west temporarily to avoid taking the oath of allegiance. The oldest, Billy, went west during the war, then returned to Elkhill while his father was still in exile in St. Louis. In 1867 he moved to Kansas City, where he was the city's comptroller, before returning to Saline County. After his surrender in 1865, Tom along with his younger brothers John and James headed west to Montana and/or Oregon to practice law, farm, and mine. They would be joined there later by four more brothers, all seeking opportunities in the Far West. Despondent and lonely, Napton wrote in his journal in 1866: "I lead a wretched life, with a heavy heart and with feeble hopes of better times. I realize now for the first time the truth of the familiar adage that misfortunes seldom come singly." Among his misfortunes: his inability to erect a permanent gravestone for Melinda, which haunted him for more than a decade.[10]

After serving a final, third term on Missouri's supreme court, Napton lost his seat by popular vote in 1880. Now seventy-two, he retired to Elkhill, to his books, and to his memories. Even into his good night, Napton would not go quietly. He immersed himself in southernized biographies of John C. Calhoun and the Virginia dynasty he so revered, and consumed Alexander H. Stephens's two-volume constitutional history of the war, which supplied an intellectual cornerstone for the emergent Lost Cause. In one of his last journal entries, he castigated the state's newest governor, former federal officer Thomas T. Crittenden, for complicity in the recent murder of the Missouri outlaw Jesse James. Napton, a lifelong conservative who had stood consistently for status quo protections for private property—even upholding repayment of Missouri civilians' wartime debts, including assessments for guerrilla depredations on public works, an unpopular ruling that cost him his seat—now bemoaned the fate of a bandit because he had publicly avowed that his postwar illegalities were an extension of the war he fought *as a guerrilla*. Sensationalized by John Newman Edwards, the partisan Democratic editor of the *Kansas City Times*, James's newest illegalities were against Missouri's Radicals, who wore the political mantle of victory, and the banks and railroad companies who benefitted from it. For Napton and other former proslavery Missourians, the death of this former Confederate was nothing less than blood sport, a murder for bounty, and only the latest crime committed in the name of overweening government. "[T]he musket and bayonet," he growled, "finally put an end to all questions except such as the majority who controlled the purse and sword choose to tolerate."[11]

Napton fully rejected this cold new world the Yankees remade. Oppressed by federals in wartime and believing he had sacrificed deeply for a just cause, Napton made a bitter transition. Like many white residents in former border slave states like Missouri and Kentucky in the years during and after the Civil War, he cast his lot by association with the South. In his family's photo album, positioned carefully among relatives now distant or long gone, Napton placed a *carte de visite* of John Wilkes Booth, the notorious assassin of Abraham Lincoln. Adjacent to it, a tintype image of Napton's oldest son, Billy, standing proudly in his Confederate frock coat. As Billy (who in 1910 wrote the county's southernized history) later recalled of his father, "I heard him say once toward the latter part of his life that there was not a drop of 'Yankee' blood in his veins—if there was 'I would take a knife and let it out' to use his own words. No native Virginian ever disliked a Yankee more than he."[12]

Napton died at Elkhill on January 8, 1883, two months shy of his seventy-fifth birthday. His children buried him in the orchard, next to Melinda, their stillborn child, and a sister, no longer forced to mix with those who remained in an unrecognizable world. Within three years of his death, after that of a second sister (who had tended to his children while Napton was banished), Napton's surviving children moved their parents' and aunt's remains and gravestones to Marshall, among the

Napton family plot, Ridge Park Cemetery, Marshall, Missouri. Photograph by Matthew Rahner.

Broken headstone of William Barclay Napton, Ridge Park Cemetery, Marshall, Missouri. Photograph by Matthew Rahner.

first interred in the newly platted cemetery. The family's war trauma did not end there. Circumstantial evidence suggests that Melinda's tragic early death deeply affected the lives of the Naptons' children. Of those nine sons who migrated to the Far West, only three ever returned to Missouri. Only three enjoyed any semblance of a normal marital life; three others lived their lives unmarried. Family members alive today whisper of alcoholism among the Napton sons. Among the Napton women, each succeeding generation bore multiple descendants with the given name Melinda, a visible lineage of defiance for whom the tragic story of their namesake is passed down. Several of these latter-day Melindas yet live. In 1910 his eldest and Confederate veteran son, Billy, would write and publish Saline County's defiant, southernized history.

Two gravestones lying side by side, one broken, the other bearing an arcane Latin inscription, breathe to us today only the faintest whispers of this war-torn narrative of loss. Yet generations of the Napton family and others who knew the hard hand of war in Missouri also knew the storm now lying silent beneath these limestone shields, its thunder having pealed over their western prairie. Like the Victorian novelist Emily Brontë wrote of another pair of star-crossed lovers parted in life by cruel fate, if one lingers round them, the soft wind breathing through the grass under a benign sky, none but those few who know would ever imagine unquiet slumbers for these sleepers in that quiet earth.

John Wilkes Booth's Death and Burials

TERRY ALFORD

John Wilkes Booth holds the record for the longest-running escape by a presidential assassin. After shooting Abraham Lincoln at Ford's Theatre on April 14, 1865, he successfully fled the scene of the crime and was not discovered until the early morning hours of April 26. Holed up in a Virginia tobacco barn and refusing to surrender, he was shot—or more accurately *executed*, given the deliberation of the act—by Sgt. Thomas "Boston" Corbett, one of the soldiers in the pursuing party.[1]

Booth was well identified at the time of his death. Two of the three officers present knew the assassin on sight. They also had photographs of him, which they placed beside his face for comparison. On the body they found Booth's diary, jewelry engraved with his name, and a check made out to him. They also took note of the dead man's broken left leg and the "JWB" tattoo on his left hand. There was no doubt the military posse had done its work. "It *is* Booth," said Col. Everton Conger, the lead detective on the scene. As one historian later stated, "It is doubtful if many murderers carried in their pockets and on their bodies more marks of absolute identification than did John Wilkes Booth."[2]

Booth's remains were sent immediately to Washington. On April 27, 1865, key government officials visited the Washington Navy Yard and boarded the USS *Montauk*, where the cadaver had been placed. Judge Advocate General Joseph Holt took statements of identification from five witnesses who had known Booth. The five were a physician, a hotel clerk, an attorney, and two naval officers.

Intimates of Booth were available in Washington who knew the assassin better than these men, but, at this early stage in

John Wilkes Booth. Courtesy of the Library of Congress.

the investigation of Booth's conspiracy, authorities did not yet know who among Booth's friends might have been involved in his plot. Therefore, although the five witnesses were only casual acquaintances of the dead man, they sufficed. After all, the murderer was a public figure. Hundreds of people knew him on sight.[3]

The biggest challenge the witnesses faced was that the body bore little immediate resemblance to the once-handsome actor. The familiar mustache was gone. In its place was a stubble of beard. The dead man's hair was matted, his clothes dirty, and his overall look unkept. He had a wild, forlorn appearance from exposure during twelve days on the run. His face mirrored the stress of the escape and the near-constant pain suffered from his leg and back injuries. Obviously, his agonies during the escape had been intense. "Booth must have suffered as much as if he had been broken on the wheel," thought Dr. J. J. Woodward, one of the doctors present. Nevertheless, all five witnesses identified the body as Booth's.[4]

Dr. John F. May proved to be the most important witness. On April 13, 1863, while Booth was filling an engagement in Washington, the actor had gone to May for treatment of a fibroid tumor located on the large neck muscle below his left ear. May excised the tumor and stitched the wound properly, leaving a neat and nearly invisible surgical repair. The wound subsequently tore open, however, during an actress's embrace in a play. This resulted in it healing as a large cicatrix formed by the process of granulation. The cicatrix had the appearance of an ugly scar or burn. May described the mark's appearance and location without seeing it, and it was found precisely where and as he stated, removing any lingering doubt as to the identity of the dead man.

"This is Booth," May said conclusively. "I have no doubt."[5]

Plans to take a photograph of the body were dropped due to the state of the remains. Gen. Thomas Eckert, chief of the War Department telegraph office, concluded "that inasmuch as there was so little likeness in the remains to the photograph[s] in existence of Booth, perhaps it would be best not to make the picture."[6]

An autopsy team headed by Dr. Joseph K. Barnes, the surgeon general of the U.S. Army, performed a formal examination of the corpse. They measured the bullet wound on Booth's neck and tracked its course. Then they removed the vertebrae (numbers three to five) impacted by the bullet. These were destined for the Army Medical Museum. The excision effectively decapitated the body. Contrary to rumor, the remains were not otherwise disturbed and were certainly never desecrated.[7]

Workmen at the navy yard had spent the afternoon preparing a pine coffin for the body. So many came forward to take a symbolic whack at driving in a nail that the nailheads, crowded as tightly together as matches in a matchbox, ran around the sides and ends of the box like thick black bands. The plan was to place Booth into the coffin, place the coffin into the ground, and put an end to Booth's infamous career. Unfortunately, the posthumous adventures of John Wilkes Booth were just getting started.

Secretary of War Edwin Stanton believed that "it would be a source of irritation to the loyal people of the country if [Booth's] body were permitted to be made the instrument of rejoicing at the sacrifice of Mr. Lincoln." He told Col. Lafayette C. Baker, head of the National Detective Police, to make the body disappear. "He don't care where it is put," Baker told a subordinate, "only so that it will not be found until Gabriel blows his horn." The government intended to give Lincoln haters no grave over which to shed their tears.[8]

Baker and a four-man crew loaded the body into a small vessel and headed down the Eastern (or Anacostia) Branch of the Potomac River. Obviously, the coffin so enthusiastically hammered together would not be needed, since everyone saw Baker also take aboard a heavy ball and chain. It appeared he intended to sink the body in the river. That was what he later told the press. It was a deliberate and successful attempt to deceive the public. *Frank Leslie's Illustrated Newspaper*, among others, spread the news by featuring on its May 20, 1865, cover a dramatic illustration of Baker dumping the body in the river. "I am able to vouch for the truth of the representation," publisher Frank Leslie assured his readers.[9]

The body was actually taken to the nearby Washington Arsenal. An old prison on the grounds had been converted during the war for use as an arms warehouse. A section of bricks was removed from the floor of the building's large wareroom and a rough pit dug there as a grave. At midnight Booth's remains, still shrouded in the army blankets furnished by the soldiers who caught him, were placed in an arms case and lowered into the pit. The hole was then filled with dirt, the bricks were replaced, the wareroom locked, and the door key delivered to Stanton.[10]

The manner in which Stanton and Baker handled matters was problematic. It was less than forty-eight hours from the time of Booth's discovery in Virginia until his burial in Washington, DC. This created unease in some minds. Why the haste? Why the big mystery? Had the government actually done its job? Was it hiding something? Senator Garrett Davis of Kentucky told his colleagues a few months later, "I want it proved that Booth was in that barn. I cannot conceive if he was in the barn, why he was not taken alive and brought to this city alive. Why so much secrecy about it?"[11]

The arsenal was remodeled in 1867. This necessitated the relocation of the body. Booth was exhumed, and a new burial spot was found in a nearby warehouse. The dead man's name was painted in black letters on the burial box. The location of the remains was carefully charted, and the body was returned to the ground. The word of all this activity was out now, however, and knowledge that he was at the arsenal, not in the river, appeared in newspapers in Washington, New York, and Chicago.[12]

The Booth family decided to appeal for the body in order to give it a proper burial. Edwin Booth, the tragedian and older brother of the assassin, was a close friend of Adam Badeau, a member of U. S. Grant's staff. Grant was then serving as interim secretary of war. Through Badeau, Edwin Booth begged Grant to show compassion for the murderer's widowed mother. "You, sir, can understand what a consolation it would be to an aged parent to have the privilege of visiting the grave of her child," he wrote. Everything would be handled with strict privacy and out of the public gaze, he promised. The appeal was touching, but, as the war wounds were still fresh, it was to no avail.[13]

Two years later President Andrew Johnson decided to settle the matter. Discredited, lame-ducked, and friendless, he concluded a few weeks before leaving office to wrap up assassination affairs by pardoning those associates of Booth, who were still in prison and returning the bodies of those executed for conspiring in Lincoln's death.

Johnson gave John H. Weaver, sexton of Christ Church in Baltimore, an order for Booth's body on February 15, 1869. The Booths, who lived in New York City, had been nominal members of Christ Church during their prewar residence in Baltimore. Weaver had earlier buried both the assassin's father, Junius Brutus Booth Sr., and his grandfather Richard Booth in a city cemetery. He was now directed to retrieve the assassin and bury him.[14]

Weaver arranged for the exhumation of the body and took it to the Washington funeral home of Harvey and Marr. It was discovered there that the gun box in which Booth had been buried was falling apart, so the remains were transferred to an unpainted wooden coffin and prepared for removal by train to Weaver's establishment in Baltimore. To reach the train station the body traveled down an alley that the funeral home shared with Ford's Theatre—the same alley Booth used to escape after shooting Lincoln. So, the old maxim was true after all! The murderer *had* returned to the scene of the crime.[15]

On February 17, 1869, the assassin's mother, Mary Ann Holmes Booth, his sister Rosalie, and his brother Joseph visited Weaver's funeral establishment in Baltimore to accept the remains. They were joined by theatrical empresario John T. Ford and several of his staff, players, and family.

Booth's body had been rehoused in a handsome mahogany case. Upon examination, it was revealed that the assassin's hair was surprisingly full and his teeth clutched together as if he were still in pain. The remains were frightful to look at yet recognizable to those who knew Booth well. Ford remarked the distinctive jaw could belong to no other person. Joseph Booth stated that the assassin had had a peculiarly shaped filling in one of his teeth. (The rest were perfect and beautifully white.) The filling was found as he described it.

Actress Blanche Chapman was present with her fiancé, Harry Ford. A younger brother of John T. Ford, Harry had been a close friend of Booth. Blanche had never met the assassin and asked Harry how he could so unequivocally recognize Booth in the blackened mass before them. "I knew Booth better than I know you," he replied. "There's no need of doctor or dentist. One look told me."[16]

The following day Weaver took the body to his receiving vault at Baltimore's Green Mount Cemetery. In winter months a body was customarily kept in such a vault until the weather improved and a time determined for the family to gather.

The conclusion of the theatrical season in summer cleared the calendars of Edwin and eldest brother Junius Brutus Booth Jr., and they set a date for the final interment. On June 26, 1869, the two brothers, together with Mary Ann and Rose, gathered at the family lot in Green Mount's Dogwood section. The assassin's father and grandfather had been relocated here from the Baltimore cemetery. The remains of three Booth children who died in the 1830s and had been buried at the family farm in Harford County were also brought to Green Mount.

Six pallbearers drawn from the city's theatrical community carried Booth's coffin from the receiving vault to the gravesite. A brick-lined excavation had been prepared for it. Nearby were long stone slabs that, when placed over the brickwork, would help maintain an even appearance at the site. The remains of the three children from the farm, all of whom died before Booth's birth, were gathered in a small single coffin. It was placed on top of his.

Reverend Fleming James gave the customary service from the Episcopalian *Book of Common Prayer*. About fifty persons, mostly ladies, were present. When the spade men filled the grave, several of the women came forward and placed floral tributes on it.[17]

A large obelisk commissioned by Edwin for his father in 1858 distinguished the site. On it appeared the names of John Wilkes

Booth and five other Booth children. These included the three children from the farm and Henry, a son who died in London in 1836 and was buried there. The name of Joseph Booth was added to it later—odd since, unlike the others, he would have his own stone when placed in the lot upon his death in 1902.

No individual marker was set up on the assassin's grave. Contrary to later rumor, this was not a requirement of the federal government. It happened due to Edwin's sense of propriety. He knew the attention it might draw—and the trouble. He allowed the grave to be adorned with small rose bushes at head and foot, but nothing else. "Place no mark there," he directed Henry W. Mears, a Weaver employee.[18]

No attempt was made to hide the location. No attempt would have been successful. Booth's interment was widely reported in the nation's press, and his burial spot, opposite the stele from that of his father, was apparent to visitors.

A controversial incident demonstrated that. On June 8, 1870, the annual Decoration Day for Confederate soldiers was held at Green Mount. "Their graves were strewed with flowers," wrote a local reporter, "but the grave that exceeded all the rest in its profuse decorations was that of J. Wilkes Booth. Upon the green mound there was a pyramid of flowers. If the richness and profusion of the emblems are to be taken as the measure of affection in which the deceased solders are held, John Wilkes Booth is the greatest hero of them all."[19]

Northerners were indignant. "We wish we could trust as unworthy of belief the story which comes from Baltimore of an act unworthy of humanity," complained the *New York Tribune*. "Certain women of that city, assembled ostensibly to decorate the grave of Rebel soldiers, devoted their fairest flowers in greatest profusion to the grave of John Wilkes Booth. Such an act, conceived in malice of those they call oppressors, [shows] these women are worthy of the men they urged and cajoled to death. The people of the North have shown no such disrespect as this to Southern soldiers. They believe them misguided, but they never thought to fix by act or word a midnight assassin higher in public esteem than the most humble of the Rebel slain."[20]

As expected, the absence of a gravestone only fired suspicion that there was no body in the grave or, if there were, it was that of an unrelated person. Booth, some speculated, was hundreds of miles away from Baltimore at this time and enjoying life. In 1872 a man alleged to be Booth was married in Franklin County,

Tennessee. He must have been a bold rascal as he felt safe enough to marry under the assassin's own name. Escape enthusiasts maintained this person was the same individual later known as John St. Helen, a Texas saloon keeper who, when he feared he was dying, confessed his identity as the murderer. St. Helen recovered and disappeared, only to be finally repurposed as David E. George, a drifter and occasional house painter who killed himself in Enid, Oklahoma Territory, in 1903.[21]

Could the mystery surrounding these claims be resolved by an exhumation and study of the Green Mount remains? The drumbeat for a scientific resolution of the question began in the 1990s. "There are intelligent, rational individuals who believe that the witnesses who identified the body that day were deceived or lying, and that the body was not that of Booth," wrote Gretchen Worden, director of the Mütter Museum of the College of Physicians of Philadelphia in 1994. Worden's collection housed among its curiosities a fragment of Booth's spine taken at the autopsy. This humble specimen made Worden a go-to person on the assassin for the media, and the voluble curator, with a bachelor's degree in anthropology but none in history, relished her role as advocate for examining the body. "Would Mary Ann Booth or any other member of her family cavil at a final examination of the body in order to settle, once and for all, a question that was so important to them at the time: 'Is it the body of John Wilkes Booth?' I think not," she said.[22]

Green Mount refused to permit an exhumation, and in May 1995 an extended hearing was held in Baltimore City Circuit Court to litigate the controversy. The assassin had no acknowledged children, thus no direct descendants with legal standing in the matter. But several distant relatives of the assassin, including a great-great-granddaughter of Edwin, petitioned for a disinterment of the body. Folklore met fact in court, and results were disastrous for the former. The "historical evidence" of the plaintiffs was exposed as mere tall tales. Judge Joseph H. H. Kaplan, who presided, quickly realized that the well-known facts of 1865–69 identifying Booth were entirely convincing.

This author was subpoenaed to testify by Green Mount and took the stand on May 25, 1995. My testimony focused in part on the three siblings from the farm who were buried with the assassin. Obviously, if Booth were dug up, they would be, too. Therefore, the petitioners sought the exhumation of four persons, an exceptional request. Other testimony showed that escape buffs had failed to account for the probability that excessive water damage at the site had rendered the remains unsuitable for testing. It was also clear that the petitioning relatives would not provide a proper DNA match.

Judge Kaplan ruled that the body should stay exactly where Booth's family put it in 1869. The following year the Maryland Court of Special Appeals in Annapolis heard oral arguments in the case and upheld Kaplan's ruling.[23]

In recent years, a custom has developed in which visitors to the gravesite leave Lincoln pennies. John Wilkes Booth has no individual marker, so the pennies are placed on the Booth monument and on the headstones and footstones of his family

Booth family plot, Green Mount Cemetery, Baltimore, Maryland. The unmarked stone with pennies, often thought to be John Wilkes Booth's grave, is actually the footstone of his sister Asia. Photograph by Melissa Winn.

members buried there. Coins for the dead go back at least to the Greeks' "Charon's Obol," a coin left with the deceased to ensure safe passage over the River Styx. Today, the practice is prevalent in military cemeteries where coins are placed as a sign of respect and camaraderie.[24] Pennies left at Green Mount have the great president's visage facing up. The point seems clear—Lincoln gets the final word in this debate.

The lingering controversies over Booth, a man who died many years ago, call to mind a quotation from Sophocles' *Antigone*, a play that tells a story about covert burying of bodies: "It is the dead, not the living, who make the longest demands upon us, since we die forever."

Of Graves and the Color Line

MARK S. SCHANTZ

Our memory of the American Civil War is cleaved by the fault line of race.[1] Clint Smith's recent book, *How the Word Is Passed: A Reckoning with the History of Slavery across America* (2021), makes clear how this double memory is etched still into our landscapes of the past. The graves of 2,200 enslaved African American children in the "Field of Angels" on the Whitney Plantation in Louisiana stand in stark and shocking contrast to the preserve of the 30,000 "Confederate heroes" who now rest at the Blandford Cemetery outside of Petersburg, Virginia. These specimens of remembrance are so distant from each other—both in geography and by design—that they seem to be recalling two entirely different histories of slavery and the Civil War. Two different Civil Wars, two distinct peoples. The Field of Angels on the Whitney Plantation in Louisiana and the Blandford Cemetery in Virginia mark out the color line of memory in places that are not directly proximate. But our divided memories of the Civil War can be laid side by side even more closely, and perhaps even more profoundly, if we keep our eyes open.[2]

In Norfolk, Virginia, the color line of memory is represented by a brick wall that separates the Elmwood Cemetery from the West Point Cemetery. I was there in March 2018 doing research for a book project when I discovered it: a ten-foot-high brick wall running at least 150 feet in length, dividing the two burial grounds. What I was looking for on that bright and windy March afternoon was the final resting place of Dr. David M. Wright, one of Norfolk's best and most respected physicians, a dedicated

Christian, good husband, and beloved father. And a slaveholding murderer. On July 11, 1863, Dr. Wright strode out of Foster & Moore's dry goods store and shot Lt. Alanson Sanborn of the Union army dead. Sanborn was leading a detachment of the 1st United States Colored Infantry on a recruiting parade to enlist more men of color for the war, and this, finally, along with the already yearlong Yankee occupation of his town, moved Dr. Wright to murder. The idea of Black troops parading through the streets, "jostling" women and children, each one of them a potential Nat Turner—these things fueled his rage.

I knew already how the story ended. The Union forces in Norfolk brought Dr. Wright before a military commission, where he was tried and convicted for murder. Despite last-minute appeals to President Abraham Lincoln, Dr. Wright walked to the gallows on October 23, 1863.[3] And his martyrdom in the white South began even before the trapdoors opened and has continued for at least a century and a half. So, I wanted to see the grave. I wanted to know how he was remembered, if there would be mention of his crime, or a vindication. Something.

That something was in Elmwood Cemetery, the cemetery for respectable, white Victorians in Norfolk established in 1853. Its neat rectangular rows of memorials, mausoleums, and markers don't quite make the grade for Elmwood as typical of a "rural cemetery," but its name and the family plots with idiosyncratic memorials help make up for that. Nowadays there is a guardhouse at Elmwood as it runs along Princess Anne Road. It's a big place. The guardhouse was closed the day I visited, and it took me a good hour of pacing, even running, briskly among the ruins to find a trace of Dr. Wright. Historians by nature are homicide detectives (but with fewer television dramas), and I was on the case. Eventually, I beat the sunset. Here was a family plot, just catching the late afternoon sun, with Dr. Wright's monument the tallest of any in the collection that included his wife, Penelope: she had a Christian cross on her memorial, of course less imposing than her husband's. Such a fitting tribute to a good, southern lady. The plot is surprisingly current; the last burial marker in the family plot is for Elizabeth Wright Talbot and dates from December 8, 1959. Dr. Wright's wife, Penelope, and descendants thus frame him as the central patriarch of the family and the one around whom they would revolve in eternity. His memorial has a base, inscriptions, and is a four-sided obelisk (taller than the observer), whose sides lean together to form

Dr. David M. Wright. Courtesy of the Virginia Museum of History and Culture.

a sharp point at the apex. It is not especially conspicuous for Elmwood and makes a neat fit with the other family memorials nearby. That's part of what makes it difficult to find, nestled among the countless other pillars and graves.

It's not simply the memorial and its style that blend into the scenery, but also the words that veil Dr. Wright's past. What we have are the familiar tropes of the mid-nineteenth-century grave marker—simple, schmaltzy, and just about as generic as they come. We learn from reading that Dr. David Minton Wright was born on April 21, 1809, and died October 23, 1863, "in the firm hope of a blissful eternity." This struck me as bizarre—how does a murderer die in hope of eternal salvation? Unless he's not actually a murderer. Shooting a white, Yankee officer who is busily recruiting Black troops (your former property, perhaps)—well, that's not really murder, that's defending one's honor. No hanging, no crime; no crime, then "a blissful hope of eternity." A defiant logic is silently at work as the sun goes down. Another element of the memorial consists of typically romantic death poetry:

Not for the dead in Christ we weep
Their sorrows are now o'er
The sea is calm the tempest past
On that eternal shore

Wright family plot, Elmwood Cemetery, Norfolk, Virginia. Photograph by Jesse Hutcheson.

Their peace is sealed their rest is sure
Within that better home
A while we weep and linger here
Then follow to the tomb

The ending of the poem—stressing the mortality of all human life—was a commonplace in American culture in the years before the Civil War. The idea that heaven was a place of rest, where all one's sorrows would pass, was also to be expected. Indeed, Dr. Wright's rather flamboyant and controversial life and death are denied fully by his memorial. There is no hint of his crime, of his trial (one might stretch to include the "tempest past" as a gesture to those events), or any details of the martyrdom that was already welling up in Virginia and throughout the South when he was executed. Unless you were a historian with specific knowledge of this crime and Dr. Wright's past, you would think this was yet another Victorian Christian burial plot. It hides more history than it reveals.

What the Wright family phalanx symbolizes, however, is the fierce will of his descendants to rehabilitate his memory and to erase any unsavory elements of his past. And no one was more zealous in defending the reputation of Dr. Wright than his grandson, by his daughter Penelope's marriage, Alexander Wilbourne Weddell (1876–1948).[4] While working as a clerk in the United States Copyright Office, Alex Weddell happened into a position in the U.S. diplomatic service and took roles as consul or ambassador for almost forty years. It was a dream career for a white southerner navigating the psychological humiliations of the post–Civil War era. During his posts abroad, however, Alex Weddell kept a sharp eye on developments in his home state and intervened numerous times on behalf of his grandfather's memory. He was aided in these campaigns by the assistance of his wife, Virginia (Chase) Steedman, in 1923, "the widow of a wealthy St. Louis manufacturer and substantial heiress in her own right."[5] With a proud heritage to defend and the means to do so, Alexander Weddell eventually became president of the Virginia Historical Society in 1944 and held that position until he and Virginia were killed in a tragic train accident in 1948. By that time, though, Weddell had not only erased the stain on his grandfather's name but had transformed him into a hero of biblical proportions. It came as no surprise when Lenoir Chambers, in an address to the Virginia Historical Society in 1965, lifted Dr. Wright to the heavens. Viewing him as a pure victim of the loathsome Yankee occupation of Norfolk, he intoned that "a great light rises from the figure of Dr. Wright as he went to the gallows: touched with inner serenity; in spirit rising above the world around him; in an indescribable sense the victor over his own destiny. It is the kind of light that lives."[6] We do well to remember that this was the state of Virginia in the same year Congress passed the national Voting Rights Act.

The soaring rhetoric of Lenoir Chambers, however, was itself grounded in the heavy historical lifting already undertaken by Alexander W. Weddell. A few early examples of the young Alex Weddell's efforts reveal both the lion and the fox. On March 30, 1901, he launched an offensive against the editor of the *Virginian-Pilot* for an article on "A Hundred Years of History" that reprinted resolutions that had been passed on July 13, 1863. Two days after Lt. Sanborn's assassination, unionists in the Portsmouth City Council offered up resolutions condemning Wright's murderous actions—which Weddell now held as a condemnation of "a man without fear and without reproach, of spotless integrity and unblemished name." He now wanted action from the newspaper. He noted, too, that he had asked an "influential friend in Portsmouth to have the resolutions expunged from the records of the Council of that place: and I am now hopeful of accomplishing."[7] Vindication was immediate and complete. The newspaper replied that the author of the piece "had only been in Virginia a few years and had no knowledge of the sentiment in reference to the matter."[8] On April 4 the paper planned to publish, by way of reparations, the March 10, 1864, "Resolutions of sympathy adopted by General Assembly, regarding the death of Dr. Wright," thus taking Virginia history back to the Civil War. In tandem with this, on May 10, 1901, the Portsmouth City Council did "expunge" its condemnation of Dr. Wright's actions and published a pamphlet titled "Expunged from the Record. David Minton Wright, M.D. 1809–1863" to trumpet the victory.[9] Fighting on two fronts, like Gen. Robert E. Lee at Chancellorsville, Alexander Weddell had scored a stunning victory on local terrain, but without a drop of bloodshed.

In 1907 Alexander Weddell invaded the North. Here he took on what he considered a scandalous article in *Century Magazine*, published in New York City. The article, by David Homer Bates, raised points that had been made in his book of the same year titled *Lincoln in the Telegraph Office*, a fascinating and sometimes cute account of a new president's engagement with a new medium of national communication. What infuriated Weddell, however, was that Bates suggested in his article that a "cabal" of southern supporters had offered a twenty-thousand-dollar bribe to a telegraph operator in Norfolk to compose a pardon cable for Dr. Wright, "a telegram which was hourly expected from President Lincoln granting a reprieve."[10] This was only one of a clutch of vexing charges that Bates had written, and Weddell took issue with all of them—more than we can consider in this brief treatment. After much ado, Weddell succeeded in having editor C. C. Buel publish something approaching a recantation of the original piece in the "Open Letters" section—not as a major article. However, Buel passed on the opportunity to accept Weddell's own vigorous and personal defense of his grandfather, including, for good measure, kind words spoken by northerners of good repute. After four months of bitter negotiating, Weddell took this as the best he could get. On a note from Buel to him dated August 6, 1907, Weddell kept the argument going in his own head. He scribbled out in his own hand no fewer than six objections to Buel's handling of this literary duel. It was one thing to manipulate a local newspaper and the "redeemed"

Brick wall separating West Point and Elmwood cemeteries, Norfolk, Virginia. Photograph by Jesse Hutcheson.

Portsmouth City Council, but quite another to take on *Century Magazine*.[11] Still, Alex Weddell had taken the defense of his grandfather's reputation national and proved to be consistent in the quest until his own tragic death in 1948.

As Alexander Weddell was taking on all comers in the name of family honor, things were happening on the other side of the brick wall. A triangle of ground to the west of Elmwood Cemetery became the site of what historian Kirk Savage notes as "the only recognizably black standing-soldier monument" in the South, and possibly the nation.[12] This terrain for the burial of Norfolk's Black residents had been a long time coming. Not until 1827 did the Common Council even find a "Potter's Field" for Black bodies, but throughout the Civil War, Black residents had no designated place for their loved ones. In 1873 the Common Council designated the area north of the Elmwood wall as "Calvary Cemetery" and as a place for Blacks, but the land was not improved, and a cemetery keeper was not appointed. It was not until 1886 when James E. Fuller, Norfolk's first African American member of the Common Council and a member of the 1st United States Colored Cavalry, put his shoulder to the task—proposing to the council in March 1886 that the twenty plots in this area be designated for the burial of African American troops and that the name be changed to West Point Cemetery. Fundraising efforts began apace, and the base of the monument was set on May 31, 1906. While James Fuller himself

Monument to African American soldiers of the Civil War and Spanish-American War, featuring a statue of William Carney of the 54th Massachusetts Volunteers, West Point Cemetery, Norfolk, Virginia. Photograph by Jesse Hutcheson.

died in 1909—still suffering from the wounds he incurred in the war—community efforts to complete the monument continued until 1920, when the monument and statue of Sgt. William Carney, runaway Norfolk slave and Medal of Honor recipient with the 54th Massachusetts Infantry for his service at Fort Wagner, graced its top.[13]

It's tempting to conjure a meeting between William Carney and James E. Fuller in prewar Norfolk or at some long-forgotten moment in their military service. They were nearly contemporaries and hailed from the same place—Carney born in 1840 in Portsmouth and Fuller born in 1843 in Norfolk. Both thirsted for freedom. Both joined the Union army. Both became sergeants (though Fuller's duties in service of the quartermaster's office did not afford much of a chance for glory). Both survived the war intact. Both were dedicated to exercising full rights of citizenship after the war. Both served in public office. After the war, though, Carney had had enough of the former slave oligarchs and lived out his days in Massachusetts, meeting his demise in 1908 (a year earlier than Fuller), dying as a result of a freakish elevator accident that crushed his leg.[14] So, while he may have had wind of what James E. Fuller was up to at the West End Cemetery, he didn't live to see his likeness perched upon the completed 1920 memorial. But what William Carney, James E. Fuller, and Norfolk's people of color had accomplished was nothing short of epic.

And it's also almost impossible to find. As I first looked for Dr. Wright's grave in Elmwood Cemetery, I completely overlooked the so-called entrance to West Point Cemetery. That's because there isn't one. You must walk around the end of the Elmwood Cemetery and flank the color line of the brick wall to find it. There is no signage directing visitors to the site, apart from a historical plaque—but it's virtually parallel to the ground so you must know it's there in the first place. The monument itself is now largely obscured from sight due to a cluster of large sycamore trees that have now grown up around it. On the far west side of the cemetery runs Armistead Avenue, and the grounds are not protected or marked by much of anything other than a thin wire fence. Trash from the road blows up among the tombstones, and I picked some of it up when I was there—Taco Bell, I recall from that day. Across Armistead Avenue, you can see the rear of several businesses and the occasional trash dumpster. Perhaps the only standing soldier monument depicting a recognizable, individual Black veteran of the Civil War has been effectively veiled.[15]

Once you find your way there, though, the site is more than worth pondering. The monument's altar inscription reads "Erected by the Norfolk Memorial Association to the Memory of OUR HEROES 1861–1865"—so, definitely not the heroes of the so-called Johnny Reb memorial in downtown Norfolk dedicated in 1907, which paid tribute to "Our Confederate Dead, 1861–1865." There's no overlapping of heroes here. There are, however, some curious historical disjunctures to be considered. We know from his pension file that Sgt. James E. Fuller was commander of the Dahlgren Post No. 4 of the Grand Army of the Republic, and that group is proudly acknowledged on the altar. However, the likely namesake of the Dahlgren Post was Union colonel Ulric Dahlgren, who hanged a local Black man for allegedly providing him with faulty intelligence for a secret raid on Richmond in the closing days of the Civil War. It seems a perverse remembrance.[16] The altar also contains two inscriptions commemorating the contributions of the Langston Camp No. 1 of United States Spanish War Vets and National Camp No. 2 United States Spanish War Vets. Here was evidence of Black men having to prove themselves to white men by fighting an imperialist war against "yellow" men in the Philippines. I was thinking then of the incredible courage of a man like James E. Fuller who, in the era of Jim Crow and in the face of political terrorism (more than four thousand documented lynchings took place in the United States between 1890 and 1940—with three of these in nearby Newport News, Virginia), took it upon himself to organize such an endeavor over a period of more than two decades. White Americans had killed Black Americans for far less effrontery.[17]

Sgt. James E. Fuller embodied Dr. David M. Wright's worst nightmare—he enlisted in the Union cause in his native Norfolk, Virginia, on December 13, 1863—just about two months after Dr. Wright's execution. In Virginia alone there would be enough Black men like Fuller to fill nine Union regiments (some nine thousand men) by the end of the Civil War—part of the decisive increment that wrote the Old South's epitaph.[18] Fuller's pension file affords glimpses into his postwar activities and about the hardships he had endured working behind the lines as a quartermaster for the 1st United States Colored Cavalry. He had at least seen some rough stuff, including the fighting at Petersburg in 1864. Despite the horrors of the war, Fuller came home, married Tamah Fuller in 1868, and together they had two children. He lived in Norfolk for his entire life after the Civil War and dedicated himself to its African American population and to his fellow veterans. He won election to the Common Council. He also battled constantly with the federal government—attempting to increase his monthly claim due to a host of physical ailments ranging from rheumatism, disease of the eyes and kidneys, and heart disease. His record reveals two rejections for an increase in his claim—which started at six dollars per month in 1895—before his final success in securing a pension of twelve dollars per month in 1907, two years before his death. Such tenacity explains a great deal about him.[19]

The constant round of physical examinations, the palpating of organs and limbs, the measuring of the pulse, the hands-on assessments of his range of motion mandated by the federal pension administrators could not have felt that much different to men who had been enslaved than what they, and their families, had endured at slave auctions. Surgeons' certificates in Fuller's file describe in minute detail his complaints (some of which were deemed "unreliable") and assigned them a numerical value for pension. The word of the physician was final in this era when professional medicine was gaining its legs. James Fuller might well claim cloudy vision or back pain or difficulty in dressing himself in the morning, but the word of the surgeon was final. Depending upon his examiner, the year he applied, and for which kind of disability, it was the veteran who was always judged and evaluated by the physician. The veteran's own assessment of his health might even be blamed on what the examiners called "vicious habit"—though Fuller himself was never confronted with such a charge. For veterans of color, however, it was now the white surgeon who performed the assessment of physical condition that in an earlier day might have been among the duties of the slave auctioneer. The nearly 150 pages in Fuller's pension file—the single largest trove of documentation of his life—is mostly about how white men touched his body and assessed his weaknesses (although here, the greater the damage, the greater the disability payment). Maybe this was just another institutional and semivisible humiliation that Black folk suffered at the hands of white folk—more insidious still because of its mundane, bureaucratic execution. It's hard to know what men like James E. Fuller felt going through that process. But it is worth pondering, I think.

Walking among the tombstones at West Point for the first time, I hadn't learned much about James E. Fuller yet, but I felt an overwhelming sense of obligation to these men whose names were surrendering to the wear of time. The only thing I could think of to do that felt right, aside from picking up trash, was to kneel before each soldier headstone and take a photo on my digital camera. Nobody really knows just how many men, women, and children are buried at West Point—I singled out the tombstones that seemed clearly marked as military graves. But I love looking at these photos of the soldier headstones, testing myself to see how many of them I can read. I feel as though if I look at them long enough, someday others will. Such is the magical thinking of memory.

The best photo of the West Point Cemetery comes full circle back to the problem of the color line. It dates from about 1910 and includes forty-one veterans of color backed up, literally, against the brick wall dividing West Point Cemetery from Elmwood Cemetery. I suspect that they might have gathered there to observe or mark the death of James E. Fuller—but that is simply my historian's intuition. I have spent hours looking at

Grand Army of the Republic Reunion Photograph (Accession #11436). Photograph by H. C. May, ca. 1910. Courtesy of the Albert and Shirley Small Special Collections Library at the University of Virginia, Charlottesville.

these aging veterans, who donned their uniforms and medals, even a saber and a flag, to be themselves a visual memorial. They look straight at the camera; there is no heroic posturing or posing—only the direct gaze of men who have served a nation whose white citizens might well have decided to put a noose around their necks and set them ablaze. By being in that space at that time, by standing up against the color line, these veterans embody something beyond words.

On one side, the living heritage of Black military service, and on the other side a memorial to one white Virginian who put his life on the line to stop that noble pursuit from becoming a reality.

Acknowledgments

This book was born over breakfast at the 2018 Society of Civil War Historians conference in Pittsburgh, Pennsylvania. Jonathan had the idea at some point in 2017, and he shared it with Brian over bagels. They sketched out an outline on a napkin (which Jonathan still has) and over the remainder of the conference began recruiting contributors. We thank the twenty-nine eminent historians who, in writing for this book, brought that initial vision about death to life.

We thank the many photographers who captured the images that make this such a beautiful volume, the private collectors who gave permission to produce images from their collections, and the many librarians, archivists, public historians, university photographers, and private collectors who helped us track down images: Megan Klintworth of the Abraham Lincoln Presidential Library, Michael Achille of the Hingham Public Library, Byron Faidley of Washington and Lee University, Roberta Schwartz of Bowdoin College, Jason Ayer of the University of South Carolina, Chris Gwinn and Gregory Goodell of Gettysburg National Military Park, Mark Losavio of NOAA, Trenton Streck-Havill of the National Museum of Health and Medicine, Rich Condon of the Reconstruction Era National Historical Park, Lori Strelecki of the Pike County Historical Society, Heather Harren of the Blue Earth County Historical Society, Michelle Krowl of the Library of Congress, Sanjay Suchak of the University of Virginia, Ryan Semmes of the Ulysses S. Grant Presidential Library, Andy Waskie of the G.A.R. Museum in Philadelphia, Jim Mundy and Keeley Tulio of the Union League of Philadelphia, Sonja Woods and Lopez Matthews of Howard University, Rachel Dworkin of the Chemung County Historical Society, and Graham Dozier of the Virginia Museum of History and Culture. Photographers and private collectors are acknowledged in the captions along with their images. Chloe Baker, class of 2022 at Christopher Newport University, did fantastic work editing many of the photographs.

Funding for this project was generously supplied through the Provost's Office and the Department of Leadership and American Studies at Christopher Newport University, the Department of History at Sam Houston State University, and the Hayek Fund at the Institute for Humane Studies.

Finally, we thank the staff, series editors, and peer reviewers at the University of Georgia Press for believing in this project and seeing it to fruition.

Notes

FOREWORD

1. Transcript of interview with L. G. Bridson, taped for BBC at the Algonquin Hotel, New York, April 1961, Robert Penn Warren Papers, Beinecke Library, Yale University, box 239, folder 4627.

2. Robert Penn Warren, "Rebuke of the Rocks" and "History among the Rocks," in Warren, *The Collected Poems*, ed. John Burt (Baton Rouge: Louisiana State University Press, 1998), 35–37.

3. Robert Penn Warren, "The Sense of the Past," edited transcript of unpublished essay, Warren Papers, box 235, folder 4507.

4. Walt Whitman, *Leaves of Grass* (San Diego: Word Cloud Classics, 2015), 445, 452.

INTRODUCTION

1. Lucy Buck, diary entry, January 12, 1862, in Elizabeth R. Baer, ed., *Shadows on My Heart: The Civil War Diary of Lucy Rebecca Buck of Virginia* (Athens: University of Georgia Press, 1997), 16.

2. Walt Whitman as quoted in Roy Morris, *The Better Angel: Walt Whitman in the Civil War* (New York: Oxford University Press, 2000), 59.

3. Ibid., 59; Nicholas Marshall, "The Great Exaggeration: Death and the Civil War," *Journal of the Civil War Era* 4 (March 2014): 3–27. On coroners and the collection of mortality statistics, see Stephen Berry, *Count the Dead: Coroners, Quants, and the Birth of Death as We Know It* (Chapel Hill: University of North Carolina Press, 2022).

4. Drew Gilpin Faust, *This Republic of Suffering: Death and the Civil War* (New York: Alfred A. Knopf, 2008), 268; J. David Hacker, "A Census-Based Count of the Civil War Dead," *Civil War History* 57, no. 4 (December 2011): 307–48; Brian Steel Wills, *Inglorious Passages: Noncombat Deaths in the American Civil War* (Lawrence:

University Press of Kansas, 2017); Jim Downs, *Sick from Freedom: African-American Illness and Suffering During the Civil War and Reconstruction* (New York: Oxford University Press, 2012); Mark Flotow, "Commentary: David Hacker's 'A Census-Based Count of the Civil War Dead,'" *Journal of the Abraham Lincoln Association* 42, no. 2 (Fall 2021): 68–84. For more recent work on the meaning and consequences of death in the Civil War era, see also Mark S. Schantz, *Awaiting the Heavenly Country: The Civil War and America's Culture of Death* (Ithaca: Cornell University Press, 2008); Angela Esco Elder, *Love and Duty: Confederate Widows and the Emotional Politics of Loss* (Chapel Hill: University of North Carolina Press, 2022); and Sarah J. Purcell, *Spectacle of Grief: Public Funerals and Memory in the Civil War* (Chapel Hill: University of North Carolina Press, 2022).

5. William A. Blair, *Cities of the Dead: Contesting the Memory of the Civil War in the South, 1865–1914* (Chapel Hill: University of North Carolina Press, 2004); John Neff, *Honoring the Civil War Dead: Commemoration and the Problem of Reconciliation* (Lawrence: University Press of Kansas, 2005); Caroline E. Janney, *Burying the Dead but Not the Past: Ladies' Memorial Associations and the Lost Cause* (Chapel Hill: University of North Carolina Press, 2008). For the canonical work on Civil War memory, see David W. Blight, *Race and Reunion: The Civil War in American Memory* (Cambridge: Harvard University Press, 2001).

6. "Compromise with the South," *Harper's Weekly*, September 3, 1864; Jonathan W. White, "Remembering the Fishing Creek Confederacy," *Pennsylvania Heritage* 40 (Summer 2014): 6–13. On Civil War graves as stubborn sites of memory, see also Neff, *Honoring the Civil War Dead*.

7. When conducting the survey of Union graves that led to the creation of the national cemetery system, Quartermaster Edmund Burke Whitman noted that "most all the information gained was from negroes who, as I was told by parties at Mt. Sterling [Kentucky], pay more attention to such matters than the white people." See Whitman notes, Records of the Office of the Quartermaster General: Records Relating to Functions: Cemeterial, 1828–1929, RG 92, entry 686, Box 1, National Archives and Records Administration (NARA). Frederick Douglass, "The Unknown Loyal Dead," in John Lobb, ed., *The Life and Times of Frederick Douglass* (London: Christian Age Office, 1882), 364; *Report of the Joint Select Committee to Inquire into the Condition of Affairs in the Late Insurrectionary States: Miscellaneous and Florida* (Washington, DC: Government Printing Office, 1872), 282. For more context, see Shawn Leigh Alexander, "T. Thomas Fortune, Racial Violence of Reconstruction, and the Struggle for Historical Memory," in Carole Emberton and Bruce E. Baker, eds., *Remembering Reconstruction: Struggles over the Meaning of America's Most Turbulent Era* (Baton Rouge: Louisiana State University Press, 2017), 59–83.

8. J. L. Donaldson to Montgomery Meigs, December 9, 1865, Records of the Office of the Quartermaster General, RG 92, entry 646A, Box 3, NARA; E. B. Whitman to J. L. Donaldson, April 29, 1866, Records of the Office of the Quartermaster General, RG 92, entry 646A, Box 3, NARA; Whitman notes, Records of the Office of the Quartermaster General: Records Relating to Functions: Cemeterial, 1828–1929, RG 92, entry 686, Box 1, NARA; J. L Donaldson to M. D. Wickersham, April 25, 1866, Records of the Office of the Quartermaster General, RG 92, entry 646A, Box 3, NARA.

9. Douglass as quoted in Lobb, ed., *Life and Times of Frederick Douglass*, 364–65.

10. Roland Bowen as quoted in Gregory Coco, ed., *From Ball's Bluff to Gettysburg and Beyond: The Civil War Letters of Private Roland E. Bowen, 15th Massachusetts Infantry* (Gettysburg: Thomas Publications, 1994).

11. Michael Brandle to Quartermaster General, April 10, 1888, in RG 92: Records of the Office of the Quartermaster General, entry 575, Box 3; Eugene Arus Nash, *A History of the Forty-Fourth Regiment New York Volunteer Infantry in the Civil War, 1861–1865* (Chicago: R. R. Donnelley & Sons, 1911), 362.

12. Weston Ferris to Edmund B. Whitman, n.d., Records of the Office of the Quartermaster General: Records of Quartermasters: Col. Edmund B. Whitman Letters and Reports received, September 1863–March 1869, RG 92, entry 646A, Box 3, NARA; Barbara A. Gannon, *The Won Cause: Black and White Comradeship in the Grand Army of the Republic* (Chapel Hill: University of North Carolina Press, 2011).

13. Micki McElya, *The Politics of Mourning: Death and Honor in Arlington National Cemetery* (Cambridge: Harvard University Press, 2016); Robert M. Poole, *On Hallowed Ground: The Story of Arlington National Cemetery* (New York: Bloomsbury, 2010).

CHAPTER 1

1. Thomas Mann, *The Magic Mountain*, trans. H. T. Lowe-Porter (New York: Knopf, 1949), 532.

2. Glenn W. LaFantasie, *Twilight at Little Round Top: July 2, 1863, The Tide Turns at Gettysburg* (New York: Vintage, 2005).

3. William C. Oates, Autobiography, Oates Family Papers, Alabama Department of Archives and History, Montgomery, Alabama (hereafter OFP).

4. Oates Sr. to William C. Oates Jr., December 24, 1900, OFP.

5. LaFantasie, *Gettysburg Requiem: The Life and Lost Causes of Confederate Colonel William C. Oates* (New York: Oxford University Press, 2006), 165–262.

6. Oates Sr. to William C. Oates Jr., December 24, 1900, OFP.

7. For a full account of the dispute over Oates's proposed monument,

see "Memories of Little Round Top," in LaFantasie, *Gettysburg Heroes: Perfect Soldiers, Hallowed Ground* (Bloomington: Indiana University Press, 2008), 172–91.

8. Joy Tutela is the editor's name. She works as a literary agent in New York and lives outside Boston.

9. Italics mine. "Monument to Confederates," *Southern Historical Society Papers* 38 (1910): 296.

10. RG 92: Office of the Commissioner for Marking Graves of Confederate Dead, Records of Cemeterial Commissions, 1893–1916, National Archives and Records Administration, Washington, DC (hereafter CMGCD).

11. L. Frank Nye to Mrs. Edgar Marburg, January 12, 1909; Oates to Jacob McGavock Dickinson, November 1, December 9, 1909, all CMGCD.

12. Oates to J. W. C. O'Neal, February 19, 23, 1909; Oates to Rufus Weaver, February 23, 1909, all CMGCD.

13. Nye to Weaver, March 2, 1909, CMGCD; Weaver to Oates, March 3, 1909, OFP.

14. Oates to Superintendent, Hollywood Cemetery, March 5, 1909; Oates to John R. Hooper, March 8, 1909; Oates to Bettie Ellyson, March 8, 1909, all CMGCD.

15. Oates Sr. to William C. Oates Jr., August 30, September 2, 1909; Oates Jr. to Georgia Whiting Saffold, ca. September 3, ca. September 21, 1909, all OFP.

16. Oates Sr. to Ellyson, January 19, 1910; Nye to Hooper, February 11, 1910; Ellyson to Oates, February 18, 1910, all CMGCD.

17. Nye to Ellyson, June 28, July 9, 1910, CMGCD.

18. *Montgomery Advertiser*, September 10, September 11, 1910; *Birmingham Ledger*, September 11, 1910; *Birmingham News*, September 12, 1910; *Montgomery Journal*, September 12, 1910.

19. Edna St. Vincent Millay to Witter Bynner, October 29, 1920, in Allan Ross Macdougall, ed., *Letters of Edna St. Vincent Millay* (New York: Harper & Brothers, 1952), 102.

CHAPTER 2

1. The location is approximately 77°14' 17" W, 39°47' 54" N.

2. Fred Hawthorne, "140 Places Every Guide Should Know," *Gettysburg Daily*, www.gettysburgdaily.com/battlefield-guides/fred-hawthorne/140-places-every-guide-should-know.

3. This book was called *Inscription at Gettysburg*. It was written by a licensed battlefield guide named Sally Walters, who worked as a public schoolteacher. My friend Coke—who was himself an author—used the same publisher as Walters, Thomas Publications, and therefore instantly knew about her book. See Sara Gould Walters, *Inscription at Gettysburg* (Gettysburg, PA: Thomas Publications, 1991).

4. Samuel Penniman Bates, *History of the Pennsylvania Volunteers,*

1861–1865 (Harrisburg, PA: B. Singerly, State Printer, 1869), 1:117–18. Acheson mustered into service of the Commonwealth on April 24. He and his comrades mustered into federal service the next day at Harrisburg.

5. Bates, *History of the Pennsylvania Volunteers,* 1:121.

6. Bates, *History of the Pennsylvania Volunteers,* 1:117–18.

7. Bates, *History of the Pennsylvania Volunteers*, 3:8–12.

8. Luther Dickey, *History of the Eighty-Fifth Regiment Pennsylvania Volunteer Infantry* (New York: J. C. and W. E. Powers, 1915), 172. John Acheson's wound did not leave him sidelined for long. He recovered and rejoined his regiment for its subsequent campaigns.

9. Robert Laird Stewart, *History of the One Hundred and Fortieth Regiment, Pennsylvania Volunteers* (Philadelphia: Franklin Binder, 1912), 4.

10. Stewart, *History of the One Hundred and Fortieth Regiment,* 301–5.

11. Stewart, *History of the One Hundred and Fortieth Regiment,* 302.

12. David Acheson to Mary Acheson, February 3, 1863, in Walters, *Inscription at Gettysburg,* 54–56.

13. David Acheson to Judge A. W. Acheson Sr., November 6, 1862, in Walters, *Inscription at Gettysburg,* 32.

14. David Acheson to Judge A. W. Acheson Sr., March 25, 1863, in Walters, *Inscription at Gettysburg,* 72.

15. Ibid.

16. Stephen W. Sears, *Chancellorsville* (Boston: Houghton Mifflin, 1996), 478.

17. Benjamin F. Powelson, *History of Company K of the 140th Regiment Pennsylvania Volunteers (1862–1865)* (Steubenville, Ohio: Carnahan, 1906), 28.

18. Stewart, *History of the One Hundred and Fortieth Regiment,* 135–36.

19. "J. B. Wilson Tells of the Reburial of Captain Acheson," *Washington (Pennsylvania) Reporter*, July 18, 1913, in Walters, *Inscription at Gettysburg*, 114.

20. Stewart, *History of the One Hundred and Fortieth Regiment,* 306–7.

21. Judge A. W. Acheson to Jane W. Acheson, November 8, 1863, in Walters, *Inscription at Gettysburg,* 121.

CHAPTER 3

1. All I knew at the time about the home guard was what I had learned from Charles Frazier's 1997 novel, *Cold Mountain*, a story set near our family farm. In Frazier's telling, and in the film made from it, the home guard bedeviled civilians who wanted to be left alone in a war in which they had no stake. Frazier's menacing home guard, more like an outlaw band than a body of soldiers, preyed on isolated women. The home

guard in Yancey County, I later learned, did in fact terrorize unionist neighbors in the name of the Confederacy, even though some among them were conscripts themselves, of uncertain and shifting loyalties.

2. These men joined the 3rd North Carolina Mounted Infantry, led by Col. George Kirk, a "home Yankee" from East Tennessee. For more on Kirk, see Phillip Shaw Palludan, *Victims: A True Story of the Civil War* (Knoxville: University of Tennessee Press, 1981), 102, 108, 122–23.

3. *Asheville News*, September 4, 1862 (available on findagrave.com).

CHAPTER 4

1. Case file of Albert D. J. Cashier, Illinois Veterans Home, Quincy, IL; RG 15, Records of the Veterans Administration, pension application file C 2,573,248, National Archives and Records Administration (hereafter NARA); https://catalog.archives.gov/id/36605129; RG 94, compiled military service record, 95th Illinois Infantry, Cashier, Albert D. J., NARA; RG 94, carded medical records, Civil War, 95th Illinois Infantry, Cashier, Albert D. J., NARA; Letters to Albert Cashier, private collection of Frank and Velma Crawford, Caledonia, IL; "Served as a Man," *National Tribune*, Nov. 25, 1915; Gerhard P. Clausius, "The Little Soldier of the 95th: Albert D. J. Cashier," *Journal of the Illinois State Historical Society* 51, no. 4 (1958); Rodney O. Davis, "Private Albert Cashier as Regarded by His/Her Comrades," *Journal of the Illinois State Historical Society* 72 (1989); Mary Catherine Lannon, "Albert D. J. Cashier and the Ninety-Fifth Illinois Infantry, 1844–1915," MA thesis, Illinois State University, 1969; "Memorial Day in Saunemin," *Daily Leader*, Pontiac, IL, May 31, 1977; "Cashier Home Dedicated in Saturday Ceremony," *Daily Leader*, Pontiac, IL, Aug. 30, 2011; and DeAnne Blanton and Lauren M. Cook, *They Fought Like Demons: Women Soldiers in the Civil War* (New York: Vintage Civil War Library, 2003).

2. It was remarkably easy for women to pass as men in nineteenth-century America. Clothing and hairstyles were so strictly gendered that the mere acts of putting on trousers and cutting hair were enough to make a woman look like a man, or at least a teenage boy. As long as passing women had access to privacy for their sanitary needs, their masquerade was usually safe. For a more detailed discussion of the means by which women, especially women in the military, passed as men, see Blanton and Cook, *They Fought Like Demons.*

CHAPTER 5

1. For a full account of the *Monitor* from conception to recovery to conservation, see Anna Gibson Holloway and Jonathan W. White, *"Our Little Monitor": The Greatest Invention of the Civil War* (Kent, Ohio: Kent State University Press, 2018).

2. See Jonathan W. White and Christopher J. Chappell, eds., "Letters

from the *Monitor*: The Civil War Correspondence of Jacob Nicklis, U.S. Navy," *Civil War History* 60 (December 2014): 436–52.

CHAPTER 6

1. David Blight, *Race and Reunion: The Civil War in American Memory* (Cambridge, MA: Harvard University Press, 2003), 68–71. I am grateful for the research assistance of Alexandra Skidmore. Professor Jonathan White and his students also provided much initial help. The editorial suggestions by Emma Reynolds were invaluable.

2. Robert Behre, "Civil War Marker Signals That 'We've come long way,'" *Charleston Post and Courier*, Dec. 31, 2015.

3. On Civil War memorialization in and around Charleston, see Thomas J. Brown, *Civil War Canon: Sites of Confederate Memory in South Carolina* (Chapel Hill: University of North Carolina Press, 2015); and Blain Roberts and Ethan J. Kytle, "Looking the Thing in the Face: Slavery, Race, and the Commemorative Landscape in Charleston, South Carolina, 1865–2010," *Journal of Southern History* 78 (Aug. 2012): 639–84.

4. Deposition of Cuffey Stoney and James Seabrook, July 27, 1868, Pension File of Julia Anna Baker Miller, Case Files of Approved Pension Applications of Widows and Other Dependents of Civil War Veterans, ca. 1861–ca. 1910, RG 15, File 123178, National Archives, Washington, DC (henceforth Julia Miller pension file).

5. *The War of the Rebellion: A Compilation of the Official Records of the Union and Confederate Armies* (Washington: Government Printing Office, 1880–1901), ser. 1, vol. 12, pt. 3, 101–3 (hereafter *OR*).

6. For other accounts of Civil War–related drownings of servicemen and civilians, see Brian Steel Wills, *Inglorious Passages: Noncombat Deaths in the American Civil War* (Lawrence: University Press of Kansas, 2017), esp. 58–61. Wills also includes detailed accounts of the sinking of the *Hunley*, the *Sultana*, and other vessels at 185–219.

7. See, for example, Pension File of Charlotte Maxwell (widow of Esau Fox), Case Files of Approved Pension Applications of Widows and Other Dependents of Civil War Veterans, ca. 1861–ca. 1910, RG 15, File 311040, National Archives, Washington, DC: the file jacket (bearing Pension Office stamp of March 1, 1893) records Esau Fox as "drowned in Stone [*sic*] River, S.C., in line of duty."

8. Court-Martial of Israel T. Halstead, U.S. Navy Courts Martial Records, RG 125, file 3804 (film M273, roll 136), National Archives, Washington, DC. For contemporaneous accounts lacking detail, see *OR*, ser. 1, vol. 35, pt. 1, 36; and *New York Times*, July 15, 1864, p. 5.

9. Court-Martial of Israel T. Halstead, Annex B, Charge and Specification of Charge, August 13, 1864; ibid., trial transcript, p. 60.

10. *New York Times*, July 15, 1864, p. 5.

11. John A. Dahlgren to Benjamin H. Hardwick, July 8, 1864, *OR*, ser.

1, vol. 15, p. 561; John A. Dahlgren to J. G. Foster, Aug. 5, 1864, Letters Received by the Secretary of the Navy, RG 45, National Archives, Washington, DC; John A. Dahlgren, review of verdict, Oct. 2, 1864, Court-Martial of Israel T. Halstead. See Navy Department Pension Office Memo, Jan. 19, 1894, "Service of Israel T Halstead," in U.S. Navy Pension File 11770, RG 15, National Archives, Washington, DC.

12. Register of Deaths, Company E, 21st USCT Infantry, Descriptive Book, Companies A–K, vol. 2, RG 94, National Archives, Washington, DC.

13. William Dudley to Adjutant General, U.S.A., Nov. 28, 1882, in Pension File of Cloy (aka Chloe or Cloe) Mitchell (widow of Flaudo, aka Flanders, Mitchell), Case Files of Approved Pension Applications of Widows and Other Dependents of Civil War Veterans, ca. 1861–ca. 1910, File 456390, RG 15, National Archives, Washington, DC.

14. Testimony of Isaac Seabrook and James Brown, June 3, 1868, Julia Miller pension file.

15. On the challenges and inquisitions faced by African American widows in the pension-application process, see Brandi Clay Brimmer, *Claiming Union Widowhood: Race, Respectability, and Poverty in the Post-Emancipation South* (Durham, NC: Duke University Press, 2020), 77–183; Tera W. Hunter, *Bound in Wedlock: Slave and Free Black Marriage in the Nineteenth Century* (Cambridge, MA: Harvard University Press, 2017), 153–59, 214–17; and Elizabeth Ann Regosin, *Freedom's Promise: Ex-Slave Families and Citizenship in the Age of Emancipation* (Charlottesville: University Press of Virginia, 2002), 85–96.

16. Esau Fox, Descriptive Book, Company E, 21st USCT Infantry, Companies A–K, vol. 2, RG 94, National Archives, Washington, DC.

17. Jacob Smith, Descriptive Book, Company E, 21st USCT Infantry, Companies A–K, vol. 2, RG 94, National Archives, Washington, DC. As Jonathan Lande has argued, desertion and mutiny among African American soldiers were more likely to be acts of legitimate resistance to authoritarian white officers than acts of disloyalty to the Union. See Lande, "Disciplining Freedom: U.S. Army Slave Rebels and Emancipation in the Civil War," PhD diss., Brown University, 2018.

18. Yael A. Sternhell, "Revisionism Reinvented? The Antiwar Turn in Civil War Scholarship," *Journal of the Civil War Era* 3 (June 2013), 239–56.

19. Kenneth E. Foote, *Shadowed Ground: America's Landscapes of Violence and Tragedy* (1997; rev. ed., Austin: University of Texas Press, 2003), 293–95.

20. Jim Downs, "Race," in "Forum: The Future of Civil War Era Studies," *Journal of the Civil War Era* 2 (March 2012): 2.

21. Bruce Suttmeier, "Ethnography as Consumption: Travel and Identity in Oda Makoto's *Nan de mo mite yarō*," *Journal of Japanese Studies* 35 (Winter 2009): 81.

CHAPTER 7

1. Barbara A. Gannon, *The Won Cause: Black and White Comradeship in the Grand Army of the Republic* (Chapel Hill: University of North Carolina Press, 2011), 178.

2. For the upwardly revised estimate of the Civil War's death toll, see J. David Hacker, "A Census-Based Count of the Civil War Dead," *Civil War History* 57 (December 2011): 307–48; Drew Gilpin Faust, *This Republic of Suffering: Death and the American Civil War* (New York: Alfred A. Knopf, 2008); John R. Neff, *Honoring the Civil War Dead: Commemoration and the Problem of Reconciliation* (Lawrence: University Press of Kansas, 2005); Caroline E. Janney, *Remembering the Civil War: Reunion and the Limits of Reconciliation* (Chapel Hill: University of North Carolina Press, 2013); George P. Sanger, ed., *The Statutes at Large, Treaties and Proclamations of the United States of America from March 1871 to March 1873* (Boston: Little, Brown, 1873), 202, 605. For a description of soldiers finding the bones of men killed in previous battles, see Frank Wilkeson, *Recollections of a Private Soldier in the Army of the Potomac* (New York: G. P. Putnam's Sons, 1887), 49.

3. Sanger, *Statutes at Large*, 545; "Proposals: For Head-Stones for National Cemeteries," *Daily State Journal* (Alexandria, VA), July 5, 1873.

4. Sanger, *Statutes at Large*, 345. Black soldiers mainly served in United States Colored Troops (USCT), though some served in state units. The 54th and 55th Massachusetts Infantry, the 5th Massachusetts Cavalry, and the 29th Connecticut Volunteers were composed of Black enlisted men and white officers. By the end of the war, a handful of African Americans received commissions. Some Black soldiers died in African American state units, such as the 1st Kansas (Colored) that later reformed as USCT units. For a summary of Black soldier service and detailed footnotes for further study, see Barbara A. Gannon, "African American Soldiers," *Essential Civil War Curriculum* (website), edited by Virginia Center for Civil War Studies at Virginia Tech, www.essentialcivilwarcurriculum.com/african-american-soldiers.html (accessed May 14, 2019).

5. William M. McKinney, ed., *Federal Statutes Annotated: Containing All the Laws of the United States of a General, Permanent, and Public Nature in Force on the First Day of January 1916* (Long Island, NY: Edward Thompson, 1917), 24. Pierre Nora, a French historian, articulated the idea of a "site of memory." For an introduction, see Pierre Nora, "Between Memory and History: Les Lieux de Mémoire," *Representations* 26 (Spring 1989): 7–24. Scholars have given little attention to Memorial Day and its evolution. For an examination of commemoration in the last decades of the twentieth century, see Gannon, *Won Cause*, 72–81.

6. Mark C. Mollan, "Honoring Our War Dead: The Evolution of the Government Policy on Headstones for Fallen Soldiers and Sailors," *Prologue* 35, no. 1 (Spring 2003), on U.S. National Archives website www.archives.gov/publications/prologue/2003/spring/headstones.html (accessed May 13, 2019).

7. U.S. Department of Veterans Affairs, National Cemetery Administration, *Federal Stewardship of Confederate Dead* (Washington, DC: n.p., 2016), 24. While this book examines Confederate graves under the care of the federal government, it represents an excellent resource on all government-issued headstones.

8. "Available Emblems of Belief for Placement of Government Headstones and Markers," U.S. Department of Veterans Affairs, National Cemetery Administration website, www.cem.va.gov/hmm/emblems.asp (accessed May 13, 2019); www.dailymail.co.uk/news/article-3715233/Faces-American-Muslims-died-fighting-country-9-11-revealed-fallen-soldier-s-father-tells-Trump-sacrificed-no-one.html. For other modern guidance on headstones, see "Headstone and Marker Inscription Abbreviations," U.S. Department of Veterans Affairs, National Cemetery Administration website, www.cem.va.gov/cem/hmm/abbreviations.asp (accessed May 14, 2019). The headstones of soldiers killed in Iraq and Afghanistan indicate their "operation," for example, Operation Iraqi Freedom.

CHAPTER 8

1. Laurel Thatcher Ulrich, *Well-Behaved Women Seldom Make History* (New York: Knopf, 2007), xxxiii; Elizabeth Leland, "Relic Hunter Salutes Union Troops: Discovery of Bones Adds to Legacy of Blacks in Civil War," *Orlando Sentinel*, January 10, 2010.

2. "Black Civil War Troops to Get Recognition in South Carolina," *Los Angeles Times*, January 3, 2010.

3. Stephen Wise, *Gate of Hell: Campaign for Charleston Harbor, 1863–1864* (Columbia: University of South Carolina Press, 1994), 140; Report, John McConihe, August 18, 1863, in *The War of the Rebellion: Official Records of the Civil War*, series I, vol. 28, 366; Luis Emilio, *History of the Fifty-Fourth Regiment of Massachusetts Volunteer Infantry, 1863–1865* (Boston: Boston Book Co., 1891), 110.

4. Emilio, *Fifty-Fourth*, 111; Charles Fox, *Record of the Service of the Fifty-Fifth Regiment of Massachusetts Volunteer Infantry* (Cambridge: Press of J. Wilson and Son, 1868), 11–12; Harriet Alonso, *Growing Up Abolitionist: The Story of the Garrison Children* (Amherst: University of Massachusetts Press, 2002), 166; *Liberator*, September 18, 1863.

5. *Liberator*, September 18, 1863; James H. Gooding to *Mercury*, November 21, 1863, and December 12, 1863, in *On the Altar of Freedom: A Black Civil War Soldier's Letters from the Front*, ed. Virginia Adams (Amherst: University of Massachusetts Press, 1991), 82, 90.

6. Emilio, *Fifty-Fourth*, 339–88, complied a complete list of the

enlisted men in his regiment, including date of enlistment and death, if known.

7. Request, Parkers Brown, December 17, 1863, in Department of the South, Letters Received, Record Group 393, National Archives; Lorien Foote, *Seeking the One Great Remedy: Francis George Shaw and Nineteenth-Century Reform* (Athens: University of Georgia Press, 2000), 120; Susie King Taylor, *Reminiscences of My Life in Camp* (Boston: n.p., 1902), 31.

8. Art Harris, "Salute to a Forgotten Black Regiment, *Washington Post*, May 30, 1989.

9. As did Emilio, Fox, *Fifty-fifth Regiment*, 115–44, compiled a roster of the men who served in the regiment.

10. Harris, "Salute to a Forgotten Black Regiment"; Douglas R. Egerton, *Thunder at the Gates: The Black Civil War Regiments That Redeemed America* (New York: Basic Books, 2016), 154.

CHAPTER 9

1. George H. Fluhr, "Rohman's Inn Shohola Brochure: Where History Happened," Miscellaneous Papers, TS Shohola Railroad and Historical Society, Shohola, PA.

2. *Official Records of the War of the Rebellion*, ser. 2, vol. 7, 488–89 (hereafter *OR*); *Elmira Daily Advertiser*, July 18, 1864; *New York Times*, July 16, 1864; *Tri-States Union* (Port Jervis, NY), July 22, 1864; Joseph C. Boyd, "Shohola Train Wreck," *Chemung County Historical Journal* (June 1964): 1253–55; Edward H. Mott, *Between the Ocean and the Lakes: The Story of the Erie* (New York: Tickner, 1899), 441.

3. *Tri-States Union*, July 22, 1864; George J. Fluhr, *Shohola: History of a Township* (Lackawaxen, PA: Alpha, 1992), 38–39; *Wayne County Herald* (Honesdale, PA), July 21, 1864; Mott, *Story of the Erie*, 442; Michael P. Gray, *The Business of Captivity: Elmira and Its Civil War Prison* (Kent, Ohio: Kent State University Press, 2001), 14–16.

4. Mott, *Story of the Erie*, 442; *Wayne County Herald*, July 21, 1864; Boyd, "Shohola Train Wreck," 1255; *OR*, vol. 7, 489.

5. Mott, *Story of the Erie*, 442; *Wayne County Herald*, July 21, 1864; Boyd, "Shohola Train Wreck," 1255; *OR*, vol. 7, 489.

6. *OR*, vol. 7, 789; Fluhr, *Shohola* 40–41; George H. Fluhr, "Miscellaneous Papers," Shohola Railroad and Historical Society.

7. *Honesdale Republic*, July 21, 1864; *Wayne County Herald*, July 21, 1864; *Tri-States Union*, July 22, 1864.

8. *Tri-States Union*, July 22, 1864.

9. Military service records for Michael Johnson and John D. Johnson (available on Fold3.com); George J. Fluhr, *Shohola Prison Train Wreck: The Great Prison Train Disaster in Pike County, Pennsylvania* (Shohola, PA: Shohola Railroad and Historical Society, 2013), 72–75.

10. *Tri-States Union*, July 22, 1864; *Wayne County Herald*, July 21, 1864. Some researchers have recently contended that Douglass Kent

may have been framed for the accident, and negligence came from railroad supervisors. This larger conspiracy involving the Erie Railroad administrators is still under investigation, and perhaps we will never know who was truly at fault. http://civilwar.gratzpa.org/2014/05/the-great-shohola-train-wreck-was-the-coal-train-in-a-hurry; https://civilwar.gratzpa.org/2014/05/the-great-shohola-train-wreck-two-elusive-participants. Phone interview with Norman Gasbarro, Nov. 3, 2021.

11. Findagrave.com entries for both Johnsons; ancestry.com genealogy created by Kathleen Powers; *Tri-States Union*, July 22, 1864; *Wayne County Herald*, July 21, 1864; https://nccivilwarcenter.org/pvt-franklin-cauble-and-the-great-shohola-pennsylvania-prison-train-wreck-july-15-1864.

12. "Burial Records in the Office of the Quartermaster General," RG 92, entry 89, box 2158, March 9, 1906.

13. For more on Oates, see chapter 1 by Glenn LaFantasie.

14. "Burial Records in the Office of the Quartermaster General," RG 92, entry 89, box 2158, May 28, 1910, Commissioner for Marking Graves; *OR*, ser. 2, vol. 7, 489.

15. Interview with George Fluhr, May 3, 2019; *Pocono Record*, July 15, 2011; https://stickettinn.client.innroad.com.

CHAPTER 10

1. *Mankato Review*, May 12, 1902.

2. *Mankato Free Press*, November 24, November 25, 1912; "Indian Monument Is formally Turned Over to City of Kato," *Mankato Free Press*, December 27, 1912.

3. *Mankato Free Press*, August 15, 1922.

4. The brewery promotion is particularly ironic given that on the day of the execution, the sale and consumption of alcohol was prohibited within a ten-mile radius of the hanging site.

5. "Marker at Hanging Site Draws Varied Comments," *Mankato Free Press*, December 27, 1937.

6. With support from the MSC student senate and the college's president, James Nickerson, the mascot was suspended and then abandoned. MSC was one of the first colleges in the country to change its Indian mascot. *Mankato Free Press*, October 14, 1971; James Nickerson, interview with author, Mankato, March 18, 2008.

7. "Councilman Wants Indian Monument Removed Perhaps to the County Museum," *Mankato Free Press*, February 16, 1971.

8. Marion Struzyk, "Indians Bring Guilt Home," *Mankato State College Daily Reporter*, June 2, 1971.

9. "Dutch Helps Foil Marker Blaze," *Mankato Free Press*, August 17, 1971.

10. For example, see Lloyd Vollmer, letter to the editor, *Mankato Free Press*, February 20, 1970; Bob and Marjorie Olson, letter to the editor,

Mankato Free Press, December 4, 1970; and Dick Meyer, letter to the editor, *Mankato Free Press*, February 19, 1971.

11. "Monument Moved," *Mankato Free Press*, October 18, 1971; Louis "Bud" Lawrence, interviews by author, Mankato, February 21 and March 8, 2006.

12. *Mankato Free Press*, November 9, 1971.

13. Dan Linehan, "Students Search for Missing Monument," *Mankato Free Press*, May 14, 2006; Dan Linehan, "Former Mayor May Know Monument's Whereabouts," *Mankato Free Press*, May 31, 2006.

14. Amanda Dyslin, "Lecture Addresses Mankato Monument Mystery," *Mankato Free Press*, April 5, 2012; Brian Ojanpa, "Ex-Mayor Christ Weighs in on Missing Dakota War Marker," *Mankato Free Press*, April 6, 2012.

15. *Mankato Free Press*, April 13, 2012.

16. "Former Mankato Mayor Explains Disappearance of Dakota 38 Monument," KEYC News 12 telephone interview, February 12, 2016.

17. The reconciliation movement in Mankato is discussed more fully in Melodie Andrews, "The U.S.-Dakota War in Public Memory and Public Space: Mankato's Journey toward Reconciliation," in Annette Atkins and Deborah K. Miller, eds., *The State We're In: Reflections on Minnesota History* (St. Paul: Minnesota Historical Society Press, 2010), 50–59.

18. *Mankato Free Press*, September 20, 1997.

19. "Protestors Call for Renaming of Sibley Park," *Mankato Free Press*, December 29, 2018. For community responses to the protest, see David Brave Heart, Megan Schnitker, Megan Heutmaker, and Scott Zellmer, "Consider Renaming Sibley Park," *Mankato Free Press*, February 1, 2019; Rick Lybeck, "My View: Protest Reminds Social Justice Can Figure into Reconciliation," *Mankato Free Press*, January 13, 2019; Linda Good, "Park's Name Needs to be Addressed," *Mankato Free Press*, February 6, 2019.

CHAPTER 11

1. *Play Ground Daily News*, May 4, 1972, p. 6D.

2. *Atlanta Constitution*, June 11, 1972, quoted in Eugene C. Harter, *The Lost Colony of the Confederacy* (Jackson: University of Mississippi Press, 1985).

3. Todd W. Walstron, *The Southern Exodus: Migration across the Borderlands after the American Civil War* (Lincoln: University of Nebraska Press, 2015), 83–113.

4. On the motivations and influences of those immigrants, see Laura Jarnagin, *A Confluence of Transatlantic Networks: Elites, Capitalism, and Confederate Migration to Brazil* (Tuscaloosa: University of Alabama Press, 2008), especially 111–80.

5. Alan P. Marcus, *Confederate Exodus: Social and Environmental Forces in the Migration of U.S. Southerners to Brazil* (Lincoln: University of Nebraska Press, 2021).

6. On the colony and its founders, see Cyrus B. Dawsey and James M. Dawsey, "The Context of the Southern Emigration to Brazil," in Cyrus B. Dawsey and James M. Dawsey, eds., *The Confederados: Old South Immigrants in Brazil* (Tuscaloosa: University of Alabama Press, 1984), 11–23.

7. For a classic work about that region and the labor strategies employed, see Emilia Viotti da Costa, *The Brazilian Empire: Myths and Histories* (Chicago: University of Chicago Press, 1985), 94–124.

8. For the political deadlocks faced by the Brazilian elites, see Jeffrey D. Needell, *The Party of Order: The Conservatives, the State, and Slavery in the Brazilian Monarchy* (Stanford: Stanford University Press, 2006), especially 167–222.

9. On Mexico's instability, see Erika Pani, "Juárez vs. Maximiliano: Mexico's Experiment with Monarchy," in Don H. Doyle, ed., *American Civil Wars: The United States, Latin America, Europe, and the Crises of the 1860s* (Chapel Hill: University of North Carolina Press, 2017), 167–84. On Cuba, Rebecca J. Scott, *Degrees of Freedom: Louisiana and Cuba after Slavery* (Cambridge, MA: Harvard University Press, 2005), 94–128.

10. Robert E. Conrad, *Destruction of Brazilian Slavery, 1850–1888* (Berkeley: University of California Press, 1972).

11. James W. Webb to William Seward, Petrópolis, January 23, 1862, in Record Group 59, National Archives microfilm publication M121, roll 29, volume 27.

12. Roberto Saba, *American Mirror: The United States and Brazil in the Age of Emancipation* (Princeton: Princeton University Press, 2021), 55–57.

13. From Karlos de Koseritz to Francisco Ignácio Homem de Mello, in *Relatórios da Administração Central das Colônias da província de S. Pedro do Rio Grande do Sul*, Arquivo Nacional, Seção de Obras Raras, p. 48.

14. Asa Thompson Oliver Sr., Find a Grave, www.findagrave.com/memorial/101273620/asa-thompson-oliver (accessed April 18, 2019). On the cemetery, see Cyrus B. Dawsey, "A Community Center Evolution and Significance of the Campo Site in the Santa Bárbara Settlement Área," in Dawsey and Dawsey, *Confederados*, 138–54.

15. A narrative about the crime and the jury can be found at Jair Toledo Veiga, "Tragédia no Sítio da Serra," in *Estudos Regionais Paulistas* (Piracicaba, 1989), 91–102.

16. For a comparison between the War of the Triple Alliance and the American Civil War, see Vitor Izecksohn, *Slavery and War in the Americas: Race, Citizenship and State Building in the United States and Brazil, 1861–1870* (Charlottesville: University of Virginia Press, 2014).

17. For about forty years, the descendants of the Confederate migrants, known as Confederados, have hosted a festival called Festa Confederada (Confederate Party), featuring country music, nineteenth-century

costumes, fried chicken, and "Confederate Dollars" that can be used to purchase items from vendors. The popular event attracts around three thousand people annually. The Confederados insist that their use of the Confederate flag does not celebrate slavery; however, resistance to that symbol has grown since the events in Charlottesville, Virginia, in 2017. During the Festa in 2019, local members of Uninegro, an antiracism organization, protested outside the cemetery. A municipal law enacted in July 2022 bans the use of racist symbols at public celebrations, thus revoking the appropriation of public funds for the Confederate festival. See "New Law Could Mark End of American Confederacy—in Brazil," *Christian Science Monitor*, August 16, 2022, www.csmonitor.com/World/Americas/2022/0816/New-law-could-mark-end-of-American-Confederacy-in-Brazil (accessed October 10, 2022).

CHAPTER 12

1. "Notes on the History of the University Cemetery," Office Administrative Files, RG 3/1/2.781, University of Virginia Small Special Collections (hereafter UVA); *Richmond Enquirer*, April 14 and April 17, 1846.

2. "Notes on the History of the University Cemetery," UVA; President's Commission on Slavery and the University, *Report to President Sullivan* (University of Virginia, 2018), 45–48, Wertenbaker quoted on p. 47.

3. *Richmond Enquirer*, Aug. 20, Oct. 1, 1861; Ervin L. Jordan Jr., *Charlottesville and the University of Virginia in the Civil War* (Lynchburg, VA: H. E. Howard, 1988), 50.

4. Jordan, *Charlottesville*, 55.

5. "Notes on the History of the University Cemetery," UVA; Jordan, *Charlottesville*, 54.

6. Mary Jane Lucas to "Nannie" [Anne Virginia Lucas], June 11, 1862, Lucas-Ashley Papers, Duke University.

7. *Richmond Dispatch*, May 14, 1866.

8. James Montgomery Bailey, *History of Danbury, Conn., 1684–1896* (New York: Burr Printing House, 1896), 419; William A. Croffut, *The Military and Civil History of Connecticut during the War, 1861–65* (New York: L. Bill, 1868), 220; Jordan, *Charlottesville*, 37.

9. *Richmond Dispatch*, May 18, 1866.

10. Caroline E. Janney, *Burying the Dead but Not the Past: Ladies' Memorial Associations and the Lost Cause* (Chapel Hill: University of North Carolina Press, 2008).

11. Sarah Ann Graves Strickler Fife diary, May 10, 1866, UVA; *Richmond Dispatch*, May 14 and 18, 1866.

12. *Richmond Dispatch*, July 6, 1866.

13. *Richmond Dispatch*, Dec. 7, 1866.

14. Stonewall Cemetery Records, Handley Regional Library, Winchester, VA; J. H. Sherrard to Mary Moncure, August 22, 1866, Ashby Family Papers, Virginia Historical Society; *Winchester Times*, October 31, 1866; *Alexandria Gazette*, June 11, 1866. Richard Ashby had

been killed in Maryland and interred there.

15. *Richmond Dispatch*, Dec. 7, 1866; United Daughters of the Confederacy Papers, 1890–1926, Accession #7130-b, UVA.

16. "Looking Back," *Daily Progress*, Oct. 1, 1951.

17. Appeal for Funds for the Soldiers' Cemetery, Ladies Confederate Memorial Association, broadside, 1890, UVA.

18. Appeal for Funds for the Soldiers' Cemetery, UVA.

19. *Baltimore Sun*, July 8, 1893.

20. *Baltimore Sun*, May 24, 1906. Approximately 2,481 university students and alumni fought for the Confederacy while 57 students and 1 professor served in the Union army. Approximately 253 African American men born in Albemarle County served in the United States Colored Troops—some of whom may have been enslaved at UVA (Black Virginians in Blue and UVA Unionists Digital Projects of the John L. Nau III Center for Civil War History, http://naucenter.as.virginia.edu/digital-projects).

21. "30 Unrecorded Graves Discovered at UVA Cemetery," NBC29 News, Nov. 2, 2012; Brendan Wolfe, "Unearthing Slavery at the University of Virginia," *UVA Magazine*, Spring 2013, accessed on Jan. 17, 2019 at http://uvamagazine.org/articles/unearthing_slavery_at_the_university_of_virginia; President's Commission on Slavery, 91.

22. President's Commission on Slavery, https://slavery.virginia.edu/memorial-for-enslaved-laborers (accessed August 10, 2021).

CHAPTER 13

1. U.S. War Department, *War of the Rebellion: Official Records of the Union and Confederate Armies*, ser. 1, vol. 43: 274, 305, 308, 314, 318 (hereafter cited as *Official Records*); Russell F. Weigley, *Quartermaster General of the Union Army: A Biography of M. C. Meigs* (New York: Columbia University Press, 1959), 306–10.

2. Mark E. Neely Jr., *The Civil War and Limits of Destruction* (Cambridge, MA: Harvard University Press, 2007), 133; Mark Grimsley, *The Hard Hand of War: Union Military Policy toward Southern Civilians* (New York: Cambridge University Press, 1995), 167–68. Today a small marker commemorates the spot of John Rodgers Meigs's death along the old Swift Run Gap road.

3. For other examples of the difficulty of identifying soldiers, civilians, and guerrillas in the field, see Brian D. McKnight and Barton A. Myers, eds., *The Guerrilla Hunters: Irregular Conflicts During the Civil War* (Baton Rouge: Louisiana State University Press, 2017); on retaliation during the war and its connection to guerrilla warfare, see Aaron Sheehan-Dean, *The Calculus of Violence: How Americans Fought the Civil War* (Cambridge, MA: Harvard University Press, 2018); Barton A. Myers, *Executing Daniel Bright: Race, Loyalty, and Guerrilla Violence in a Coastal Carolina Community* (Baton Rouge: Louisiana

State University Press, 2009); and Lorien Foote, *Rites of Retaliation: Civilization, Soldiers, and Campaigns in the American Civil War* (Chapel Hill: University of North Carolina Press, 2021).

4. "Diary of John Rodgers Meigs," Montgomery C. Meigs Papers, Library of Congress, Washington, DC, reel 16; Mary A. Giunta, ed., *A Civil War Soldier of Christ and Country: The Selected Correspondence of John Rodgers Meigs, 1859–1864* (Urbana: University of Illinois Press, 2006), 243; S. Emlen Meigs, "Maj. John Rodgers Meigs, Corps of Engineers, U.S. Army," *Professional Memoirs, Corps of Engineers, United States Army, and Engineer Department at Large* 7, no. 35 (September–October, 1915), 644–46.

5. *Daily Intelligencer*, October 8, 1864.

6. Jas. W. Forsyth to J. H. Taylor, October 4, 1864, *Official Records*, ser. 1, vol. 43: 274.

7. John Singleton Mosby, *Mosby's Memoirs: The Memoirs of Colonel John Singleton Mosby* (New York: Barnes and Noble, 2006), 185; James A. Ramage, *Gray Ghost: The Life of Col. John Singleton Mosby* (Chapel Hill: University of North Carolina Press, 1999), 209–10.

8. E. M. Stanton to William H. Seward, October 6, 1864, *Official Records*, ser. 1, vol. 43: 305.

9. E. M. Stanton to J. A. Dix, October 7, 1864, *Official Records*, 43: 318.

10. *Cleveland Morning Leader*, October 11, 1864.

11. Philip H. Sheridan, *Personal Memoirs of P. H. Sheridan* (New York: Charles L. Webster, 1888), 50–52.

12. Giunta, *Civil War Soldier*, 250–51; "The Killing of Lieutenant Meigs, of General Sheridan's Staff—Proof That It Was Done in Fair Combat," *Southern Historical Society Papers* 9, no. 2 (February 1881): 77–79; for another postwar account of the incident, see Peter Cline Kaylor, "The Killing of Lieutenant Meigs, 1864" (circa 1925), *John W. Wayland Virginia Valley Records*, Rockingham Supplement (Shenandoah Publishing House, 1930), 187–96; for another account that attributes the Meigs shooting to Shaver, see *Staunton Spectator*, March 11 and 18, 1879. This account was written by Dr. Thomas H. B. Brown of the *Bridgewater Enterprise* newspaper. The Brown piece records Martin's name incorrectly. For a specific Union army account, see James E. Taylor, *With Sheridan Up the Shenandoah Valley in 1864: Leaves from a Special Artist's Sketchbook and Diary* (Dayton, OH: Morningside Bookshop, 1989). The *Frank Leslie's Illustrated Newspaper* sketch artist attached to Sheridan's 1864 Valley command used Shaver's account and attributed the fatal shot to Shaver in his work as well. Taylor, after careful investigation, including walking the ground of the incident with a member of Shaver's regiment postwar, concluded that Meigs's death was not an assassination, as Sheridan had maintained after the war.

13. Giunta, *Civil War Soldier*, 250–51; "The Killing of Lieutenant Meigs," 77–79.

14. Giunta, *Civil War Soldier*, 249–53.

15. *National Republican*, June 8, 1868.

16. John Rodgers Meigs, Find a Grave, www.findagrave.com/memorial/4472/john-rodgers-meigs (accessed December 17, 2018); Robert M. Poole, *On Hallowed Ground: The Story of Arlington National Cemetery* (New York: Bloomsbury, 2010); Micki McElya, *The Politics of Mourning: A Death and Honor in Arlington National Cemetery* (Cambridge, MA: Harvard University Press, 2016).

17. Diary of John Rodgers Meigs, Montgomery C. Meigs Papers, Library of Congress, Washington, DC, reel 16.

18. Craig Swain, ed. "The Death of Lt. Meigs," www.hmdb.org/marker.asp?marker=15121 (accessed December 17, 2018).

19. Montgomery Cunningham Meigs, Find a Grave, www.findagrave.com/memorial/2287/montgomery-cunningham-meigs (accessed December 17, 2018).

20. On Montgomery C. Meigs, see Robert O'Harrow Jr., *The Quartermaster: Montgomery C. Meigs, Lincoln's General, Master Builder of the Union Army* (New York: Simon & Schuster, 2016); Russell F. Weigley, *Quartermaster General of Union Army: Biography of M.C. Meigs* (New York: Columbia University Press, 1959); Poole, *On Hallowed Ground*, 93.

21. S. Emlen Meigs, "Maj. John Rodgers Meigs," 644–46.

CHAPTER 14

1. The author wishes to acknowledge the generous assistance of Professor Lucas E. Morel of Washington and Lee University, and Dr. Lynn Rainville, professor of anthropology and director of institutional history and the museums at the university.

2. Donald Hopkins, *Robert E. Lee in War and Peace: The Photographic History of a Confederate and American Icon* (El Dorado Hills, CA: Savas Beatie, 2013), 142–45; Mary Bandy Daughtry, *Gray Cavalier: The Life and Wars of General W. H. F. "Rooney" Lee* (Cambridge, MA: Da Capo Press, 2002), 49–50; Robert E. Lee to Mary Custis Lee (November 8, 1856, April 1 and 17, May 2, June 3, 1860), to William Henry Fitzhugh Lee (April 2, 1860), to Annie Carter Lee (August 27, 1860), and to Eleanor Agnes Lee (June 8, 1860), in Francis Ray Adams, "An Annotated Edition of the Personal Letters of Robert E. Lee, April 1855–April 1861," PhD diss., University of Maryland, 1955, 1:202, 2:595, 600, 617, 626, 630, 642, 684.

3. Rose Mortimer Ellzey MacDonald, *Mrs. Robert E. Lee* (New York: Ginn, 1939), 166; John Perry, *Lady of Arlington: The Life of Mrs. Robert E. Lee* (Sisters, OR: Multnomah Press, 2001), 251, 264; REL to MCL (March 27 and April 5, 1863), in Clifford Dowdey and L. H. Manarin, eds., *Wartime Papers of Robert E. Lee* (Boston: Little, Brown, 1961), 419, 428; William Preston Johnston, in J. W. Jones, *Personal Reminiscences, Anecdotes, and Letters of Gen. Robert E. Lee* (New York: D. Appleton,

1875), 444; Richard A. Reinhart, "Robert E. Lee's Right Ear and the Relation of Earlobe Crease to Coronary Artery Disease," *American Journal of Cardiology* 120 (May 22, 2017): 327–30; and "Historical Implications of a Failing Heart: Robert E. Lee's Medical History in Context of Heart Disease, Medical Education and the Practice of Medicine in the Nineteenth Century," National Museum of Civil War Medicine, www.civilwarmed.org/surgeons-call/lee/#_edn44.

4. REL to the Trustees of Washington College (August 24, 1865), in Robert E. Lee Jr., *Recollections and Letters of General Robert E. Lee* (New York: Doubleday, Page, 1904), 181–82; Washington College Trustee Minute Book, August 4, 1865, p. 149; and Washington College Records of Board of Trustees, Feb. 21, 1845–Sept. 1873, pp. 152, 153–54, 165–66 (September 20 and October 2, 1865), Special Collections, Leyburn Library, Washington and Lee University; Jones, *Personal Reminiscences*, 86; MCL to Emily Mason, in MacDonald, *Mrs. Robert E. Lee*, 204.

5. REL to G. W. Leyburn, in Jones, *Personal Reminiscences*, 214; "To the Hon. John W. Brockenbrough" (April 26, 1866, and June 19, 1867), Washington College Trustee Minute Book, Leyburn Library; Catharine Roach, "Robert E. Lee's Financial Impact on Washington College," *Washington and Lee Spectator* (Fall 2014): 9; *Richmond Times*, August 31, 1866.

6. REL to Robert E. Lee Jr. (June 8, 1867, in *Recollections and Letters*, 260; REL to Charles Carter Lee (September 16, 1867) and to Edward Lee Childe (January 16, 1868), Papers of the Lee Family, Jessie Ball duPont Library, Stratford Hall; REL to Martha Williams (October 4, 1867), in *"To Markie": The Letters of Robert E. Lee to Martha Custis Williams*, ed. Avery Craven (Cambridge, MA: Harvard University Press, 1933), 76; REL to Prof. J. L. Campbell (September 9, 1867) and to CCL (September 16, 1867), Leyburn Library; REL to Edward Lee Childe (February 19 and March 8, 1870), Papers of the Lee Family, Jessie Ball duPont Library, Stratford Hall; Charles Bracelen Flood, *Lee: The Last Years* (Boston: Houghton Mifflin, 1981), 223.

7. J. Rainey to brother (March 1870), in J. Rainey Correspondence, Library of Congress; William Preston Johnson, "Memoranda of Conversations with General R. E. Lee" (March 18, 1870), in Gary W. Gallagher, ed. *Lee the Soldier* (Lincoln: University of Nebraska Press, 1996), 32; Trustee Minutes, April 19, 1870, Washington College Records of Board of Trustees, Feb. 21, 1845–Sept. 1873 (p. 269), Leyburn Library; REL to Mildred Childe Lee (March 21, 1870) and WHFL (March 22, 1870) in Robert E. Lee Jr., *Recollections and Letters*, 384–87.

8. Johnston, "Death and Funeral of General Lee," in Franklin L. Riley, ed., *General Robert E. Lee after Appomattox* (New York: Macmillan, 1922), 207.

9. "Our Great Loss," *Charleston Daily News,* October 14, 1870; "Latest from Lexington," *Richmond Dispatch,* October 15, 1870; Marshall

Fishwick, *Lee after the War* (New York: Dodd, Mead, 1963), 219–20.

10. William Preston Johnson, "Death and Funeral of General Lee," 215–21; "The Funeral of Gen. Lee," *Richmond Dispatch*, October 17, 1870; John Esten Cooke, *A Life of Gen. Robert E. Lee* (New York: D. Appleton, 1871), 501–5; "The Funeral Services of General Robert Edward Lee, at Lexington, Va.," *Frank Leslie's Illustrated Magazine*, November 5, 1870.

11. "Letter from Lexington," *Richmond Dispatch*, October 20, 1870.

12. Carolyn S. Kazmierczak, "Robert E. Lee and His Horse Traveller," *HistoryNet*, www.historynet.com/robert-e-lees-horse-traveller.htm.

13. Douglas W. Bostick, *Memorializing Robert E. Lee: The Story of Lee Chapel* (Charleston: Joggling Board, 2005), 43, 51; Christopher R. Lawton, "Constructing the Cause, Bridging the Divide: Lee's Tomb at Washington College," *Southern Cultures* 15 (Summer 2009): 12, 20–22; "The History of the Flags in Lee Chapel and Museum," https://my.wlu.edu/lee-chapel-and-museum/about-the-chapel/history-of-lee-chapel-flags.

14. Daniel, "Oration," in *Ceremonies Connected with the Inauguration of the Mausoleum and the Unveiling of the Recumbent Figure of General Robert Edward Lee at Washington & Lee University, June 28, 1883* (Richmond: West Johnston, 1883); "A Salute to the Day," *Richmond Dispatch*, June 28, 1883.

15. "Bombast," *New National Era*, November 10, 1870; David W. Blight, *Frederick Douglass' Civil War: Keeping Faith in Jubilee* (Baton Rouge: Louisiana State University Press, 1989), 229; Edmunds, in "Mrs. R. E. Lee," *Congressional Globe*, 41st Congress, 3rd session (December 13, 1870), 74; "The Death of General Lee," *Chicago Tribune*, October 14, 1870; "The Grief at Lee's Death," *Atlanta Constitution*, October 15, 1870; Michael A. Ross, "The Commemoration of Robert E. Lee's Death and the Obstruction of Reconstruction in New Orleans," *Civil War History* 51 (June 2005): 135, 148.

16. "Views in Lexington, Virginia," *Frank Leslie's Illustrated Magazine*, June 30, 1883; Matthew Haag, "Dallas Can Remove Robert E. Lee Statue, Judge Rules," *New York Times*, September 7, 2017; Nicholas Fandos, "Baltimore Mayor Had Statues Removed in 'Best Interest of My City,'" *New York Times* (August 16, 2017); Gregory S. Schneider, "Northam Calls Lee Statues 'Offensive,' Promotes Efforts to Boost Black History," *Washington Post*, January 9, 2020.

17. REL to MCL, December 27, 1856, in "Personal Letters," 1:245.

18. "Lee and His Slaves," *New-York Tribune*, March 26, 1866. Slavery, and especially the whipping incident, would only emerge as problems for the Lee legacy and Lee biographers many years after Lee's death. In James McCabe's *Life and Campaigns of General Robert E. Lee* (1866), the longest references to slavery emerge from Lee's correspondence about exchanges of black prisoners of war in 1864, about the proposed emancipation of southern slaves as a condition for their enlistment in 1865, and about his argument to Francis Preston Blair that slavery was

no part of his reasons for declining command of federal forces in 1861. John Esten Cooke's *A Life of Gen. Robert E. Lee* (1871) was even more sparing on Lee's connection to slavery. Cooke quoted Lee's 1856 letter on the "moral & political evil" of slavery but dismissed any further discussion of slavery as "a worn-out and wearisome story" (24). Emily Mason's *Popular Life of Gen. Robert Edward Lee* (1872) only cites the 1856 letter. Edward Lee Childe's *The Life and Campaigns of General Lee* (1873) also quoted the 1856 letter but added a denial that slavery "was the real subject of the strife" between North and South (17). One of the most influential of the nineteenth-century Lee biographers, J. William Jones, in his *Personal Reminiscences of General Robert E. Lee* (1874), was the sparest of all, citing only Lee's response to Blair and an obituary from the *New York Herald,* which claimed that "as a slaveholder, he was beloved by his slaves for his kindness and consideration" (63).

Not until Fitzhugh Lee's *General Lee* (1894) was there even so much as an oblique reference to the slaves of the Custis estate, and not until Robert E. Lee Jr.'s *Recollections and Letters of General Robert E. Lee* in 1904 was there any substantial allusion to his father having been made executor of George Washington Parke Custis's will, with responsibility for emancipating the Custis slaves "after the expiration of so many years"—and even that only served to open an opportunity to quote from one of his father's letters, insisting on the necessity of the emancipation (89–90). In 1908 Thomas Nelson Page waved off the Custis slaves in a single sentence and went on to compare Lee favorably (and inaccurately) with Ulysses Grant, who "is said to have continued in the possession of slaves until they were emancipated by the Government of the United States" (*Robert E. Lee: The Southerner*, 31, 46).

Not until the first volume of Douglas Southall Freeman's *R. E. Lee* in 1934 was the whipping episode finally unveiled, and even then only as an example of how "false stories were spread" (390–92). Margaret Sanborn's admirable (and neglected) *Robert E. Lee: A Portrait* (1966) spoke candidly about the Custis slaves but could not admit that the whipping took place. ("To have whipped a slave would have been as abhorrent to Lee as to his accusers"). From that point on, however, it became impossible to portray Lee in the old fashion as the kindly and indulgent master who embraced slavery only with his fingertips. Alan Nolan's *Lee Considered: General Robert E. Lee and Civil War History* (1991) devoted an entire chapter to "Lee and the Peculiar Institution." Michael Fellman's *The Making of Robert E. Lee* (2000) also included a chapter on both Lee and slavery and the whipping incident, and Elizabeth Brown Pryor's *Reading the Man: A Portrait of Robert E. Lee through His Private Letters* (2007) was almost cinematic in her description of the whipping (269–73). Even Emory Thomas's more temperate treatment of Lee and slavery in *Robert E. Lee: A Biography* (1995) could not dodge Lee's involvement with slavery and the whipping incident (176–78). It has now become a fixed star in the Lee constellation.

19. REL to Robert E. Lee Jr. (March 12, 1868), in Robert E. Lee Jr., *Recollections and Letters*, 306.

20. Scott Jaschik, "Race, History and Robert E. Lee," *Inside Higher Ed* (May 29, 2018); Andrew Adkins, "Report Calls for Major Changes in How W&L Teaches and Presents Its History," *Roanoke Times*, May 18, 2018; Peter J. Boyer, "The Complicated History of Washington & Lee University," *Weekly Standard*, November 19, 2018; Toni Locy, "Letting Go of Robert E. Lee at Washington and Lee University," *The Nation*, June 25, 2020; "Brandon Hasbrouck, "Both Namesakes of Washington and Lee University Perpetrated Racial Terror. The School Should Be Renamed," *Washington Post*, July 4, 2020; Elizabeth Bell, "Washington and Lee Faculty Vote to Change the University's Name," *Richmond Times-Dispatch*, July 6, 2020.

21. Johnny Diaz, "Board of Washington and Lee University Votes to Keep Lee's Name," *New York Times*, June 4, 2021, www.nytimes.com/2021/06/04/us/washington-lee-university-names.html.

22. Pat Thomas, "No Name Change at Washington and Lee," WDBJ-7, June 4, 2021, www.wdbj7.com/2021/06/04/washington-and-lee-university-will-not-change-name.

23. Dean Golembeski, "Washington and Lee Keeps Name, Black Alumni React," *Best Colleges*, June 8, 2021, www.bestcolleges.com/blog/washington-and-lee-university-keeps-name; Sandy Hausman and Nick Gilmore, "Washington & Lee University to Keep Its Name," WVTF, June 4, 2021, www.wvtf.org/news/2021-06-04/washington-lee-university-to-keep-its-name; Brandon Hasbrouck, "White Supremacy Was on Trial at Washington and Lee University. It Won," *Slate*, June 7, 2021, https://slate.com/news-and-politics/2021/06/white-supremacy-washington-and-lee-robert.html.

CHAPTER 15

1. Ruth Ann Stewart and David M. Kahn, *Richard T. Greener, His Life and Work* (New York: National Park Service, 1980).

2. See Katherine Reynolds Chaddock, *Uncompromising Activist: Richard Greener, First Black Graduate of Harvard College* (Baltimore: Johns Hopkins University Press, 2017).

3. Frederick Grant, quoted in Marquis James, *Merchant Adventurer: The Story of W. R. Grace* (Wilmington, DE: Scholarly Resources Books, 1993), 202.

4. Richard T. Greener, "First Meeting of the Committee of 100," *Grant Monument Association Minute Book, No. 1*, July 28, 1885.

5. "Act of the Majority of the Grant Association," March 3, 1886, National Park Service, Grant Monument Association, Manhattan Historical Sites Archive.

6. H. W. Brands, *The Man Who Saved the Union: Ulysses Grant in*

War and Peace (New York: Doubleday, 2012), 634–35.

7. See Chaddock, *Uncompromising Activist*, 108–10.

8. Howard Dodson, Christopher Moore, and Roberta Yancy, *The Black New Yorkers* (New York: John Wiley and Sons, 2000), 222–24.

9. Richard T. Greener to Sir, April 12, 1890, form letter to five architects; Stewart and Kahn, *Richard T. Greener*, 13–14.

10. *Congressional Record*, 51st U.S. Congress, 2nd session (Dec. 10, 1890), 238, 240, 241.

11. "President Grace Resigns," *New York Times*, Nov. 27, 1891; "Secretary Greener Out," *New York Age*, Feb. 22, 1892.

12. See Chaddock, *Uncompromising Activist*, 116.

13. "The Negro Left Out in the Cold," *Charleston (SC) Sunday News*, May 16, 1897.

14. See Chaddock, *Uncompromising Activist*, 126–60.

CHAPTER 16

1. There is no Wharton biography currently. General sketches of his life may be found in Ezra J. Warner, *Generals in Gray* (Baton Rouge: Louisiana State University Press, 1959), 331; and William C. Davis, "Gabriel Colvin Wharton," in *The Confederate General*, ed. William C. Davis (Harrisburg, PA: National Historical Society, 1991), 120–21.

2. Biographical detail on Ann "Nannie" Radford may be found in Minnie Adams Fitting, *The Radford Letters: A Radford Family History* (Blacksburg, VA: Pocahontas Press, 2001), *passim.*

3. For decades this correspondence lay unknown in the attic of the Whartons' home ("Glencoe," in Radford, Virginia). Discovered in 1988, it is now in the hands of their great-great-granddaughter Susan Bell of Wellesley, MA. Substantial portions are available in William C. Davis and Sue Heth Bell, eds., *The Whartons' War: The Civil War Correspondence of General Gabriel C. Wharton and Anne Radford Wharton, 1863–1865* (Chapel Hill: University of North Carolina Press, 2022).

CHAPTER 17

1. "War Record of Old Baldy," *The Pony Express* (Placerville, CA) 17, no. 8 (January 1951): 7.

2. "War Record of Old Baldy," George Gordon Meade Collection, microfilm roll 12, U.S. Army Heritage and Education Center, Carlisle, Pennsylvania (all notes hereinafter from microfilm roll 12 cited as USAHEC); Michael A. Cavanaugh Jr., "Old Baldy: General George Gordon Meade's War Horse," *North-South Trader*, March–April 1982, 12; Anthony Waskie, "Old Baldy: General George Gordon Meade's War Horse and the Story of the Post #2 Mule," self-published (document in possession of the author), available at the General Meade Society's website: https://generalmeadesociety.org/old-baldy.

3. George Meade to the Commander of the George G. Meade Post, no.

1, March 12, 1883, George Gordon Meade Post No. 1 Records (Collection 1805.004.001), box 1, Union League of Philadelphia, Philadelphia, PA (all notes hereinafter cited as George Meade, GAR Post, Union League); *Providence Evening Press*, July 31, 1861. Colonel Hunter was then commanding a cavalry division.

4. George Meade, GAR Post, Union League; Waskie, "Old Baldy"; George Gordon Meade to John Sergeant Meade, November 14, 1861, George G. Meade Collection (Collection 0410), series 1, box 1, Historical Society of Pennsylvania, Philadelphia (all notes hereinafter cited as GGM to JSM, HSP). Meade was stationed in Maryland at this time and was commanding a brigade of Pennsylvania Reserves.

5. "General Meade's Charger," *Washington Standard* (Olympia, WA), February 9, 1883; Waskie, "Old Baldy." A canter is a controlled gait that is faster than a trot but slower than a gallop.

6. GGM to JSM, November 14, 1861; George Gordon Meade to Margaretta Meade, December 2, 1861, George G. Meade Collection (Collection 0410), series 1, box 1, Historical Society of Pennsylvania, Philadelphia (all notes hereinafter cited as GGM to MM, HSP). During the course of the war, Meade owned at least three horses, Baldy, Blacky, and a brown Morgan. Later in the winter of 1861, Meade purchased Blacky, "a fine black horse," from a trader who came to the army's camp.

7. GGM to MM, August 31, 1862, HSP; Waskie, "Old Baldy." Waskie cites a privately held letter from Meade to Samuel Ringwalt recounting his wounding at the battle of Glendale on June 30, 1862. General Meade was wounded during the battle but was riding Blacky, not Baldy. Meade noted that Blacky's wound was so severe that it remained open for eighteen months until it fully healed.

8. GGM to MM, September 18, 1862, HSP.

9. "War Record of Old Baldy," *The Pony Express* (Placerville, CA) 17, no. 8 (January 1951): 7; "Old War Horses," *Republican and Herald* (Pottsville, PA), May 24, 1892; "War Record of Old Baldy," USAHEC.

10. GGM to MM, September 23, 1862, HSP.

11. Harry W. Pfanz, *Gettysburg: The Second Day* (Chapel Hill: University of North Carolina Press, 1987), 142–44; Paul G. Oliver to Col. George G. Meade Jr., May 16, 1882, Gettysburg National Military Park Library, Gettysburg, Pennsylvania. There is considerable confusion in both the primary and secondary accounts as to when Baldy was injured during the battle of Gettysburg. On the afternoon of July 2, Gen. Daniel Sickles ordered the forward movement of his Third Corps to a new position that occupied the ground from Devil's Den, through the Wheatfield and Peach Orchard, and then running parallel to Emmitsburg Road. Meade did not approve of this forward movement and struggled to bolster the Third Corps line against the wave of Confederate assaults. Shortly after 3:00, Meade, accompanied by his chief engineer, Gen. Gouverneur K. Warren, rode along Cemetery Ridge toward Little Round Top to survey the terrain. At this time, Baldy was not saddled

or ready for immediate use. Gen. Alfred Pleasonton, the cavalry commander, loaned Meade his horse, Bill. Reportedly, Bill plunged under the Confederate fire, and Meade, unaccustomed to riding the horse, lurched from the saddle. Paul Oliver, one of Meade's aides, recounted Meade having a conversation with Gen. John Newton, then commanding the First Corps, as an artillery shell exploded near the general. Oliver did not indicate that this shell wounded Baldy.

12. George Meade, GAR Post, Union League; Sgt. McEarney, Chief of Mounted Orderlies, Army of the Potomac, August 13, 1894, folder 16, box 2, George G. Meade Collection, Historical Society of Pennsylvania, Philadelphia.

13. GGM to MM, July 8, 1863, HSP.

14. GGM to MM, April 24, 1864, HSP; George Meade, GAR Post, Union League; "War Record of Old Baldy," USAHEC. Melloy served in the 1st Pennsylvania Cavalry.

15. GGM to MM, September 24, 1861, HSP; George Meade, GAR Post, Union League; Freeman Cleaves, *Meade of Gettysburg* (Norman: University of Oklahoma Press, 1960), 293. Ringwalt had been assigned to Meade as a quartermaster in September 1861. Cleaves stated that Meade paid three dollars per week in the fall and winter season when Ringwalt provided oats for Baldy, and one dollar per week during the grazing season.

16. GGM to MM, July 7, 1864, HSP.

17. Cleaves, *Meade of Gettysburg*, 339. Among those who ascribe at least fourteen wounds to Baldy, and record him traveling with Meade through the Overland Campaign, include DiFebo in "Old Baldy: A Horse's Tale," Worman in *Civil War Animal Heroes*, and Cavanaugh in "Old Baldy." These authors fail to read Meade's letters, which, as noted, indicate that the general sent Baldy to Pennsylvania in April 1864. While Baldy recovered from his war wounds on the farm in Downingtown, Meade relied on the brown Morgan and Blacky, his show horse. In fact, in the Grand Review of the Armies, May 23–24, 1865, Meade rode Blacky.

18. George Meade, GAR Post, Union League; *Daily City News* (New Castle, PA), December 19, 1882. The Meade family resided at a home on Delancey Street, the house given to his wife during the war, and they spent their summers in a cottage in Jenkintown, north of the city.

19. "Unveiling of the Equestrian Statue of Major General George Gordon Meade, October 18, 1887," Fairmount Park Art Association (Philadelphia: Allen, Lane & Scott, 1887), 14. Beginning in 1866, Meade served as a commissioner at Fairmount Park.

20. "General Meade's Charger," *Washington Standard* (Olympia, WA), February 9, 1883.

21. Notable mourners included President Ulysses S. Grant, Philip Sheridan, Andrew Humphreys, and the governor of Pennsylvania.

22. "An Equine Hero," *Brainerd Dispatch* (Brainerd, MN), July 29, 1916; "Old Baldy," *Brown County* (Hiawatha, KS), December 25, 1879;

Joseph Ripley Chandler Ward, *History of George G. Meade Post No. One, Department of Pennsylvania, Grand Army of the Republic* (Philadelphia, 1889), 81–83. This parade was in honor of President Grant, who had just returned from his world tour.

23. "General Meade's Charger," *Washington Standard* (Olympia, WA), February 9, 1883.

24. James C. Wray, "Securing the Head of Major General George G. Meade's Veteran War Horse," George Gordon Meade Post No. 1 Records (Collection 1805.004.001), box 1, Union League of Philadelphia, Philadelphia, (all notes hereinafter cited as Wray, Union League). Henrietta Meade wrote to Davis.

25. Wray, Union League. Awash in holiday sentiment, the two men presented Davis's son a copy of *Robinson Crusoe* and his wife a box of fine confectionery before departing. It seems that in addition to Baldy's head, the veterans also secured his front two hooves. One hoof is on display at the Old York Road Historical Society in Jenkintown, Pennsylvania, and the location of the second hoof is unknown (Waskie, "Old Baldy").

26. Wray, Union League; Resolution, George G. Meade Post No. 1, March 4, 1883, George Gordon Meade Post No. 1 Records (Collection 1805.004.001), box 1, Union League of Philadelphia, Philadelphia.

27. "General Meade's Charger," *Washington Standard* (Olympia, WA), February 9, 1883; "Warhorse, Old Baldy to Get Monument," *Gettysburg Times*, July 5, 1932.

28. "General Meade's Old War Horse," *Hartford Courant*, March 2, 1883.

29. "Old Baldy Returns to Philadelphia Museum," *Philadelphia Inquirer*, September 27, 2010; Dane DiFebo, "Old Baldy: A Horse's Tale," in *Pennsylvania Magazine of History and Biography* 135 (October 2011): 550–52; Gene C. Armistead, *Horses and Mules in the Civil War: A Complete History with a Roster of More Than 700 Horses* (Jefferson, NC: McFarland Press, 2013), 110–11; Waskie, "Old Baldy"; Linda Wheeler, "Resolution on Ownership of Old Baldy," *Washington Post*, March 25, 2010.

30. "Old Baldy Returns to Philadelphia Museum," *Philadelphia Inquirer*, September 27, 2010; DiFebo, "Old Baldy," 550–52; Armistead, *Horses and Mules in the Civil War*, 110–11; Waskie, "Old Baldy." For more information on the GAR Museum in Philadelphia, see https://garmuslib.org.

31. Drew Gilpin Faust, "Equine Relics of the Civil War," in *Southern Cultures: The Fifteenth Anniversary Reader* (Chapel Hill: University of North Carolina Press, 2008), 392; Earl J. Hess, "Revitalizing Traditional Military History in the Current Age of Civil War Studies," in *Upon the Fields of Battle: Essays on the Military History of America's Civil War*, ed. Andrew S. Bledsoe and Andrew F. Lang (Baton Rouge: Louisiana State University Press, 2018), 20–42; Earl J. Hess, ed., *Animal Histories*

of the Civil War Era (Baton Rouge: Louisiana State University Press, 2022).

32. Faust, "Equine Relics of the Civil War," 393.

33. Charles G. Worman, *Civil War Animal Heroes: Mascots, Pets and War Horses* (Lynchburg, VA: Schroeder, 2011), 150–52, 177–78. Traveller also participated in the funeral procession for his master. Traveller stepped on a nail and contracted tetanus, and consequently had to be put down. Little Sorrell's bones are buried on the parade grounds at VMI.

CHAPTER 18

1. I am indebted to the friendship of John Cross, secretary of development and college relations at Bowdoin College, for information about all things Chamberlain, and especially the second gravestone.

2. A. Wilson Greene, *From the Crossing of the James to the Crater*. Vol. 1 of *A Campaign of Giants: The Battle for Petersburg* (Chapel Hill: University of North Carolina Press, 2018), 192.

3. Alice Rains Trulock, *In the Hands of Providence: Joshua L. Chamberlain and the American Civil War* (Chapel Hill: University of North Carolina Press, 1992), 208–10.

4. OR 40 (2); 216–17, 236. Grant forwarded his order to Secretary of War Edwin Stanton.

5. Joshua Lawrence Chamberlain to Frances Caroline Adams, June 19, 1864, Special Collections, Hawthorne-Longfellow Library, Bowdoin College.

6. Robert F. Reilly, MD, "Medical and Surgical Care During the American Civil War, 1861–1865," *Baylor University Medical Center Proceedings* 29, no. 2 (2016): 138.

7. For an excellent essay on invisible and visible wounds pertaining to Chamberlain, see Sarah Handley-Cousins, "Wrestling at the Gates of Death: Joshua Lawrence Chamberlain and Nonvisible Disability in the Post–Civil War North," *Journal of the Civil War Era* 6 (June 2016), 220–42.

8. Diane Monroe Smith, *Fanny and Joshua: The Enigmatic Lives of Frances Caroline Adams and Joshua Lawrence Chamberlain* (Gettysburg, PA: Thomas Publications, 1999), 173.

9. Smith, *Fanny and Joshua*, 70–71.

10. Joshua Lawrence Chamberlain to Governor Israel Washburn Jr., July 14, 1862, Maine State Archives, Augusta, Maine.

11. James M. McPherson, *For Cause and Comrade: Why Men Fought in the Civil War* (New York: Oxford University Press, 1997), viii.

12. Joshua Lawrence Chamberlain to Governor Israel Washburn, July 14, 1862, Maine State Archives.

13. Trulock, *In the Hands of Providence*, 304–7. I am grateful to Patrick A. Schroeder, Appomattox Court House National Historical Park historian, for helping me sort out the truth and fiction of this event.

14. See Stephen Cushman's chapter, "Joshua Lawrence Chamberlain Repeats Appomattox," in *Belligerent Muse: Five Northern Writers and How They Shaped Our Understanding of the Civil War* (Chapel Hill: University of North Carolina Press, 2014), 147–63. Cushman examines the changes in the various versions of Chamberlain's lectures and writings on the surrender at Appomattox.

15. Joshua Lawrence Chamberlain, "The New Education," Presidential Inauguration Address, Bowdoin College, September 1871, 1–2.

16. On the "Drill Rebellion," see Charles C. Calhoun, *A Small College in Maine: Two Hundred Years of Bowdoin* (Brunswick, ME: Bowdoin College, 1993), 191–95.

17. Trulock, *In the Hands of Providence,* 376.

18. Smith, *Fanny and Joshua,* 351–52.

19. Trulock, *In the Hands of Providence,* 378–79.

CHAPTER 19

1. On John Brown, see David S. Reynolds, *John Brown, Abolitionist: The Man Who Killed Slavery, Sparked the Civil War, and Seeded Civil Rights* (New York: Vintage Books, 2005); and on Andrew see Henry Greenleaf Pearson, *The Life of John A. Andrew: Governor of Massachusetts, 1861–1865* (Boston: Houghton, Mifflin, 1904); Stephen D. Engle, "'Under Full Sail': John Andrew, Abraham Lincoln, and Standing by the Union," *Massachusetts Historical Review* 19 (2017): 43–82; Julia Ward Howe, "The Great Agitation. IV. Recollections of the Antislavery Struggle," *The Cosmopolitan: A Monthly Illustrated Magazine* 7 (July 1889): 278–85; *Report of the Select Committee of the Senate Appointed to Inquire into the Late Invasion and Seizure of the Public Property at Harpers Ferry*, Committee no. 278, 36th Congress, 1st session (Washington, DC, 1860). Known as the Mason Committee, members interviewed Andrew along with several other political leaders, including William Seward and Henry Wilson.

2. *Appleton's Journal of Literature, Science, and Art* 14 (October 1875): 441; Luther Stephenson Jr., *Addresses and Papers* (Togus, ME: 1885), 18–23; *Hingham Journal*, May 13, 2010; John M. Hamrogue, "John A. Andrew: Abolitionist Governor, 1861–1865," (PhD diss., Fordham University, 1974), 250–52.

3. *Speeches of John A. Andrew at Hingham and Boston Together with His Testimony before the Harper's Ferry Committee of the Senate, in Relation to John Brown* (Boston: Republican State Committee, 1860).

4. Frederic H. Hedge, "John Albion Andrew," *Monthly Religious Magazine* 38 (Dec. 1867): 435; *Boston Daily Advertiser*, Oct. 31, 1867; *The Independent*, Nov. 7, 1867; Hamrogue, "John A. Andrew," 252; *Appleton's Journal*, 441; *Massachusetts Ploughman and New England Journal of Agriculture*, Nov. 6, 1869; Mount Auburn Cemetery Interment Records, November 2, 1867; *New York Observer and Chronicle*, Nov. 7, 1867; Pearson, *The Life of John A. Andrew*, 2:329–30.

5. Stephenson, *Addresses and Papers*, 18–23; James L. Bowen, *Massachusetts in the War, 1861–1865* (Springfield, MA: Clark W. Bryan, 1889), 983.

6. Stephenson, *Addresses and Papers*, 18–23; *Hingham Journal*, May 13, 2010; Bowen, *Massachusetts in the War*, 983; *Appleton's Journal*, 441.

7. Stephenson, *Addresses and Papers*, 18–23; Patrick Browne, "Grave of Governor John Andrew," *Historical Digression Blog*, Feb. 8, 2012; Thomas Bouve et. al., *History of the Town of Hingham, Massachusetts* (Hingham, MA: Hingham Historical Society, 1893), 1:347; *The Independent*, Nov. 11, 1875.

8. "John Albion Andrew," *Massachusetts Civil War Monuments Project Blog*, Feb. 4, 2018; *Hingham Journal*, May 13, 2010; Browne, "Grave of Governor John Andrew," Feb. 8, 2012; Bouve, *History of the Town of Hingham, Massachusetts*, 1:347; Bowen, *Massachusetts in the War*, 983; Stephenson, *Addresses and Papers*, 18–23; *The Aldine: The Art Journal of America*, Jan. 1, 1879; *The Independent*, Nov. 11, 1875.

9. *Appleton's Journal*, 441; *Massachusetts Ploughman and New England Journal of Agriculture*, Nov. 6, 1869; Pearson, *The Life of John A. Andrew*, 2:239–30; Hamrogue, "John A. Andrew," 252.

10. Laura Elizabeth Howe, Richards Maud Howe Elliott, and Florence Howe Hall, *Julia Ward Howe, 1819–1910* (Boston: Houghton Mifflin, 1915), 1:187–89.

11. *Dwight's Journal of Music*, Boston, Dec. 7, 1867, p. 150.

12. Ibid.

13. *Hingham Journal*, May 13, 2010.

14. Governor Deval Patrick's State of the Commonwealth Address, January 17, 2013, *Boston Globe*, January 13, 2017.

15. Albert Gallatin Browne, *Sketch of the Official Life of John Andrew as Governor of Massachusetts* (New York: Hurd and Houghton, 1868), 71–72; *Northwestern Christian Advocate*, Aug. 28, 1907.

16. Harriet Beecher Stowe, *The Lives and Deeds of Our Self-Made Men* (Hartford, CT: Worthington, Dustin, 1872), 326.

CHAPTER 20

1. William C. Rives to Judith Rives, May 1, 1864, William C. Rives Papers, Library of Congress Manuscripts Division, copy in White House of the Confederacy research files; Mrs. Burton Harrison, *Recollections Grave and Gay* (New York: Charles Scribner's Sons, 1916), 182. Also *Richmond Daily Dispatch*, May 2, 1864, p. 1, c. 6, and an anonymous eyewitness letter, April 30, 1864, excerpted in Alexander Autographs, October 3, 2001, lot 706.

2. Mrs. Jefferson Davis, *Jefferson Davis: A Memoir by His Wife* (New York: Belford, 1890), 2:496–97.

3. C. Vann Woodward, ed., *Mary Chesnut's Civil War* (New Haven: Yale University Press, 1980), 504. In a May 8, 1864, letter to a friend,

Varina Davis described Joseph as "my most beautiful and promising child." In *Jefferson Davis Private Letters, 1823–1889*, ed. Hudson Strode (New York: Harcourt, Brace & World, 1966), 137.

4. Mary H. Mitchell, *Hollywood Cemetery: The History of a Southern Shrine* (Richmond: Virginia State Library, 1985), chapters 1 and 2.

5. Woodward, *Chesnut*, 602; Harrison, *Recollections*, 181–82.

6. Hollywood Cemetery Company Minute Book, 1847–1868, Virginia Museum of History and Culture, 401; also published in Dunbar Rowland, *Jefferson Davis, Constitutionalist: His Letters, Papers, and Speeches* (Jackson: Mississippi Department of Archives and History, 1923), 6:267.

7. *Alexandria (Virginia) Gazette*, May 17, 1866, p. 1, c. 1; Mitchell, *Hollywood Cemetery*, 59, specifies the cost of the stone as forty dollars.

8. *Richmond Daily Dispatch*, July 16, 1866, p. 1, c. 6.

9. Lynda Lasswell Crist et al., eds., *The Papers of Jefferson Davis* (Baton Rouge: Louisiana State University Press, 1971–2015), 12:204 (hereafter *PJD*).

10. *Richmond Daily Dispatch*, June 1, 1867, p. 1, c. 1; *PJD*, 12:208.

11. Hollywood Cemetery Company Minute Book, 1868–1892, Virginia Museum of History and Culture, 23 and 16–29.

12. *Richmond Daily Dispatch*, May 30, 1868, p. 1, c. 2.

13. *PJD*, 14:143.

14. *PJD*, 14:45.

15. *Richmond Daily Dispatch*, March 27, 1885, p. 5, c. 1; April 10, 1887, p. 8, c. 2; May 26, 1887, personals and briefs.

16. "The Tomb of the Little Boy," *Staunton (Virginia) Spectator*, January 22, 1890, p. 1, c. 6.

17. See Donald E. Collins, *The Death and Resurrection of Jefferson Davis* (Lanham, MD: Rowman & Littlefield, 2005); and Charles Reagan Wilson, "The Death of Southern Heroes: Historic Funerals of the South," *Southern Cultures* 1, no. 1 (Fall 1994): 5–8.

18. *Richmond Daily Dispatch*, December 19, 1889, p. 1, c. 3; Hollywood Cemetery Company Minute Book, 1868–1892, 371–72; Varina Howell Davis to J. Taylor Ellyson, December 21, 1889, Eleanor S. Brockenbrough Library, Museum of the Confederacy, under the management of the Virginia Historical Society.

19. Jefferson Davis Monument Association [JDMA] Minute Book, 2, 5, Eleanor S. Brockenbrough Library, Museum of the Confederacy, under the management of the Virginia Historical Society; Collins, *Death and Resurrection*, 92–93.

20. JDMA Minute Book, 22, 31.

21. Collins, *Death and Resurrection*, chapter 4; Edison H. Thomas, "The Story of the Jefferson Davis Funeral Train," reprint from *L&N Magazine*, February 1955.

22. John O. Peters, *Richmond's Hollywood Cemetery*. (Richmond: Valentine Richmond History Center, 2010), 97–98.

23. M. Anna Fariello, "Personalizing the Political: The Davis Family Circle in Richmond's Hollywood Cemetery," in *Monuments to the Lost Cause: Women, Art, and the Landscapes of Southern Memory*, ed. Cynthia Mills and Pamela H. Simpson (Knoxville: University of Tennessee Press, 2003), 116–32.

24. John M. Coski, "The Tortuous Tale of the Jefferson Davis Monument," *American Civil War Museum Magazine*, Spring 2017, 11–17; Gaines M. Foster, *Ghosts of the Confederacy: Defeat, the Lost Cause, and the Emergence of the New South, 1865–1913* (New York: Oxford University Press, 1987), 158–59.

25. "With Davis Statue Down, Stoney Vows to Finish Job," *Richmond Times-Dispatch*, June 12, 2020, A1.

CHAPTER 21

1. Allan Nevins and Milton Thomas, eds., *The Diary of George Templeton Strong*, 4:266 (Dec. 24, 1869).

2. John Kelly, "'Lincoln in the Bardo' Novel Has People Flocking to a Georgetown Cemetery," *Washington Post*, Apr. 17, 2017.

3. Stanton to John Adams Dix, Oct. 26, 1861, Dix Papers, Columbia University.

4. Ibid.

5. Ellen Stanton to Kate Hutchison, Jan. 5, 1862, in *Ellen Hutchison Stanton Letters, 1845–1869*, ed. Catherine Stanton Richert (Akron, OH: n.p., 2014), 162–63.

6. Stanton to Oella Wright, March 24, 1862, in Pamphila Wolcott, "Edwin M. Stanton: A Biographical Sketch by his Sister," 179–80 (typescript at Ohio History Center).

7. Stanton to Dr. WC Van Bibber, Apr. 28, 1862, telegrams sent by the secretary of war, National Archives microfilm M473, reel 78.

8. Stanton to Lincoln, June 29, 1862, Lincoln Papers, Library of Congress.

9. Stanton to Dr. WC Van Bibber, July 10 and 11, 1862, telegrams sent by the secretary of war, National Archives microfilm M473, reel 79; Stanton to James Hutchison, July 11, 1862, ibid.

10. *Pittsburgh Gazette*, July 17, 1862, quoting *New York World*.

11. William E. Gienapp and Erica L. Gienapp, eds., *The Civil War Diary of Gideon Welles, Lincoln's Secretary of the Navy: The Original Manuscript Edition* (Urbana: University of Illinois Press, 2014), 3. The manuscript version is now available through the website of the Library of Congress.

12. Gideon Welles to Anna Welles, July 13, 1862, Welles Papers, Library of Congress.

CHAPTER 22

1. Elizabeth Keckley, *Behind the Scenes; or, Thirty Years a Slave, and Four Years in the White House* (New York: G. W. Carleton, 1868), 240. As will be discussed in this essay, Elizabeth Keckly's surname appears with different spellings in different sources. She signed her surname as "Keckly," but *Behind the Scenes* was published under the surname "Keckley." For the purposes of this article, her name is spelled "Keckly" in reference to the woman herself, and "Keckley" in citations of *Behind the Scenes.*

2. The community in Maryland in which the National Harmony Memorial Park is located is variously recorded as Landover and Hyattsville. Landover will be used in this article for historical consistency.

3. Keckley, *Behind the Scenes*, 45.

4. Keckley, *Behind the Scenes*, 210.

5. Keckley, *Behind the Scenes*, 191, 209, 204. Keckly estimated Mary Lincoln's debts to be seventy thousand dollars.

6. Keckley, *Behind the Scenes*, xiv; Jennifer Fleischner, *Mrs. Lincoln and Mrs. Keckly: The Remarkable Story of the Friendship between a First Lady and a Former Slave* (New York: Broadway Books, 2003), 316; Mary Lincoln to Rhoda White, May 2, 1868, quoted in *Mary Todd Lincoln: Her Life and Letters*, ed. Justin G. Turner and Linda Levitt Turner (New York: Fromm International, 1972, 1987), 472; Elizabeth Keckly to Jesse W. Weik, April 2, 1891, container 30, group V, Herndon-Weik Collection of Lincolniana, Manuscript Division, Library of Congress.

7. John E. Washington, *They Knew Lincoln* (New York: E. P. Dutton, 1942), 212, 216–17.

8. Paul E. Sluby Sr., *History of the Columbian Harmony Society and of Harmony Cemetery, Washington D.C.* (Washington, DC, 2001), revised edition of Paul E. Sluby Sr. and Stanton L. Wormley Jr., *The Columbian Harmony Society: A Brief History* (1976); Washington, *They Knew Lincoln*, 215; Keckley, *Behind the Scenes*, 24. Originally located on what is now Florida Avenue NW, in the late 1850s the Columbian Harmony Cemetery moved to another location on Rhode Island Avenue NE, after new ordinances prohibited the establishment of new cemeteries within the boundaries of the city of Washington and made continued operation difficult for existing cemeteries within city limits. The Rhode Island Avenue site was located outside of the then-city of Washington but still within the District of Columbia.

9. Stansil and Lee of Buffalo, NY, republished *Behind the Scenes* in 1931. See Library of Congress online catalog record at https://lccn.loc.gov/53054284. Robert T. Lincoln, the only surviving child of Abraham and Mary Lincoln, died in 1926. "Bizarre Lincoln Story Is Traced. 'Sob Sister' Revealed as Writer of Tragic Tale of Widow," *Evening Star*

(Washington, DC), November 11, 1935; John E. Washington, "Ample Proof of Reality of Elizabeth Keckley," *Evening Star* (Washington, DC), November 15, 1935; Washington, *They Knew Lincoln*, 223–24.

10. For more on the sale and move of the Columbian Harmony Cemetery, see Paul E. Sluby Sr., *History of the Columbian Harmony Society*, 43–52.

11. Paul E. Sluby Sr., *History of the Columbian Harmony Society*, 45; "Columbian Harmony Cemetery," Wikipedia entry, https://en.wikipedia.org/wiki/Columbian_Harmony_Cemetery (accessed March 23, 2019); Robert Malesky, "On This Spot: Cemeteries in the City," Bygone Brookland blog, http://bygonebrookland.com/on-this-spot-cemeteries-in.html (accessed March 23, 2019). Keckly's son George passed for a white man to enlist in the Union army under the name George Kirkland. He was killed at the battle of Wilson's Creek in August 1861.

12. Frances Smith Foster, "Autobiography after Emancipation: The Example of Elizabeth Keckley," in *Writing Self, Writing Nation*, vol. 1 of *The Elizabeth Keckley Reader*, ed. Sheila Smith McKoy (Hillsborough, NC: Eno, 2016), 34.

13. *The Elizabeth Keckley Reader*, published by Eno Publishers, includes two volumes: *Writing Self, Writing Nation* (2016) and *Artistry, Culture and Commerce* (2017).

14. Tamika Y. Nunley, "Elizabeth Keckly's Union War," in *New Perspectives on the Union War*, ed. Gary W. Gallagher and Elizabeth R. Varon (New York: Fordham University Press, 2019), 39–62.

15. "Elizabeth Keckly Gravesite," Surratt Society Homepage, www.surrattmuseum.org/elizabeth-keckly-gravesite (accessed May 20, 2019).

16. Jordan Grant, "Elizabeth Keckley: Businesswoman and Philanthropist," Smithsonian Institution, National Museum of American History blog, March 22, 2016, https://americanhistory.si.edu/blog/elizabeth-keckley-businesswoman-and-philanthropist (accessed September 9, 2019).

CHAPTER 23

1. Frederick Douglass, address at Lincoln birthday celebration at Brooklyn, New York, February 13, 1893, *The Standard Union* (Brooklyn), February 14, 1893.

2. James Oakes, *The Crooked Path to Abolition: Abraham Lincoln and the Antislavery Constitution* (New York: W. W. Norton, 2021); Jonathan W. White, *A House Built by Slaves: African American Visitors to the Lincoln White House* (Lanham, MD: Rowman & Littlefield, 2022); David S. Reynolds, *Abe: Abraham Lincoln in His Times* (New York: Penguin Press, 2021); Michael Burlingame, *The Black Man's President: Abraham Lincoln, African Americans, and the Pursuit of Racial Equality* (New York: Pegasus Books, 2021).

3. *The Life and Times of Frederick Douglass* (Hartford: Park Publishing, 1881), 436.

4. Frederick Douglass, eulogy for Lincoln, delivered at Manhattan's Cooper Union on June 1, 1865, manuscript, Douglass Papers, Library of Congress.

5. Horace White, "Recollections of Lincoln," *Magazine of History* 3, no. 2 (February 1906): 72.

6. Henry C. Whitney, *Lincoln the Citizen* (New York: Baker & Taylor, 1908), 231.

7. *Philadelphia Inquirer*, February 22, 1861.

8. Washington, *They Knew Lincoln* (New York: E. P. Dutton, 1942), 128.

9. Washington correspondence, January 17, 1864, *New York Anglo-African*, January 30, 1864.

10. Audrey Elisa Kerr, *The Paper Bag Principle: Class, Colorism, and Rumor and the Case of Black Washington, D.C.* (Knoxville: University of Tennessee Press, 2006), 53. For a history of intraracial discrimination in Washington, see *ibid.*, 37–117.

11. *Alton (Illinois) Telegraph*, January 15, 1855.

12. Margaret Hunter, "The Persistent Problem of Colorism: Skin Tone, Status, and Inequality," *Sociology Compass* 1 (2007): 237–54.

13. Roy P. Basler et al., eds., *The Collected Works of Abraham Lincoln* (New Brunswick, NJ: Rutgers University Press, 1953–55), 4:277.

14. Lincoln to Welles, Washington, March 16, 1861, *ibid.*, 4:288.

15. Lincoln to Chase, Washington, November 29, 1861, *ibid.*, 5:33.

16. Washington, *They Knew Lincoln*, 131–32.

17. Henry C. Whitney, *Life on the Circuit with Lincoln* (Boston: Estes & Lauriat, 1892), 32.

18. Recommendation, October 24, 1862, Basler, *Collected Works of Lincoln*, 5:474.

19. Endorsement, December 17, 1862, on a letter drafted by a staff member to John A. Dix, December 16, 1862, in Basler, *Collected Works of Lincoln*, 6:8–9, www.christies.com/en/lot/lot-5698208.

20. Washington correspondence, January 14, 1864, *Chicago Tribune*, January 19, 1864.

21. Samuel Wilkeson, "How Mr. Lincoln Indorsed the Negro," *Janesville (Wisconsin) Gazette*, July 23, 1867.

22. See Phillip W. Magness and Sabastian Page, "Mr. Lincoln and Mr. Johnson," *New York Times* blog (February 1, 2012).

23. A few years ago, when a Black man sued an employer, alleging that by calling him "boy" the employer showed racial animus, the U.S. Supreme Court, in sending the case back to trial, noted: "The speaker's meaning may depend on various factors including context, tone of voice, local custom and historical usage." R. L. Johnson, "How Racist Is 'Boy'? It's Always Hard to Say," *The Economist*, November 1, 2010.

24. Washington, *They Knew Lincoln*, 132.

25. Frederick Douglass, eulogy for Lincoln, Douglass Papers.

26. Douglass, *Life and Times*, 364.

27. John Eaton, *Grant, Lincoln, and the Freedmen* (New York: Longmans, Green, 1907), 175–76.

28. Clarence Lusane, *The Black History of the White House* (San Francisco: City Lights Books, 2011), 198.

29. *Boston Liberator*, April 1, 1864.

30. *Boston Daily Advertiser*, April 13, 1864, copied *ibid.*, April 15, 1864.

31. Reminiscences of John W. Forney in a lecture delivered in November 1865 before the Ladies' Soldiers' Aid Society of Weldon, Pennsylvania, *Sandusky (Ohio) Register*, December 13, 1865.

32. Washington correspondence, March 4, *New York Evening Post*, March 4, 1864, copied in the *Cleveland Leader*, March 5, 1864.

33. Lincoln to Michael Hahn, Washington, March 13, 1864, in Basler, *Collected Works of Lincoln*, 7:243.

34. Booth told this to David Herold, who in turn told it to his attorney, who then told Louis J. Weichman. Louis J. Weichman, *A True History of the Assassination of Abraham Lincoln and of the Conspiracy of 1865* (New York: Knopf, 1975), 148.

35. "Impeachment of the President," House Report no. 7, 40th Congress, 1st session (1867): 674.

36. Manuscript of a speech, [ca. December 1865], Douglass Papers.

CHAPTER 24

1. "Death of Samuel James," October 20, 1839, Diary Number 2, Basil Manly Sr., Manly Family Papers, W. S. Hoole Special Collections, University of Alabama, Tuscaloosa.

2. "College Burial Ground," October 21, 1839, Diary Number 2; Manly, Second Annual President's Report to University of Alabama Board of Trustees; Diary Number 2; James B. Sellers, *History of the University of Alabama, 1818–1902* (Tuscaloosa: University of Alabama Press, 1953), 1:91.

3. Manly, Second Annual President's Report; Basil Manly and John P. Boyle, University Survey, 1852, accessed in Historical Maps of Alabama, Cartographic Research Lab, University of Alabama, Tuscaloosa.

4. Second Annual President's Report; "Death of Maam Lydia," January 31, 1839, Diary Number 2; L. C. Garland to Mrs. Neilson, July 4, 1864, Letterbook of Landon Cabell Garland, vol. 3, pt. 1, 1863–1864, Landon Cabell Garland Letters, Hoole Special Collections.

5. "Death—Jack," May 5, 1843, Diary Number 2.

6. Albert J. Raboteau, *Slave Religion: The Invisible Institution in the Antebellum South* (New York: Oxford University Press, 1980), 230; "Arrival of Servant Mary," April 10, 1838, and "Death—Bosyey," November 22, 1844, Diary Number 2; Hilary Green, "The Burden of the University of Alabama's Hallowed Grounds," *Public Historian* 42 (November 2020): 36–37.

7. Robert Mellown, *The University of Alabama: A Guide to the Campus and Its Architecture* (Tuscaloosa: University of Alabama Press, 2013), 60–61.

8. "Death of a Student," July 6, 1844, Diary Number 2.

9. July 5, 1844, Meeting, Faculty Minutes, vol. 4 (1842–1854), RG 154, Hoole Special Collections.

10. A. James Fuller, *Chaplain for the Confederacy: Basil Manly and Baptist Life in the Old South* (Baton Rouge: Louisiana State University Press, 2000), 167–68, 177; Sellers, *History of the University of Alabama*, 39–40; December 31, 1838, Meeting, and March 1, 1839, Meeting, Faculty Minutes, vol. 3 (1838–1841).

11. August 24, 1840, Meeting, and January 1, 1841, Meeting, Faculty Minutes, vol. 3 (1838–1841).

12. Fuller, *Chaplain for the Confederacy*, 168; Thomas Waverly Palmer, *A Register of the Officers and Students of the University of Alabama* (Tuscaloosa: University of Alabama, 1901), 71, 106.

13. Sellers, *History of the University of Alabama*, 91–92.

14. Sellers, *History of the University of Alabama*, 281–88.

15. See "Cemetery's Iron Gate and Fence at the University of Alabama Campus," photograph, 1890, and "University Cemetery," photograph, 1950, Hoole Special Collections; Sellers, *History of the University of Alabama*, 91; Max Clarke and Gary Alan Fine, "'A' for Apology: Slavery and the Collegiate Discourses of Remembrances—The Cases of Brown University and the University of Alabama," *History and Memory* 22 (Spring/Summer 2010), 99.

16. Gilbert Cruz, "Professor Wants UA to Apologize for Slavery," *Tuscaloosa News*, March 17, 2004.

17. Alfred L. Brophy, "The University and the Slaves: Apology and Its Meaning," in *The Age of Apology: Facing Up to the Past,* ed. Mark Gibney, Rhoad E. Howard-Hassmann, Jean-Marc Coicaud, and Niklaus Steiner (Philadelphia: University of Pennsylvania Press, 2009), 118–19; Ellen Griffith Spears and James C. Hall, "Engaging the Racial Landscape at the University of Alabama," in *Slavery and the University: Histories and Legacies*, ed. Leslie M. Harris, James T. Campbell, and Alfred L. Brophy (Athens: University of Georgia Press, 2019), 299, 304–5.

18. Brophy, "The University and the Slaves," 114–15.

19. Clarke and Fine, "'A' for Apology," 98, 100.

20. Brophy, "The University and the Slaves," 114.

21. Brophy, "The University and the Slaves," 116–17; Clarke and Fine, "'A' for Apology," 99.

22. Clarke and Fine, "'A' for Apology," 102; Brophy, "The University and the Slaves," 116–17; Cruz, "Professor Wants UA to Apologize."

23. Faculty Senate, Minutes, March 16 and April 20, 2004.

24. "University of Alabama Apologizes for Slave Past," NBCNews.com, April 20, 2004.

25. Jamon Smith, "Slavery Marks University Past," *Tuscaloosa News*, April 7, 2006; "Slavery Cemetery Plaque," Campus Historical Markers, University Libraries, University of Alabama, Tuscaloosa.

26. Smith, "Slavery Marks University Past."

27. Clarke and Fine, "'A' for Apology," 83.

28. See Sarah Elizabeth Tooker, "Professor Leads Racial Tour," *Crimson White,* February 5, 2013; Ellen Coogan, "Cemetery Serves as Reminder of History, Hope for Future," *Crimson White*, September 13, 2013; Alyssa Locklar, "On-campus Gravesite Recalls Antebellum University," *Crimson White*, January 24, 2012; Mark Hammontree, "Exhibit Captures History of Slavery at University," *Crimson White*, February 8, 2014; "The University Must Acknowledge Its Own History, Good and Bad," *Crimson White*, October 17, 2014.

29. Elayne Smith, "The Names in the Schoolhouse Door: UA Students Question Building Names," *Crimson White*, February 22, 2016; CW Editorial Board, "Our View: Rename Morgan Hall for Harper Lee," *Crimson White,* February 22, 2016; Isabelle Beauregard, "The UDC Boulder Represents Our Campus," *Crimson White*, February 20, 2017; Isabelle Garrison, "Monumental Debate: Students Divided over Necessity," *Crimson White*, September 1, 2017.

30. "Why Nott? Confronting a Campus Building's Legacy of White Supremacy," public lecture, UA Honors College, University of Alabama, Tuscaloosa, September 6, 2017; Ruben Tarajano, "Our University Must Further Its Recognition of the History of Slavery," *Crimson White*, February 19, 2018.

31. Year End Report of the Community and Legislative Affairs Committee, 2017–18, Faculty Senate, University of Alabama, March 2018.

32. Clarke and Fine, "'A' for Apology," 83; Faculty Senate, Proposal to Establish a Commission on Race, Slavery, and Civil Rights at the University of Alabama, October 16, 2018; Faculty Senate, Minutes, November 13, 2018; Green, "The Burden," 34.

33. Karen L. Cox, *Dixie's Daughters: The United Daughters of the Confederacy and the Preservation of Confederate Culture* (Gainesville: University Press of Florida, 2019), 49.

34. Jessa Reid Bolling, "UA Board of Trustees Authorizes Removal of Three Confederate Plaques," *Crimson White*, June 8, 2020; Stephanie Taylor, "University of Alabama Removes Confederate Monument," *Tuscaloosa News*, June 9, 2020.

35. Jessa Reid Bolling, "Trustees Rename Manly Hall, Ignore UCW Suggestions," *Crimson White*, November 13, 2020.

36. James Baldwin, *The Fire Next Time* (1963; reprint, New York: Vintage International, 1993), 81.

CHAPTER 25

1. The cemetery can be located on the Find a Grave website at www.findagrave.com/cemetery/2178695/otho-thomas-cemetery/map. The cemetery is on private property.

2. I purchased the items from Iron Horse Military Antiques, owned by Jeff McArdle.

3. Find a Grave was the original source that said Lamar was buried in

Burkittsville's Union Cemetery. The entry has since been corrected to indicate his Otho Thomas resting place, but Lamar's birthdate remains inaccurately listed as September 11, 1811, on the Find a Grave site, and mistakenly states he was forty-nine when he died, www.findagrave.com/memorial/33286802/samuel-calvin-lamar; Jacob Mehrling Holdcraft, *Names in Stone: 75,000 Cemetery Inscriptions from Frederick County, Maryland* (Baltimore, MD: Genealogical Publishing, 2002), 2:690.

4. U.S. War Department, *The War of the Rebellion: A Compilation of the Official Records of the Union and Confederate Armies,* series 1, 2:107. Stone's command was in some flux as units were assigned to other locations or broken up; Rev. Stephen G. Abbott, A.M., *The First Regiment New Hampshire Volunteers in the Great Rebellion* (Keene, NH: Sentinel Printing, 1890), 128–29.

5. Abbott, *The First Regiment New Hampshire Volunteers*, 162.

6. Joseph L. Harsh, *Sounding the Shallows: A Confederate Companion for the Maryland Campaign of 1862* (Kent, OH: Kent State University Press, 2000), 126. The exact population of Frederick City was 8,142.

7. The accounts are written on two different pieces of paper, 9 7/8 by 15 inches in size, and are folded in half. Both sides of each sheet are used. John Crown's and Curtis Wheeler's statements are written in bold, florid hand on one sheet of paper. The other sheet contains the statements of Charles E. Bready and George C. Bready written in a much smaller, tighter hand. On this sheet is also written, in the same hand, "The above statements were made to me by the several parties and committed to writing as stated. Wm. F. Greeley, Lieut., Co. E., 1 N.H.V.," indicating the officer wrote this document.

8. Raynors' Historical Collectible Auctions, Auction #2021-05, May 21, 2021, Lot #245. Jeff McArdle, mentioned in note 2, alerted me to the presence of the account for sale. Davis's account was taken down on one side of a sheet of paper measuring 7 7/8 by 9 3/4 inches. It is also written in Lt. Greeley's hand.

9. *The Diary of Jacob Englebrecht* (Frederick, MD: Historical Society of Frederick County, 2001), 2:909; Samuel Webster compiled service record, Record Group 94, Records of the Adjutant General's Office, Compiled Service Records, National Archives and Records Administration, Washington, DC. Hereinafter cited as NARA and CSR.

10. *The Diary of Jacob Englebrecht*, 2:922.

11. Webster CSR.

12. Charles S. Davis CSR.

13. William F. Greeley CSR; William F. Greeley pension file, Record Group 15, Records of the Veterans Administration, Pensions, NARA.

14. Consolidated Lists of Civil War Draft Registration Records, "Counties of Allegheny, Washington, Frederick, and Carroll," August 1863, Record Group 110, NARA; John O. Crown CSR, Record Group 109, NARA; 1870 Census of the United States, Frederick Ward 4, Frederick, Md. Roll: M593_586, p. 82A. Capt. Elijah White's 35th Battalion operated

primarily as partisan rangers in Loudoun County, VA, during the war, with some attached service with the Army of Northern Virginia.

15. Charles E. Bready obituary, *The News* (Frederick, MD), August 18, 1916, p. 5; information on George C. Bready comes from Ancestry.com, *U.S. City Directories, 1822–1995*.

16. Thomas Harwood CSR, Record Group 109, NARA.

17. Lamar's family information comes from the 1860 Census of the United States, Buckeystown District, Frederick County, MD, p. 869; Harsh, *Sounding the Shallows*, 114; information about Annie Mary Lamar Bready is found at www.findagrave.com/memorial/144572393/annie-mary-bready.

18. Abbott, *The First Regiment New Hampshire Volunteers*, 162. Abbott incorrectly remembered that the shooting took place on July 5, 1861.

CHAPTER 26

1. William B. Napton (hereafter WBN) to Melinda Napton, December 5, 7, 9, 11, 14, 16, 1860, January 7, February 3, April 15, 19, 1861, William B. Napton Papers, box 1, Missouri Historical Society, St. Louis (hereafter Napton Papers).

2. On the Camp Jackson affair, see Christopher Phillips, *Damned Yankee: The Life of General Nathaniel Lyon* (1990; reprint, Baton Rouge: Louisiana State University Press, 1996), 178–93.

3. Ibid., 215–64 passim.

4. Napton Journals (original), vol. 3, December 30, 1862, entry, Napton Papers.

5. *Marshall Democrat*, July 3, 1861; *(Columbia) Missouri Statesman*, January 16, 1863, June 9, 1882; William B. Napton Jr., *Past and Present of Saline County* (Indianapolis: B. F. Bowen, 1910), 141–63, 205–6, 899–900; Oath of Allegiance and Bond of J. W. Napton, June 3, 1862, United Daughters of the Confederacy, Missouri Division, Collection, Mss. 3188, folder 206, Western Historical Manuscripts Collection, Joint Collection—State Historical Society of Missouri/University of Missouri, Center for Missouri History, Columbia, Missouri (hereafter SHSM); Saline County, Missouri, Militia Enrollments, 1865–1866, microfilm reel ML-423, p. 312; and Record of Missouri Confederate Veterans, United Daughters of the Confederacy, Missouri Division, Saline County, microfilm reel M-145, both at Missouri State Archives, Columbia (hereafter MSA).

6. W. A. Wilson to Benjamin Loan, November 28, 1862, Record Group 109: War Department Collection of Confederate Records, Union Provost Marshals' File of Papers Relating to Individual Civilians, microfilm publication F1375, reel 201, National Archives and Records Administration, Washington, DC (hereafter NARA); Napton Journals (typescript), p. 277, Napton Papers; WBN to H[amilton]. R. Gamble, March 14 [1863], Record Group 133: Adjutant General's Records,

Correspondence—Miscellaneous, Enrolled Missouri Militia, 40th Regiment, box 85, folder 1, MSA; *Report of the Committee of the House of Representatives of the Twenty-second General Assembly of the State of Missouri, Appointed to Investigate the Conduct and Management of the Militia* (Jefferson City: State Printer, 1864), 249.

7. Napton Journals (original), vol. 3, December 31, 1862, entry, Napton Papers.

8. R. R. Spedden to Hamilton R. Gamble, March 2, 1863; Special Order No. 41, June 3, 1863; Alexander Lowry to Allen Blacker, August 13, 1863, all in Record Group 133 (Adjutant General's Records), Correspondence—Miscellaneous, Enrolled Missouri Militia, 40th Regiment, box 15, MSA.

9. WBN to F[ranklin]. A. Dick, May 25, 1863, and Statement of Mr. W. B. Napton, June 6, 1863, both in Record Group 110: Provost Marshals' Papers, microfilm publication F1375, reel 201, NARA; "Domestic Chronology," March 30, April 30, 1864, February 22, December 31, 1868, and Harry P. Napton, "Sketch," both in box 1, Napton Papers; *(Columbia) Missouri Statesman*, May 22, 1863; WBN to John F. Snyder, October 18, 1864, Dr. John F. Snyder Collection, MHS; Napton Journals (typescript), pp. 239, 314, 318, Napton Papers.

10. Napton Jr., *Past and Present of Saline County*, 899–900; "Domestic Chronology," January 11, 1863, May 3, 1865, June 8, 1866, May 9, October 26, 1867, May 20, 1872, Napton Papers; Eighth and Tenth U.S. Censuses, 1860 and 1880, Population Schedule, Saline County, Mo., NARA; William B. Napton Jr. to Walter Williams, August 5, 1910, private collection; Napton Journals (typescript), 899.

11. *(Columbia) Missouri Statesman*, January 12, 1883; Napton Journals (typescript), 980, 983, 997, Napton Papers; T. J. Stiles, *Jesse James: The Last Rebel of the Civil War* (New York: A. A. Knopf, 2003), 388–92 passim.

12. Napton Family photographic album, undated, private collection, and William B. Napton Jr. to Harry P. Napton, March 18, 1902, microfilm reel 37, both in Napton Papers.

CHAPTER 27

1. *New York Tribune*, April 28, 1865.

2. James O. Hall, "Identification of John Wilkes Booth," typescript, n.d., author's collection.

3. Terry Alford, *Fortune's Fool: The Life of John Wilkes Booth* (New York: Oxford University Press, 2015), 323–40.

4. *New York Daily Graphic*, April 13, 1876.

5. *(Washington) National Tribune*, May 6, 1915. May's statement in *The Lincoln Assassination: The Evidence*, ed. William C. Edwards and Edward Steers Jr. (Urbana: University of Illinois Press, 2009), 849–51.

6. *Washington Evening Star*, March 21, 1891.

7. *New York Clipper*, May 20, 1865; *(New York) Pomeroy's Democrat*,

October 5, 1870. Barnes published the autopsy in his *Surgical and Medical History of the War of the Rebellion* (1875).

8. Stanton testimony, *Impeachment Investigation,* May 18, 1867, p. 409; *Chicago Daily Tribune*, Feb. 17, 1889.

9. *Frank Leslie's Illustrated Weekly*, May 20, 1865.

10. George L. Porter, "How Booth's Body Was Hidden," *Columbian Magazine* 4 (April 1911): 70–73.

11. *Congressional Globe*, July 28, 1866, p. 4292.

12. *Chicago Tribune*, May 28, 1867; *Washington Evening Star*, Oct. 3, 1867; *Baltimore Sun*, January 14, 1913.

13. Booth to Grant, Baltimore, Sept. 11, 1867, *The Papers of Ulysses S. Grant,* ed. John Y. Simon (Carbondale: Southern Illinois University Press, 1991), 17:315–16.

14. *Brooklyn Daily Eagle*, Jan. 14, 1877.

15. *Washington Evening Star*, Feb. 16, 1869; *Washington Post,* March 25, 1901.

16. George Ford, *These Were Actors* (New York: Library Publishers, 1955), 301.

17. *New York Clipper*, July 3, 1869; *Baltimore American*, March 2, 1902.

18. Alford, *Fortune's Fool*, 332.

19. *Baltimore American*, June 9, 1870.

20. *New York Tribune*, June 10, 1870.

21. C. Wyatt Evans, *The Legend of John Wilkes Booth: Myth, Memory, and a Mummy* (Lawrence: University Press of Kansas, 2004), 23–25, 30–32, 128–31, passim.

22. Gretchen Worden, "Is It the Body of John Wilkes Booth?" *Transactions and Studies of the College of Physicians of Philadelphia* 16 (December 1994): 67, 82.

23. Francis J. Gorman, "The John Wilkes Booth Exhumation Case," November 7, 1996, www.gw-law.com/blog/john-wilkes-booth-exhumation-case (accessed Feb. 11, 2019).

24. Sam Tetrault, "Coins on Graves: What They Mean and Why People Leave Them," July 8, 2021, www.joincake.com/blog/coins-on-graves/ (accessed July 22, 2021).

CHAPTER 28

1. This essay is deeply indebted to the exploration of the "color line" offered by W. E. B. Du Bois, *The Souls of Black Folk* (1903; New York: Library of America, 1990).

2. Clint Smith, *How the Word Is Passed: A Reckoning with the History of Slavery across America* (New York: Little, Brown, 2021), 52–84, 118–72.

3. The Sanborn-Wright case may be found in the National Archives in Washington, DC, Record Group 153, Case MM 631.

4. See Alexander Wilbourne Weddell Papers, Virginia Museum of History and Culture, Richmond, VA. The Weddell collection comprises fifty-five archival boxes of materials and is enormous in scope and detail. The correspondence cited in this essay is contained in box 55, "Family Miscellany" and "genealogical materials." I wish to thank particularly Ms. Jennifer Huff, archivist at the VMHC, for her enthusiastic and expert help on this project.

5. From Weddell Papers finding guide, p. 2.

6. Lenoir Chambers, "Notes on Life in Occupied Norfolk, 1862–1865," *Virginia Magazine of History and Biography* 73 (April 1965): 143.

7. Alexander Weddell to Editor of the *Virginian-Pilot*, March 30, 1901, Weddell Papers, box 55.

8. Editor of the *Virginian-Pilot* to Alexander Weddell, (date covered by another document), and Editor of the *Virginian-Pilot*, April 9, 1901, Weddell Papers, box 55.

9. "Expunged from the Record. David M. Wright, M.D. 1809–1863," Weddell Papers, box 55. The "Expunged from the Record" document would be reprinted again by Alexander Weddell from his posting in Mexico City in 1925.

10. David Homer Bates, *Lincoln in the Telegraph Office: Recollections of the United States Military Telegraph Corps During the Civil War* (New York: Century, 1907), 153.

11. Weddell Papers, box 55.

12. Kirk Savage, *Standing Soldiers, Kneeling Slaves: Race, War, and Monument in Nineteenth-Century America*, new ed. (Princeton: Princeton University Press, 2018), 187.

13. I am grateful to Professor Cassandra Newby-Alexander of Norfolk State University for her piece "Remembering Norfolk's African American Cemeteries" and for her helpful email correspondence with respect to this project. See www.racetimeplace.com/cemeteryhistory.htm.

14. A sketch of William Carney's postwar life may be found in Douglas R. Egerton, *Thunder at the Gates: The Black Civil War Regiments That Redeemed America* (New York: Basic Books, 2016), 314–17.

15. See www.norfolk.gov/Facilities/Facility/Details/52 for informative maps and views of the West Point Cemetery. Other maps and views are available on Google Earth. I wish to thank Troy Valos, archivist of the Sergeant Memorial Collection at the Slover Public Library in Norfolk for pointing me to these images and for directing me to the *Norfolk Landmark*, Wednesday Morning, March 31, 1886, on the actions of the Common Council: "On Motion of Mr. Fuller, Section 20 in West Point Cemetery Was Donated to the Union Veterans and Hall Association."

16. On this incident see Ervin L. Jordan Jr., *Black Confederates and Afro-Yankees in Civil War Virginia* (Charlottesville: University Press of Virginia, 1995), 286–87.

17. See *Lynching in America: Confronting the Legacy of Racial Terror*, 3rd ed. (Montgomery, AL: Equal Justice Initiative, 2017), for a superb overview. See page 43 for the Newport News lynching number.

18. Jordan, *Black Confederates and Afro-Yankees*, 268.

19. I am grateful to Professor Jonathan White and his students for finding James E. Fuller's pension file in full for me at the National Archives.

List of Contributors

TERRY ALFORD received his PhD in history from Mississippi State University and did postdoctoral work in family history at the University of California, Davis. He is a founding board member of the Abraham Lincoln Institute and the author of *Prince among Slaves* (1986), *Fortune's Fool* (2015), and *In the Houses of Their Dead* (2022). Alford received the 2010 Outstanding Faculty of Virginia Award from the State Council on Higher Education.

MELODIE ANDREWS is an emerita history professor at Minnesota State University, Mankato, where she taught public history, early America, and women's history. She co-edited volumes 1 and 2 of *The Papers of Thomas A. Edison* and has written journal articles on women and technology. She has contributed essays to a number of historical anthologies, writing on women's suffrage and Minnesota history. She has also edited over sixty history books for young readers.

EDWARD L. AYERS has been named National Professor of the Year, received the National Humanities Medal from President Obama at the White House, served as president of the Organization of American Historians, and won the Bancroft Prize for distinguished writing in American history. The author of *The Thin Light of Freedom* (2017), he is university professor and president emeritus at the University of Richmond.

DEANNE BLANTON retired from the National Archives and Records Administration in Washington, DC, after thirty-one years of service as a reference archivist specializing in eighteenth- and nineteenth-century U.S. Army records. With Lauren Cook, she is co-author of the groundbreaking book *They Fought Like Demons: Women Soldiers in the American Civil War* (2002). Blanton has appeared in nearly a dozen Civil War and women's history documentaries for cable channels and public broadcasting.

DAVID W. BLIGHT is Sterling Professor of American History at Yale University, author of the Bancroft Prize–winning *Race and Reunion: The Civil War in American Memory* (2001), and the Pulitzer Prize–winning *Frederick Douglass: Prophet of Freedom* (2018).

MICHAEL BURLINGAME, holder of the Chancellor Naomi B. Lynn Distinguished Chair in Lincoln Studies at the University of Illinois Springfield, has published twenty Lincoln books, among them *Abraham Lincoln: A Life* (2008), *The Inner World of Abraham Lincoln* (1997), *Lincoln and the Civil War* (2011), *The Black Man's President: Abraham Lincoln, African Americans, and the Pursuit of Racial Equality* (2021), and *An American Marriage: The Untold Story of Abraham Lincoln and Mary Todd* (2021).

KATHERINE REYNOLDS CHADDOCK is distinguished professor emerita at the University of South Carolina. She is the author of numerous articles and books on higher education history and the lives of notable educators. Most recent are *Uncompromising Activist: Richard Greener* (2017) and *The Spingarn Brothers: White Privilege, Jewish Heritage and the Struggle for Racial Equality* (2022).

JOHN M. COSKI worked for thirty-three years as historian at the Museum of the Confederacy and the American Civil War Museum in Richmond, Virginia, beginning his career there as a guide at the "White House of the Confederacy." He is the author, among other books, of *The Confederate Battle Flag: America's Most Embattled Emblem* (2005).

WILLIAM C. DAVIS is author or editor of more than fifty books in Civil War and southern history, most recently coediting (with Sue Heth Bell) *The Whartons' War: The Civil War Correspondence of General Gabriel C. Wharton and Anne Radford Wharton, 1863–1865* (2022). He is a retired professor of history and former executive director of the Virginia Center for Civil War Studies at Virginia Tech.

DOUGLAS R. EGERTON is professor of history at Le Moyne College and the author of eight books, including the Lincoln Prize co-winner, *Thunder at the Gates: The Black Civil War Regiments That Redeemed America* (2016), *The Wars of Reconstruction: The Brief, Violent History of America's Most Progressive Era* (2014), and *Year of Meteors: Stephen Douglas, Abraham Lincoln, and the Election That Brought on the Civil War* (2010). He is currently writing a biography of Thomas Wentworth Higginson.

STEPHEN D. ENGLE is author of the prizewinning *Gathering to Save a Nation* (2016) as well as a forthcoming biography of John Albion Andrew entitled *In Pursuit of Justice*. He is a professor of history and director of the Alan B. and Charna Larkin Symposium on the American Presidency at Florida Atlantic University in Boca Raton.

BARBARA A. GANNON is an associate professor of history at the University of Central Florida. She is the author of *The Won Cause: Black and White Comradeship in the Grand Army of the Republic* (2011), which received the Wiley-Silver Prize from the University of Mississippi for the best first book in Civil War history, as well as *Americans Remember Their Civil War* (2017).

MICHAEL P. GRAY is professor of history at East Stroudsburg University. His books include *The Business of Captivity: Elmira and Its Civil War Prison* (2001) and *Crossing the Deadlines: Civil War Prisons Reconsidered* (2018). He edits the Voices of the Civil War series with the University of Tennessee Press. Gray is the founder of HistoryFit, which integrates personal and group fitness with history tours that interplay physical challenges with critical moments in our nation's past.

HILARY GREEN is the James B. Duke Professor of Africana Studies at Davidson College. Previously, she worked at the University of Alabama, where she created the Hallowed Grounds Project. She is the author of *Educational Reconstruction: African American Schools in the Urban South, 1865–1890* (2016). Her current book project examines how African Americans remembered and commemorated the Civil War.

ALLEN C. GUELZO is the Thomas W. Smith Distinguished Research Scholar and director of the Initiative on Politics and Statesmanship in the James Madison Program in American Ideals and Institutions at Princeton University. A three-time winner of the Gilder Lehrman Lincoln Prize, he is the author of *Abraham Lincoln: Redeemer President* (1999), *Lincoln's Emancipation Proclamation: The End of Slavery in America* (2004), *Fateful Lightning: A New History of the Civil War and Reconstruction* (2012), *Gettysburg: The Last Invasion* (2013), *Reconstruction: A Very Short Introduction* (2018), and *Robert E. Lee: A Life* (2021).

ANNA GIBSON HOLLOWAY served for many years as curator of the award-winning USS *Monitor* Center at The Mariners' Museum in Newport News, Virginia. She is the co-author (with Jonathan W. White) of *"Our Little Monitor": The Greatest Invention of the Civil War* (2018). She received her PhD from the College of William & Mary and currently serves as a maritime historian with the federal government in Washington, DC.

VITOR IZECKSOHN is professor in the graduate program of social history at the Federal University of Rio de Janeiro. He is the author of *Slavery and War in the Americas: Race, Citizenship, and State Building in the United States and Brazil, 1861–1870* (2014) as well as two earlier books published in Brazil. His work engages in debates about the new Brazilian military history and the process of internationalization in the U.S. Civil War.

CAROLINE E. JANNEY is the John L. Nau III Professor of the American Civil War and director of the John L. Nau Center for Civil War History at the University of Virginia. She has published seven books, including *Remembering the Civil War: Reunion and the Limits of Reconciliation* (2013) and *Ends of War: The Fight of Lee's Army after Appomattox*, which won the 2022 Gilder Lehrman Lincoln Prize.

BRIAN MATTHEW JORDAN is associate professor of Civil War history and chair of the Department of History at Sam Houston State University in Huntsville, Texas. He is the author or editor of several books, including *Marching Home: Union Veterans and Their Unending Civil War* (2015), which was a finalist for the 2016 Pulitzer Prize in history, and *A Thousand May Fall: An Immigrant Regiment's Civil War* (2021).

MICHELLE A. KROWL is the Civil War and Reconstruction specialist in the Manuscript Division at the Library of Congress. She received her PhD in history from the University of California, Berkeley, and has authored several publications relating to the Civil War as well as Theodore Roosevelt; Quantico, Virginia; and the World War II Memorial in Washington, DC.

GLENN W. LAFANTASIE is the Richard Frockt Family Professor of Civil War History emeritus at Western Kentucky University. He is the author of *Twilight at Little Round Top* (2005), *Gettysburg Requiem: The Life and Lost Causes of Confederate Colonel William C. Oates* (2006), and *Gettysburg Heroes: Perfect Soldiers, Hallowed Ground* (2008), among other books and articles. He is at work on a book about Abraham Lincoln, Ulysses S. Grant, and the crisis of the Union.

JENNIFER M. MURRAY is a military historian with a specialization in the Civil War at Oklahoma State University. She is the author of *On a Great Battlefield: The Making, Management, and Memory of Gettysburg National Military Park, 1933–2013* (2014) and co-editor of the forthcoming *Civil War Memories in a Polarized America.* Murray is currently writing a biography of George Meade, tentatively titled *Meade at War.*

BARTON A. MYERS is a professor of history at Washington and Lee University in Lexington, Virginia. He is the author of the awarding-winning *Executing Daniel Bright: Race, Loyalty, and Guerrilla Violence in a Coastal Carolina Community, 1861–1865* (2009), *Rebels against the Confederacy: North Carolina's Unionists* (2014), and co-editor (with Brian D. McKnight) of *The Guerrilla Hunters: Irregular Conflicts During the Civil War* (2017).

TIMOTHY J. ORR is associate professor of military history at Old Dominion University in Norfolk, Virginia. He is editor of *Last to Leave the Field: The Life and Letters of First Sergeant Ambrose Henry Hayward* (2010) and co-author of the national best-seller *Never Call*

Me a Hero: A Legendary American Dive-Bomber Pilot Remembers the Battle of Midway (2017). For eight years, he worked as a seasonal park ranger at Gettysburg National Military Park.

CHRISTOPHER PHILLIPS is the John and Dorothy Hermanies Professor of American History and the University Distinguished Research Professor in the Arts, Social Sciences, and Humanities at the University of Cincinnati. He is the author of seven books, including *The Rivers Ran Backward: The Civil War and the Remaking of the American Middle Border* (2016), which won the Tom Watson Brown Book Award, and co-editor (with Jason L. Pendleton) of *The Union on Trial: The Political Journals of William Barclay Napton, 1829–1883* (2005).

MARK S. SCHANTZ is professor of history at Birmingham-Southern College. He is the author of *Awaiting the Heavenly Country: The Civil War and America's Culture of Death* (2008) and is currently writing a book on the murder of Lt. Alanson Sanborn in Union-occupied Norfolk, Virginia, on July 11, 1863.

DANA B. SHOAF is the editor in chief for HistoryNet, the editor of *Civil War Times* magazine, and can be seen on his magazine's "First Monday" *Civil War Times* Facebook broadcasts. He frequently speaks on a variety of Civil War topics. He has appeared on C-SPAN and has served as a Civil War consultant to the Smithsonian Institution, Library of Congress, and the National Archives.

WALTER STAHR, an honors graduate of Stanford University and Harvard Law School, practiced law for twenty years, mainly in Washington, DC, and Hong Kong. He then turned to writing and is the author of prizewinning biographies of John Jay, William Henry Seward, Edwin Stanton, and Salmon Chase. Both the Seward and Stanton books won the Seward Prize for Civil War Biography, and the Chase book received the Cooley Prize.

MICHAEL VORENBERG teaches history at Brown University and is the author of *Final Freedom: The Civil War, the Abolition of Slavery, and the Thirteenth Amendment* (2001) and *The Emancipation Proclamation: A Brief History with Documents* (2010). His book on the struggle to end the American Civil War will be published by Alfred A. Knopf in 2024.

JONATHAN W. WHITE is professor of American studies at Christopher Newport University. He is the author or editor of sixteen books, including *To Address You as My Friend: African Americans' Letters to Abraham Lincoln* (2021), and *A House Built by Slaves: African American Visitors to the Lincoln White House* (2022), which won the 2023 Gilder Lehrman Lincoln Prize. He serves as vice chair of The Lincoln Forum and on the Ford's Theatre Advisory Council, and won the 2019 State Council of Higher Education for Virginia's Outstanding Faculty Award.

RONALD C. WHITE is the author of two *New York Times* bestselling presidential biographies: *A. Lincoln: A Biography* (2009) and *American Ulysses: A Life of Ulysses S. Grant* (2016). He is also the author of *Lincoln's Greatest Speech: The Second Inaugural* (2002), a *New York Times* Notable Book, *The Eloquent President: A Portrait of Lincoln through His Words* (2005), and *Lincoln in Private: What His Most Personal Reflections Tell Us about Our Greatest Presiden*t (2021), recipient of the Barondess/Lincoln Award. His biography, *On Great Fields: The Life and Unlikely Heroism of Joshua Lawrence Chamberlain*, will be published in 2023.

Index

UnCivil Wars

Weirding the War: Stories from the Civil War's Ragged Edges
edited by Stephen Berry

Ruin Nation: Destruction and the American Civil War
by Megan Kate Nelson

America's Corporal: James Tanner in War and Peace
by James Marten

The Blue, the Gray, and the Green: Toward an Environmental History of the Civil War
edited by Brian Allen Drake

Empty Sleeves: Amputation in the Civil War South
by Brian Craig Miller

Lens of War: Exploring Iconic Photographs of the Civil War
edited by J. Matthew Gallman and Gary W. Gallagher

The Slave-Trader's Letter-Book: Charles Lamar, the Wanderer, and Other Tales of the African Slave Trade
by Jim Jordan

Driven from Home: North Carolina's Civil War Refugee Crisis
by David Silkenat

The Ghosts of Guerrilla Memory: How Civil War Bushwhackers Became Gunslingers in the American West
by Matthew Christopher Hulbert

Beyond Freedom: Disrupting the History of Emancipation
edited by David W. Blight and Jim Downs

The Lost President: A. D. Smith and the Hidden History of Radical Democracy in Civil War America
by Ruth Dunley

Bodies in Blue: Disability in the Civil War North
by Sarah Handley-Cousins

Visions of Glory: The Civil War in Word and Image
edited by Kathleen Diffley and Benjamin Fagan

Household War: How Americans Lived and Fought the Civil War
edited by Lisa Tendrich Frank and LeeAnn Whites

Buying and Selling Civil War Memory in Gilded Age America
edited by James Marten and Caroline E. Janney

The War after the War: A New History of Reconstruction
by John Patrick Daly

The Families' Civil War: Northern African American Soldiers and the Fight for Racial Justice
by Holly A. Pinheiro Jr.

Sand, Science, and the Civil War: Sedimentary Geology and Combat
by Scott Hippensteel

A Man by Any Other Name: William Clarke Quantrill and the Search for American Manhood
by Joseph M. Beilein Jr.

Final Resting Places: Reflections on the Meaning of Civil War Graves
edited by Brian Matthew Jordan and Jonathan W. White